7. Protecting Inventory **197**
   Introduction   197
   Legal Duties   199
   The Plan   199
     Preparation   200
       Natural Emergencies   200
       Technological Emergencies   200
       Incited Emergencies   201
       Planning Team   201
   The Assessment   202
   Theft   205
     Types Of Theft Threats   205
     Assessing The Threat   206
     Countering The Threats   207
       Crime Prevention Through Environmental
         Design (CPTED)   207
       Collusion Theft   210
       Background Checks   212
   Recap   216
   Review Questions   217

Appendix A—Inventory 219
Appendix B—Formulae 227
Bibliography 235
Index 237

ABOUT THIS BOOK

Essentials of Inventory Management and Control has been written to introduce the (i) new stockroom/warehouse manager; (ii) non-financial inventory control individual; or (iii) the small business owner to the fundamental nature of inventory from a financial, physical, forecasting, and operational standpoint. The ultimate goal of this book is to present immediately usable information in the areas of forecasting, physical control and layout, problem recognition, and resolution. These materials should enable you to:

- Understand that modern practice discourages holding large quantities of inventory and encourages only having amounts on-hand required for current needs.
- Grasp the significance of controlling actual, on-hand inventory as both a physical object (shelf count) and as an intangible object (record count and monetary worth).
- Understand the fundamental differences between finished goods inventories in the retail/distribution sectors and raw materials and work-in-process inventories found in the manufacturing environment.

- Apply basic formulae to calculating inventory quantities.
- Recognize and analyze dysfunctions within your own operation.
- Employ basic problem-solving techniques toward issue resolution.
- Control the physical location of inventory in a more efficient manner.
- Protect your operation from natural, technological, or incited crises.

Max Muller is an attorney who has served as chief executive or operations officer for companies distributing products as diverse as food to automated teller machines to safety equipment. Mr. Muller has also developed or revised more than 20 seminars that focus on areas of warehousing, inventory control, facilities management, project management, employment law, disaster planning, and occupational safety and health. These courses have been presented to more than 100,000 people throughout the United States, England, Canada, and Scotland. Mr. Muller has published articles in several business magazines and newsletters. He is an authorized General Industry Outreach Trainer of the Occupational Safety and Health Administration, Department of Labor. Mr. Muller has been an attorney, businessman, educator, and consultant for more than 27 years.

CHAPTER 1

Inventory as Both a Tangible and an Intangible Object

Introduction

The objective of this chapter is to provide you with a basic understanding of the nature of inventory as both a tangible, physical item actually kept within the facility ("real life" or "shelf count") and as an intangible item existing within the company's records ("paper life" or "record count"). Since you frequently make purchasing, sales, customer service, production planning, and other decisions based on whether or not an item is shown as being in-house *as per your records*, an item's paper life can be just as important as its real life.

Inventory—Who Needs It?

All organizations keep inventory. "Inventory" includes a company's raw materials, work in process, supplies used in operations, and finished goods.

1

Inventory can be something as simple as a bottle of glass cleaner used as part of a building's custodial program or something complex such as a mix of raw materials and subassemblies used as part of a manufacturing process.

Inventory Costs

Inventory brings with it a number of costs. These costs can include:

- Dollars
- Space
- Labor to receive, check quality, put away, retrieve, select, pack, ship, and account for
- Deterioration, damage, and obsolescence
- Theft

Inventory costs generally fall into ordering costs and holding costs. Ordering, or acquisition, costs come about regardless of the actual value of the goods. These costs include the salaries of those purchasing the product, costs of expediting the inventory, and so on. For a complete discussion of ordering costs see Chapter 5, Planning and Replenishment Concepts. For a complete discussion of carrying costs see Chapter 2, Inventory As Money.

As discussed in Chapter 2, holding costs include the cost of capital tied up in inventory (the opportunity cost of money[1]); storage costs such as rent; and costs of handling the product such as equipment, warehouse and stockkeeping staff, stock losses/wastage, taxes, and so on.

As discussed in Chapter 5, acquisition/ordering costs come about regardless of the actual value of the goods. These costs in-

clude the salaries of those purchasing the product, costs of expediting the inventory, and so on.

The Purpose of Inventory

So why do you need inventory? As discussed in a just-in-time manufacturing environment, inventory is considered waste. However, in environments where an organization suffers from poor cash flow or lacks strong control over (i) electronic information transfer among all departments and all significant suppliers, (ii) lead times, and (iii) quality of materials received, inventory plays important roles. Some of the more important reasons for obtaining and holding inventory are:

• *Predictability:* In order to engage in capacity planning and production scheduling, you need to control how much raw material, parts, and subassemblies you process at a given time. Inventory buffers what you need from what you process.

• *Fluctuations in demand:* A supply of inventory on hand is protection: You don't always know how much you are likely to need at any given time, but you still need to satisfy customer or production demand on time. If you can see how customers are acting in the supply chain, surprises in fluctuations in demand are held to a minimum.

• *Unreliability of supply:* Inventory protects you from unreliable suppliers or when an item is scarce and it is difficult to ensure a steady supply. *Whenever possible* unreliable suppliers should be rehabilitated through discussions or they should be replaced. Rehabilitation can be accomplished through master purchase orders with timed product releases, price or term penalties for nonperformance, better verbal and electronic communications between the parties, etc. This will result in a lowering of your on-hand inventory needs.

- *Price protection*: Buying quantities of inventory at appropriate times helps avoid the impact of cost inflation. Note that contracting to assure a price does not require actually taking delivery at the time of purchase. Many suppliers prefer to deliver periodically rather than to ship an entire year's supply of a particular stockkeeping unit (SKU) at one time. (Note: The acronym "SKU," standing for "stockkeeping unit," is a common term in the inventory world. It generally stands for a specific identifying numeric or alpha-numeric identifier for a specific item.)

- *Quantity discounts:* Often bulk discounts are available if you buy in large rather than in small quantities.

- *Lower ordering costs:* If you buy a larger quantity of an item less frequently, the ordering costs are less than buying smaller quantities over and over again. (The costs of holding the item for a longer period of time, however, will be greater.) See Chapter 5, Planning and Replenishment Concepts. In order to hold down ordering costs and to lock in favorable pricing, many organizations issue blanket purchase orders coupled with periodic release and receiving dates of the SKUs called for.

Types of Stock

Inventory basically falls into the overall categories of raw materials, finished goods, and work-in-process. Remember:

- *Raw materials:* Used to produce partial products or completed goods.

- *Finished product:* This is product ready for current customer sales. It can also be used to buffer manufacturing from predictable or unpredictable market demand. In other words, a manufacturing company can make up a supply of toys during the year for predictably higher sales during the holiday season.

- *Work-in-process (WIP):* Items are considered to be WIP during the time raw material is being converted into partial product, subassemblies, and finished product. WIP should be kept to a minimum. WIP occurs from such things as work delays, long movement times between operations, and queuing bottlenecks.

Other categories of inventory should be considered from a functional standpoint:

- *Consumables:* Light bulbs, hand towels, computer and photocopying paper, brochures, tape, envelopes, cleaning materials, lubricants, fertilizer, paint, dunnage (packing materials), and so on are used in many operations. These are often treated like raw materials.

- *Service, repair, replacement, and spare items (S&R Items):* These are after-market items used to "keep things going." As long as a machine or device of some type is being used (in the market) and will need service and repair in the future, it will never be obsolete. S&R Items should not be treated like finished goods for purposes of forecasting the quantity level of your normal stock.

Quantity levels of S&R Items will be based on considerations such as preventive maintenance schedules, predicted failure rates, and dates of various items of equipment. For example, if an organization replaced its fluorescent tubes on an as-needed, on-failure basis, it would need a larger supply of these lights on hand at all times. However, if the same company re-lamped all of its ballasts once per year, it would buy a large quantity of tubes at one time and only keep a small supply on hand on an ongoing basis.

Since S&R Items are never "obsolete" or "dead" until the

equipment or device they are to be used for is no longer in service, these items should not be included in calculating dead stock
levels. See Chapter 2, pages 34–38.

- *Buffer/safety inventory:* This type of inventory can serve
  various purposes, such as:

—compensating for demand and supply uncertainties.

—holding it to "decouple" and separate different parts of
your operation so that they can function independently from
one another. See Exhibit 1–1.

- *Anticipation Stock:* This is inventory produced in anticipation of an upcoming season such as fancy chocolates
  made up in advance of Mother's Day or Valentine's Day.
  Failure to sell in the anticipated period could be disastrous because you may be left with considerable
  amounts of stock past its perceived shelf life.
- *Transit Inventory:* This is inventory en route from one
  place to another. It could be argued that product moving
  within a facility is transit inventory; however, the common meaning of the concept concerns items moving
  within the distribution channel toward you and also outside of your facility or en route from your facility to the
  customer.

Transit stock highlights the need to understand not only
how inventory physically moves through your system, but also
how and when it shows up in your records. If, for example, 500
widgets appeared as part of existing stock while they were still
en route to you, your record count would include them while
your shelf count would be 500 widgets short.

How could stock show up as being a part of inventory before it actually arrives? The answer lies in when did title to the

Exhibit 1-1. Points Along the Channel of Distribution Where Buffer Stock Is Needed to Decouple Operations

⬆ ⬆ ⬆ ⬆ ⬆ ⬆ ⬆

Suppliers	Allows Procurement time to prepare purchase orders, place orders, and control timing and modes of delivery. Protects against uncertainties in lead times.	**Procurement (purchasing)**
Procurement (purchasing)	Provides time to plan and produce items while Procurement is interacting with Suppliers. Prevents downtime and allows for a continuous flow.	**Production**
Production	Provides Marketing with product to sell while Production is producing items for future sale.	**Marketing**
Marketing	Provides Distribution with the product Marketing has sold. Immediate customer satisfaction.	**Distribution**
Distribution	Offers the Intermediary items to deliver to the Consumer/End User.	**Intermediary (e.g., UPS, truck line, rail line, etc.)**
Intermediary (e.g., UPS, truck line, rail line, etc.)	Satisfies the Consumer/End User with product while it is waiting for deliveries from the Intermediary.	**Consumer/End User**

widgets transfer to you? Did title transfer when the product left the shipper's dock, or did it transfer only after the items arrived at your site and were signed for? If title transferred when the

What Article 2-319 States	What It Means
(1) Unless otherwise agreed, the term "F.O.B." (which means "free on board") at a named place, even though used only in connection with the stated price, is a delivery term under which:	
(a) when the term is F.O.B. the place of shipment, the seller must at that place ship the goods in the manner provided in this article and bear the expense and risk of putting them into the possession of the carrier; or	This is F.O.B. Origin and means that title shifts to the buyer when the goods are deliverd to the carrier. Risk of loss while the product is in transit then shifts to the buyer. When the buyer receives notice of the shipment having been made the goods are then often shown as being a part of the buyer's total inventory. The transit inventory now has a paper life within the buyer's system even though it is still not in the buyer's facility. Buyers will purchase F.O.B. Origin in order to control shipping methods, timing, and costs.
(b) when the term is F.O.B. the place of destination, the seller must at his own expense and risk transport the goods to that place and there tender delivery of them in the manner provided in this article.	This is F.O.B. Destination and means that title and risk of loss while the goods are in transit stay with the seller until the product reaches the buyer's dock and is accepted. Unless the buyer's system reflects items in transit, the goods have neither a real nor a paper life within the system.

product left the shipper's dock, and it was then counted as part of your total inventory, your total record count would not match your shelf count. For example, (a) a stockkeeper did not understand that an item's paper life had floated ahead of its real life and (b) did not have a breakdown of items on hand, on order, in transit, and immediately available, the (c) stockkeeper would find a mismatch between the shelf and record counts. Inappropriate adjustments might then be made.

The Uniform Commercial Code (UCC) governs the transfer of title to product. The UCC has been adopted by most states. Article 2 of the UCC covers the sale of goods.

Tracking the Paper Life

In order for you to gain an understanding of the relationship between an item's real life and its paper life within your own system, you should follow a single item on its path through that system. In other words, track an item's physical movement through your facility while noting what is happening to its paper life during that same time period. You will be able to discover when one of these lives moves ahead of the other and when there are system errors such as an item is moved but there is no paperwork authorizing that action.

Exhibit 1–2 provides an example of what could happen if an item's paper life and real life begin to leapfrog ahead or behind one another without the stockkeeper understanding the process.

As can be seen from the example in Exhibit 1–2, an item's real life and paper life can leapfrog around one another. It is important to understand that these lives can exist independently of one another, and to comprehend your own system, you must trace how both product and information move through the sys-

Exhibit 1-2. Real Life and Paper Life Leap Frog

Carr Enterprises operates six days per week, Monday through Saturday. It has an inventory system that is updated at 4:45 P.M. every day. In spite of the daily updating, the record count and the shelf count in Small Stock Room #1 are often out of balance.

Carr's warehouse manager, Nate, has decided to count everything in Small Stock Room #1 every Friday. He does so for two months. At the end of that time he is angry—the numbers still don't match.

Carr hires Shawn, an ace inventory detective, to help track down the source of the problem. Nate is flabbergasted. He believes he is counting very carefully, and if there is a problem, it is with the computer. Nate declares to anyone who will listen that "the computer is always wrong."

On Monday at 5:15 P.M., Shawn suggests that they examine an item that seems to be out of balance from the previous week's count.

Nate declares, "I'll show you one." Thrusting a brand new inventory Stock Status Report in front of Shawn's nose, Nate states, "Look at these widgets. It says there are 12 of them in stock. When we counted them last week there were 12 of them. I looked at this report this morning, and it said there were 13 of them. Now it says there are 12 of them, but I just looked in the stock room and there are actually 15 of them. See, I told you—the computer's always wrong."

Shawn asks if he can see Nate's count sheet with the widgets on it from the previous week. The sheet looks like this:

Stock Status Report					
Location	**Part Number**	**Description**	**U/M**	**Quantity**	
AB1002	9063	Gidgets	ea	127	
AB1003	2164	Gadgets	ctn	36	
AB1004	1878	Widgets	ea	~~10~~	12
AB1005	9201	Doodads	dz	98	
AB1006	5769	Whoohahs	pkg	~~105~~	101

Shawn asks what the notations mean.

Nate replies that when the wrong quantity was on the count sheet, he would "X" it out, write in the correct quantity, and turn the sheet into data entry.

Shawn asked when Nate turned his sheets in. Nate replied, "Friday—why?"

Shawn said, "I understand that you turn the sheets in on Friday. I'm asking, what *time* do you turn them in?" Nate says he does it at about 5 P.M. Thinking Shawn is criticizing him, Nate defensively states, "Hey, they're busy in data entry from 4:30 or so. They're doing cut-off and updates and stuff like that. So I wait until they're done."

Shawn asks when Nate's count sheets are keyed into the system. Nate says he doesn't know.

Shawn asks Hillary, the data entry clerk, when Nate's sheets are keyed in. Hillary replies that she doesn't put Nate's work on the front burner, "if you know what I mean." Shawn persists. He asks again, "who keys Nate's count sheets in and when are they done?" Hillary replies that she works on Saturday but leaves the sheets for Carolyn, the other data entry clerk, to input on Monday.

Shawn asks Hillary if she entered any widgets into the system on Saturday. She says she entered three of them into the system on Saturday.

Shawn asks Carolyn how she handles inputting Nate's

Cont. on page 12

Cont. from page 11

information. She replies that she pulls up the item on her computer screen, checks to see if the total in the computer matches Nate's handwritten amount and if it doesn't, she changes the amount in the system to match Nate's number.

Shawn charts-out the flow of real life and paper life for the widgets, and he comes up with the following:

Day	Record Count	Shelf Count	Notes
Friday @ close of business	10	12	At the start of business on Friday, the system believes there are 10 widgets. There are actually 12. Nate does not note a plus or minus amount on his count sheet. He X's through the 10 and writes in 12. He does not turn in his count sheets until after the system has been updated for that day. At the close of business on Friday, the system still believes there are 10 widgets. There are actually 12.
Saturday @ close of business	13	15	No one enters Nate's information on Saturday. Nate does not know this—he hasn't checked. Three widgets are added into the system on Saturday. At the close of business on Saturday, the system believes there are 13 widgets in stock. There are actually 15.
Monday morning	13	15	Monday morning's Stock Status Report reflects Saturday's numbers. During the day on Monday, Carolyn wipes out the record of 13 and enters the quantity of 12 from Nate's sheets.
Monday @ close of business	12	15	When the system is updated at 4:45 P.M. on Monday, the stock record and new Stock Status Report reflects that there are 12 widgets. There are actually 15. When Nate began counting on Friday the system was off by 2, and when all was said and done, it was off by 3![2]

Exhibit 1-3. Tracking the Paper Life

Instructions: At each stage of the flow chart below note:

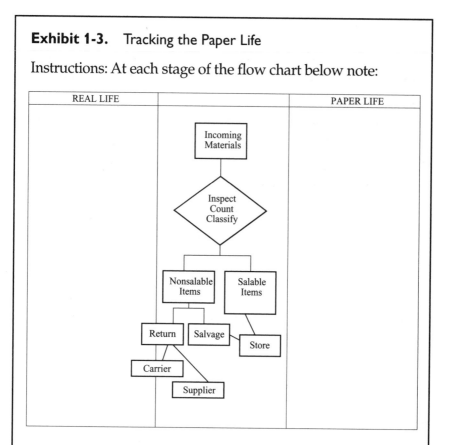

1. Where is the item physically?

2. What pieces of paper(s) authorize that?

3. When is information entered into your computer system?

4. Who is supposed to write something down? What are they supposed to write down? When were they supposed to write it down? Who are they supposed to give the piece of paper to? What is that person supposed to do with it? When are they supposed to pass the piece of paper along?

5. Does any item change its unit of measure within the

Cont. on page 14

Cont. from page 13

system even though it retains the same physical form. For example: Item *X* is purchased by the master case. When it is entered into the database, a conversion table converts each case into the four cartons within the master case. However, for ease of handling, the cartons remain in the master case for storage. Visually this item appears as a single unit while it will be sold or used as four separate items.

6. After the paper chase, where is the item physically?

tem. See Exhibit 1–3 for a simple method of breaking down a portion of your system to gain an understanding of your physical item and data base float times.

Electronic Data Interchange

Stockkeepers who do not understand how and when an item's paper life is first created within a system become even more confused if there is no hard paper copy audit trail they can follow. How could:

- an order be placed?
- an order be accepted?
- confirmation of the order be given?
- shipping instructions be given?
- notice of shipping arrangements be given?
- a paper life be created for an item in advance of it entering the facility?

All occur without there being any hard paper copies of these transactions existing. All of these events and more can occur in a paperless environment through electronic data interchange.

Electronic data interchange (EDI) is where routine business transactions are sent over standard communication lines (such as telephone lines) between computers within a company or between your computer and that of a vendor.

An example of EDI within a company is at the time of order entry, information about that order is electronically transmitted to shipping or operations for order selection and shipping, to accounting for billing purposes, to sales for order verification, and so on.

An example of EDI with a vendor is you electronically place an order directly from your computer into the vendor's computer. The vendor's computer then electronically confirms the order and transmits information about the order to the vendor's shipping and accounting departments. The vendor's computer also electronically notifies a carrier of the upcoming shipment. The carrier's computer electronically confirms the pickup and provides the vendor with pickup and delivery information. The vendor's computer then notifies your computer of the date, time, etc. of the upcoming delivery. All of this would be accomplished without any human intervention other than the original placement of the order.

For EDI to work, all of the system participants must agree to strict rules regarding message content, format, and structure.

recap   The objective of this chapter was to point out that inventory exists within your system as both a physical item and as an item existing within your records.

There are many reasons for obtaining and holding inventory, and inventory can play a variety of roles within the life of any organization.

In order to control and manage the items coming into, through, and out of your facility, it is important to understand not only where an item is physically located at any given time, but also how that existence is being acknowledged within the system.

❓ REVIEW QUESTIONS

1. Inventory costs generally fall into: 1. (d)
    (a) sales expenditures.
    (b) work in process.
    (c) line during the annual physical inventory.
    (d) ordering costs and holding costs.

2. **True or False**
    EDI is where routine business transactions are sent
    over standard communication lines.   2. (a)
    (a) True
    (b) False

3. **True or False**
    Service and repair stock must never be retained
    beyond 5 years from date of purchase.   3. (b)
    (a) True
    (b) False

4. True or False

Anticipation stock is inventory en route from
one place to another.   4. (b)
  (a) True
  (b) False

5. Which Article of the Uniform Commercial Code
governs the sale of goods?   5. (c)
  (a) 9
  (b) 1
  (c) 2
  (d) 117

NOTES

1. If you have $2 million tied up in inventory, you cannot earn money (interest) on that money. If you could earn 10 percent interest on that $2 million, you could earn $200,000. Not being able to is an opportunity cost.

2. If you are going to note stock quantity changes but the information will not be input before there are intervening inventory events, you must use a "plus/minus" notation system, e.g., +3; –4; ±0. By using a plus/minus notation system, the data entry clerk will add or subtract from the then current amount, which will already include any intervening events.

CHAPTER 2

Inventory as Money

Introduction

Why should you care about the financial aspects of inventory? Because inventory is money.

Even if you do not have a financial background, it is important to understand and appreciate that inventory information in financial statements can be useful in the operation of your business. A basic understanding of how inventory appears on the balance sheet and its impact on the income statement and cash flow statement will improve your ability to have the right item in the right quantity in the right place at the right time.

Accounting for Inventories

There are three basic types of inventory:

1. Raw Materials—**raw materials inventory** is made up of goods that will be used in the production of finished products, e.g., nuts, bolts, flour, sugar.

2. Work in Process —**work in process inventory, or WIP,** consists of materials entered into the production process but not yet completed, e.g., subassemblies.

3. Finished Goods—**finished goods inventory** includes completed products waiting to be sold, e.g., bar stools, bread, cookies.

Most inventory fits into one of these general buckets, yet the amount of each category varies greatly depending on the specifics of your industry and business. For example, the types of inventory found in distribution environments are fundamentally different from those found in manufacturing environments. Distribution businesses tend to carry mostly finished goods for resale while manufacturing companies tend to have less finished goods and more raw materials and work in progress. Given these differences, it is natural that the accounting choices vary between distribution and manufacturing settings.

How Inventory is Valued

In order to assign a cost value to inventory, you must make some assumptions about the inventory on hand. Under the federal income tax laws, a company can only make these assumptions once per fiscal year. Tax treatment is often an organization's chief concern regarding inventory valuation. There are five common inventory valuation methods:

1. **First-in, First-out (FIFO)** inventory valuation assumes that the first goods purchased are the first to be used or sold regardless of the actual timing of their use or sale. This method is most closely tied to actual physical flow of goods in inventory. See Exhibit 2–1.

2. **Last-in, First-out (LIFO)** inventory valuation assumes that the most recently purchased/acquired goods are the first to be used or sold regardless of the actual timing of their use or sale. Since items you have just bought often cost more than those purchased in the past, this method best matches current costs with current revenues. See Exhibit 2–1.

3. **Average Cost Method** of inventory valuation identifies the value of inventory and cost of goods sold by calculating an average unit cost for all goods available for sale during a given period of time. This valuation method assumes that ending inventory consists of all goods available for sale. See Exhibit 2–2.

**Average Cost = Total Cost of Goods ÷ Total Quantity of Goods
Available for Sale   Available for Sale**

4. **Specific Cost Method (also Actual Cost Method)** of inventory valuation assumes that the organization can track the actual cost of an item into, through, and out of the facility. That ability allows you to charge the actual cost of a given item to production or sales. Specific costing is generally used only by companies with sophisticated computer systems or reserved for high-value items such as artwork or custom-made items.

5. **Standard Cost Method** of inventory valuation is often used by manufacturing companies to give all of their departments a uniform value for an item throughout a given year. This method is a "best guess" approach based on known costs and expenses such as historical costs and any anticipated changes coming up in the foreseeable future. It is not used to calculate actual net profit or for income tax purposes. Rather, it is a working tool more than a formal accounting approach.

Inventory on the Balance Sheet

The balance sheet shows the financial position of a company on a specific date. It provides details for the basic accounting equation: Assets = Liabilities + Equity. In other words, assets are a company's resources while liabilities and equity are how those resources are paid for.

• Assets represent a company's resources. Assets can be in the form of cash or other items that have monetary value—including inventory. Assets are made up of (a) current assets (assets that are in the form of cash or that are easily convertible to cash within one year such as accounts receivable, securities, and inventory), (b) longer-term assets such as investments and fixed assets (property/plant/equipment), or (c) intangible assets (patents, copyrights, and goodwill).

• Liabilities represent amounts owed to creditors (debt, accounts payable, and lease-term obligations).

• Equity represents ownership or rights to the assets of the company (common stock, additional paid-in capital, and retained earnings).

Inventory is typically counted among a company's *current assets* because it can be sold within one year. This information is used to calculate financial ratios that help assess the financial health of the company (see pp. 27–31). Note, however, that the balance sheet is not the only place that inventory plays a role in the financial analysis of the company. In fact, inventory shows up on the income statement in the form of *cost of goods sold*.

Inventory on the Income Statement

The income statement is a report that identifies a company's revenues (sales), expenses, and resulting profits. While the balance sheet can be described as a snapshot of a company on *a specific date* (June 30, for example), the income statement covers *a given period of time* (June 1 through June 30). The *cost of goods* sold is the item on the income statement that reflects the cost of inventory flowing out of a business.

The old saying, "it costs money to make money," explains the cost of goods sold. You make money by using or selling inventory. That inventory costs you something. Cost of goods sold (on the income statement) represents the value of goods (inventory) sold during the accounting period. See Exhibit 2–3.

The value of goods that are *not sold* is represented by the ending inventory amount on the balance sheet calculated as:

$$\text{Ending Inventory} = \text{Beginning Inventory} + \text{Purchases} - \text{Cost of Goods Sold}$$

This information is also useful because it can be used to show how a company "officially" accounts for inventory. With it, you can back into the cost of purchases without knowing the actual costs by turning around the equation as follows:

$$\text{Purchases} = \text{Ending Inventory} - \text{Beginning Inventory} + \text{Cost of Goods Sold}$$

Or, you can figure out the cost of goods sold if you know what your purchases are by making the following calculation:

$$\text{Cost of Goods Sold} = \text{Beginning Inventory} + \text{Purchases} - \text{Ending Inventory}$$

Finally, as you sell/use inventory and take in revenue for it, you subtract the cost of the items from the income. The result is your gross profit.

Exhibit 2–1 FIFO vs. LIFO vs. Average Cost Method of Inventory Valuation Example

Assume the following inventory events:

- November 5   Purchased 800 widgets at $10.00/unit—Total *cost* $8,000
- November 7   Purchased 300 widgets at $11.00/unit—Total *cost* $3,300
- November 8   Purchased 320 widgets at $12.25/unit—Total *cost* $3,920
- November 10   Sold 750 units of goods at $15.00/unit
- November 14   Sold 460 units of goods at $15.55/unit
- November 15   Purchased 200 widgets at $14.70/unit—Total *cost* $2,940
- November 18   Sold 220 units of goods at $14.45/unit

Basic Events:

Date	Units Purchased		
	#Units	Cost/Unit	Total Cost
11/5	800	$10.00	$8,000
11/7	300	11.00	3,300
11/8	320	12.25	3,920
11/15	200	14.70	2,940
Total	1,620	N/A	$18,160

Date	Units Sold		
	#Units	Cost/Unit	Total Cost
11/10	750	Varies By	
11/14	460	Valuation	
11/18	220	Method	
Total	1,430	N/A	N/A

Exhibit 2–1 FIFO vs. LIFO vs. Average Cost Method of Inventory Valuation Example

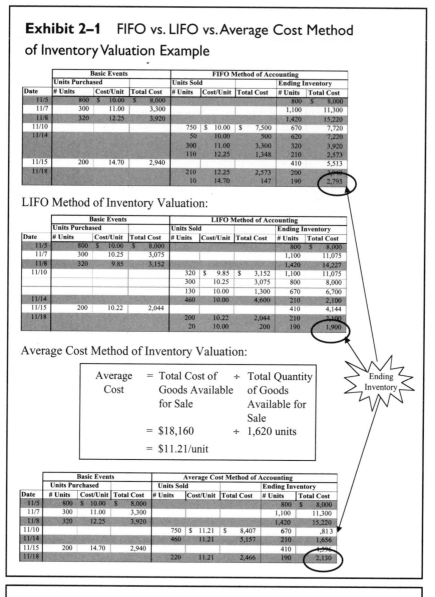

| | Basic Events | | | FIFO Method of Accounting | | | | |
| | Units Purchased | | | Units Sold | | | Ending Inventory | |
Date	# Units	Cost/Unit	Total Cost	# Units	Cost/Unit	Total Cost	# Units	Total Cost
11/5	800	$ 10.00	$ 8,000				800	$ 8,000
11/7	300	11.00	3,300				1,100	11,300
11/8	320	12.25	3,920				1,420	15,220
11/10				750	$ 10.00	$ 7,500	670	7,720
11/14				50	10.00	500	620	7,220
				300	11.00	3,300	320	3,920
				110	12.25	1,348	210	2,573
11/15	200	14.70	2,940				410	5,513
11/18				210	12.25	2,573	200	2,940
				10	14.70	147	190	2,793

LIFO Method of Inventory Valuation:

| | Basic Events | | | LIFO Method of Accounting | | | | |
| | Units Purchased | | | Units Sold | | | Ending Inventory | |
Date	# Units	Cost/Unit	Total Cost	# Units	Cost/Unit	Total Cost	# Units	Total Cost
11/5	800	$ 10.00	$ 8,000				800	$ 8,000
11/7	300	10.25	3,075				1,100	11,075
11/8	320	9.85	3,152				1,420	14,227
11/10				320	$ 9.85	$ 3,152	1,100	11,075
				300	10.25	3,075	800	8,000
				130	10.00	1,300	670	6,700
11/14				460	10.00	4,600	210	2,100
11/15	200	10.22	2,044				410	4,144
11/18				200	10.22	2,044	210	2,100
				20	10.00	200	190	1,900

Average Cost Method of Inventory Valuation:

$$\text{Average Cost} = \frac{\text{Total Cost of Goods Available for Sale}}{\text{Total Quantity of Goods Available for Sale}}$$

$$= \$18,160 \div 1,620 \text{ units}$$

$$= \$11.21/\text{unit}$$

| | Basic Events | | | Average Cost Method of Accounting | | | | |
| | Units Purchased | | | Units Sold | | | Ending Inventory | |
Date	# Units	Cost/Unit	Total Cost	# Units	Cost/Unit	Total Cost	# Units	Total Cost
11/5	800	$ 10.00	$ 8,000				800	$ 8,000
11/7	300	11.00	3,300				1,100	11,300
11/8	320	12.25	3,920				1,420	15,220
11/10				750	$ 11.21	$ 8,407	670	,813
11/14				460	11.21	5,157	210	1,656
11/15	200	14.70	2,940				410	1,596
11/18				220	11.21	2,466	190	2,130

Ending Inventory

Exhibit 2–2 Calculating Cost of Goods Sold

	FIFO	LIFO	Avg Cost Method
Cost of Goods Purchased	$18,160	$18,160	$18,160
Minus: Ending Inventory	2,793	1,900	2,130
Cost of Goods Sold	$15,367	$16,260	$16,030

Exhibit 2–3   Sample Balance Sheet and Income Statement

Balance Sheet (assumes FIFO Method of Accounting)

Assets		Liabilities and Equity	
Cash	$5,000	Accounts Payable	$10,000
Accounts Receivable	11,500	Notes Payable	7,500
Inventory		Current Portion of	
(per FIFO method)	2793	Long Term Debt	3,050
Other Current Assets	7,000	Total Current	
Total Current Assets	26,293	Liabilities	20,550
Investments	1,800	Long Term Debt	30,500
Property, Plant, &		Long Term	
Equipment (net)	53,000	Lease Obligations	12,250
Deferred Charges	1,000	Total Liabilities	$63,300
Patents, Goodwill	1,200		
Total Assets	$83,293	Shareholders' Equity	$19,993
		Total Liabilities	
		and Equity	$83,293

Income Statement	FIFO	LIFO	Avg. Cost Method
Revenues	$21,582	$21,582	$21,582
Less: Cost of Goods Sold	15,367	16,260	16,030
Gross Profit	6,215	5,322	5,552
Less:			
Selling, General and			
Administrative Expenses	2,500	2,500	2,500
Depreciation and			
Amortization Expenses	1,250	1,250	1,250
Goodwill Expense	553	553	553
Profit Before Taxes	1,912	1,019	1,249
Less: Federal Income Tax			
(assume 40%)	765	408	500
After-Tax Income	$1,147	$611	$749

Conclusions

1. By valuing its inventory under the FIFO method of inventory valuation, this company would have earned an extra $536 or $398 in after-tax income than under the LIFO or Average Cost methods of inventory valuation, respectively.

2. By valuing its inventory under the LIFO method of inventory valuation, this company would pay $357 or $92 less in federal income taxes than under the FIFO or Average Cost methods of inventory valuation, respectively.

Ratio Analyses and What They Mean

Is something good or is it bad? To answer this question we often compare one thing to another. That is what a "ratio" is: It is an expression of how many of one item is contained within another.

Ratios can be used in the business world by selecting parts of an organization's finacial statements and comparing one set of financial conditions to another. A company's financial statements contain key aspects of the business. By reviewing these aspects, you can determine an organization's economic well-being. One way of reviewing these financial conditions is to compare one to another through dividing one by the other. For example, if you had $200 cash and $100 worth of debts, you could divide the cash (assets) by the debt (liabilities) getting a ratio of 2 to 1. In other words, you have twice as many assets as you do liabilities.

Ratios are useful tools to explain trends and to summarize business results. Often third parties, such as banks, use ratios to determine a company's credit worthiness. By itself, a ratio holds little meaning. However, when compared to other industry and/or company-specific figures or standards, ratios can be powerful in helping to analyze your company's current and historical results. Companies in the same industry often have similar liquidity ratios or benchmarks, as they often have similar cost structures. Your company's ratios can be compared to:

1. Prior period(s)
2. Company goals or budget projections
3. Companies in your industry
4. Companies in other industries
5. Companies in different geographic regions

In particular, here are three ratios that are useful when assessing inventory.

1. **Current Ratio.** The current ratio assesses the organization's overall liquidity and indicates a company's ability to meet its short-term obligations. In other words, it measures whether or not a company will be able to pay its bills. Technically speaking, the current ratio indicates how many dollars of assets we have for each dollar of liabilities that we owe. The current ratio is calculated as follows:

Current Ratio = Current Assets ÷ Current Liabilities

Current Assets, refers to assets that are in the form of cash or that are easily convertible to cash within one year, such as accounts receivable, securities, and inventory. *Current Liabilities* refers to liabilities that are due and payable within twelve months, such as accounts payable, notes payable, and short-term portion of long-term debt.

Standards for the current ratio vary from industry to industry. Companies in the service industry that carry little or no inventory typically have current ratios ranging from 1.1 to 1.3—that is, $1.10 to $1.30 in current assets for each dollar of current liabilities. Companies that carry inventory have higher current ratios. Manufacturing companies are included in this latter group and often have current ratios ranging from 1.6 to 2.0; not only do they have inventory in the form of finished goods ready for sale, but they also carry inventory of goods that are not yet ready for sale. Generally speaking, the longer it takes a company to manufacture the inventory and the more inventory it must keep on hand, the higher the current ratio.

What the current ratio might mean:

A low current ratio may signal that a company has liquidity problems or has trouble meeting its short- and long-term obligations. In other words, the organization might be suffering from a lack of cash flow to cover operating and other expenses. As a result, accounts payable may be building at a faster rate than receivables. Note, however, that this is only an indicator and must be used in conjunction with other factors to determine the overall financial health of an organization. In fact, some companies can sustain lower-than-average current ratios because they move their inventory quickly and/or are quick to collect from their customers and therefore have good cash flow.

A high current ratio is not necessarily desirable. It might indicate that the company is holding high-risk inventory or may be doing a bad job of managing its assets. For example, fashion retailers may have costly inventory, but they might also have significant trouble getting rid of the inventory—if the wrong clothing line was selected for example. This makes it a high-risk company, forcing creditors to require a bigger financial cushion.

Further, if a high current ratio is a result of a very large cash account, it may be an indication that the company is not reinvesting its cash appropriately. Even if the current ratio looks fine, other factors must be taken into consideration, as liquidity problems might still exist. Since ratios look at quantity, not quality, it is important to look at what the current assets consist of to determine if they are made up of slow-moving inventory. In order to assess inventory's impact on liquidity, another test of liquidity should be taken into account—the Quick Ratio (or Acid Test).

2. **Quick Ratio or Acid Test.** The quick ratio compares the organization's most liquid current assets to its current liabilities. The quick ratio is calculated as follows:

Quick Ratio = (Current Assets – Inventories) ÷ Current Liabilities

Assume that an industry that sells on credit has a quick ratio of at least 0.8. In other words, the company has at least 80¢ in liquid assets (likely in the form of accounts receivable) for every $1 of liabilities. Industries that have significant cash sales (such as grocery stores) tend to be even lower. As with the current ratio, a low quick ratio is an indicator of cash flow problems, while a high ratio may indicate poor asset management as cash may be properly reinvested or accounts receivable levels are out of control. An organization's ability to promptly collect its accounts receivable has a significant impact on this ratio. The quicker the collection the more liquidity it has.

3. **Inventory Turnover Ratio.** The inventory turnover ratio measures, on average, how many times inventory is replaced over a period of time. In its simplest sense, an inventory turn occurs every time an item is received, is used or sold, and then is replaced. If an SKU came in twice during the year, was used/sold, and then replenished, that would be two turns per year. If this happened once per month, it would be twelve turns per year, and so forth.

Inventory turnover is an important measure since the ability to move inventory quickly directly impacts the company's liquidity. Inventory turnover is calculated as follows:

Inventory Turnover Ratio = Cost of Goods Sold ÷ Average Inventory

Essentially, when a product is sold, it is subtracted from inventory and transferred to cost of goods sold. Therefore, this ratio indicates how quickly inventory is moving for accounting purposes. It does not necessarily reflect how many times actual physical items were handled within the facility itself. This is true because the cost of goods sold number may include items you sold but never physically handled. For example, items that we purchase and

then have drop-shipped directly at our customer's site aren't ever handled within our facility. A more accurate measure of how many times actual physical inventory turned within the site would be:

$$
\begin{array}{c} \textbf{Actual Physical} \\ \textbf{Inventory Turnover Ratio} \end{array} = \begin{array}{c} \textbf{Cost of Goods Sold} \\ \textbf{from Inventory Only} \end{array} \div \begin{array}{c} \textbf{Average} \\ \textbf{Inventory} \end{array}
$$

Note that if the inventory has increased or decreased significantly during the year, the average inventory for the year may be skewed and not accurately reflect your turnover ratio going forward. Also, if the company uses the LIFO method of accounting, the ratio may be inflated because LIFO may undervalue the inventory.

Unlike the current ratio and quick ratio, the inventory turnover ratio does not adhere to a standard range. Organizations with highly perishable products can have inventory turns of 30 times a year or more. Companies that retain large amounts of inventory or that require a long time to build their inventory might have turns of only two or three times a year. In general, the overall trend in business today is to reduce carrying costs by limiting the amount of inventory in stock at any given time. As a result, both individual inventory turnovers and industry averages in this area have increased in recent years.

It is important to understand, however, that many factors can cause a low inventory turnover ratio. The company may be holding the wrong type of inventory, its quality may be lacking, or it may have sales/marketing issues.

Obsolete Stock

Any stockkeeper who has had to repeatedly move really slow moving or outright dead stock out of the way or finds herself

hurting for space because obsolete product eats up square foot after square foot knows that these items "just gotta go."

Why You Have Been Told Not to Dispose of It

Why is the dead stock still here? The three reasons most often given as to why the product can't be disposed of are:

1. It's already paid for.
2. We might use it someday.
3. We might sell it someday.

These explanations seem logical and the idea of throwing away dead stock may be counterintuitive. Indeed, there are some very real practical problems with simply hauling it off to the dumpster.

Problems with Convincing Decision Makers That "Its Gotta Go"

Decision makers often have difficulty with disposing of dead inventory because it will adversely impact the balance sheet and deplete resources considered to be valuable for lending purposes.

- *Impact of write off* Anything that appears as an asset on the balance sheet has an accounting value. This value, consisting of an item's original cost minus depreciation, is called the "book value." It is irrelevant that the item may actually be worthless to either a customer or as part of a manufacturing process. If it has a one-dollar value on the books, then disposing of dead inventory has an accounting consequence to our organization.

If we sell dead inventory that has a monetary value at a deep discount, throw it away, or give it away to a charity, we will

have to immediately write-off the book value of those items, which will, of course, have a negative impact on the financial statements.

If your organization is sensitive to making extraordinary adjustments to the balance sheet and never or seldom writes off dead inventory, you may have a difficult time ever convincing any decision maker to dispose of these items. The decision maker will simply not be willing to "take the hit on the books."

• *Organization's capital structure*   Almost everyone has heard the expression, "cash is king." The problem for many organizations is that cash flow doesn't always keep up with our needs.

Often organizations raise operating capital by borrowing against (a) their accounts receivable and (b) the book value of the inventory they are carrying.

"Accounts receivable" are the amounts due from customers resulting from normal sales activities. Depending on the industry, banks will generally lend up to 75 percent of the value of accounts receivable due in ninety days or less.

Bankers will also lend against the book value of inventory. The willingness to lend against this asset is not as straightforward as with accounts receivable. The more complex nature of these transactions comes from the fact that in accordance with accepted accounting practices, we should value inventory at the *lower* of cost or fair market value. Therefore, dead stock should logically be valued at a fair market value of zero dollars no matter what it originally cost.

In spite of generally accepted accounting practices and even though parts of your inventory have no real market value (and should be valued at zero dollars), bankers will often loan your organization 50 to 60 percent of the value of the inventory *as that value is shown on the books.* So, companies will sometimes continue to carry dead stock so as to retain this artificial value on

the books. This is an area most stockkeepers will not have any direct control over. However, the arguments below may overcome the need to keep inventory values artificially high.

Arguments in Favor of Disposing of Dead Stock

Strong arguments can be made in favor of disposing of nonproductive stock including recapture of space, better use of labor and equipment, plus a reduction in the costs associated with having inventory sitting around.

- Recapture of space

  In terms of space utilization, there are some simple mathematical facts to keep in mind:

  —Multiplying an item's length times its width tells you the amount of square feet the item is occupying.

  —Multiplying an item's length times its width times its height tells you the amount of cubic space it is occupying.

If you were to actually figure out the cubic space taken up by dead product, you would gain a powerful argument in favor of disposing of this inventory. To bolster the argument, you may want to ask your organization's financial officer how much the company is paying per square foot for rent. Multiplying the square footage being consumed by dead product times the rent per square foot often results in a truly eye-opening dollar amount. Providing actual numbers to a decision maker is far more effective than speaking in generalities like, "dead stock is taking up a lot of space." Pointing out that obsolete stock is "taking up 4,000 square feet" or "represents $2,000 per month in per square foot costs" should help you convince your decision maker that "its gotta go."

- Efficient utilization of labor and machine resources

  Not only does obsolete inventory take up a lot of space, it can also get in the way of workers. Repeatedly moving obsolete product out of the way hurts efficient use of both labor and machine time.

  Too often, in trying to argue against keeping obsolete stock, stockkeepers will state generalities like, "it takes us a lot of time to move that stuff around." How long is "a lot of time"? Is it an hour a day, four hours per week? Without specific numbers your arguments will sound hollow.

  As many business writers have noted, "You cannot control what you do not measure." There are two things to do to get specific time and dollar amounts you need to:

  —During each week for one month, every time you or your staff move dead product out of the way, measure the amount of direct labor that goes into that effort. Remember, if two workers are working together to move the items and they work for fifteen minutes, that represents fifteen minutes times two, or thirty minutes of direct labor.

  —At the end of the month, divide the total amount of labor hours by four to determine a weekly average. To determine the amount of yearly labor involved in moving dead stock, multiply the weekly average times the number of weeks in a year your company operates.

Once again, obtain base information from your financial officer and multiply the average hourly wage you pay your workers, including benefits, times the annual labor number. The result will make a rather impressive argument as to how the organization can save thousands of dollars per year by disposing of its dead stock.

- Reduction of carrying costs (the K Factor)

  The K Factor represents the number of pennies per inventory dollar per year a company is spending to house its inventory. It is generally expressed as a percent. In other words, a K Factor of 25 percent means that you are spending 25¢ per inventory dollar per year to house your inventory. A one dollar dead item that sits on your shelf for a year would cost you 25¢ that year, a total of 50¢ at the end of the second year, a total of 75¢ at the end of the third year, and so on.

There are two ways of computing the K Factor—a traditional method in which you add together various expenses directly related to carrying inventory and a rough rule-of-thumb method. See Exhibit 2–4.

Exhibit 2–4 Methods of Determining the Cost of Carrying Inventory

Traditional Accounting Method		Rule-of-Thumb Method
Warehouse Space	$ 130,000	20% + Prime Lending Rate
Taxes	65,000	= K Factor
Insurance	40,000	
Obsolescence/Shrinkage	23,000	
Material Handling	64,800	
Cost of Money Invested	200,000	
Total Annual Costs	$ 522,800	

$$\frac{\text{Total Annual Costs}}{\text{Ave Inventory Value}} = \frac{\$522,800}{\$2,000,000} = 26\% \text{ K Factor}$$

Since it always costs something to carry inventory, it is obvious that the longer dead stock remains in your facility, the more it will cost. Two approaches can be used to effectively argue this point:

1. Demonstrate the impact of carrying costs on your existing dead stock. This addresses the "We've already paid for it," argument in favor of retaining dead stock. See Exhibit 2–5 and Exhibit 2–6.

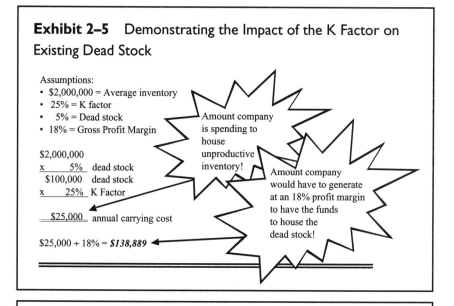

Exhibit 2–5 Demonstrating the Impact of the K Factor on Existing Dead Stock

Assumptions:
• $2,000,000 = Average inventory
• 25% = K factor
• 5% = Dead stock
• 18% = Gross Profit Margin

$2,000,000
x   5%   dead stock
$100,000   dead stock
x   25%   K Factor

  $25,000   annual carrying cost

$25,000 ÷ 18% = *$138,889*

Amount company is spending to house unproductive inventory!

Amount company would have to generate at an 18% profit margin to have the funds to house the dead stock!

Exhibit 2–6 Creating an Inventory Analysis Report Listing Dead Stock

SKU #	DESCRIPTION	QUANT ON HAND	UNIT COST	DOLLAR VALUE OF PRODUCT IN HOUSE	MONTHLY USAGE	PROJECTED ANNUAL USAGE	MONTHS SUPPLY ON HAND

2. Demonstrate that if the product remains long enough, even selling it at a profit will not recapture your original cost. This addresses the "We might need it someday," and, "We might sell it someday," arguments in favor of retaining dead stock. See Exhibit 2–7.

In Exhibit 2–5, a percentage is used to indicate the amount of dead stock in the facility. Note, however, it is always more convincing to a decision maker if you use actual lists and dollar amounts to demonstrate those items that are dead rather than using a generality like a rough percentage. See Exhibit 2-6.

Methods of Disposal

Various approaches to disposing of dead stock exist:

- Sell at net price
- Temporarily raise commissions for salespeople
- Discount the price
- Return to vendor
- Donate it
- Write it off
- Auction

It is important to remember something about convincing decision makers of anything. Ordinarily, when reports or other information flow up a chain of command, the level of detail at each level *decreases*. Generally, each higher level of management wants to see less and less information with which to make decisions. You should resist providing only minimal data in making arguments regarding dead stock. This is a time to let the detail do the talking.

Exhibit 2–7 Demonstrating the Impact of the K Factor on Items Sold at a Profit but after Remaining in Stock for Long Periods of Time

Assumptions:
- 720 pairs of earmuffs purchased at $2.25 per pair ($1,620 original cost)
- Earmuffs have remained unsold for 2 years
- We hope to sell at a 30% gross profit per pair ($2.93 pair)
- 25% K factor

$1,620 x 25% = $405 per year in carrying cost

$405 ÷ 720 pairs = 56¢ per year, per pair in additional carrying cost expense

Additional cost after one year:
$2.25 + $0.56 = $2.81/pair (720 pairs x $2.81/pair = $2,023)

Additional cost after two years:
$2.81 + $0.56 = $3.37/pair (720 pairs x $3.37/pair = $2,426)

Costs are going up $0.002 per day ($0.56 ÷ 365 days/yr)

$2.93   sales price
−2.25   original cost
$0.68   gross profit expected

$0.68 ÷ $0.002 = breakeven at 340 days—after 340 days there is no profit at all!

Original cost: $2,500

Cost including carrying costs after two years:
$4,449 ($2,023 + $2,426)
Revenue from selling earmuffs at $2.93/pair: $2,110
($2.93/pair x 720 pairs)

Loss on sale made after inventory has been in-house for two years even though sale made at 30% gross profit on original cost: $2,339

Carrying Cost and Purchasing

Although you should only have the minimum amount of inventory on hand required for either production or distribution, be careful not to purchase small quantities over and over again. Buying small amounts frequently will lead to an excessive cost of replenishment (the "R Factor").

A simple example of how an excessive R Factor can be created would be the following:

Assumptions:

It costs a certain amount of money per line item, per purchase order to buy something. Assume $2.59 per line item, per purchase order for this example. See Exhibit 2-8, Determining the R Factor.

You Purchase 1 million widgits per year.

If you bought all 1 million widgits at one time, the R Factor would be $2.59 since there was only one purchase order with one line item on it.

If you bought 250,000 widgits at a time, the R Factor would be $10.36. That is because you would have four purchase orders with one line item each at a cost of $2.59 each.

If you bought 1 million widgits one at a time at an R Factor of $2.59 each the replenishment cost would be $2,590,000!

Because of the R Factor, modern purchasing dictates that you buy larger quantities on fewer purchase orders, but with suppliers releasing items on a prearranged schedule or on demand.

Ultimately, the point at which your cost of carrying inventory matches the cost of purchasing it is the proper economic order quantity of that item. See Chapter 5, Planning and Replenishment Concepts, Replenishment Costs.

recap The objective of this chapter was to provide you with highlights of the most basic accounting concepts you, as a stockkeeper, must understand to successfully discuss and plan inventory values with your colleagues.

Although you may never participate in the preparation of month- or year-end financial statements, it is in your own self-interest to review these statements and think about how the inventory values reflected impact your operation.

And finally, whenever discussing either buying more stock or getting rid of dead stock, it is always more persuasive to use actual numbers than to deal in generalities. Remember, "if you can measure it, you can control it."

❓ REVIEW QUESTIONS

1. A balance sheet is best described as: 1. (b)

   (a) A report that identifies a company's revenues (sales), expenses, and resulting profits for a given period of time.

   (b) A report that shows the financial position of a company on a specific date.

   (c) A report that shows the relationship between inventory on-hand and on-order.

   (d) A report that identifies the number of items per level and number of tiers of product on a pallet.

2. An income statement is best described as: 2. (a)

   (a) A report that identifies a company's revenues (sales), expenses, and resulting profits for a given period of time.

   (b) A report that shows the financial position of a company on a specific date.

(c) A report that shows the relationship between inventory on-hand and on-order.

(d) A report that identifies the number of items per level and number of tiers of product on a pallet.

3. True or False   3. (a)

The K Factor represents the number of pennies per inventory dollar per year a company is spending to house its inventory.

(a) True

(b) False

4. True or False   4. (a)

The K Factor is generally expressed as a percent.

(a) True

(b) False

5. Current Assets ÷ Current Liabilities is the formula for which ratio?   5. (b)

(a) Inventory Turn Ratio

(b) Current Ratio

(c) Quick Ratio

CHAPTER 3

Physical Location and Control of Inventory

Introduction

If you can't find an item you can't count it, fill an order with it, or build a widgit with it. This chapter is about setting up a system that allows you to put items where they will do the most good for your organization.

If you cannot control the location of your product or raw materials from both a physical and a recordkeeping standpoint, then your inventory accuracy will suffer.

To sustain inventory accuracy on an ongoing basis you must:

1. formalize the overall locator system used throughout the facility

2. track the storage and movement of product from

a. receipt to storage

b. order filling to shipping or to staging at a point-of-use

3. maintain timely records of all item storage and movement

The objective of this chapter is to provide you with a working knowledge of (i) three key stock locator systems (which relate to the overall organization of SKUs within a facility and their impact on space planning); (ii) item placement theories dealing with the specific arrangement of products within an area of the warehouse (should the box be over here or over there?); and (iii) some practical methods of attaching addresses to stock items and how to tie an item number to its location address.

Common Locator Systems

The purpose of a material locator system is to create procedures that allow you to track product movement throughout the facility. Although going by many names, the most common "pure" systems are *memory*, *fixed*, and *random*. A type of fixed system is the *zone* system. The *combination* approach is a common mixture of the fixed and random systems.

In considering which locator system will work best, you should attempt to maximize:

- Use of space
- Use of equipment
- Use of labor
- Accessibility to all items
- Protection from damage
- Ability to locate an item
- Flexibility
- The reduction of administrative costs

Maximizing all of these considerations at the same time is difficult, if not impossible. Often each of these concerns creates

---

Exhibit 3–1 Examples of Valid Storage Considerations in Conflict

- Scenario One—*Accessibility versus Space*: Charmax, Inc. wishes to have its entire product as easy to get to as possible for order filling purposes. It therefore attempted to have a "picking face" (a front line, visible position from which the product can easily be selected) for each item. In order to actually create a picking face for each SKU, Charmax would have to assign a specific location for every product appearing on all of its pick tickets, with no two items being placed one on top of another, and no item being placed behind another. Charmax quickly realized that it lacked sufficient space in its facility to have a specific position for every item it carried.

- Scenario Two—*Use of Labor Versus Protection from Damage*: Alana Banana Enterprises wishes to reduce labor hours by putting into place efficient product handling procedures. Its intent is to develop standard operating procedures so that workers will only handle SKUs four times: once when it is received, once when stored, once when

---

Cont. on page 46

conflicts with one or more of the others. For example, you may wish to store all cylinders together in order to utilize the same equipment to handle them or locate them together for ease of getting to and retrieving them. However, if the chemical nature of the contents of these cylinders prohibits them from being stored in the same area, safety and protection of property concerns overcome other considerations . Exhibit 3–1 provides scenarios in which several valid considerations are in conflict.

Cont. from page 45

picked, and once when loaded. However, in order to protect SKUs from bruising, items must be placed into protective cartons for storage. SKUs are not picked in full carton quantities so workers have to remove various quantities at different times from the cartons. Empty cartons must then be stacked, cleaned, restacked, and taken back to the receiving area for reuse. These protective measures add a number of labor intensive steps to the process.

• Scenario Three—*Ability To Locate an Item Versus Space Utilization*: Racquetballers America wants to assign a specific home to each of its products for inventory control purposes. However, it has a small stockroom. Racquetballers realizes that if it uses a fixed storage location approach it must assign sufficient space to store the maximum amount of any one of its SKUs that will ever be on hand at one time in that location. If it uses a random location approach where items can be placed one on top of another or behind one another, then it will maximize its use of space. Racquetballers decides using its limited space is more important than putting in the extra labor and administration necessary to keep track of where everything is as it moves around the floor.

The stockkeeper should select a locator system that provides the best solution given the tradeoffs between conflicting objectives. No one system is "right." What is best will depend on considerations such as:

• Space available

• Location system (See the "Impact On Physical Space" discussions in this chapter.)

- Dimensions of product or raw materials stored

- Shape of items

- Weight of items

- Product characteristics, such as stackable, toxic, liquid, crushable

- Storage methods, such as floor stacked, racks, carousels, shelving

- Labor availability

- Equipment, including special attachments available

- Information systems support

Every company has a limited amount of space available for stock storage. Some locator systems use space more effectively than do others. When choosing your locator system, you need to think carefully about how much space it will use. The following pages show several types of locator systems and evaluate the strengths and weaknesses of each type.

Memory Systems

Basic Concept—Memory Systems

Memory systems are solely dependent on human recall. Often they are little more than someone saying, "I think it's over there."

The foundations of this locator system are simplicity, relative freedom from paperwork or data entry, and maximum utilization of all available space. Memory systems depend directly on people and only work if several or all of the conditions listed in Exhibit 3–2 exist at the same time.

Exhibit 3–2 Conditions Under Which Memory Systems Will Work

- Storage locations are limited in number.
- Storage locations are limited in size.
- The variety of items stored in a location is limited.
- The size, shape, or unitization (e.g., palletization, strapping together, banding, etc.) of items allows for easy visual identification and separation of one SKU from another.
- Only one or a very limited number of individuals work within the storage areas.
- Workers within the storage area do not have duties that require them to be away from those locations.
- The basic types of items making up the inventory does not radically change within short time periods.
- There is not a lot of stock movement.

Impact on Physical Space—Memory Systems

The most complete space utilization is available through this system. Why? Because no item has a dedicated location that would prevent other SKUs from occupying that same stock location position if it were empty (either side-to-side or up-and-down).

Pros—Memory Systems

- Simple to understand
- Little or no ongoing paper-based or computer-based tracking required

- Full utilization of space
- No requirement for tying a particular stocking location, identifier, bin, slot, drawer, rack, bay, spot, to a specific SKU
- Requirements of single item facilities (such as a grain silo) can be met

Cons—Memory Systems

- The organization's ability to function must strongly rely on the memory, health, availability, and attitude of a single individual (or a small group of people).
- Significant and immediate decreases in accuracy result from changes in the conditions set out in Exhibit 3–2.
- Once an item is lost to recall, it is lost to the system.

Despite its limitations, a memory system may be as efficient as any other, particularly if there are only a limited number of different SKUs within a small area.

Fixed Location Systems

Basic Concept—Fixed Location Systems

In pure fixed location systems, every item has a home and nothing else can live there. Some (not pure) fixed systems allow two or more items to be assigned to the same location, with only those items being stored there.

Impact on Physical Space—Fixed Location Systems

If quantities of any given SKU are large, then its "home" may consist of two or more storage positions. However, collectively all of these positions are the only places where this item may ex-

ist within the facility, and no other items may reside there. Basically, everything has a home and nothing else can live there.

Fixed location systems require large amounts of space. There are two reasons for this:

- Honeycombing
- Planning around the largest quantity of an item that will be in the facility at one time

Honeycombing is the warehousing situation where there is storage space available but not being fully utilized due to:

Cause	Description
• **Product shape**	**Physical characteristics cut down on stackability and prevent use of cubic space or prevent placing one item against another.**
• **Product put away**	**Product not stacked or placed in a uniform manner causing loss of vertical or horizontal space.**
• **Location system rules**	**Situation where a location is empty but no other item may be placed there since it is not the second item's assigned home.**
• **Poor housekeeping**	**Trash, poorly placed desks, etc. force empty space around it.**

Honeycombing is unavoidable given location system trade-offs, product shape, and so on. The goal of a careful layout is to minimize how often and to what extent this happens.

Honeycombing occurs both horizontally (side-to-side) and vertically (up-and-down), robbing us of both square feet and cubic space. See Exhibit 3–3.

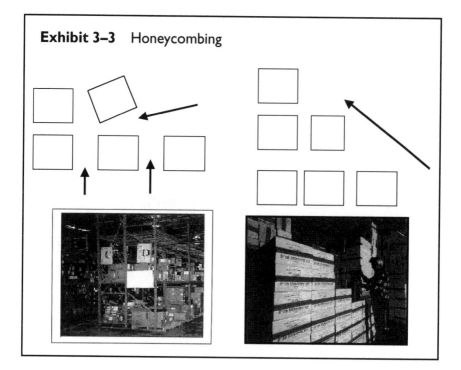

Exhibit 3–3 Honeycombing

There are two simple methods of determining the level of honeycombing within your own facility. One deals with a simple ratio analysis, the other with cubic space. See Exhibits 3–4 and 3–5.

The other thing that causes the fixed system to require significant space is the necessity of planning around the largest quantity of an item that will be in the facility at one time. Each SKU will have an assigned location or locations. This "home" must be large enough to contain the total cubic space the item will fill-up at the time that the largest quantity of that item will be in the facility at one time. In other words, if a thousand cases of widgits are all in the warehouse at the same time, the home of the widgits has to be large enough to hold them all. Therefore, the total space required for all items in a fixed system will be the total cubic space of one hundred percent of all SKUs as though the maximum quantity of each of them was in the facility at one time.

Exhibit 3–4   Determining Impact of Honeycombing—Ratio Method

Determine the impact of honeycombing on your present facility.

1. Count the number of locations you currently have set up to store items—both horizontally and vertically. Include all locations whether full, partially full, or empty.

2. Count the number of empty positions.

3. Divide the number of empty locations by the total storage positions you have. The result will be your honeycombing ratio.

$$\text{Honeycombing Ratio} = \frac{\text{Empty Storage Locations}}{\text{Total Storage Locations}}$$

$$\text{Example:} \quad \frac{847}{1,200} = .294 \text{ or about } 30\% \text{ Honeycombing Ratio}$$

That ratio represents the percentage of empty space within the storage portion of your stockroom(s). Determining this ratio provides you with a baseline. If you decide to change your storage philosophy, change your storage mechanisms (for example, from racks to floor stacking, or from racks to shelving). You can then determine the new ratio and measure improvement in space utilization.

Space planning for an entire inventory in a dedicated location environment is done around a one year time period. Stated differently, all of the space needed for all of the widgits has to be added

Exhibit 3–5 Determining Impact of Honeycombing—Square Footage Method

Globus, Inc. has 16,000 cubic feet (ft³) of storage space. Globus has a fixed locator system and has divided the storeroom into 490 storage locations with the following sizes (and empty locations):

No of Locations	Ft³	Total Cu Ft	Empty Locations
400	20	8,000	65
50	50	2,500	15
25	100	2,500	5
15	200	3,000	8
490		16,000	93

The honeycombing ratio on a location basis is:

$$\frac{\text{Empty Spaces}}{\text{Total Spaces}} = \frac{93}{490} = 19\%$$

Cont. on page 54

to all of the space needed for the gidgits, and that space has to be added to all of the room needed for the doodads, and so on.

Pros—Fixed Location Systems

- Immediate knowledge of where all items are located (This system feature dramatically reduces confusion as to where "to put it," "where to find it," which increases

Cont. from page 53

The honeycombing ratio on a ft³ basis is:

$$\frac{\text{Empty Spaces x ft}^3}{\text{Total ft}^3} = \frac{(65 \times 20 \text{ ft}^3) + (50 \times 15 \text{ ft}^3) + (5 \times 100 \text{ ft}^3) + (8 \times 200 \text{ ft}^3)}{16{,}000 \text{ ft}^3}$$

$$= \frac{1{,}300 + 750 + 500 + 1{,}600}{16{,}000}$$

$$= \frac{4{,}150}{16{,}000}$$

$$= \ 26\%$$

The ratio method is a relatively simple approach to determining a rough estimate of honeycombing. However, the ratio method doesn't account for the fact that storage spaces within a given facility come in various sizes. A more precise method to determine honeycombing is to calculate the amount of unused cubic feet.

---

efficiency and productivity, while reducing errors in both stocking and order fulfillment.)

- Training time for new hires and temporary workers reduced.

- Simplifies and expedites both receiving and stock replenishment because predetermined put-away instructions can be generated.

- Allows for controlled routing of order fillers. Exhibit 3–5 provides an example of how a fixed location system can assist an organization in fulfilling an order quickly.

- Allows product to be aligned sequentially (for example, SKU001, SKU002, SKU003).

- Allows for strong control of individual lots, facilitating *first in first out* ("FIFO") control, if that is desired. Lot control can also be accomplished under a random location system. However simpler, more definitive control is possible using the dedicated location concept.

- Allows product to be positioned close to its ultimate point-of-use. Product positioning is discussed in the "Item Placement Theories" section of this chapter.

- Allows product to be placed in a location most suitable to an SKU's size, weight, toxic nature, flammability, or other similar characteristics.

Cons—Fixed Location Systems

- Contributes to honeycombing within storage areas.

- Space planning must allow for the total cubic volume of all products likely to be in a facility within a defined period of time.

- Dedicated systems are somewhat inflexible. If you have aligned product by sequential numbering and then add a subpart or delete a numbered SKU, then you must move all products to allow for the add-in or collapse out locations to fill-in the gap.

Basically, fixed or dedicated location systems allow for strong control over items without the need to constantly update location records. That control must be counterbalanced by the amount of physical space required by this system.

Exhibit 3–6 Controlling Order Filling Operations Through Specific Item Placement

Scenario One Shawn Michael Irish Linens, Inc. has two sections of select rack on which it randomly places product. This organization uses the *whole order* method of order filling in which a single picker pulls each item on the pick ticket/work order for an entire order, marshalling it together as the order filler travels from storage location to storage location. No planning has gone into item placement. Consequently, heavy items that should be picked first are commingled with light, crushable items that should be selected last. In addition, work orders/pick tickets do not display SKUs to be picked in any particular order. The filler must run up and down the aisle trying to pull product in some semblance of order. Therefore, a typical order run, where product was located in positions 1, 5, 10, 11, 15, and 20 may look like this:

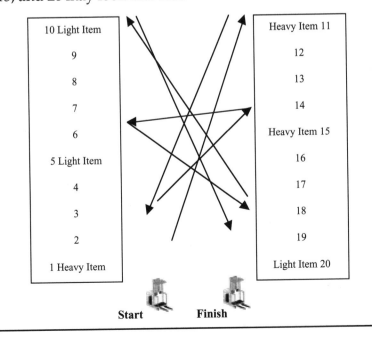

10 Light Item	Heavy Item 11
9	12
8	13
7	14
6	Heavy Item 15
5 Light Item	16
4	17
3	18
2	19
1 Heavy Item	Light Item 20

Start   **Finish**

If product was placed into assigned positions with the heaviest items appearing first, lighter ones last, and the pick ticket routed the filler sequentially, then the pull would look more like this:

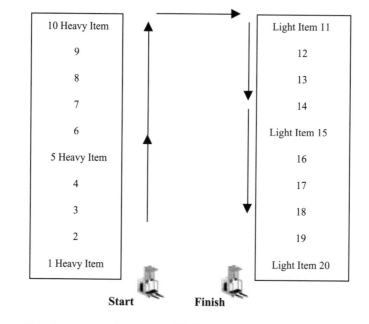

This layout and route will decrease travel time and will allow for efficient use of labor and for product protection.

Zoning Systems

Basic Concept—Zoning Systems

Zoning is centered around an item's characteristics. Like a fixed system, only items with certain characteristics can live in a particular area. Items with different attributes can't live there.

An SKU's characteristics would cause the item to be placed within a certain area of the stockroom or at a particular level

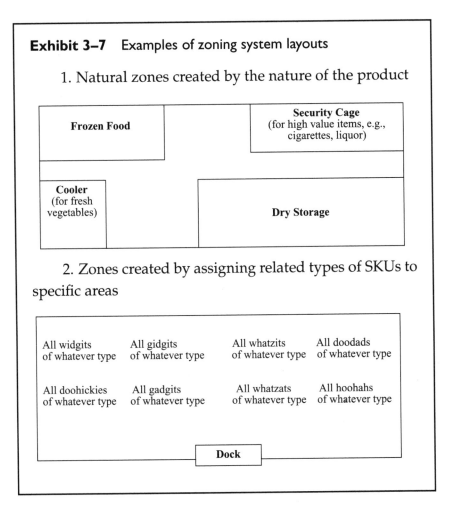

Exhibit 3–7   Examples of zoning system layouts

1. Natural zones created by the nature of the product

| Frozen Food | Security Cage (for high value items, e.g., cigarettes, liquor) |

| Cooler (for fresh vegetables) | Dry Storage |

2. Zones created by assigning related types of SKUs to specific areas

| All widgits of whatever type | All gidgits of whatever type | All whatzits of whatever type | All doodads of whatever type |
| All doohickies of whatever type | All gadgits of whatever type | All whatzats of whatever type | All hoohahs of whatever type |

Dock

within a section of shelving or rack section. See Exhibit 3–7. For example, irregular shaped SKUs might be placed in lower levels to ease handling, or all items requiring the use of a forklift for put away or retrieval might be located in a specific area and on pallets.

Impact on Physical Space—Zoning Systems

As with dedicated systems, (see the discussion for *Impact on Physical Space—***Fixed Location Systems** on pages 53–55) the

more you tightly control where a particular item will be stored, the more you will contribute to honeycombing or to the need to plan around maximum quantities.

Pros—Zoning Systems

- Allows for the isolation of SKUs according to such characteristics as size, variety, flammability, toxicity, weight, lot control, private labeling, and so on.
- Allows for flexibility moving items from one zone to another quickly or in creating different zones efficiently.
- Allows for the addition of SKUs within a zone (unlike a fixed system) without having to move significant amounts of product to create room within an assigned location or within a sequentially numbered group of items. It also does not require the collapsing of space if an item is deleted.
- Allows for flexibility in planning: Although items are assigned to a general zone, because they do not have a specific position they must reside in, there is no need to plan around one hundred percent of any given item's cubic requirements.

Cons—Zoning Systems

- Zoning is not always required for efficient product handling. You may be adding needless administrative complexity by utilizing zoning.
- Zoning may contribute to honeycombing.
- Zoning requires updating of stock movement information.

Basically zoning allows for control of item placement based on whatever characteristics the stockkeeper feels are important.

Random Location Systems

Basic Concept—Random Location Systems

In a random system nothing has a home, but you know where everything is. Pure random location systems allow for the maximization of space since no item has a fixed home and may be placed wherever there is space. This allows SKUs to be placed above or in front of one another and for multiple items to occupy a single bin/slot/position/rack. The primary characteristic of a random locator system that makes it different from a memory system is that each SKU identifier is tied to whatever location address it is in while it is there. In other words, memory systems tie nothing together, except in the mind of the stockkeeper. Random systems have the flexibility of a memory system coupled with the control of a fixed or zone system. Essentially an item can be placed anywhere so long as its location is accurately noted in a computer database or a manually maintained paper-based card file system. When the item moves, it is deleted from that location. Therefore, an SKU's address is the location it is in while it is there.

Impact on Physical Space—Random Location Systems

Because items may be placed wherever there is space for them, random locator systems provide us with the best use of space and maximum flexibility while still allowing control over where an item can be found.

Planning space around a random locator system is generally based on the cubic space required for the average number of SKUs on-hand at any one time. Therefore, in planning space requirements around a random locator system, you need to discern from our inventory records what our average inventory levels are and what products are generally present within that

Exhibit 3–8 Planning a Storage Area Around a Fixed or a Random Location System

Hammer Company manufactures widgits. It has broken down its bill-of-materials, the listing of all of the pieces and parts required to build a widgit, and has come up with the following list:

SKU #	Description	Container	Dimensions	Total Cubic Ft	Maximum Expected At One Time	Total Cubic Ft Req Fixed System	Total Ft Space Req Random System
12345	Gidgit	Box	2'x3'x1'	6 cu ft	50	300	90
54321	Whazzit	Carto•	4'x4'x4'	64 cu ft	100	6,400	1,920
67890	Whozzit	Case	3'x4'x2'	24 cu ft	25	600	180
09876	Doodad	Box	2'x3'x1'	6 cu ft	50	300	90
						7,600	2,280

If Hammer Co was going to store product in fixed positions, it would have to plan around a minimum of 7,600 cubic feet of actual storage space. Although each of these items is required to produce Hammer Company's products, they are not all needed at the same time. On average Hammer only has on-hand 30 percent of any of the above items at any one time. If it used a random locator system it would plan for approximately 2,280 cubic feet of actual storage area.

average. By multiplying the cubic footage of each of those items by the quantity of each usually onhand, you can determine our space required. See Exhibit 3–8.

Pros—Random Location Systems

- Maximization of space.
- Control of where all items are at any given time.

Cons—Random Location Systems

- Constant updating of information is necessary to track where each item is at any given time. Updating must be accomplished through manual paper-based recording, bar code scanning, or data entry intensive updating. See pages 84–86 regarding maintenance of product location information.
- May be unnecessarily complicated if your organization has a small number of SKUs.

Basically, random location systems force a tradeoff between maximization of space and minimization of administration.

Combination Systems

Basic Concept—Combination Systems

Combination systems enable you to assign specific locations to those items requiring special consideration, while the bulk of the product mix will be randomly located. Very few systems are purely fixed or purely random.

Conceptually you are trying to enjoy the best features of the fixed and random systems. You achieve this by assigning only selected items to fixed homes—but not all items. Therefore, you only have to plan around the maximum space required by the

selected items instead of that required by all items. For the items not in fixed homes, you can plan around the average quantities you expect to have on a daily, ongoing basis. So, the fixed system is used for the selected items and the random system for everything else.

A common application of the combination system approach is where certain items are an organization's primary product or raw materials line and must be placed as close as possible to a packing/shipping area or to a manufacturing work station. Those items are assigned a fixed position, while the remainder of the product line is randomly positioned elsewhere. See Exhibit 3–9 for typical scenarios for utilizing a combination locator system.

Exhibit 3–9 Typical Scenarios Involving Combination Location Systems

Scenario One: Barash Foods decided to speed up its order filling efforts by changing where product was located in relationship to the shipping dock. First it determined which 15 percent–20 percent of its product lines showed up on 80 percent of its orders. (See "A-B-C Categorization" on pages 66–67 for an explanation of the 80/20 Pareto's Law concept.) These items would be assigned to fixed positions close to the point-of-use (shipping dock), while those items found in only 20 percent of the orders would be randomly stored.

Barash had to decide if these fixed homes would be large enough to hold 100 percent of the cubic space necessary to house a product if the maximum quantity of it was in the facility at one time during the year. The company decided it could not devote that much space per product in

---

Cont. on page 64

Cont. from page 63

the limited area closest to the point-of-use. It therefore decided to allow for 100 percent of the space needed for one week's worth of product movement for the fixed location SKUs. In other words, while still having to follow the fixed location system rule that space must exist for 100 percent of the cubic space required for the maximum quantity of an item expected during a given time period, it controlled the space and quantity by shortening the time frame.

Random items were stored in accordance with the general rule that random space is planned around the average quantity expected in an area during a defined time period. In this case the time period was one year.

Scenario Two: Charmax Manufacturing is a "job shop" electronics manufacturer. It manufactures special order items and often will only produce one, never to be repeated run of an item. Therefore, some specific raw materials inventories required for any given production run may never be needed in the future. However, the company uses many common electronics components such as resisters, transistors, and solder in most of the final assemblies it produces. Its physical plant is very small.

Charmax carefully reviews its master production schedule to determine when various subassemblies and final assemblies will be produced. It then analyzes the bill-of-materials (the recipe of components) for the sub- or final assemblies, and orders as much specific purpose items as possible on a to be delivered just-in-time basis. This holds down the quantity of nonstandard inventory it will have in-house at any one time.

Charmax then establishes fixed positions for working

stock, both special order and standard stock items, during a production cycle around the appropriate workstations. Where working stock would consume too much space around a work area, working reserve stock is placed in zone locations close to the workstations. Regular, general use product, such as resisters and transistors, is stored in random order.

This combination location system—which is comprised of fixed, zone and random storage for working, working reserve and general stock—allows Charmax to maximize its use of space at any given time.

Common Item Placement Theories

Locator systems provide a broad overview of where SKUs will be found within a facility. Physical control of inventory is enhanced by narrowing the focus of how product should be laid out within any particular location system. As with locator systems, item placement theories (where should a particular item or category of items be physically positioned) go by many different names in textual as well as in trade literature. By whatever name, most approaches fall into one of three concepts: inventory stratification, family grouping, and special considerations.

Inventory Stratification

Inventory stratification consists of two parts:

- A-B-C categorization of SKUs.
- Utilizing an SKU's unloading/loading ratio.

A-B-C Categorization

This item placement approach is based on "Pareto's Law." In 1907, an Italian sociologist and economist by the name of Vilfredo Pareto (1848–1923) wrote his belief that 80 to 85 percent of Italy's money was held by only 15 to 20 percent of the country's population. He called the small, wealthy group the "vital few" and everyone else the "trivial many." This ultimately came to be known as the "80–20 Rule" or Pareto's Law. The concept stands for the proposition that within any given population of things, approximately 20 percent of them have 80 percent of the "value" of all of the items concentrated within them, and that the other 80 percent only have 20 percent of the value concentrated within them. "Value" can be defined in various ways. For example, if the criterion is money, then 20 percent of all items represent 80 percent of the dollar value of all items. If the criterion is usage rate, then 20 percent of all items represent the 80 percent of the items most often used/sold.

Accordingly, for efficient physical inventory control, using popularity (speed of movement into and through the facility) as the criterion, the most productive overall location for an item is a storage position closest to that item's point-of-use. SKUs are separated into A-B-C categories, with "A" representing the most popular, fastest moving items (the "vital few"), "B" representing the next most active, and "C" the slow-movers.

Providing product to outside customers is often the chief objective of a distribution environment. Therefore, the point-of-use would be the shipping dock, with SKUs being assigned in the manner shown in Exhibit 3–10. In a manufacturing environment, a work station would become the point-of-use, with the most active, most often required raw materials positioned in near proximity to it.

In order to separate an inventory into A-B-C categories, it is

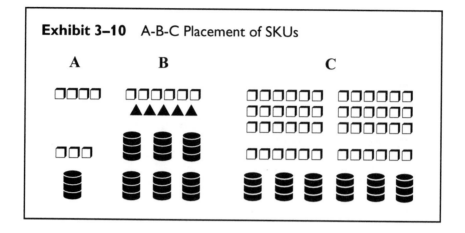

Exhibit 3–10 A-B-C Placement of SKUs

necessary to create a sorted matrix that presents all SKUs in descending order of importance and allows for the calculation of those items representing the greatest concentration of value. Exhibit 3–11 represents selected rows of a complete listing of SKUs shown in Appendix A.

Before attempting to understand how the matrix is mathematically constructed, you first have to explore what information the matrix is presenting. Unless otherwise stated, all references are to Exhibit 3–10.

What the Matrix Shows

• Column A is merely a sequential listing of the number of SKUs in the total population. In the example there are 300 items. If an organization had 2,300 SKUs, Column A of its matrix would end with row 2,300.

• Recall that there are two components within Pareto's Law. The first component refers to the percentage of all items that a certain number of items represent, and the second component represents the percentage value that the same grouping of items has when compared to the value of all other items combined.

Exhibit 3–11   Categorization for Item Placement by Popularity *

A	B	C	D	E	F	G
Line No.	Part No.	Description	Annual Usage	Cumulative Usage	% Total Usage	% Total Items
1	Part 79	Product A	8,673	8,673.00	6.3%	0.3%
2	Part 133	Product B	6,970	15,643.00	11.3%	0.7%
3	Part 290	Product C	5,788	21,431.00	15.5%	1.0%
·						
·						
·						
17	Part 70	Product Q	1,896	64,915.00	47.0%	5.7%
18	Part 117	Product R	1,888	66,803.00	48.4%	6.0%
19	Part 134	Product S	1,872	68,675.00	49.7%	6.3%
20	Part 170	Product T	1,687	70,362.00	50.9%	6.7%
21	Part 182	Product U	1,666	72,028.00	52.1%	7.0%
22	Part 28	Product V	1,646	73,674.00	53.3%	7.3%
·						
·						
·						
30	Part 278	Product AD	997	82,919.00	60.0%	10.0%
·						
·						
·						
93	Part 295	Product CJ	325	123,350.00	89.3%	31.0%
94	Part 30	Product CK	325	123,675.00	89.5%	31.3%
95	Part 11	Product CL	323	123,998.00	89.8%	31.7%
96	Part 192	Product CM	321	124,319.00	90.0%	32.0%
97	Part 96	Product CN	321	124,640.00	90.2%	32.3%
98	Part 40	Product CO	298	124,938.00	90.4%	32.7%
·						
·						
·						
272	Part 86	Product JG	6	138,053.00	99.9%	90.7%
273	Part 32	Product JH	6	138,059.00	99.9%	91.0%
274	Part 129	Product JI	5	138,064.00	99.9%	91.3%
275	Part 164	Product JJ	5	138,069.00	100.0%	91.7%
276	Part 283	Product JK	5	138,074.00	100.0%	92.0%
277	Part 252	Product JL	5	138,079.00	100.0%	92.3%
·						
·						
·						
298	Part 151	Product KG	—	138,134.00	100.0%	99.3%
299	Part 61	Product KH	—	138,134.00	100.0%	99.7%
300	Part 165	Product KI	—	138,134.00	100.0%	100.0%

Complete listing shown in Appendix A.

Column G reflects the first aspect. For example, 30 items represent 10 percent of 300. Therefore, Column G, Row 30 shows 10 percent of all 300 items.

Column F reflects the second aspect. For example, the first three items (Rows 1, 2, and 3) of Column A have a combined value (usage rate) of 15.5 percent. That 15.5 percent is shown at Row 3 of Column F. (How the 15.5 percent is arrived at is explained below in "Creating the Matrix.")

• After creating the matrix, a review of Column F leads to decisions as to where the cut-off should be for each (A-B-C) category. There is no rule of thumb. The decision is a common sense, intuitive one. In Exhibit 3–11, since 19 of all items represented almost 50 percent of the value of all items (see Row 19, Column F), it seems appropriate to cut off the A category at that number. It would have been just as appropriate to cut it off at Row 20, Column F, which shows 50.9 percent.

Creating the Matrix

• Most application software programs include a report generator module that allows various fields of information, such as SKU identifiers, descriptions, and quantities, to be extracted from the general database and saved in a generically formatted (ASCII)[1] file. This information may then be exported into one of the commonly available spreadsheet software programs such as Excel,® or Lotus.® Rather than undertaking the data entry required to input the information found in Columns B, C, and D, you should use your report generator to obtain this information, and then export it into a spreadsheet program.

• Column A—reflects the number of SKUs being analyzed. It is organized in ascending numeric sequence (1, 2, 3 . . .).

• Column B—SKU number/identifier.

- Column C—SKU description.
- Column D—Annual usage quantity of the SKU.

In a retail/distribution environment where the inventory is comprised of finished goods, Column D will contain the immediately preceding 12 months' usage quantities. This is based on the rule of thumb that the product lines will remain relatively unchanged during the upcoming 12-month period. The immediately preceding 12 months' usage rates will reflect any product trends and is more timely than using the immediate past calendar year's rates.

In a manufacturing environment, raw materials, components, and sub-assemblies used during the past 12 months may not be required during the upcoming 12 months. Therefore, the data for Column D must be derived from the master production schedule (the projection of what is to be built and in what quantities). After determining what will be built and in what quantities, examine the bill-of-materials (BOM), the recipe of what pieces and parts will actually go into the items to be manufactured. The data necessary for Column D is ascertained by multiplying the appropriate items in the BOM times the quantity of items to be built.

Column D is sorted in descending order, with the highest use item appearing at the top and the most inactive item at the bottom.

Column D is the sort field. However, if only Column D was sorted, the information in it would become disassociated from the SKUs the data represents, which information is reflected in Columns B and C. Therefore, the sort range includes columns B, C, and D so that all related information is sorted together.

- E—Cumulative total of Column D.

In order to derive the percentage value that a number of items have compared to the value of all items, it is necessary to

establish that overall value as well as the value that any given number of items added together may possess. This is what Column E does.

Note that the first row of Column E is the same as the first row of Column D. Note that adding together the first two rows of Column D results in the second row of Column E. The sum of the first three rows of Column D equals the third row of Column E. The sum of the first seventeen rows of Column D results in the data in row seventeen of Column E, and so forth.

The data shown in row 300 of Column E reflects the usage value of all 300 items added together. The information on any given row of Column E reflects the value of all of the preceding SKUs added to the value of that specific row's value.

- F—This is the second aspect of Pareto's Law. It reflects the percentage value that a grouping of items has when compared to the value of all other items.

Column F is derived by dividing every row of Column E by the last value of Column E. In other words, the first value in Column F (6.3 percent) results from dividing the first row of Column E (8,673) by the last row of Column E (138,134). The value found in row two of Column F is derived from dividing the amount shown in row two of Column E (15,643) by the last row of Column E (138,134), and so forth. Using arithmetic terminology, each row of Column E acts as a numerator, the last row of Column E is the denominator, and the quotient is found in Column F.

- G—This is the first aspect of Pareto's Law. It reflects the percentage of all items compared with all other items. In other words, 3 is 1 percent of 300.

Column G is derived by dividing every row of Column A by the last number in Column A. In other words, the first value

in Column G (0.3 percent) results from dividing the first row of Column A (1) by the last row of Column A (300). The value found in row two of Column G is derived from dividing the amount shown in row two of Column A (2) by the last row of Column A (300), and so forth.

- After creating the chart, you look down Columns F and G and decide where you want to place the cutoff for categories A, B, and C. Product would then be arranged according to which category it is in.

- Appendix B sets out the formulae necessary to create the matrix for 300 SKUs in Microsoft Excel®.

Utilizing an SKU's Unloading/Loading Ratio

Even more efficiency in physical inventory control can be achieved through placing items within the A-B-C zones according to that SKU's unloading to loading ("unloading/loading") ratio. The unloading/loading ratio reflects the number of trips necessary to bring an item to a storage location compared with the number of trips required to transport it from a storage point to a point-of-use. If one trip was required to bring in and store a case of product, but 10 trips were required to actually take its contents to a point-of-use, the unloading/loading ratio would be 1 to 10 (1:10). Substantial reductions in handling times can be achieved through application of this principle. See Exhibit 3–12.

The closer the unloading/loading ratio is to 1:1, the less it matters where an item is stored within an A-B-C zone because the travel time is the same on either side of the storage location. The more the ratio increases, the more critical it is to place an item closer to its point-of-use. Assuming 7 productive hours of labor within an 8-hour work shift, a reduction of even 30 sec-

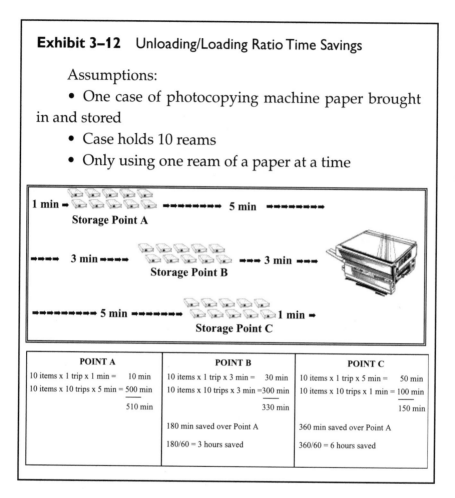

Exhibit 3–12   Unloading/Loading Ratio Time Savings

Assumptions:
- One case of photocopying machine paper brought in and stored
- Case holds 10 reams
- Only using one ream of a paper at a time

POINT A	POINT B	POINT C
10 items x 1 trip x 1 min = 10 min	10 items x 1 trip x 3 min = 30 min	10 items x 1 trip x 5 min = 50 min
10 items x 10 trips x 5 min = 500 min	10 items x 10 trips x 3 min =300 min	10 items x 10 trips x 1 min = 100 min
510 min	330 min	150 min
	180 min saved over Point A	360 min saved over Point A
	180/60 = 3 hours saved	360/60 = 6 hours saved

onds in travel time every 5 minutes will result in a timesaving of 42 minutes. See Exhibit 3–13.

Family Grouping

An alternative to the A-B-C approach is the family grouping/ like product approach. This approach to item placement positions items with similar characteristics together. Theoretically, similar characteristics will lead to a natural grouping of items, which will be received/stored/picked/shipped together.

Exhibit 3–13　Practical Effect of Inventory Layout Changes

If a change in procedure, layout, product design, paperwork, or any other factor saved 30 seconds every 5 minutes, how much time would you save each day?

- Assume 7 actual work hours per day
- 60 minutes x 7 hours = 420 minutes
- 420 minutes / 5 minutes = 84 segments
- 84 x 30 seconds = 2,560 seconds
- 2,560 seconds / 60 seconds = 42 minutes

Saving 30 seconds every 5 minutes saves 42 minutes per day!

Groupings can be based on:

- Like characteristics—widgits with widgits, gidgits with gidgits, gadgits with gadgits.
- Items that are regularly sold together—parts needed to tune-up a car.
- Items that are regularly used together—strap with sports goggles.

Pros—Family Grouping

- Ease of storage and retrieval using similar techniques and equipment.
- Ease of recognition of product groupings.
- Ease of using zoning location systems.

Cons—Family Grouping

- Some items are so similar they become substituted one for the other such as electronics parts.

- Danger of properly positioning an active item close to its point-of-use but consuming valuable space close to that area by housing far less active "family member" items with their popular relative.
- Danger of housing an active product with its inactive relatives far from the popular SKU's point-of-use, all for the sake of keeping like items together.
- An item can be used in more than one family.

Using Inventory Stratification and Family Grouping Together

Effective item placement can often be achieved through tying both the inventory stratification and family grouping approaches together. For example, assume order-filling personnel travel up and down a main travel aisle, moving into picking aisles to select items, and then back out to the main aisle to proceed further. Also assume that there are 12 brands of Gidgits that are all stored in the same area for purposes of family grouping. Pareto's Law indicates that not all brand of Gidgits will be equally popular. Consequently, using both the inventory stratification and family grouping concepts together, the most popular Gidgit brands are positioned closer to the main travel aisle and the least popular furthest from it. The end result is a more efficient overall layout.

Special Considerations

A product's characteristics may force us to receive/store/pick/ship it in a particular manner. The product may be extremely heavy or light, toxic or flammable, frozen, odd in shape, and so on.

Even with items requiring special handling or storage such as frozen food stored in a freezer, the inventory stratification and

family grouping concepts can and should be employed to ensure efficient inventory layout.

Location Addresses and Sku Identifiers

Significance

You simply cannot control what you can't find. Major contributing factors to the success of inventory systems are:

- Adequate, appropriate identification markings on SKUs, including both SKU number and stockkeeping unit of measure. These markings allow a worker to quickly and easily identify an item without having to read and translate product descriptions and confusing pack size designations. This ease of recognition reduces errors and the time required for either stock selection of put-away.

- Adequate, appropriate identification markings on bin/slot/floor/rack/drawer/shelf locations. Just like the address on a house, the address of a specific location in the stockroom lets you quickly find the "tenant" or "homeowner" SKU you are looking for.

- Procedures tying any given SKU to the location it is in at any given time. How does the post office know where to send mail to someone after they have moved? Obviously, the relocated person fills out a change of address form. In much the same manner, you must set up a procedure that tells your system where a product lives, and if it moves—where to.

- Procedures tying a single SKU to multiple locations in which it is stored. If you have two homes, you let your friends know the addresses. Your friends then put that information together in their address books. You must do the same thing for products residing in two or more locations within the building.

- A system for tracking items, on a timely basis, as they change locations. Whatever form your "change of address" form takes, it has to be filled out and processed quickly.

- Package advertising that does not obscure SKU identifier codes.

- Use of simple marking systems that are easy to read and understand. You should avoid complicated marking systems that are difficult to read, understand, recall, or are conducive to numerical transposition. For example, markings such as "12/24 oz" and "24/12 oz" are quantity oriented coding employing numbers describing the quantity and size of the inner packages. However, such numbers are easily reversed or transposed, and are not intuitively understood.

If you incorporate these elements into your inventory systems, you can expect:

- Decreased labor costs related to search time for product. These search-time savings manifest themselves not only when you search for an individual item, but most definitely when product is located in multiple unspecified locations.

- Decreased labor costs associated with searching for appropriate storage locations.

- Elimination of the unnecessary purchase of items that are already in the facility but are undiscovered when needed.

- Correct selection of SKUs during order filling.

- Correct selection of pack size(s) during order fulfillment.

All of the above lead to more accurate inventory tracking, less wasted time to correct errors, and an increase in customer satisfaction.

Keys to Effectively Tying Together SKUs and Location Addresses

In order to keep track of where SKUs are at any given time, it is necessary to:

1. Clearly mark items with an SKU identifier.

2. Clearly mark items with a unit of measure such as pack size.

3. Clearly mark location addresses on bins/slots/shelves/racks/floor locations/drawers/and so on.

4. Tie SKU numbers and location addresses together either in a manual card file system or within a computerized database.

5. Update product moves on a real-time basis with bar coding coupled with radio frequency scanners (see Chapter 4, The Basics of Bar Coding) or with stock movement reporting (see the section in this chapter on *updating product moves*, pages 84–86).

Clearly Mark Items with an SKU Identifier; Clearly Mark Items with a Unit of Measure

Too often managers believe that workers can read a product's markings and packaging and actually understand what they are looking at. The end result of this belief is error after error. To eliminate many of these identification miscues, you need to clearly mark out items with an identifying number and a unit of measure. Workers will make far fewer errors matching a number on a box to the same number on a piece of paper than they will trying to match words or abbreviated descriptions.

The SKU identifier is generally an organization's own internal identifying code for the item rather than a manufacturer's or customer's number for that SKU. Although the SKU number

---

Exhibit 3–14   Marking SKUs

By manufacturer

• Manufacturer prints or affixes plain, human readable label on the item and/or a bar code label with coding on the items. Manufacturer obtains labels or you provide them.

At vendor site

• Vendor from whom you obtain the product prints or affixes your plain, human readable label on the item and/or a bar code label with coding on the items. Manufacturer obtains labels or you provide them.

At time of receiving

• Everything comes through receiving—it is a natural node. That convergence allows you the opportunity to affix plain, human readable label on the item and/or a bar code label with coding on the items.

• You can have all product that turns even once during the year marked in this manner, with faster moving items (12 turns a year) all marked within a few weeks.

---

itself is often adequate for identification purposes, in manufacturing it may be necessary to also include lot and serial numbers to aid in quality control. Lot and serial numbers make it possible to track manufacturing batch, date, location, and inspector. Exhibit 3–14 reflects various methods of getting items actually labeled or marked.

Markings related to unit of measure (such as each/pair/ dozen/barrel/ounce/pound/cylinder/barrel/case) also serve to greatly reduce error in picking and shipping.

Exhibit 3–15   Alpha-Numeric Variations

$0 \rightarrow 9 = 10$

$00 \rightarrow 99 = 100$ $10 \times 10 = 100$

$000 \rightarrow 999 = 1{,}000$ $10 \times 10 \times 10 = 1{,}000$

$A \rightarrow Z = 26$

$AA \rightarrow ZZ = 676$ $26 \times 26 = 676$

$AAA \rightarrow ZZZ = 17{,}576$ $26 \times 26 \times 26 = 17{,}576$

Clearly Mark Location Addresses On Bins/Slots/Shelves/Racks/Floor Locations/Drawers

Just as you could not find a house in a city if its address was not clearly identified, you cannot find a storage location unless its address is clearly marked or easily discerned in some other manner. The addressing or location system you choose should have an underlying logic that is easy to understand. Addresses should be as short as possible, yet they should convey all needed information.

You should first consider whether the system will be all numeric, all alphabetic (alpha), or alpha-numeric. In deciding which system to adopt, consider the following:

• All numeric systems require sufficient digit positions to allow for future growth. Because each numeric position only allows for 10 variations (0-9), numeric systems sometimes become too lengthy. In other words, since a single numeric position only allows 10 variations, if you required 100 different variations (for 100 different SKUs), you would need 2 digit positions, representing 00 through 99 (10 x 10). One thousand variations would require three numeric positions, 000 through 999, and so on. See Exhibit 3–15, Alpha-Numeric Variations.

• Systems that are completely alphabetic allow for 26 variations per position, A through Z (assuming only capital letters). Two alphas together, AA through ZZ (26 x 26), allow for 676 variations. Three alphas, AAA through ZZZ, allow for 17,576 variations. See Exhibit 3–15, Alpha-Numeric Variations. Although alphas provide numerous variations in a short address, systems that are completely alphabetic are visually confusing (HFZP).

• Alpha-numeric systems often provide for visual differentiation while allowing sufficient variations in a short address.

• *Caution:* While alpha systems require fewer characters to hold the same number of variations, they are more error prone. For example: Is that the number zero or the letter *O*? A "one" or the letter *l*? A two or the letter *Z*? A *P* or an *R*? A *Q* or an *O*? If you are only dealing with a computer system, then characters are "cheap," and you could use only numerics to avoid confusion. However, if part of your system will involve human readable labels, placards, or markings where a long string of numbers might present a problem or where you are trying to keep a bar code label short, you might have to balance out the merits of shorter alpha-numeric systems against longer pure numeric systems.

Exhibit 3–16 presents some common location addressing systems for racks or shelving.

Exhibits 3–17 and 3–18 present common location addressing systems for bulk storage.

Tie SKU Numbers and Location Addresses Together

The placement of identifiers on both product and physical locations creates an infrastructure by which you can track product as it moves. The next step is marrying together an SKU number

Exhibit 3–16   Addressing Racks, Drawers, and Shelving

APPROACH	EXPLANATION
"Street Address" 03A02B02	03 A 02 B 02 Room Aisle Rack Tier Slot (City) (Street) (Building) (Floor) (Apartment) Although this is a lengthy address if an automated storage and retrieval system (AS/RS) is used, then detailed exact spot information is required for the selector arm to find the desired load.
"Rack-Section-Tier-Bin" 030342	03 03 4 2 Rack Section* Tier Bin *A rack section is that portion of the weight bearing horizontal support between two upright supports.
Room/Bldg-Rack-Bin AA001 **Rack-Bin** AA001	A A 001 Rm/Bldg Rack Bin AA 001 Rack Bin These last two systems are short, simple, and easy to remember, but they do not provide tier information.

and the location(s) where that item is located. This can be easily accomplished by using a simple 3 x 5 card file system (which should be computerized as soon as possible). See Exhibit 3–19.

Exhibit 3–17 Bulk Storage Grid Addressing System

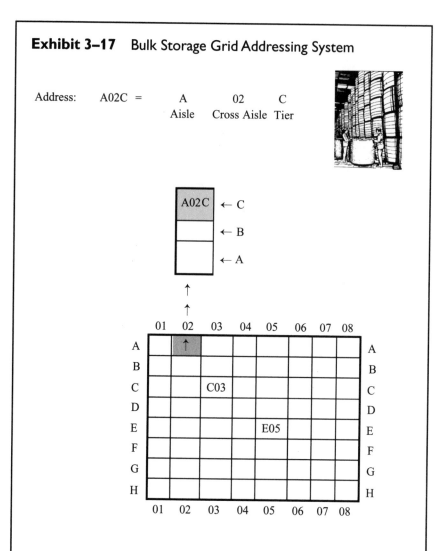

Address: A02C = A 02 C

Aisle Cross Aisle Tier

• In bulk storage areas, you can utilize a simple grid denoted with placards on walls or on the building's structural supports to find an address on the floor. This is done through two lines bisecting on a flat plain.

• For vertical addresses, you triangulate three lines.

• The above is applied geometry (Cartesian Coordinates) developed by René Descartes, the famous French mathematician.

Exhibit 3–18   Bulk Storage Quadrant Addressing System

NWNW	NWNE	NENW	NENE
	N W	NE	
NWSW	NWSE	NESW	NESE
SWNW	SWNE	SENW	SENE
	S W	SE	
SWSW	SWSE	SESW	SESE

Entrance

Quadrant addresses are read right to left—the Northeast Quadrant of the Southeast Quadrant is written as "SENE."

Update Product Moves

A final step in managing inventory is tracking it as it is added to, deleted, or moved. This challenge exists for any organization whether or not the company uses manual tracking, computerized approaches, or bar coding.

The best generally available approach for real-time tracking of items as they move is using bar coding mobile scanners with radio frequency (RF) capability. See Chapter 4, The Basics of Bar Coding.

If RF capable bar coding is not available, then updating can be accomplished as follows:

• Portable bar code scanners that capture the information within the scanner mechanism or on a disk in the scanner. The information is then uploaded into the computerized database either through the communications ports on the scanner and computer, or by loading the scanner disk into the computer.

Exhibit 3–19   Simple Card File Tracking System

SKU#	QUANT	LOC
SKU 3	135	LOC 1
	87	LOC 2
	965	LOC 3

SKU#	QUANT	LOC
SKU 2	27	LOC 1
	57	LOC 2

SKU#	QUANT	LOC
SKU 1	1235	LOC 1
	187	LOC 2
	187	LOC 3
	543	LOC 4

Cards are marked with all SKU numbers. Cards will be indexed in ascending number sequence—lowest SKU number in the front of the file box and the highest SKU number appearing last. All locations and quantities for that specific item are noted. As SKUs are added-to or moved, card file information is updated as often as possible. Updates should occur at least twice daily, for example, during the lunch hour and at the end of the workday.

• Manually captured, paper-based information (see Exhibit 3–20) is entered into the database through keying (data entry by a human being).

Exhibit 3–20   Simple Stock Movement Report

STOCK MOVEMENT REPORT

SKU# _____

DATE _____   TIME _____

QUANT _____

FROM _____   TO _____

• Manually captured, paper-based information is manually written onto file cards.

No matter what method is used, it is imperative that information relative to inventory additions, deletions, or movement be inputted into the system as soon as possible. To the greatest extent possible, the shelf count (what is actually in the facility and where it is) should match the record count (the amount reflected in the main database records). The longer the time lag between inventory movement and information capture and updating of the record count, the greater the chance for error, lost product, and increased costs.

recap   Organizations should carefully consider specific item placement within an overall location system in order to maximize each SKU's accessibility while being mindful of that item's point-of-use, unloading/loading ratio, relationship to similar items, or characteristics requiring special handling.

Organizations lacking procedures that identify the location of each SKU within the facility suffer from excessive labor costs, "lost" product causing additional items to be purchased to cover for those on-site but unavailable when required, poor customer service, and general confusion. Controlling product location and movement centers around establishing an overall locator system that effectively reflects the organization's basic inventory nature such as finished goods in a retail/distribution environment or raw materials and sub-assemblies in a manufacturing facility. Often legitimate operational and storage objectives are in conflict with one another resulting in final location system decisions made on the basis of a series of tradeoffs.

And finally, each item's present location must be identified with that SKU's identifier, with address and quantity changes being updated on an ongoing, timely basis.

? REVIEW QUESTIONS

1. Honeycombing is best described as: 1. (c)
   (a) product unevenly stacked.
   (b) matrix racking or shelving layout.
   (c) empty space in usable storage areas.
   (d) the number of items per level and the number of tiers of product on a pallet.

2. Memory location systems: 2. (b)
   (a) are simple and efficient.
   (b) are human dependent.
   (c) require updating of location information.
   (d) are useful when a large number of different SKUs must be quickly located.

3. Regarding random locator systems,:   3. (b)

    (a) each item has an assigned home in a random zone.

    (b) an item's home is the location it is in while it is there.

    (c) an SKU's storage location must be planned around the maximum quantity of that item expected to be on-site during a defined time period.

    (d) only certain items may be placed in the bulk storage areas of the facility.

4. In relationship to its unloading/loading ratio, an SKU should be placed closer to its point of use if the ratio is: 4. (a)

    (a) 1:28.

    (b) 1:1.

    (c) 3:15.

    (d) 28:28.

5. Pareto's Law holds that: 5. (c)

    (a) 80 percent of all items account for 80 percent of the dollar value of 20 percent of those items.

    (b) 20 percent of all items account for 20 percent of the usage value of 80 percent of those items.

    (c) 80 percent of all items contain 20 percent of the value of those items.

    (d) a fixed locator system is operationally efficient 20 percent of the time for 80 percent of all items.

NOTE

1. American Standard Code of Information Interchange (ASCII) is the basic 128 character set understood by all computer systems.

CHAPTER 4

The Basics of Bar Coding

Introduction

Errors and time increase dramatically the more often a human being is involved in identifying an object, inputting that information into a database, and then modifying the knowledge to keep track of changes in location, pack size, quantity, and so on.

The less you rely on human intervention to identify items, input information, and track data, the more timely and accurate your records will be. Bar coding is a major tool in capturing critical data quickly and accurately.

The time and dollar savings that would be realized if your organization could eliminate the time and errors noted above will often pay for a bar coding system. See Exhibit 4–1. The speed of information capture and the accuracy of bar coding are often sufficient reasons to cost justify installing bar coding within your operation.

Exhibit 4–1   Data Entry Comparisons Assuming a 12-Character Field

	Key-Entry	**OCR**	**BAR Code**
Speed	6 seconds	4 seconds	.3 seconds to 2 seconds
Error Rate	1 character error in 300 characters entered	1 character error in 10,000 characters entered	1 character error in 15,000 to 36 trillion characters entered

Bar coding is an optical method of achieving automatic identification. It relies on visible or invisible light being reflected off of a printed pattern. The dark bars or dark areas within the pattern absorb light, and the intervening spaces or areas reflect light. The contrasting absorption and reflection is sensed by a device that "reads" this reflected pattern and decodes the information.

Bar coding is not the only automated method of identifying inventory. For example, there is also optical character reading, machine vision, magnetic stripe, surface acoustic wave, and radio frequency tags. See Exhibit 4–2.

This text will only deal with one dimensional, linear bar coding—probably the most commonly used method of automated inventory identification and control.

Bar code systems generally consist of three components: the code itself, the reading device(s), and the printer(s). The objective of this chapter is to provide you with a working knowledge of (i) elements of a bar code symbol; (ii) the fundamentals of the more commonly used linear bar code languages/symbologies in the inventory control world; (iii) printing and scanning (reading) basics; and (iv) some practical bar code applications.

Exhibit 4–2 Various Automated Methods of Identifying Inventory

Technology	How It Works	For Your Information
Optical Character Reading (OCR)	Numbers, letters, and characters are printed in a predetermined, standard character style or font. Like a bar code the image is illuminated and the reflection is sensed and decoded.	• Allows for both human and machine readability • 10 characters per inch data density • Slower read rate than bar codes • Higher error rate than bar codes • Very sensitive to print quality
Machine Vision	Cameras take pictures of objects, encode, and send them to a computer for interpretation.	• Very accurate under the right light conditions • Reads at moderate speed • Expensive
Magnetic Stripe	A magnetic stripe, like those on credit cards, is encoded with information.	• Proven technology • Readable through grease and dirt • Relatively high density of information—25 to 70 characters per inch • Information can be changed • Must use a contact reader making high speed reading of many items impractical • Not human readable

Cont. on page 92

Cont. from page 91

Surface Acoustic Wave (SAW)	Data is encoded on a chip that is encased in a tag. In response to a radar pulse from a reader with a special antenna, the tag converts the pulse to an ultrasonic acoustic wave. Each tag is uniquely programmed so that the resulting acoustic wave has an amplitude matching the chip's code. The wave is converted back to an electromagnetic signal sent back to the reader.	• Can be used in highly hazardous environments such as high heat and acid baths • Can be read up to 6 feet away • No line of sight required • Physically durable
Radio Frequency Tag	Data is encoded on a chip that is encased in a tag. In response to a radar pulse from a reader with a special antenna, a transponder in the tag sends a signal to the reader.	• Tags can be programmable or permanently coded • Can be read up to 30 feet away • No line of sight required • Physically durable—life in excess of 10 years

Elements of a Bar Code Symbol

Why can you easily read the sentence, "Inventory control is fun"? You can read that sentence because you recognize the alphabet used and understand the rules of grammar and sentence construction utilized. A bar code "symbology" or language is very similar because it has a fixed alphabet made up of various patterns of dark bars and intervening light spaces coupled with rules for how it is presented.

There are many types of bar codes, not all of which are the linear symbols most commonly found in the inventory control world. For example:

Appearance of common one-dimensional, linear types of bar code patterns:

Appearance of common two-dimensional, matrix and stacked bar code patterns:

Presently, linear bar codes are the most commonly used for general inventory control purposes.

Structure of a Generic Bar Code Symbol

The entire pattern is called the "symbol." Each bar or space is called an "element."

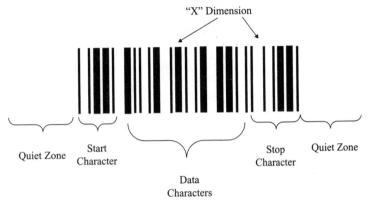

Quiet Zone

Symbols can be read from left to right or right to left. A bar code scanner (reader) must make a number of measurements in order to decode the symbol accurately. The quiet zones on each side of the symbol gives the scanner a starting point from which to start its measurement.

Start and Stop Characters

In order for codes to be read from either direction or top to bottom or bottom to top in a vertically oriented symbol ↕, start and stop characters tell the scanner where the message begins. It is customary for the character on the left or at the top of the symbol to be the start character, and the one on the right or bottom to be the stop character.

Data Characters

The data characters are the actual message within the code. These can be letters of the alphabet, numbers, symbols (+, −, /, =), or a combination of all three.

"X" Dimension

The narrowest bar or space in a bar code is called the "X" dimension. This width can run from 5 mils to 50 mils. A mil is one-thousandth of an inch.

This is a very important width because it determines how wide each narrow and wide bar or space will be. The narrow bars/spaces are a single "X" in width, while the wide bars/spaces can be two, three, or four "Xs" wide. Therefore, an element (a bar or space) can be a single "X" or several "Xs."

The larger the "X" dimension of a symbol the easier it is to read.

Symbologies—Bar Coding Structural Rules

Just as there are rules for how an English sentence is structured, for the relationship of upper case to lower case letters, and for punctuation, there are similar rules governing bar codes. These rules are set out in a "symbology." A symbology controls how information will be encoded in a bar code symbol.

Just as there are different languages such as French, English, Spanish, Italian, Russian, Japanese, and Chinese, there are different symbologies. Common symbologies found in the inventory world are Code 39, Code 128, Interleaved 2 of 5, and UPC.

Symbologies are like typefaces with different character sets and separate printing characteristics. Some symbologies only present numbers. Some have numbers, uppercase alphabetics (A–Z), and limited special characters. Others have both upper and lowercase alphabetics (A–Z, a–z), numbers, and a wide range of special characters. Some symbologies only allow for a set number of characters in a pattern, while others allow for variable length messages.

Discrete and Continuous Symbologies

Bar codes can either be discrete or continuous. Characters in a discrete code start with a bar and end with a bar, and they have a space between each character. Characters in a continuous code start with a bar, end with a space, and have no gap between one character and another. The primary significance of the difference is that a discrete code is easier to print and read, but you can get more characters per inch with a continuous code.

Which of the following is easier to read?

<small>Symbologies</small> Symbologies Symbologies Symbologies

The word on the far left is the most difficult to read but has the greatest amount of information in the smallest amount of space, which is a good thing on a bar code label with limited space available. The word on the far right is the easiest to read, would allow for a more forgiving print job (for example, if the ink spread on the label surface between each letter, we would still be able to read it), but it takes up more space. Discrete symbologies are easier to print and read, but they take up more space.

Symbology Summary

The rules of a particular symbology control are:

- Character set—which alphabetics, numbers, and special characters are in the symbology?
- Symbology type—discrete or continuous? See Exhibit 4–3.
- Number of element widths—how many different "Xs" are there in the wide bars/spaces?

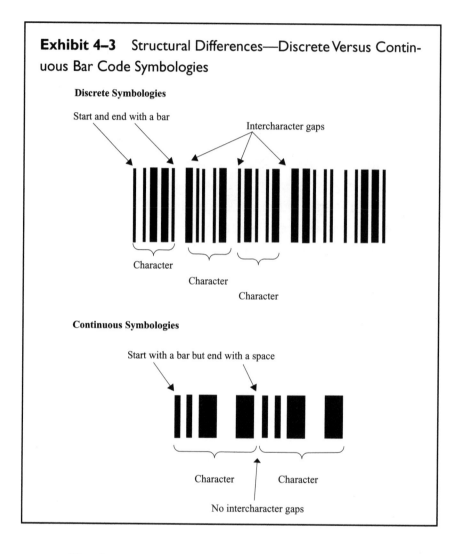

Exhibit 4–3 Structural Differences—Discrete Versus Continuous Bar Code Symbologies

Discrete Symbologies

Start and end with a bar

Intercharacter gaps

Character

Character

Character

Continuous Symbologies

Start with a bar but end with a space

Character

Character

No intercharacter gaps

- Fixed or variable lengths of characters in a pattern?
- Density—how many characters can appear per inch?

Popular Symbologies Found in the Inventory World

There are dozens of bar code symbologies. Many have failed in the marketplace because a large number of printer and scanner suppliers will not support them. Others are owned by individ-

ual companies that control and limit their use. Others have specialized uses like Postnet used by the U.S. Postal Service. Some are widely supported and accepted in the inventory control world.

Universal Product Code/European Article Numbering System

Without question, when dealing with point-of-sale identification of product (as in a grocery or other retail store), the bar code used is the Universal Product Code (UPC). A very similar code, which will eventually be interchangeable with UPC, is the European Article Numbering System (EAN).

The UPC symbology is highly structured and controlled, and it is only used in general merchandise retailing. It is an all numeric, fixed length (11 characters) symbology. The UPC symbol is physically arranged into two halves. The left half has six numbers that identify the manufacturer or packager. The right half identifies the product. See Exhibit 4–4. You have to license the right to use the UPC from the Uniform Code Council (UCC), an organization created by the grocery industry.

The UPC is not suitable for inventory control use within a warehousing or manufacturing facility where there is a need for variable length messages, alpha-numeric coding, flexible identification patterns, and so on.

Code 39

This symbology is the most widely used bar code in nonretail applications. It was first introduced in 1975.

Most stockkeepers will be able to find a Code 39 software to interface with their existing application software systems. In other words, you should be able to find a Code 39 bar code package that will allow you to continue to use your existing in-house software, numbering systems, and internal procedures.

Code 39 is sometimes referred to as "3 of 9 Code" because

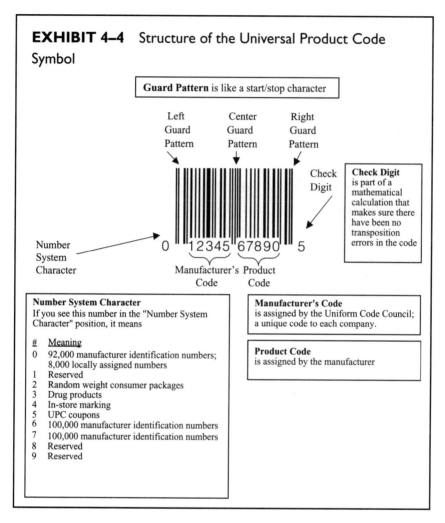

EXHIBIT 4–4 Structure of the Universal Product Code Symbol

Guard Pattern is like a start/stop character

Left Guard Pattern   Center Guard Pattern   Right Guard Pattern

Check Digit

Check Digit is part of a mathematical calculation that makes sure there have been no transposition errors in the code

Number System Character

0 1 2 3 4 5 6 7 8 9 0 5

Manufacturer's Code   Product Code

Number System Character
If you see this number in the "Number System Character" position, it means

#	Meaning
0	92,000 manufacturer identification numbers; 8,000 locally assigned numbers
1	Reserved
2	Random weight consumer packages
3	Drug products
4	In-store marking
5	UPC coupons
6	100,000 manufacturer identification numbers
7	100,000 manufacturer identification numbers
8	Reserved
9	Reserved

Manufacturer's Code
is assigned by the Uniform Code Council; a unique code to each company.

Product Code
is assigned by the manufacturer

three of the nine elements (bars or spaces) making up a Code 39 character are wide and the other six are narrow.

Code 39 was the first alphanumeric symbology developed. Among its most important features are:

- Entire alphabet in uppercase letters
- All numerics, e.g., 0 through 9
- Seven special characters: –, ., *, $, /, +, %, and a character representing a blank space

- Discrete symbology
- Allows variable length symbols
- Allows two messages to be decoded and transmitted as one ("concatenation")
- Can be printed in a wide variety of technologies
- Although there are only 43 data characters in the basic Code 39 set, by using certain characters as internal codes, it is possible to encode all 128 ASCII (American Code of Information Interchange) characters used by computers. This feature is cumbersome and is not widely used.
- Self checking, which means a single printing defect cannot cause an error where one character is mistaken for another

Code 128

This code, introduced in 1981, is the preferred symbology for most new bar code applications. It is one you should seriously consider if your business is going to enter into the world of bar coding.

This symbology has many desirable features, such as:

- It uses three start codes to allow the encoding of all 128 ASCII characters without cumbersome procedures. Therefore, you can use the entire alphabet in both upper and lower case, all ten numerics, and all special characters. Each printed character can one of three meanings.
- There is high data density and continuous symbology that uses the least amount of label space for messages of six or more characters
- Tests have shown this to be a highly readable code with high message integrity.

- Code 128 has become one of the two standard bar code symbologies used to identify the contents of corrugated boxes. (The other standard for corrugated shipping boxes is Interleaved 2 of 5 symbology.)
- Code 128 allows for concatenation.

Which Symbology is Right for Your Organization?

Each symbology has its strengths and weaknesses. There is no one "right" bar code language that will fit every organization's needs.

A starting point in reviewing appropriate symbologies actually begins with your own industry. Has your industry selected a particular type of symbology? For example, the automotive industry has been using Code 39 since 1980. You can obtain guidance from trade associations in your industry segment.

The reason to start with a symbology accepted by your industry is that direct application software and hardware will have been written or created for the specific requirements of your business. It is the old question, "Why recreate the wheel?"

If no symbology dominates your industry, then the real questions become What do you want the system to do for you? and How large is your budget?

Scanning Basics

Something has to read a bar code. That something is a scanner. These electro-optical devices include a means of illuminating the symbol and measuring reflected light.

A scanner projects a tiny spot of light that crosses the bar code symbol and then measures the exact width of the bars and spaces. The measurement is determined by the amount of re-

flectance off of the dark and light bars and spaces. Software in either the scanner or in a separate plug-in device then translates the visual (analog) signal into a digital one a computer can understand, and it decodes what symbology (language) it is reading and the message contained in the pattern.

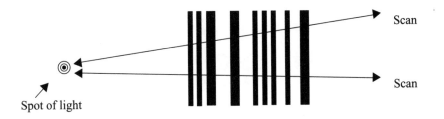

Light reflected is converted from an analog voltage (visual) format to a digital waveform for decoding.

The spot of light must not be larger than the "X" dimension being used for that label or you will get misreads.

Scanner might believe that both narrow bars are a single wide element and that the space is merely an ink void printing error.

Scanners must be purchased so that they match the "X" dimension that will be used for printing labels or for printing directly onto a surface.

Scanners can either be manual (where the user supplies the scanning motion) or automatic (where the device provides the scanning motion). See Exhibit 4–5.

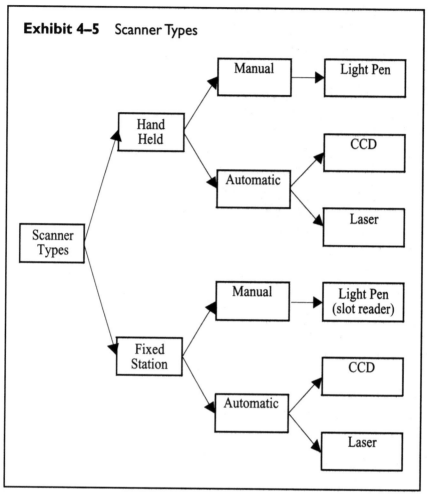

Exhibit 4–5 Scanner Types

Cont. on page 104

Printing Basics

Bar code printing can be done by the user on-site or by an off-site third party vendor.

On-site printing generally occurs close to where product is either being received or shipped—it's point-of-use.

There are five basic on-site bar code print technologies: direct thermal, thermal transfer, dot matrix impact, ink jet, and laser (Xerographic). See Exhibit 4–6.

Cont. from page 103

- Light pen (wand scanner)
  —Makes contact with the label or surface on which pattern is printed
  —Inexpensive
  —Durable
  —Can be tied into various decoder types of equipment

- Charge Coupled Device (CCD)
  —Has a depth of field of several inches so you do not have to make contact with the label or other surface. Therefore, you can read through shrink wrap, which is common in warehousing operations.
  —Floods symbol with light and reflectance illuminates photodetectors in the CCD scanner. Can read very high bar code densities
  —Moderate cost

- Lasers
  —Project a beam of energy off of a rotating prism or oscillating mirror
  —Depth of field of several feet
  —Expensive but versatile

Off-site, commercial printers use a wide variety of printing techniques.

See Chapter 3, Exhibit 3–13 for a discussion of methods to affix bar code labels.

Exhibit 4–6   Common Bar Code Print Technologies

- **Direct Thermal**—Overlapping dots are formed on a heat-sensitive substrate (label or other foundation) by selectively heating elements in a printhead.
- **Thermal Transfer**—Same concept as direct thermal except the image is transferred to the substrate from a ribbon that is heated by the elements in the printhead.
- **Dot Matrix Impact**—A moving printhead with rows of hammers that creates images through multiple passes over a ribbon.
- **Ink Jet**—A fixed printhead sprays tiny droplets of ink onto a substrate.
- **Laser (Xerographic)**—A controlled laser beam creates an image on an electrostatically charged, photoconductive drum. The charged areas attract toner particles that are transferred and fused onto the substrate.

Bar Code Applications

It is far more important that you understand what you want to accomplish with bar codes than for you to understand all of the technical aspects of them.

Think of all of the bits and pieces of information you need to know in order to control inventory in a distribution environment. For example:

- Manufacturer
- Supplier
- SKU number
- Description

- Pack size
- Ship to address
- Bill To address
- Credit terms
- Identification of receiving clerk, stock replenishment worker, order filler, shipping clerk
- Shipper
- Carrier
- Quantity
- Throughput rates, e.g., pieces per hour
- Time, date
- Location
- Purchase order identification

Think of all the information you need to control material in a manufacturing environment. For example:

- Particular bill of materials
- SKU number
- Quantity
- Work in process (WIP)
- Individual tasks
- Throughput rates
- Scrap
- Time, date
- Which machine
- Which process
- Location
- Machine instructions
- Job number

All of the above can be given a bar code identifier.

Bar code labels and markings can be printed directly on forms, boxes, the product itself, or on labels that are then affixed to forms, boxes, items themselves, individual parts of items, and so on.

A quick and easy way to begin using bar codes is through the use of scan boards or menu cards. A scan board or menu card is merely a sheet of paper or heavier card stock that contains on it information in both machine readable (bar code) and human readable (plain alpha-numeric text). See Exhibit 4–7 for examples of common scan boards/menu cards.

Exhibit 4–7 Common Types of Bar Code Scan Boards/ Menu Cards

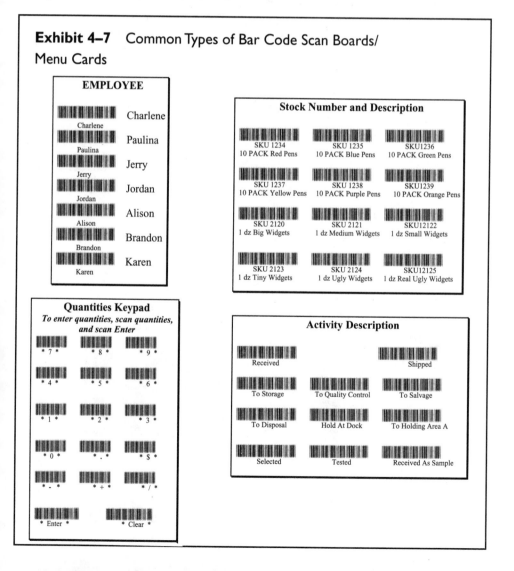

Examples of Using Bar Codes

- Receiving—Shipping

1. Employee scans in their own identity off of scan board or identification badge.

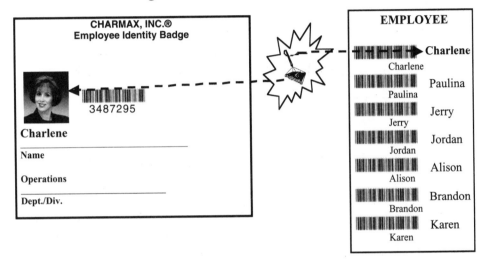

2. Employee scans product code from either items themselves or from scan board.

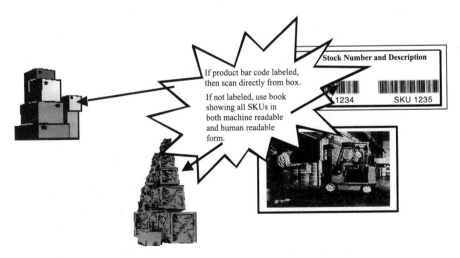

3. Employee scans in quantity.

4. Employee scans in activity (received, shipped, etc.).

- Tracking Multiple Activities at the Same Time in a Manufacturing Setting

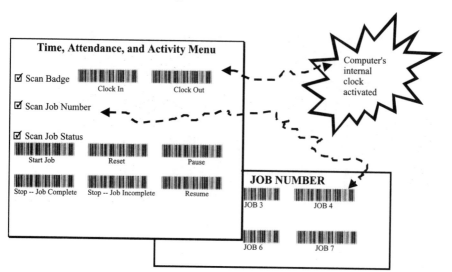

1. Employee scans in their identity.

2. Employee scans in either "Clock In" or "Clock Out." This starting/stopping time can be noted by the computer's internal clock. In addition, the computer's internal calendar notes the date.

(a) This information could be automatically routed to accounting for payroll purposes.

(b) This information will be captured for the particular job in question. That information can then be used as a part of various variance reports such as projected starting time versus actual starting time, projected ending time versus actual ending time, and so on. See Chapter 6, page 162 for a discussion of variance reports.

3. Employee scans in Job Number.

4. Employee scans in Job Status.

5. When employee scans in "Stop—Job Complete," system could begin, for example, a backflush of all raw materials used

as part of the job just completed. See Exhibit 6–1 on p. 172 for more information on backflushing.

- Using Bar Coding as Part of a Maintenance Program

1. Bar codes are assigned to each part of the maintenance procedure and to various parts (engines, for example) of the piece of equipment in question.

2. Employee then uses a Time, Attendance, and Activity Menu to track the maintenance tasks.

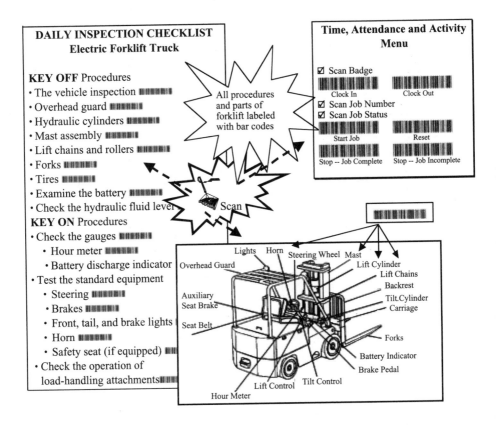

- Bar Coding and Physical Inventory and Cycle Counting

1. Bar code markings in both machine readable and human readable form are placed on both the storage locations (shelves, racks, drawers, bins) and on the product itself.

2. A counter equipped with a portable scanner:

   a. Scans in the identity of the SKU.

   b. Enters the quantity through a keypad on the scanner. The record count and shelf count can be compared in a variety of ways:

      (1) The shelf count as captured by the scanner and counter can be transmitted into the system by way of radio frequency at the time of information capture, or it can be uploaded from the scanner at a later time. The computer system would then generate an exception report of those items where the record and shelf counts did not match.

      (2) Scanners are small computers. Because of that they can contain software allowing them to have the record count stored within them. As the scanner reads the bar code and the counter enters the quantity information, the scanner could immediately compare the record count and shelf count. If there was a discrepancy, the scanner could alert the counter either through audible tones, flashing lights, or LED displays. The counter could then immediately initiate a recount.

recap   The objective of this chapter was to provide you
with an overview of bar coding, various popular
symbologies, and basic bar code applications.

The set of rules for how the bars and spaces of a bar code
language, its symbology, are arranged dictates how much and
what type of data can be displayed within a particular symbol.
The language that is most appropriate to your industry will be
determined by how much data and in what form that information must be displayed on your goods, inventory, or other materials.

Many industry segments such as automotive and retail
sales have selected the symbology felt to be most appropriate for
their respective needs. Often it is more economical and efficient
to adopt the symbology commonly found within your own industry segment.

In applying bar coding to your system, you are only limited
by your imagination—and your wallet. Applications can be simple ones involving scan boards or can be complex, utilizing laser
scanners, radio frequency, and sophisticated sharing of information throughout the system at the time of information capture.

? REVIEW QUESTIONS

1. What appears on both sides of a bar code symbol to give the
scanner a starting point from which to start its measurements?

1. (c)

(a) "X" Dimension
(b) A 3 of 9 interleave
(c) Quiet zones
(d) An aperture

2. **True or False**

   There are only five types of bar code languages. 2. (b)
   (a) True
   (b) False

3. **True or False**

   The most widely used bar code symbology for
   nonretail applications is Code 39. 3. (a)
   (a) True
   (b) False

4. **True or False**

   A discrete symbology starts with a bar and ends
   with a bar.

   4. (a)

   (a) True
   (b) False

5. Which symbology is the most widely used for retail
   point of sale transactions? 5. (a)
   (a) Universal Product Code
   (b) Code 39
   (c) Code 128
   (d) Codabar

CHAPTER 5

Planning and Replenishment Concepts

Introduction

The objective of this chapter is to provide basic approaches to forecasting inventory levels and to undertaking stock replenishment. With the proper techniques, you will have the right item, in the right quantity, at the right time, and in the right place.

Replenishment Costs

As discussed in Chapter 2, Inventory as Money, every day that an item remains in your stockroom it costs you money in the form of a carrying cost (K Factor). If you take that concept to its ultimate extreme, it would make sense to only buy items exactly when you need them. Multiple smaller quantity purchases of the same item certainly hold down your carrying costs. However, it hurts your cost of replenishment—the expenses associated with buying things.

It costs money to buy things. That sounds absurdly simple when you first read it. However, the cost of purchasing product exceeds the actual price paid for it. Expenses related to purchasing include the salaries of the purchasing staff, rent, and other overhead expenses attributable to the purchasing department. See Exhibit 5-1.

In fact, the more often you buy, the greater your internal costs. For example, if you purchased one million widgets all at the same time, your purchasing or replenishment cost (R Factor) would be the cost per line item, per purchase order (PO). See Exhibit 5–1.

- If the per line, per PO cost is $5.00, then your cost to buy all one million widgets at one time would be $5.00.
- If you were to buy the same one million widgets 250,000 at a time, then your R Factor would be $5.00 times four (four POs with one line item each) or $20.00.
- If you purchased the widgets one at a time, the cost would be one million times $5.00 or five million dollars.

Order size versus frequency of purchase shifts the cost burden from the K Factor to the R Factor and vice versa. In other words:

- If you buy smaller quantities more often, your purchasing costs go up—or your R Factor increases.
- If you buy larger quantities less often, you have a higher inventory level for a longer period of time, so your carrying costs go up—or your K Factor increases.

In a perfect world the K Factor and the R Factor would be equal. Although this is difficult to achieve, an organization attempting to have the correct amount of product at the overall lowest cost will strive for that balance.

Exhibit 5–1 Calculating the R Factor

The cost of replenishment is calculated on a per item, per order basis. This is because it takes the same amount of internal effort to determine how much of each item you desire, from which supplier, at what pricing, terms, and so on, no matter which item is being considered and no matter how many items there are on any given PO. Therefore, if the R Factor is $5.00 per item, per order, and there is a single line item on an order, the replenishment cost is $5.00. If there are two items, it's $10.00. If there are three items, it's $15.00, and so on.[1]

To calculate the cost of replenishment, include:

Annual cost of purchasing department labor	220,000
Annual cost of purchasing department overhead	
(rent, utilities, equipment allocation, etc.)	$179,000
Annual cost of expediting stock items	$ 25,000
Total annual costs	$424,000
Number of purchase orders created per year	
for stock (assume):	10,000
Average number of different stock items	
per order (assume):	x 8
Total number of times stock items were ordered:	80,000

$$\frac{\text{Total Annual Costs}}{\text{Total Times Stock Items Were Ordered}} = \xrightarrow{\text{R Factor}} = \frac{\$424,000}{80,000} = \boxed{\begin{array}{c}\$5.30 = \\ \text{R Factor}\end{array}}$$

Case Study: Balancing Carrying and Replenishment Costs

A dispute has arisen at the Charmax Co. between the purchasing and warehouse managers.

Charmax's receiving ends at 5:00 PM. At 4:45 PM, a 40-foot trailer is backed up to the dock. The doors are opened to reveal three levels of floor-stacked boxes extending from floor to ceiling, back to front.

Joe, the warehouse manager, realizes that it will take four workers at least two hours to hand unload the trailer. Virtually all of that time will be on an overtime basis.

Joe reviews the truck's manifest and determines what items on the trailer are needed for delivery tomorrow morning. He discovers that there are only three boxes on the trailer that are truly required for tomorrow's business. He asks Tracy, the truck driver, if he helped to load the trailer. Tracy replies that he did. Joe asks if Tracy remembers where those three boxes are. With a smile, Tracy replies that they are located in the nose of the trailer.

Joe decides not to incur the overtime. He will have the trailer unloaded in the morning.

Betty, the sales manager, hears that the three items will not be shipped to Acme, a large and important customer. She storms into the warehouse and demands that the trailer be unloaded.

Joe explains the overtime situation. Betty replies that Joe should have scheduled the trailer to arrive earlier in the day. Joe replies that the buyer, Bill, handles traffic management as part of the purchase of the product. Betty angrily says she doesn't much care. Joe had told her that the product would be here today for delivery tomorrow. "You promised me," Betty says, "so that's what I prom-

ised the customer. Now unload the trailer." Joe reluctantly does so.

Later, Joe confronts Bill and demands that product be brought in palletized or unitized or in some other manner so it can be unloaded quickly. Joe argues that since internal handling is a major component in computing the cost of carrying inventory, unitization will help cut Charmax's costs.

Bill responds that he has to buy the product as he is buying it now. He argues that to palletize the product would increase the costs per unit of product. He also points out that since the product already extends to the top of the trailer, that the added height of three levels of pallets at approximately four inches each, would force him to buy less per order so that it will all fit on a trailer. Therefore, he will have to buy less and buy it more often driving up his replenishment costs. Ill-will and stalemate result.

Suggested Solutions:

1. Joe and Bill should coordinate traffic management so that loads match the labor, equipment, time resources, and constraints of the organization. By lowering handling costs the company will reduce overall carrying costs.

2. Both Joe and Bill need to specifically determine their respective costs.

   (a) Joe can determine the handling portion of the K Factor by :
      (1) Determining the average time it takes to hand unload a trailer.
      (2) Multiplying the average hand unloading time times the number of trailers during the year.

Cont. on page 120

Cont. from page 119

(3) Multiplying the total hand unloading time times the average hourly labor rate being paid the warehouse personnel.

(4) Determining the average time it would take to unload unitized loads.

(5) Multiplying the average unitized unloading time times the number of trailers during the year.

(6) Multiplying the total unitized unloading time times the average hourly labor rate being paid the warehouse personnel.

(7) Comparing the annual labor costs involved for hand unloading to the annual labor costs of unitized unloading to determine the total dollar savings.

(b) Bill can determine his added replenishment costs associated with smaller loads purchased more often.

(c) A fair comparison can then be made as to which route is the most advantageous for the overall organization.

3. Alternatives meeting the needs of both parties might be developed. For example, if slip-sheets (thin cardboard or plywood sheets the same length and width as a pallet) were used, Bill might be able to overcome the size of load and volume problem, while Joe could automate the unloading process.

Inventory Types

In the worlds of distribution, retailing, and replacement parts, an organization deals with finished goods. In the manufacturing world an organization deals with raw materials and subassemblies. Considerations of what to buy, when to buy it, in what quantities, and so on are dramatically different in these two worlds.

In distribution you are concerned with having the right item, in the right quantity. Issues relating to having the item at the right time and place are often dealt with by simply increasing safety stock on-hand. That is not a good solution because it leads to wasted money and space. However, traditional formulae used in computing inventory requirements in a distribution environment focus on item and quantity rather than place and time. In manufacturing, you are concerned with having the right item, in the right quantity, at the right time, in the right place.

Demand for finished goods and spare parts for replacements are said to be "independent," while demand for items in the manufacturing world are said to be "dependent." Understanding these distinctions will assist you in forecasting your procurement needs.

Independent demand is influenced by market conditions outside the control of your organization's operations. The demand for the widgets your organization sells will be independent of the demand for your gadgets, doodads, and whatchamacallits. Your products are independent of one another. In this environment you must have the right item in the right quantity.

Dependent demand is related to another item. The demand for products built up or created from raw materials, parts, and assemblies is dependent on the demand for the final product. You would not need one item if you did not also require another,

both of which would go into an assembly or finished product. In this environment you must have the right items in the right quantities at the time in order to complete a finished product.

A chair can be used as an example of the above. The demand for the number of chairs you need is independent from the number of tables that you need because quantity required is influenced by the demand in the market for each item. The demand for chair legs, or seats, or rails is mathematically dependent on the demand for *finished* chairs. Four legs and one seat are required for each chair.

Dependent and independent demands demonstrate very different usage and demand patterns.

Independent demand calls for a *replenishment* approach to inventory management. This approach assumes that market forces will exhibit a somewhat fixed pattern. Therefore, stock is replenished as it is used in order to have items on hand for customers.

Dependent demand calls for a *requirements* approach. When an assembly or finished item is needed, then the materials needed to create it are ordered. There is no fixed pattern because an assembly created in the past may never be produced again.

The nature of demand, therefore, leads to different concepts, formulae, and methods of inventory management.

Independent Demand Inventory

Order-Point Formulae

Order point formulae are used to determine how much of a given item needs to be ordered where there is independent demand. In these formulae a reorder point (ROP) is set for each item. The ROP is the lowest amount of an item you will have on hand and on order before you reorder.

A Simple Min-Max Inventory System

Order point formulae are based on some relatively simple concepts.

Imagine that all of a particular SKU are kept in a single bin. If no reorder point was set, then the entire batch would be used up without any order being placed. The organization would then be unable to sell or use that item during whatever time frame was required to order and bring the SKU in—the lead time. It would therefore make sense to adopt a two-bin system with Bin 1 containing working stock and Bin 2 containing working reserve. The amount of product in Bin 2 would be equal to your usage rate during that item's lead time.

In a two-bin system, if all goes as it should, then immediately upon using the first item from Bin 2, you would reorder a quantity equal to both Bins 1 and 2. As you use the last item in Bin 2, the order arrives and you refill both bins. This assumes that lead time is exact, there are no vendor stockouts or backorders, and that there are never any defects. That assumption is, of course, often false. Therefore, a true order-point system is a three-bin system, with the Bin 3 containing safety stock.

Bin 3, safety stock, relates to Bin 2 since Bin 3 is to make up for uncertainties in lead time and defects. Mathematically safety stock is 50 percent of working reserve. (The average between having nothing in Bin 2 and having it at 100 percent full is 50 percent.) However, companies adjust safety stock levels to coincide with their actual experience.

Bins can be mathematically created or can reflect actual physical separation of items in the stockroom.

A simple formula for determining the ROP reflects the above concepts.

(Usage x Lead Time) + Safety Stock = ROP

In the above formula lead time is shown as a percentage of a month, as follows:

1 week = 0.25 = 25%	4 weeks = 1.00 = 100%
2 weeks = 0.50 = 50%	5 weeks = 1.25 = 125%
3 weeks = 0.75 = 75%	6 weeks = 1.50 = 150%

Example 1:

Assume:
- Usage rate of 1,200 items per month
- Lead time of 3 weeks

Step-by-Step Calculation:
- Calculate weekly usage. Assume a 4-week month. 1,200 items ÷ 4 weeks = 300 items per week ➜ therefore Bin 1 or working stock should contain at least 300 items
- Calculate working reserve: Given 3 weeks of lead time, working reserve should be 1,200 items x 0.75 = 900 items
- Calculate safety stock, use 50 percent of working reserve as a guideline (900 items x 50% = 450 items)
- Calculate ROP: (1,200 items x 0.75) + 450 items = ROP 1,350 items

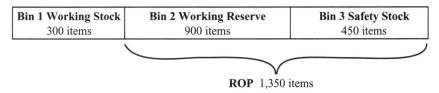

Bin 1 Working Stock	Bin 2 Working Reserve	Bin 3 Safety Stock
300 items	900 items	450 items

ROP 1,350 items

Example 2:

Assume:
- Usage rate of 1,200 items per month
- Lead time of 1 week

Step-by-Step Calculation:
- Calculate weekly usage. Assume a 4-week month. 1,200 items ÷ 4 weeks = 300 items per week ➜ therefore Bin 1 or working stock should contain at least 300 items
- Calculate working reserve: Given 1 week of lead time, working reserve should be 1,200 items x 0.25 = 300 items
- Calculate safety stock, use 50 percent of working reserve as a guideline (300 items x 50% = 150 items)
- Calculate ROP: (1,200 items x 0.25) + 150 items = ROP 450 items

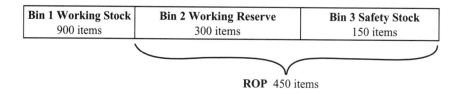

Bin 1 Working Stock	Bin 2 Working Reserve	Bin 3 Safety Stock
900 items	300 items	150 items

ROP 450 items

The ROP is the "minimum" (min) in a "minimum-maximum" (min-max) inventory control system. In these systems there is a minimum below which you will not let your stock level fall; and there is a maximum above which you will not have items on hand or on order.

In order to compute the maximum in these systems, you must first determine how often you will place orders. This time period is called the *review cycle*.

The review cycle is the length of time between reviews of when you wish to order product. The formula to determine the review cycle is:

$$\frac{\text{Total Purchases from Vendor for a Year}}{\text{Discount Quantity}} = \text{Review Cycle}$$

The unit of measure reflecting total purchases from a vendor can be dollars, pieces, pounds, units, or whatever your organization uses. The discount quantity is the minimum amount you have to order of that unit of measure in order to be granted a discount.

Review cycle example:

$$\frac{200,000}{5,000} = 40 \text{ reviews per year}$$

And, by dividing 40 reviews by 52 weeks equals a review roughly every 1.3 weeks. When the review actually occurs will also depend on factors such as seasonality.

The maximum in these systems is also represented by a simple formula.

ROP + Usage During the Review Cycle = Maximum

Maximum Point Example 1: **Assume:**	**Maximum Point Example 2:** **Assume:**
• Usage rate of 1,200 items per month • Review cycle every 1.3 weeks • ROP equals 1,350 items	• Usage rate of 1,200 items per month • Review cycle every 1.3 weeks • ROP equals 450 items
$\dfrac{1,200 \text{ items}}{4 \text{ wks}} = 300 \text{ items used per week}$	$\dfrac{1,200 \text{ items}}{4 \text{ wks}} = 300 \text{ used per week}$

300 items x 1.3 weeks
    = 390 items used during
    review cycle
	300 items x 1.3 weeks
	    = 390 used during
	    review cycle

1,350 items + 390 items
    = 1,740 items max
	450 items + 390 items
	    = 840 items max

By setting a min-max for each item in your inventory, you can create a simple method of ordering products having independent demand.

Economic Order Quantity (EOQ) Formula

In 1915, F. W. Harris of General Electric developed the Economic Order Quantity formula (EOQ) to help stockkeepers in determining how much product to buy.

To calculate EOQ, assume:

$$A = \text{Total Value of SKU Per Year}$$
$$K = \text{Carrying Cost (The K Factor)}$$
$$R = \text{Replenishment Cost (The R Factor)}$$
$$P = \text{Price Per Unit}$$

Basic Formula:

$$EOQ = \sqrt{\frac{2AR}{P^2K}}$$

This formula and its variations allow you to determine the following:

- the optimal quantity to order
- when it should be ordered
- the total cost
- the average inventory level
- how much should be ordered each time
- the maximum inventory level

The EOQ model is based on several assumptions:

- the demand rate is constant (no variations), recurring, and known.
- the carrying cost and ordering cost are independent of the quantity ordered (no discounts).
- the lead time is constant and known. Therefore, the ordering times given result in new orders arriving exactly when the inventory level reaches zero.

- formula can handle only one type of item at a time.
- orders arrive in a single batch (no vendor stockouts or backorders).

A simple example of the basic formula is:

$$A = \$36,000$$
$$K = 15\%$$
$$R = \$75$$
$$P = \$25$$

$$EOQ = \sqrt{\frac{2AR}{P^2K}} = \sqrt{\frac{2(\$36,000)(\$75)}{(\$25)^2(0.15)}} = \sqrt{\frac{5,475,000}{93.75}} = \sqrt{58,400}$$
$$= 242 \text{ units per order}$$

Since the above assumptions do not reflect the real world, mathematicians have developed variations of the basic formula. See Exhibit 5–2.

Exhibit 5–2   Variations of the Basic EOQ Formula

Inventory Variable Formulae and Examples

For the below formulae and examples, assume:

A = Total Value of SKU Per Year	= \$36,000
K = Carrying Cost (The K Factor)	= 15%
R = Replenishment Cost (The R Factor)	= \$75
P = Price Per Unit	= \$25

Optimum Number of Orders Per Year =

$$\sqrt{\frac{AK}{2R}} = \sqrt{\frac{(\$36,000)(0.15)}{2(\$75)}} = \sqrt{\frac{5,475}{150}} = \sqrt{36.5} = 6.4 \cong 6 \text{ per order}$$

Optimum Number of Dollars Per Order =

$$\sqrt{\frac{2AR}{K}} = \sqrt{\frac{2(\$36,000)(\$75)}{0.15}} = \sqrt{\frac{5,475,000}{0.15}} = \sqrt{36,500,000} \cong \$6,041.52$$

How to Set Up an EOQ Worksheet in Microsoft® Excel®

Here's a tip . . . by setting up a permanent worksheet in Microsoft® Excel® or similar spreadsheet program, you will be able to quickly calculate important EOQ information simply by entering variable values for A, K, R, and P under the "Insert Value" column.

Based on the cell placement as noted below, you can calculate each quantity by entering the following formulae:

Economic Order Quantity ➜ type: = SQRT((2*E4*E8)/((E10 ^ 2)*E6))

Optimum Number of Orders Per Year ➜ type: = SQRT((E4*E6)/(2*E8))

Optimum Number of Dollars Per Order ➜ type: = SQRT((2*E4*E8)/E6)

Screen Shot I Illustrates worksheet set up including formulae input

Screen Shot II   Illustrates example of completed worksheet. Values were entered for the variables A, K, R, and P. The worksheet then updated itself as the formulae were already input:

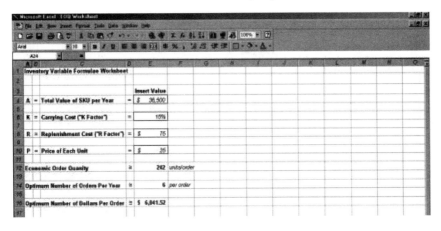

Dependent Demand Inventory

Materials Requirements Planning

Controlling not only what item is purchased and in what quantities, but also the timing of its arrival through computerized systems is called *materials requirements planning* (MRP). This concept of the right item, in the right quantity, and at the right time was first introduced by Joseph Orlicky in 1975.

Independent demand inventory management is customer oriented. The objective of ROP rules and formulae is high customer service levels and low operating costs. Dependent demand systems, however, are manufacturing oriented. The objective of dependent demand inventory control is to support the master production schedule. Even if you have a low stock level of an item, it won't be ordered unless and until it is needed to produce something for the master schedule—a true requirements philosophy of inventory control. MRP dependent demand inventory control is directed inward rather than outward like ROP inventory control. See Exhibit 5–3.

Exhibit 5–3 Contrasting Order Point with MRP Systems

	ORDER POINT	MRP
Demand	Independent	Dependent
Order Philosophy	Replenishment	Requirements
Forecasting	Based on past demand	Based on master schedule
Control Concept	ABC categorization	All items are equally important
Objectives	Meet customer needs	Meet manufacturing needs
Lot Sizing	EOQ	Individual item requirements
Demand Pattern	Consistent	Random but predictable
Inventory Type	Finished goods/ spare parts	Work in progress/ raw materials

---

MRP Elements

Key concepts in understanding MRP are the *master production schedule* and the *bill of materials*.

The *master production schedule* sets out what will be built, when, and in what quantities. It can either cover short or long time horizons.

- Short horizon—planning of initial requirements sets out:
  —final product requirements
  —schedule for production of components
  —purchase order priorities
  —short term capacity requirements

- Long horizon—estimating long term requirements sets out:

—long term production capacity required

—long term warehouse capacity required

—long term staffing required

—long term money required

The *bill of materials* (BOM) is the recipe of raw materials, parts, subassemblies, and so on required to build or make something.

There are levels to each BOM. See Exhibit 5–4 and Exhibit 6–1 on page 165 for a discussion of how inventory is relieved from stock after each level of the BOM is completed. This is a technique called "backflushing."

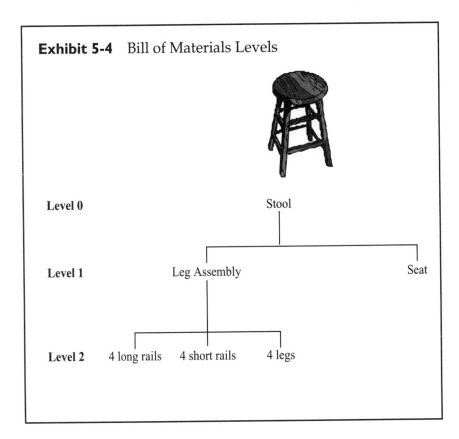

Exhibit 5-4   Bill of Materials Levels

Level 0   Stool

Level 1   Leg Assembly   Seat

Level 2   4 long rails   4 short rails   4 legs

MRP's chief advantage over the ROP approach is that it lets you customize your ordering strategy for raw materials, parts, and so on with different demand characteristics such as lead times. The ROP approach answers the questions of *what* and *how much*:

On Hand	60	or	60
On Order	100		50
Required	130		130
Available	30		−20

ROP does not answer the question of *when*:

On Hand	60	or	60
On Order	100 due in		50 due on
	on Nov. 15th		Nov. 1st
Required	130 *needed by*		100 needed by
	Nov. 5th		Nov. 5th
			30 *needed by Nov. 15th*
Available			10 on Nov. 5th
when needed	−70		−20 on Nov. 15th

MRP allows purchases to be made as and when needed to ensure that items will arrive when needed. It accomplishes this by setting up time phasing charts within the computer system. See Exhibit 5–5.

Exhibit 5-5 Time Phasing Chart for a Single Item Within a MRP System

Assumptions:

- 12-week production schedule
- 10 units of this item are required each week for production
- Starting balance of 70 units
- One week lead time

As evidenced by the first chart, you do not need to buy and hold any of the items in question until Week 7. Week 7's production will bring our balance of inventory on hand to zero.

Time Phasing Chart Without Release of Purchase Order

	0	1	2	3	4	5	6	7	8	9	10	11	12	Week Number
		10	10	10	10	10	10	10	10	10	10	10	10	Gross Requirements
														Scheduled Receipt
	70	60	50	40	30	20	10	0	-10	-20	-30	-40	-50	Inventory on Hand
														Planned Order Release

Time Phasing Chart With Release of Purchase Order

	0	1	2	3	4	5	6	7	8	9	10	11	12	Week Number
		10	10	10	10	10	10	10	10	10	10	10	10	Gross Requirements
								100						Scheduled Receipt
	70	60	50	40	30	20	10	100	90	80	70	60	50	Inventory On Hand
						100								Planned Order Release

In the second chart, a purchase order is released during Week 6. The product arrives during Week 7, and you are ready for production as Week 8 begins.

The above charts demonstrate that by timing the release of the PO for a specific item, that item can be brought in only when needed. This holds our inventory levels down.

MRP has evolved into three somewhat distinct systems:

• **MRP—an inventory control system**	**Overall characteristics:** —**Master Production Scheduling** —**Master Requirements Planning** —**Capacity Requirements Planning** —**Executing Capacity Plans** —**Executing Material Plans** **These systems are sometimes called closed-loop systems. See Exhibit 5–6.** **Overall characteristics:** —**Business Plan** —**Sales and Operations Planning** —**Simulation**
• **Enterprise Resource Planning (ERP) And Other Just-In-Time (JIT) Inventory Systems—manufacturing resource-planning systems**	**ERP and other JIT systems are used to plan and control all resources: cash, labor, inventory, facilities, and capital equipment.** **Overall Characteristics:** —**Investment Management** —**Plant Maintenance** —**Quality Management** —**Personnel Planning & Development** —**Materials Management** —**Sales and Distribution** —**Financial Accounting** —**Controlling**

An example of MRP would be a decision to build one bar stool in your garage on Saturday.

The decision to build a single unit of something on a given day is the master schedule.

Included in your thinking was the fact that if you had all of

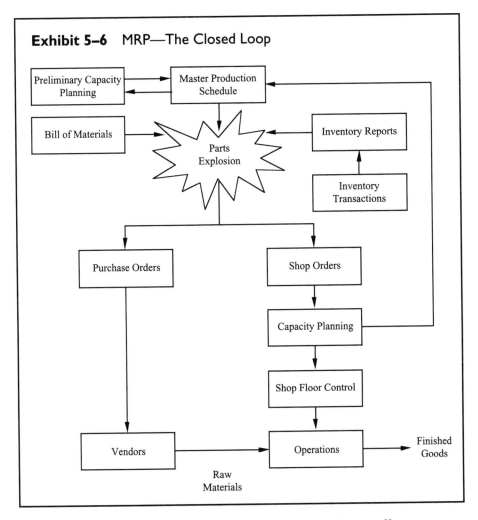

Exhibit 5–6   MRP—The Closed Loop

the pieces, parts, and tools necessary, you could actually accomplish the task. That is rough-cut capacity planning.

You then draw-up and define what parts are required for the task. See Exhibit 5–4. This is your bill of materials.

The next step is a parts explosion where you review your on-hand inventory levels to initially determine if any POs must be prepared and released.

You then engage in detailed capacity planning to decide if you can proceed or if the master schedule, capacity, or the planned release of POs must be changed.

Ultimately, all parts, equipment, and so on come together and the stool is built.

MRP works well because it is a forward-looking system. The predictability of events allows for careful planning and a reduction in unnecessary inventory.

A major drawback of MRP and JIT systems is that they are highly data dependent. Not only do you have to have *all* of the data easily available on an ongoing basis, but in addition, the information must be accurate and timely. Organizations lacking a strong software/hardware infrastructure will have difficulty in fully implementing an MRP system.

Just-In-Time (JIT) Inventory Systems

JIT was first developed within Toyota's manufacturing operations by Taiichi Ohno in the 1970s as a means of meeting customer demands with minimum delay. In its original form, it referred to the production of goods, assemblies, and subassemblies to meet exactly the customer's demand in terms of time, quality, and quantity. With a JIT system, the "buyer" can be the actual end user or another process along the production line.

JIT goes further than MRP, because you control not only the right item, in the right quantity, at the right time, but you also bring that SKU to the right place. Under this time-based concept, an item appears exactly when it is needed—not before, not after.

The American Production and Inventory Control Society (APICS) has the following definition of JIT:

> . . . a philosophy of manufacturing based on planned elimination of all waste and continuous improvement of productivity. It encompasses the successful execution of all manufacturing activities required to produce a final product, from design engineering to delivery

and including all stages of conversion from raw material onward. The primary elements include having only the required inventory when needed; to improve quality to zero defects; to reduce lead time by reducing setup times, queue lengths and lot sizes; to incrementally revise the operations themselves; and to accomplish these things at minimum cost.

There are many benefits to a JIT system, including:

- Reduction of stockouts
- Reduction of inventory levels
- Reduction of need for material handling equipment
- Reduction of time frames between delivery and production
- Significant quality improvement
- Employee inclusion in continuous quality improvement

JIT is a management philosophy rather than a technique.

The fact that certain words and acronyms have come to be used somewhat interchangeably can be confusing to anyone not in the manufacturing world. Do those terms/acronyms have individual, stand alone characteristics differentiating one from another? Most certainly they do, however, grappling with the details of what separates one particular type of manufacturing philosophy from another closely related theory won't further your understanding of the basic concepts of inventory management and control.

The terms/acronyms *MRP III, Computer Integrated Manufacturing, Lean Manufacturing, Short Cycle Manufacturing, Just-in-Time, JIT, Enterprise Resource Planning, ERP,* and so on all relate to the fundamental notions that:

- manufacturing activities should be integrated.
- the actions and decisions of each department should complement all other departments.
- information should flow both internally throughout the organization and externally to/from suppliers/customers electronically rather than through:

—the movement of hard paper copies, or

—through individual software (accounting) modules whose data do not flow into one another both automatically and in real time.

- suppliers are reliable and raw materials are without defect.
- all employees follow the philosophy of continuous quality improvement in all aspects of the operation.

Let's concentrate on how these concepts—by whatever name—relate to inventory. They all regard inventory as *waste*.

Today JIT has come to mean producing with a minimum of waste. "Waste" is used in the broadest sense and includes any nonvalue adding activities. For example, storing, inspecting, and counting materials doesn't change the items; therefore, those actions add no value. There are seven types of waste JIT systems strive to eliminate:

- Overproduction—producing more than needed. Wasted money, effort, space, etc.
- Waiting time—decreases productivity and efficiency.
- Transportation—double and even triple handling of an item from one storage position to another.
- Processing— what are the interfaces between parties, de-

partments, you, and your suppliers? The fewer and faster the better.

- Inventory—stock simply sitting around does no one any good.
- Motion—reduce motions such as those involved in looking for materials.
- Defects—defective goods not only cost money directly, but they also cause stops and delays.

Implementing JIT

Take the following steps to introduce a JIT type system into your manufacturing facility:

1. Stabilize and level the production schedule.

- All work centers should have a uniform load through constant daily production.
- Prevent changes in the production plan for some period of time.
- Produce roughly the same mix of products each day, using a repeating sequence if several products are produced on the same line. This is often called "mixed model assembly."
- Change the quantity of end-item inventory to meet demand fluctuations rather than through fluctuations in production levels.

2. Reduce or eliminate setup times.

- Strive to create single digit setup times (less than 10 minutes).

3. Reduce lot sizes (manufacturing and purchase).

- Reducing setup times allows economical production of smaller lots.
- Close cooperation with suppliers is necessary to achieve reductions in order lot sizes since more frequent deliveries will be called for. In JIT systems, the old, adversarial methods of purchasing will not work. In traditional approaches buyers buy an item here and another item there through a series of disconnected negotiations over price, delivery quality, and terms. In JIT systems, larger quantities and types of items are purchased from fewer vendors. The larger purchases give the buyer more economic leverage while providing the supplier with enough financial incentive to become the buyer's business partner. Both parties recognize the critical needs, costing, pricing, quality concerns, and so on of the other.

4. Reduce lead times (production and delivery)
- Production lead times can be reduced by:
  —moving work stations closer together.
  —applying group technology and cellular manufacturing concepts.
  —reducing the number of jobs waiting to be processed at a given machine ("queue" length).
  —improving the coordination and cooperation between successive processes, such as, reducing delivery times by inducing suppliers to have distribution centers/warehouses closer to your operation.

5. Engage in strong preventive maintenance
- Machine and worker idle time should be used to maintain equipment and prevent breakdowns.

6. Cross-train to create a flexible work force

- Workers should be trained to:
  —operate several machines.
  —perform maintenance tasks.
  —perform quality inspections.

7. Require supplier quality assurance and implement a zero-defects quality program.

- Since there are no buffers of safety stock, errors leading to defective items must be eliminated.

8. Use a control system such as a kanban (card) system to convey parts between work stations in small quantities (ideally, one unit at a time).

Inventory Objectives

Inventory in and of itself is not waste. *Unnecessary* inventory is waste. A key question is: What is unnecessary in the context of your organization?

In manufacturing operations, inventory in excess of that needed to support current operations or research and development efforts would certainly be waste. However, is the inventory of a distributor that uses immediate availability of a large cross-section of items as an effective, profitable marketing tool, "unnecessary?"

Your company should have a "zero-tolerance" inventory policy. That is, it will not accept any inventory over a stated target. But what is the target? Is it zero-tolerance from a days supply of inventory on-hand? Is it a zero-tolerance from a dollars invested standpoint (turns per year)? Is it zero-tolerance from an order fill rate of 97 percent?

For an organization to actually have useful inventory, it must understand its own objectives for the product it will have

on-hand, on-order, or in-transit at any one time. What inventory level is required for your organization to profitably and effectively operate?

Until the answers to these questions are determined, it will be difficult to get everyone within the organization to work toward the common, shared goal of eliminating inventory waste.

recap Organizations establish techniques for forecasting their product level needs based on the nature of the demand characteristics of those items.

Formulae for ensuring that you have the right item, in the right quantity, in the right place, at the right time can range from relatively simple min-max models to highly sophisticated computer-dependent systems.

For individuals not directly involved in purchasing, successful inventory control doesn't so much flow from actually using the various formulae, but rather from understanding what outcomes are supposed to result from their use.

? REVIEW QUESTIONS

1. Independent demand is best described as: 1. (c)
   (a) erratic purchasing of inventory.
   (b) one item is needed because of its relationship to another item.
   (c) items are impacted by market conditions outside the control of your organization's operations, and they are therefore independent of operations.
   (d) demand for items outside of their normal review cycle.

2. Just-in-time manufacturing results in: 2. (a)
    (a) right item, right quantity, right place, right time.
    (b) right item, right quantity, right place.
    (c) right item, right quantity.
    (d) larger inventory levels.

3. Independent demand calls for a(n) _____ approach to inventory management.

                               3. *replenishment*

4. Dependent demand calls for a(n) _____ approach to inventory management.

                               4. *requirements*

5. The reorder point is the   5. (c)
    (a) point in time when a product review is undertaken.
    (b) largest quantity of an item you will have on hand or on order.
    (c) lowest quantity of an item you will have on hand or on order before you reorder
    (d) lowest quantity at which you can obtain a discount from a vendor

6. The bill of materials is: 6. (b)
    (a) another name for a purchase order.
    (b) the recipe of raw materials and subassemblies that make up a finished product.
    (c) the schedule of what will be built, when, and in what quantities.
    (d) an accounts payable concept.

7. JIT systems regard inventory in excess of current production and R & D needs to be: 7. (c)
  (a) safety stock.
  (b) FIFO inventory.
  (c) waste.
  (d) part of the kanban system.

NOTE

1. This method of calculating the R Factor takes a straight average. It implies that every PO requires the same time and effort. Companies that calculate items using activity based costing would probably develop the R Factor using a blended average.

CHAPTER 6

Why Inventory Systems Fail and How to Fix Them

Introduction

The objective of this chapter is to provide you with an understanding of the nature of inventory accuracy and the working tools to "fix" your inventory system. If all items are moving through a properly operating system, then it doesn't matter what the characteristics of an SKU are—expensive item, inexpensive item, fast mover, slow mover, long lead time, critical—the *shelf count* of the item (actual balance on-hand stock levels) and *record count* (how many your records say are supposed to be here) will match.

The traditional method of determining if actual balance on-hand stock levels match book/record levels is to take an annual physical inventory. As a method of correcting inventory accuracy problems, this costly and time consuming effort is riddled with deficiencies. Why? Consider the following:

• Accuracy is often defined in dollars rather than in actual physical units. As discussed in Chapter 1, the dollar value of product does not reflect exactly what items are in house. For example, imagine you sent out a thousand cases of peaches to a customer rather than the thousand cases of pears actually requested. An annual inventory would reflect an overall dollar value roughly equal to whatever it would have been even if the correct item had been shipped. Therefore, our shelf count is off a thousand over for one SKU and a thousand under for another with no discrepancy in accuracy—if accuracy is measured in dollars.

• Misidentification of product. As discussed in Chapter 3, product within a facility is misidentified for a variety of reasons. During annual inventories, misidentification often occurs because inexperienced counters assisting with the effort do not recognize items, misunderstand package descriptions, and so on.

• Misidentification of units of measure. Incorrect quantities are often written down during annual inventories because counters simply do not understand an SKU's pack size, pack size descriptions, or abbreviations on packaging.

• Discrepancies "adjusted away." Perhaps the greatest problem with using the annual inventory as a method for establishing accuracy is that it provides no method for backtracking through physical and paper transactions to determine why an item's shelf count and its record count do not agree—a twelve month time period is simply too long of an audit trail. Consequently, if the reason for a discrepancy cannot be immediately found during the inventory, an adjustment is made with the underlying cause of the error never being corrected.

At the end of an annual inventory, after all of the adjustments have been made and after the lights have been turned off,

you have an inventory shelf and record count that agree. At least they agree until the next morning when the same system that spawned the discrepancies found during the effort reasserts itself and a new group of errors is born.

Albert Einstein, the famous physicist, once said, "A problem stated is a problem half-solved." Modern business writers like Peter Drucker have expressed a similar view, "A problem analyzed is a problem half-solved." The sentiment expressed in these sayings, that reviewing the nature of inventory problems is a key step in solving them, provides you with a good starting point in resolving your own inventory-related issues. Consider the following:

Inventory System Failures—Example Case

The following paragraph events have been numbered for ease of reference.

1. Big Hammer, Inc. manufactures and distributes widgets. Manufacturing occurs at its Los Angeles, CA, plant. It distributes from two separate locations. One of these locations is in Kansas City, MO, and has been part of Big Hammer for many years. The other location is in New York, NY, and is the surviving portion of Paulex Co., a distribution company just purchased by Big Hammer.

2. Marc, Big Hammer's president, has just reviewed operating reports from all three locations and is upset. It seems that the inventory accuracy level at all three locations is off. The end result is delayed production, too much inventory, and poor customer service. In addition, various department heads in all three locations clash with one another. In order to get everything straightened out, he hires the consulting firm of Alana, Eric, and Shawn.

3. Alana goes to KC. Eric goes to NY. Shawn goes to LA.

4. The trio immediately discovers that NY is using a different software system than LA and KC. In addition, the LA/KC software was designed for distribution, not manufacturing. However, some modifications have been made to the LA/KC software to help with manufacturing applications.

5. The NY system allocates inventory on a real-time basis. In other words, as a pick ticket is generated for an item, the quantity in question is allocated to a specific order and is not available for any other customer—its paper life ceases.

6. The LA/KC system is a batch system. Items are relieved from stock at the time the system is updated. This usually occurs once per day when billing is done. A modification to the system backflushes[1] some items out of stock during the manufacturing cycle.

7. Eric wanders around the NY location and observes the following:

8. Sales people, customer service personnel, clerical staff, and others freely roam through all stockrooms. Eric notices that some nonstockroom personnel fill their own orders, grab samples for customers, and put things back into the facility that they have previously removed.

9. Eric observes that some of these individuals document their actions immediately, while others document nothing, and others turn in necessary paperwork—later.

10. Eric observes Sally, a sales person, peering intently into her computer screen. He hears her utter an oath and declare out loud, "I just saw a whole bunch of SKU #1234 out there a little while ago." She then creates a manual invoice within the software system, prints it, walks out into the stockroom, fills the order she has just created, delivers it to customer Acme Widgets of

the World, and later drops the signed delivery copy on the desk of her accounts receivables clerk.

11. Eric observes an angry exchange between the warehouse manager and the accounting manager of the NY location. They were arguing over a negative stock balance for SKU #1234.

12. Eric also observes Sally angrily telling the warehouse manager that one of her customers, Widgets, Gidgets, Gadgets and Such, was shorted 10 widgets on an order it received "just a little while ago."

13. Alana has also observed some interesting things in KC.

14. Alana has observed two different order fillers attempting to fill orders for the same item—from the same empty shelf.

15. At 5 P.M. one evening, Alana was standing behind Carmen, the company's billing clerk. Carmen's inbox contained several inches of delivery slips ready for processing. Carmen got up and began to make preparations to go home. Alana asked her what she was doing. Carmen replied, "It's 5 P.M. I'm going home."

Alana said, "But you still have a lot of work in your inbox."

"So what? I'll work on it tomorrow," Carmen indignantly responded.

"But you'll mess up the warehouse if you don't get those slips processed tonight," Alana stated.

Angrily, Carmen stated, "I work in accounting. I don't work in the warehouse."

Alana asked, "How long would it take you to do those?"

Carmen glanced at her inbox and replied, "About 30 minutes."

"Please stay and get them done," Alana cajoled.

"I can't even if I wanted to," Carmen said. "I'm not allowed any overtime."

Bill, one of Carmen's co-workers chimes in and says, "Why can't you get your work done during the day?"

Furious, Carmen turns on Bill and says, "Hey, you sort and distribute the mail every morning, run photocopies of all incoming checks while fighting with people over our one copy machine, and prepare and go out to make the daily deposit like I do; and, then let's see if you can get your stuff done."

16. Hanging around the warehouse, Alana observed that receiving was done on a manual basis; and there wasn't always a copy of a PO in the warehouse to support incoming loads.

Alana noticed on several occasions that when the receiving staff did not have all appropriate paperwork for an item, they would simply put it away or move it off to the side. Then later, or the next day, they would hunt down all of the appropriate documentation and turn everything in to the data entry people for entry into the system.

Like Eric, Alana also observed nonstockroom individuals filling their own orders.

17. Alana also observed a curious exchange between Franklin, the accounting manager, and Carmen, the billing clerk.

While attempting to create an invoice for an item, Carmen's computer screen flashed an error message indicating that she was trying to bill for something that had a zero stock balance in the system. The software would not let her bill for an item it did not reflect as being available for the subject sale.

Carmen called Franklin over. She showed him the signed delivery slip indicating that the item had, in fact, been delivered.

Franklin stated, "Those people in the warehouse can't get anything right." He then proceeded to manually override the system and entered the SKU (SKU #4567) and quantity in question (10). Franklin then directed Carmen to try again. The invoice was created without any further problems.

Mid-morning of the next day the stock records began to show that there were 10 of SKU #4567 in the facility. A telemarketing sales person sold 10 SKU #4567s that afternoon. A pick ticket was generated for the order. The order filler could not find any of SKU #4567 in the warehouse. A stock adjustment form is processed to take these ten items out of stock.

18. Alana overhears a telephone conversation between Carmen and a customer. The customer wants to return five SKU #9876s and wants to ensure that it is not charged for them. Carmen notes the information, prepares a pickup slip, and issues a credit to the customer's account.

Later that day, a salesperson sells five SKU #9876's. A pick ticket was generated for the order. The order filler could not find any of SKU #9876s in the warehouse. A stock adjustment form is processed to take these five items out of stock.

19. Meanwhile, Shawn has been talking to Ichiro, the inventory control clerk in LA. Ichiro is frustrated. He works hard at his job but can't seem to track work in process.[2] Consequently, he is never sure how much of any particular item the company has available for production purposes.

20. Shawn observes a worker disassembling a sub-assembly. He asks the worker what he is doing. The worker replies that there is a rush order they lack all of the raw materials for, so they are disassembling some less important assemblies to cannibalize the required parts.

Shawn asks if the products being disassembled are from other orders. The worker replies that they are. Shawn asks about any paperwork that was generated to support whatever it is the worker is doing. The worker replies that he doesn't know.

Discussion of Example Case

After events, note problem identification and discussion.

Event #1. Big Hammer, Inc. manufactures and distributes widgets. Manufacturing occurs at its Los Angeles, CA, plant. It distributes from two separate locations. One of these locations is in Kansas City, MO, and has been part of Big Hammer for many years. The other location is in New York, NY, and is the surviving portion of Paulex Co., a distribution company just purchased by Big Hammer.

Any organization that has several locations must clearly identify the answers to the "who, what, when, where, why, and how" questions: Who is doing what? When are they doing it? Where are they doing it? Why are they doing it? and How are they doing it? If these questions are not answered materials and information will not flow smoothly between and among the organization's separate departments. See pages 169–172.

Event #2. Marc, Big Hammer's president, has just reviewed operating reports from all three locations and is upset. It seems that the inventory accuracy level at all three locations is off. The end result is delayed production, too much inventory, and poor customer service. In addition, various department heads in all three locations clash with one another. In order to get everything straightened out, he hires the consulting firm of Alana, Eric, and Shawn.

Although consultants are helpful in most instances, by applying the concepts contained within this chapter, you should be able to resolve many system problems your organization may be currently experiencing.

Event #3. Alana goes to KC. Eric goes to NY. Shawn goes to LA.

Event #4. The trio immediately discovers that NY is using a different software system than LA and KC. In addition, the LA/KC software was designed for distribution, not manufacturing. However, some modifications have been made to the LA/KC software to help with manufacturing applications.

Trying to integrate different software systems is always difficult. Once again, any organization hoping to achieve that result must clearly lay out the timing and sequencing of the information flow within the system.

In addition, the demand patterns for items in a distribution world and those in a manufacturing environment are radically different. See the discussion of inventory types on pages 119–20. Purchasing patterns for finished goods and spare parts in a distribution are based on past usage patterns. See the discussion of independent demand inventory on pages 120–24. Purchasing patterns for the raw materials and sub-assemblies used in manufacturing are based on the master production schedule. See the discussion of dependent demand inventory on pages 128–40. Different concepts and formulae are used for each type of inventory and, therefore, software designed for one or the other or specifically written for a combination environment should be used whenever possible.

Event #5. The NY system relieves inventory on a real-time basis. In other words, as a pick ticket is generated for an item, the quantity in question is allocated to a specific order and is not available for any other customer—its paper life ceases.

The central problem often encountered in real time systems is that there is often a time lapse between the creation of a pick ticket and the actual removal of the product from the shelves.

Since the items on the pick ticket were immediately allocated[3] to that order, with their paper life ceasing (see pages 9–15), those SKUs will actually be sitting on the shelves but won't appear in the then current record count.

Somewhere in the software files is the information: total items on hand, items allocated, and items actually available for sale or use. The problem is that *not everyone in the organization has access to this information!* If (a) staff members are allowed to fill their own orders, and (b) do not understand how it is possible to check the then current stock records and see a lower number of items than are actually sitting in plain view, then (c) they will stop believing in the record count, will only believe their eyes, and will raid product allocated for other orders.

Event #6. The LA/KC system is a batch system. Items are relieved from stock at the time the system is updated. This usually occurs once per day when billing is done. A modification to the system backflushes some items out of stock during the manufacturing cycle.

The most significant issue created by batch software systems is that items are physically gone from the shelves/building but still appear in the record count until the system is updated. The longer the length of time between updates, the more out of balance the shelf count and the record count are.

Backflushing works well *if* the backflush occurs at each level of the bill of materials. See the discussion of Event 19 on pages 163–64.

Event #7. Eric wanders around the NY location and observes the following:

Event #8. Sales people, customer service personnel, clerical staff, and others freely roam through all stockrooms. Eric notices that some non-stockroom personnel fill their own orders, grab samples for cus-

tomers, and put things back into the facility that they have previously removed.

Any organization hoping to continuously have its shelf count match its record count simply must stop all unauthorized personnel from touching anything in a stockroom or warehouse. And, authorized personnel must have a paper- or computer-based document before placing anything into or removing anything from storage areas. These points cannot be overstated. They are imperative to inventory accuracy.

Event #9. Eric observes that some of these individuals document their actions immediately, while others document nothing, and others turn in necessary paperwork—later.

Documentation created after something has been placed into or removed from a facility creates all sorts of problems. For example:

a. If an item is physically removed without a document deleting it from inventory, then sales people, production schedulers, and others will believe that the item is still available for sale or use. They will then generate pick tickets for its selection. Order fillers will then waste their time looking for items that do not exist. The order fillers will generate adjustment forms leading to the items being deleted from inventory. Eventually, when the original documentation goes through the system, it causes these same items to be deleted from inventory—again. Your shelf count and record count are now almost hopelessly out of balance.

b. If an item is placed into the stockroom without accompanying paperwork, then the subject SKU is unavailable for sale or use—since no one knows its there.

Event #10. Eric observes Sally, a sales person, peering intently into her computer screen. He hears her utter an oath and declare out

loud, "I just saw a whole bunch of SKU #1234 out there a little while ago." She then creates a manual invoice within the software system, prints it, walks out into the stockroom, fills the order she has just created, delivers it to customer Acme Widgets of the World, and later drops the signed delivery copy on the desk of her accounts receivables clerk.

Event #10 is an example of someone in a real time software scenario that does not understand how it is possible to have a stock record (in the computer or hard paper copy) that reflects a stock balance lower than the actual number of items on the shelves. Recall that the discrepancy is due to the time period between the creation of a pick ticket with its allocation of product to an order and the physical removal of the SKUs from the stockroom.

Event #11. Eric observes an angry exchange between the warehouse manager and the accounting manager of the NY location. They were arguing over a negative stock balance for SKU #1234.

Since this is a real time system, when Sally created a manual pick ticket she caused the system to allocate and delete the subject SKU. If the stock balance was zero when Sally did this, her actions have caused the balance to go into a negative.

As discussed in Event #17 of this section, Sally's actions have also created the potential for a much different problem in an entirely different department of the organization. By forcing a manual invoice through the system and dropping off a delivery slip for billing, Sally has created the potential for a billing clerk to try to create an invoice for product that the system has never received into itself. Many accounting programs will not let an invoice be created for product that has never been received.

Event #12. Eric also observes Sally angrily telling the warehouse manager that one of her customers, Widgets, Gidgets, Gadgets

and Such, was shorted 10 widgets on an order it received "just a little while ago."

In Event #10 it should be obvious that the product Sally took had already been allocated to a different customer (Customer #1) than the one she was taking care of at that time (Customer #2). Sally's actions caused her to raid Customer 1's order, causing a stockout for one of her own customers—Customer 1.

Event #13. Alana has also observed some interesting things in KC.

Event #14. Alana has observed two different order fillers attempting to fill orders for the same item—from the same empty shelf.

It is common in batch systems that are only updated once per day and in which there is no way to easily check (without going to look) the availability of an item, for multiple orders to be written against the same "phantom" items. This also creates the danger of multiple adjustments adding to the overall confusion.

Event #15. At 5 P.M. one evening, Alana was standing behind Carmen, the company's billing clerk. Carmen's inbox contained several inches of delivery slips ready for processing. Carmen got up and began to make preparations to go home. Alana asked her what she was doing. Carmen replied, "It's 5 P.M., I'm going home."

Alana said, "But you still have a lot of work in your inbox."

"So what? I'll work on it tomorrow," Carmen indignantly responded.

"But you'll mess up the warehouse if you don't get those slips processed tonight," Alana stated.

Angrily, Carmen stated, "I work in accounting. I don't work in the warehouse."

Alana asked, "How long would it take you to do those?"

Carmen glanced at her inbox and replied, "About 30 minutes."

"Please stay and get them done," Alana cajoled.

"I can't even if I wanted to," Carmen said. "I'm not allowed any overtime."

Bill, one of Carmen's co-workers chimes in and says, "Why can't you get your work done during the day?"

Furious, Carmen turns on Bill and says, "Hey, you sort and distribute the mail every morning, run photocopies of all incoming checks while fighting with people over our one copy machine, and prepare and go out to make the daily deposit like I do; and, then let's see if you can get your stuff done."

A number of issues are raised by the Event #15 scenario, such as:

a. The morning following an incident like the one described will find everyone who deals with inventory—sales, accounting, production scheduling, customer service, and purchasing—making decisions on information they believe is as current as the night before when the system was updated. The reality is that the information is no more current than the last time Carmen made it to the bottom of the in-basket. If she hasn't made it to the bottom of her basket in several days, then the records and operations are really suffering.

The problem is made worse by the fact that roughly 20 percent of our inventory will represent 80 percent of our most important items. (See also pages 63–65 in Chapter 3.) Therefore, not only does our shelf count not match our record count, but they don't match regarding some of our most important items.

b. Another problem revealed by the incident is that the organization does not recognize the importance of getting all receiving and shipping into and out of the building on both a real life and paper life basis every day. This is indicated by those du-

ties assigned to Carmen that cause her not to complete her inventory related tasks on a daily basis. Although these duties are important, they should be performed by someone whose actions do not have the ripple effect that Carmen's actions have throughout the entire organization.

Event #16. Hanging around the warehouse, Alana observed that receiving was done on a manual basis; and there wasn't always a copy of a PO in the warehouse to support incoming loads.

Alana noticed on several occasions that when the receiving staff did not have all appropriate paperwork for an item, they would simply put it away or move it off to the side. Then later, or the next day, they would hunt down all of the appropriate documentation and turn everything in to the data entry people for entry into the system.

Like Eric, Alana also observed nonstockroom individuals filling their own orders.

Virtually every organization has a purchase order system. And, in virtually every organization anyone with the authority to buy something is repeatedly told to have a PO for everything. In spite of those facts, in many organizations product comes in daily without any supporting documentation. This causes confusion, inefficient receiving operations, and separates an item's real life from its paper life. (See also Chapter 1.) There should be either a hard copy or a record of the PO in the computer system available to receiving for all items that arrive at the stockroom.

When an item's real life becomes separated from its paper life, people begin to ship or use product that has not been received; to put away product that has not been received so that no one knows it is available for sale or use, creates an environment where inventory clerks and accounting personnel are making adjustment after adjustment to the record count.

Event #17. Alana also observed a curious exchange between Franklin, the accounting manager, and Carmen, the billing clerk.

While attempting to create an invoice for an item, Carmen's computer screen flashed an error message indicating that she was trying to bill for something that had a zero stock balance in the system. The software would not let her bill for an item it did not reflect as being available for the subject sale.

Carmen called Franklin over. She showed him the signed delivery slip indicating that the item had, in fact, been delivered.

Franklin stated, "Those people in the warehouse can't get anything right." He then proceeded to manually override the system and entered the SKU (SKU #4567) and quantity in question (10). Franklin then directed Carmen to try again. The invoice was created without any further problems.

Mid-morning of the next day the stock records began to show that there were 10 of SKU #4567 in the facility. A telemarketing sales person sold 10 SKU #4567s that afternoon. A pick ticket was generated for the order. The order filler could not find any of SKU #4567 in the warehouse. A stock adjustment form is processed to take these ten items out of stock.

From Event #16, it appears here that someone delivered an item that had not yet gone through the paperwork receiving cycle. Then when Carmen tried to bill for it, the software would not let her.

Instead of researching what had actually happened, Franklin overrode the system and put in a quantity of 10. Carmen's billing then deleted the 10 items.

When the receiving paperwork finally made it through the system it created a quantity of 10 items that were no longer in the building. These 10 phantom items were then sold—maybe more than once.

When the 10 items could not be found, additional paperwork had to be initiated to delete the SKUs from the system.

All of the above issues are caused, in part, by a lack of understanding on the part of various staff members of how the timing and sequencing of the system works.

Event #18. Alana overhears a telephone conversation between Carmen and a customer. The customer wants to return five SKU #9876s and wants to ensure that it is not charged for them. Carmen notes the information, prepares a pickup slip, and issues a credit to the customer's account.

Later that day, a salesperson sells five SKU #9876's. A pick ticket was generated for the order. The order filler could not find any of SKU #9876s in the warehouse. A stock adjustment form is processed to take these five items out of stock.

Although application software systems vary widely in how items are accounted for, many systems place an item back into stock (in the data base) when a credit is issued against that item. By issuing a credit, Carmen caused the software system to place the five SKUs back into stock—even though they had not yet been returned to the building.

Again, a lack of understanding regarding timing and sequencing of software and events causes terrible dysfunctions to stockroom operations.

Event #19. Meanwhile, Shawn has been talking to Ichiro, the inventory control clerk in LA. Ichiro is frustrated. He works hard at his job but can't seem to track work in process. Consequently, he is never sure how much of any particular item the company has available for production purposes.

As indicated in Event #4, a key problem Ichiro faces is that the company is using two separate methods of relieving items from stock. One method is batch, while the other is a backflush of some items. Recall that *backflushing* refers to a software technique where raw materials and other components going into a

particular sub-assembly or final product are relieved from stock when that sub-assembly/product is completed.

As indicated in the discussion of Event #6, if a batch system is not updated with some degree of frequency, it is difficult to understand what is available without actually looking. This problem can be overcome through software modules that advise the stockkeeper of those SKUs that have gone into completed orders. This report shows a running total for each SKU that has been drawn down that day. Once the system is updated, then a new report begins.

The key issue regarding backflushing is, does the backflush occur at every level of the bill of materials? See Exhibit 6–1. (A similar example is also used in Exhibit 5–4.) If the backflush only goes down one level, but no backflush occurred at that next lower level, then all materials below that level will still appear to be in stock. In reality they have been used up.

Event #20. Shawn observes a worker disassembling a sub-assembly. He asks the worker what he is doing. The worker replies that there is a rush order they lack all of the raw materials for, so they are disassembling some less important assemblies to cannibalize the required parts.

Shawn asks if the products being disassembled are from other orders. The worker replies that they are. Shawn asks about any paperwork that was generated to support whatever it is the worker is doing. The worker replies that he doesn't know.

Exhibit 6–1 Backflushing

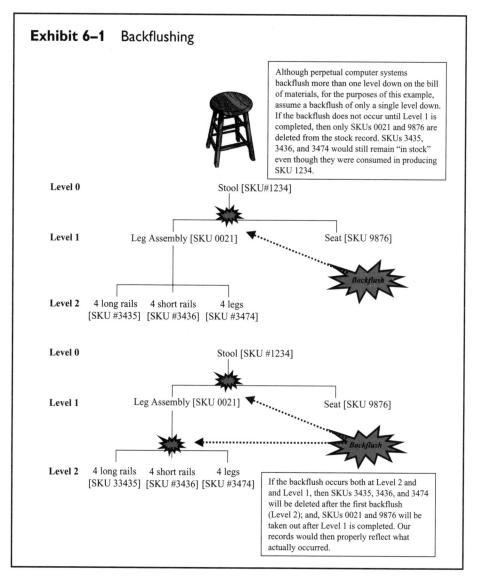

Although perpetual computer systems backflush more than one level down on the bill of materials, for the purposes of this example, assume a backflush of only a single level down. If the backflush does not occur until Level 1 is completed, then only SKUs 0021 and 9876 are deleted from the stock record. SKUs 3435, 3436, and 3474 would still remain "in stock" even though they were consumed in producing SKU 1234.

Level 0   Stool [SKU#1234]

Level 1   Leg Assembly [SKU 0021]   Seat [SKU 9876]

Backflush

Level 2   4 long rails   4 short rails   4 legs
[SKU #3435] [SKU #3436] [SKU #3474]

Level 0   Stool [SKU #1234]

Level 1   Leg Assembly [SKU 0021]   Seat [SKU 9876]

Backflush

Level 2   4 long rails   4 short rails   4 legs
[SKU 33435] [SKU #3436] [SKU #3474]

If the backflush occurs both at Level 2 and and Level 1, then SKUs 3435, 3436, and 3474 will be deleted after the first backflush (Level 2); and, SKUs 0021 and 9876 will be taken out after Level 1 completed. Our records would then properly reflect what actually occurred.

Metrics

"You can't control what you don't measure." Peter Drucker

Before doing *anything* toward establishing methods to discover, analyze, and fix any discrepancies between actual on-hand stock lev-

els and database record levels, you should take a snapshot of where you are *now*. There are two sets of numbers you should develop that relate to (a) inventory record accuracy (IRA) and (b) fill rate.

IRA is a reflection of how well your shelf count and record count match. In other words, do your stock records accurately reflect what is actually in the stockroom?

Fill rate is a reflection of how effective your inventory is. Did you have what you needed when you needed it?

Inventory Record Accuracy

Test Counting

A quick, accurate method of establishing your current IRA is to perform a test count:

- Select 100 SKUs that represent a cross-section of all items. In other words, select all sorts of items—fast movers, slow movers, expensive items, inexpensive items, and those with both long and short lead times to acquire.
- Count all 100 in all locations where they are located. Measure accuracy by considering actual units on the floor—not dollar value.
- Divide the number of accurate counts by the total number of counts. Accurate counts mean where the record count and the shelf count exactly match.
- Quotient is your inventory record accuracy. See Exhibit 6–2.

Tolerances

How accurate does accuracy have to be? You may think, at first, that *accurate* means that 100 percent of the time your stock records match your shelf counts. Consider, however, your feelings about counting a large container of nails.

Exhibit 6–2   Test Counting To Establish Inventory Record Accuracy

$$\frac{\text{Accurate Counts}}{\text{Total Counts}} = \frac{\text{Inventory}}{\text{Record}} \quad \frac{87}{100} = .87 = 87\% \text{ IRA}$$

In counting a large container of nails, would you actually count each nail individually? It is more probable that you will (a) weigh out one pound of nails, (b) count the number of nails in a pound, (c) weigh all of the nails, and (d) then compute the total number of nails by comparing the number of nails in a pound to the number of pounds of nails in the container. Will your computation capture the exact number of nails in the container? Probably not. Do you really care? Probably not. Why? Because of the nature of the SKU in question, in this case nails, is low cost, easy to acquire, and hard to count individually (if there is a large quantity of them). Therefore, you would probably be willing to accept some percentage of tolerance in your numbers. If you were within ±5 percent of a perfect match between the record count and the shelf count, would you be satisfied? Probably so. Would you be equally satisfied applying the same approach to a large container of diamonds? Of course not.

Many organizations allow a variance or tolerance in considering IRA. That is, they allow a plus-minus percentage of accuracy they find acceptable. These tolerances can be set using dollars, actual units, or some combination of the two. Most accountants use dollars. Stockkeepers should use actual units: It's either here or it isn't.

Few organizations accept a tolerance of greater than ±5 percent on any item. In other words, a 95 percent tolerance should

be the lowest variance from a 100 percent accuracy level you will accept for any item no matter what its characteristics.

If you will accept tolerances, they must be set for each item or category of item with great care. Consider the following factors:

- Dollar value: The higher the dollar value, the more accuracy you will demand.
- Usage rate: Usage rate can actually be argued in two ways:

  —The Higher-the-Usage-Rate-the-Lower-the-Tolerance-Level Argument: If you are using a large quantity of an item you will want to always know how much is available so there is never a stockout.

  —The Lower-the-Usage-Rate-Lower-the-Tolerance-Level Argument: If an item is not moving very quickly, then why should there be any discrepancy between shelf and record count? A low variance percentage for a slow moving item will alert everyone to a problem quickly as opposed to waiting for a crisis. This argument assumes that if there are stockouts on higher moving products, then the situation will alert everyone anyway.

- Lead time: The longer the lead time, the lower the tolerance level. A long lead time requires more working reserve and safety stock. See also Chapter 5.

- Level on bill of materials: The higher something is on the bill of materials, the more overall value it has. Therefore, the higher on the bill of materials an SKU is, the lower the tolerance.

- Criticality: Some items are critical for reasons other than dollar value, usage rate, or lead time. A safety equipment company may only sell a few biohazard cleanup suits

per year, but when they are needed they are needed immediately.

- Combination of the above

Example: Considering Tolerances

Read the following scenario:

Melvin, President of Megawatts, Inc., doesn't believe in allowing any tolerances in his inventory levels. His friend, Sarah, President of Bright Lights Co., does.

A cross-section of 100 items was counted in each of these companies' facilities.

The actual stock count on 87 SKUs in each facility matched the respective companies' stock records.

Bright Lights allowed a variance of ±2 percent on 5 of the 13 items that were not 100 percent accurate. The count of these 5 fell within their respective tolerances.

$$\text{Megawatts:} \quad \frac{87}{100} = 87\% \text{ accuracy}$$

$$\text{Bright Lights:} \quad \frac{92}{100} = 92\% \text{ accuracy}$$

Melvin argues that Sarah's higher IRA level is artificial and doesn't really reflect accuracy.

Sarah's approach does reflect an acceptable level of accuracy if the tolerances were carefully set. As in the container of nails example, if we (1) weighed a large container of nails and determined there were 14,003 nails, (2) entered that total into our

records, (3) reweighed the nails and determined there were 14,010 nails, would we change our records? Probably not. The second total would fall within an acceptable tolerance.

Impact of Tolerances on Adjustments

Once you have set tolerances, you should not make adjustments to your records when a discrepancy between shelf and record counts falls within the variance allowed. If an item does fall outside of the tolerance range, you would hunt down the reason for the discrepancy and adjust the record if necessary. See Exhibit 6–3.

Fill Rates

Although matching shelf count to record count is one way of measuring inventory, it does not indicate if you have the items you need when you need them. Simple fill rate calculations achieve that objective. The fill rate looks at the qualitative nature of your inventory efforts.

Fill Rate Formulae

Simple Fill Rate:

$$\text{Fill Rate} = \frac{\text{Items Shipped on a Given Day}}{\text{Items Ordered for Shipment on a Given Day}} \quad \frac{417 \text{ Items Shipped}}{447 \text{ Items Ordered}} = 0.93 = 93\% \text{ Fill Rate}$$

The above indicates that you had 93 percent of the items you needed on the day they were required.

The fill rate can reflect the availability of a single item or a grouping of items.

Exhibit 6–3 Tolerances and Adjustments

Assume that a count was made of ten SKUs, with the results being as follows:

SKU #	RECORD COUNT	ACTUAL COUNT	% DEVIATION	% TOLERANCE ±	HIT/MISS
1	1,200	1,128	−6%	2%	M
2	2,217	2,106	−5%	5%	H
3	317	304	−4%	5%	H
4	8,947	8,679	−3%	2%	M
5	100	98	−2%	5%	H
6	567	561	−1%	2%	H
7	100	100	0%	0%	H
8	1,367	1,381	+1%	0%	M
9	1,432	1,461	+2%	2%	H
10	185	191	+3%	5%	H

SKUs 1, 4, and 8 fell outside of their tolerances. For example, if the count for SKU 1 would have fallen within the range of 1,176 to 1,224, a ±2 percent of the record count, then it would have been a hit. It was not. Therefore, you would research why the discrepancies exist and adjust your records if necessary.

All of the other SKUs fell within their tolerances. However, only SKU 7 was exactly correct. You would still not make any adjustments to any SKUs where there was a hit. The variance percentages you set should allow you a comfortable range in which you can tolerate some up or down differences. Often pluses and minuses cancel one another out over time.

Stockouts Per Year:

$$\text{Stockout \%} = \frac{\begin{array}{c}\text{Number of Days}\\ \text{Where all Orders Were}\\ \text{Not Shipped Complete}\\ \hline \text{Total Number of}\\ \text{Shipping Days}\\ \text{During the Year}\end{array}}{} \quad \frac{34}{200^4} = 0.17 = 17\%$$

This indicates that you were unable to send all orders out complete 17 percent of the time. Stated more positively, you were able to send orders out complete 83 percent of the time.

Tools with Which to Uncover System Dysfunctions

To solve problems you need to engage in:

- Fact finding—what is happening now?
- Problem finding—what is wrong with what is going on?
- Solution finding—how can we fix what is wrong?

So far this chapter has focused on (a) beginning to analyze inventory problems in an intellectual, intuitive, "gut feel" manner, and (b) developing some measurements with which to understand your current level of inventory accuracy and availability. This is part of fact finding.

Another way of determining what is actually happening at your facility is to create a number of charts.

Charts, by their very nature, allow you to analyze things. However, you need to guard against "paralysis by analysis." If

everything is equally important, then nothing is important. In other words, you should only chart things that are really important to controlling inventory items, trends, operational undertakings, and so on.

Run Charts

Run charts allow you to measure a variable that changes over time.

A run chart is an x–y axis chart with the unit of measure appearing on the vertical y-axis, and the timeframe running along the horizontal x-axis. The unit of measure can be anything you wish to track such as stockouts, errors, labor hours, pieces, pounds, or gallons. The timeframe can also be whatever you desire it to be such as seconds, minutes, hours, days, weeks, months, or years. See Exhibit 6–4.

Flow Charts

Flow charts allow you to analyze the sequence of a set of events. A flow chart does not necessarily show the interdependence of events or which events are going on at the same time as others.

Flow charts are easier to understand than written procedures.

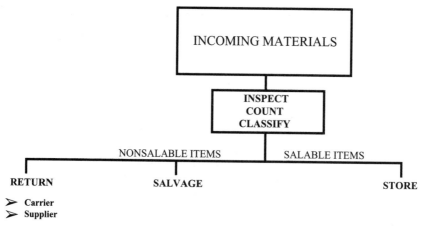

Exhibit 6–4   Run Charts

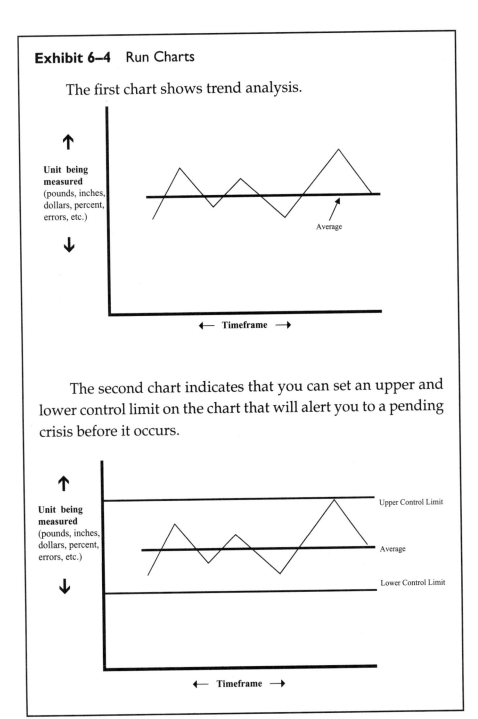

The first chart shows trend analysis.

The second chart indicates that you can set an upper and lower control limit on the chart that will alert you to a pending crisis before it occurs.

Caution:

• You do not have to use traditional flow chart symbols. Be consistent however, with the symbols you do use or you will confuse yourself and others. Provide a key to symbols.

• Have version control. If flow charts are not revised as procedures change, they are worthless.

Logic Charts

Logic charts are flow charts that show the interrelationships of events.

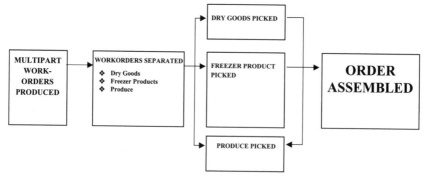

Variance Reports

Variance reports compare an expectation with what actually occurred.

Variance reports can be based on any factor necessary for tracking an expectation. Some factors are dollars, labor, consumption rates, lines/pieces per hour, or trucks per day.

VARIANCE REPORT				
			VARIANCE	
DESCRIPTION	PROJECTED	ACTUAL	AMOUNT	PERCENT
TOTAL				

Cycle Counting

After becoming familiar with your system through utilization of the techniques described in this chapter, you should be ready to systematically approach "fixing" whatever might be causing discrepancies between your shelf and record counts.

The most systematic method of solving inventory problems and enjoying a consistently high IRA is cycle counting. Cycle counting is simply counting a statistically significant cross-section of your inventory frequently.[5]

This continuous counting leads to the discovery of discrepancies soon after they arise. By catching an error quickly, you can backtrack through both the paperwork and the stock movement of the item(s) to determine why that SKU's paper life became separated from its real life. Once the cause of the error is identified, it can be eliminated.

Since this is a continuous process, as one cause of error after another is eliminated the system begins to operate more and more smoothly. Eventually all items move through a series of procedures that work.

Cycle counting is different than an annual inventory in several ways:

Annual Inventories

- Objectives

    —The objective of the annual physical inventory is to produce a financial valuation of the inventory on a given day.

    —Every item must be counted as part of the annual inventory.

    —The 12-month long audit trail of the annual physical is too long for any serious effort made at uncovering why

an error occurred or even when—did it happen yesterday, last month, ten months ago?

Cycle Counting

- Objectives:
    —Discover discrepancies soon after they occur
    —Identify causes of errors
    —Correct conditions causing errors
    —Continuous process improvement
    —Minimum of 95 percent accuracy on ALL items
    —Correct statement of inventory assets
    —Eliminate annual inventory. Most accounting firms will allow an organization to stop taking annual physical inventories once the company has established a mature cycle counting program. Generally, a company will cycle count for at least twelve months. Then, an annual physical inventory is taken and the numbers from the annual are compared with the cycle count figures. If they match, then in the future the accounting firm will merely test count once per year for valuation purposes.
- Not every item in the building has to be counted as part of a cycle count, only a statistically significant cross-section of all items.

Cycle Count Methodologies

There are a number of cycle count methodologies.

- Control Group
- Location Audit

- Random Selection
- Diminishing Population
- Product Categories
- A-B-C Categorization

A key point to remember is that no matter what cycle count methodology you eventually choose to follow, when you first begin and your inventory record accuracy is low, you *will not* count a large number of items per day. This is because it will take time to recount, review paperwork, talk to people, and do all of the other things necessary to determine why an item's record count and shelf count do not match. Why count fifty items a day if you can only count and reconcile ten of them? As your record accuracy increases, and more and more items match their record counts, you can comfortably count more items each day.

Any cycle count methodology will assist you in achieving high levels of IRA. However, not every method works in every company setting. For example:

Assumptions:
- You wish to cycle count each item 4 times per year
- Cycle count 200 days per year (4 days/wk x 50 wks = 200 count days)
- 10,000 SKUs
- 3 cycle counters working 7 hours per day
- Company A has 10,000 items that are unitized and in single locations within the stockroom
- It takes Company A an average of 2 minutes to count an item
- Company B has 10,000 items that are not unitized, would

have to be counted in "onesy-twosy," and each item is found in multiple locations throughout the facility

- It takes Company B an average of 5 minutes to count an item

Company A	Company B
10,000 SKUs x 4 counts/yr = 40,000 counts	10,000 SKUs x 4 counts/yr = 40,000 counts
40,000 counts ÷ 200 days = 200 counts/day	40,000 counts ÷ 200 days = 200 counts/day
200 counts/day x 2 minutes = 400 minutes	200 counts/day x 5 minutes = 1,000 minutes
400 minutes ÷ 60 minutes = 7 hours/day	1,000 minutes ÷ 60 minutes = 17 hours/day
7 hrs/day ÷ 3 counters = 2.33 hours/day each	17 hrs/day ÷ 3 counters = 6 hrs/day each

Treating all items equally and counting them four times per year may work for Company A; however, it seems like an unreasonable burden for Company B.[6]

You should select a method that fits your own organization's resources and inventory types.

Control Group Cycle Counting Method

No matter which method you eventually decide to use, always start with a small scale counting test run. By using a control group approach you will be able to:

1. Immediately identify significant system problems such as unrestricted access to the stockroom, major timing problems

related to when product is moved, and when records of the move are updated.

2. Develop an understanding of the who, what, when, where, why, and how of the way your system actually works.

3. When you first begin cycle counting you will probably make adjustments only to find that you made a mistake. It is much simpler to correct errors related to only a few SKUs rather than hundreds of them.

Control Group Procedure

- Select 100 items as a control group. **IMPORTANT:** The SKUs selected must be a true cross-section of the entire population of items they represent such as some expensive items, some inexpensive, some fast movers, some slow, or some with a long lead time, etc.
- Count only ten items per day. Use a Control Group Count Tracking Sheet. See Exhibit 6–5.
- Count for 100 days.
- Stats: 10 x 100 = 1,000 counts
- "Cycle" is 10 days
- Each item counted 10 times during test

Because you have tracked the same items over and over again, at the conclusion of your control group cycle count you should be able to eliminate major systems problems and have a good understanding of how your overall inventory system is working.

The control group approach should only be used as a starting point and not as an ongoing cycle count method. The reason for this is that the control group is not statistically large enough to actually represent your entire inventory.

Exhibit 6–5   Control Group Count Tracking Sheet

	SKU #	DESCRIPTION	1	2	3	4	5	6	7	8	9	10
1	BD79	Widget	✓	✓								
2	QD455	Gidget	✓	✓								
3	XD110	Gadget	✓	✓								
4	PD418	Thig-a-ma-jig	✓	✓								
5	AC123	Doohickey	✓	✓								
6	ZG23	Receiver	✓	✓								
97	HG786	Receiver Mount	✓									
98	LK951	Miniplexer	✓									
99	LK236	Multiplexer	✓									
100	DK47	Radome	✓									

Now you are ready to select a cycle count method that bests suits your own organization's needs.

Location Audit Cycle Counting Method

In this approach you divide the stockroom(s) up in some logical method—rooms, racks, bins, and so on. See Exhibit 6-6. Then on each counting day you count the SKUs found in those areas.

All items are treated equally. In other words, selection of those items included on that day's count is based solely on the item being located in the area counted. No other characteristics such as cost, usage rate, and so on are considered.

The length of the cycle depends on how many areas are to be counted. For example, if you were counting by rack, one rack per day, and there were 45 racks, then the entire cycle would be 45 days. You would then start over again.

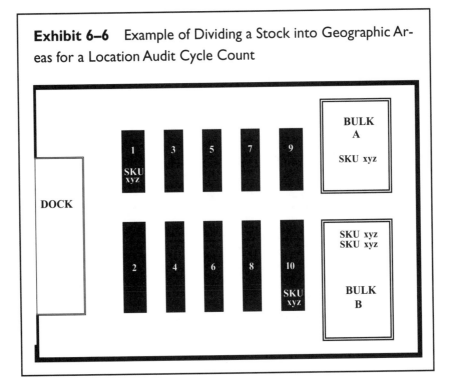

Exhibit 6–6   Example of Dividing a Stock into Geographic Areas for a Location Audit Cycle Count

The location audit approach has two significant benefits:

1. This approach does not require detailed recordkeeping of whether or not you have counted a specific item or the exact number of times you have counted it. It is administratively simple to follow.

2. This approach serves as a double audit because you are checking the quantity of an item at the same time that you are checking to make sure it is in the right location in your facility. Product that has been misplaced can be "discovered" sooner than the annual inventory through the use of this method.

Two separate approaches are possible regarding how much of any selected SKU gets counted:

1. Only count the SKU in the location being cycle counted that day.

Example: Count only the quantity of SKU xyz in Rack 1. (See Exhibit 6–6) Item xyz located in Rack 10 and in both bulk storage areas ignored.

This first approach requires a higher level of sophistication within your own inventory control system. Your system must allow you to identify not only how much of an item you have, but also each location it is located in and how much of it is in each location. See also Chapter 3, Physical Location and Control of Inventory.

This first approach forces you to keep your shelf count and record count accurate on an ongoing basis.

2. Count the selected SKU in all locations where it may be located throughout the facility.

Example: Quantities of SKU xyz counted in Racks 1 and 10 and in both bulk areas.

With either locational audit approach, the warehouse will be counted wall-to-wall during the cycle. However, this does not mean that *all* items in the stockroom during that cycle will actually be counted.

Not all items in the stockroom during the cycle will be counted because items will arrive into and leave from areas already counted or to be counted during the cycle. In other words, SKUs will be coming in behind you and moving away from in front of you as you go through the count.

Does it matter if every item in the stockroom is counted during a location audit cycle? It does not matter that all items are not counted during any particular cycle because of the large

number of items that are counted during that cycle. Remember that in cycle counting you are interested in looking at the *system* not individual SKUs within the system. Whether or not a SKU's shelf and record counts match is merely a way of determining if the system is actually working. Therefore, as long as you count a statistically significant number of the total items in the stockroom, you will accomplish the cycle count objective.

Random Selection Cycle Counting Method

This is probably the easiest form of cycle counting. The items selected for counting are totally random. However, the SKUs selected must be a true cross-section of the entire population of items they represent: some expensive items, some inexpensive, some fast movers, some slow movers, some with a long lead time.

The cycle is generally one year with a statistically significant number of SKUs being counted during that time frame. For example,

- 10,000 total SKUs
- 200 counting days
- Therefore, 50 items/day counted (10,000 ÷ 200 = 50)
- 10,000 total counts during the year—a statistically significant number!

All items are treated equally. Product characteristics like dollar value and usage rate are ignored.

Diminishing Population Cycle Counting Method

This is a versatile approach. It can be used as a stand-alone procedure or used as part of the product category approach or the A-B-C approach, which are both explained later in this chapter.

The basic concept is to:

1. Count each item in a defined population before counting any item over again.

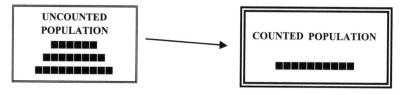

2. Then you begin the count all over again

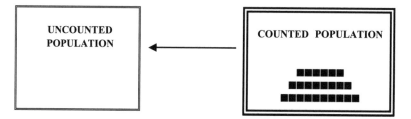

The diminishing population technique ensures all items in the population are counted at least once per cycle.

The number of times the total population is counted during a year depends on the size of the total number of items there are and how many days you are willing to count. See Exhibit 6–7.

The larger the number of items counted per day the more cycles can be completed during the year.

Product Categories Cycle Counting Method

To this point in our cycle count discussion we have ignored an item's characteristics. In the product categories approach, the organization decides on what categories it wishes to place SKUs into based on some characteristics, such as by manufacturer or by type of use (the "criteria").

Exhibit 6–7 Diminishing Population Cycle Counting

EXAMPLE:	EXAMPLE:	EXAMPLE:
• 900 total SKUs	• 900 total SKUs	• 900 total SKUs
• 200 counting days in cycle	• 100 counting days in cycle	• 50 counting days in cycle
• 900 ÷ 200 = 4.5 > 5 items/day	• 2 cycles per year	• 4 cycles per year
• 1,000 total counts/yr	• 900 ÷ 100 = 9 items/day	• 900 ÷ 50 = 18 items/day
	• 1,800 total counts/yr	• 3,600 total counts/yr

Items matching the criteria are counted either on the basis of:

(a) a single event, e.g., only items whose balance-on-hand equals zero, or

(b) using the diminishing population technique for each separate category: all of the widgets this week, all of the gadgets next week, all of the gidgets the week after, and so on.

The number of items to be counted can vary or be set by the number of items in the group divided by the number of days in the cycle. See Exhibit 6–7.

Cycle can be a single day or a defined number of times per year.

Single Criteria

You should be careful of using single event characteristics in defining categories. For example:

Criteria: Only cycle count items on that day's purchase orders.

Benefits:

1. Ensures that correct quantity is being ordered.

2. Allows for count when stock level at a low point. Makes it easier to count.

Problems:

a. Only the fastest moving items receive attention. Expensive but slower use items might be ignored until there is a crisis.

b. A true cross section of all types of SKUs won't be represented until a large part of the year will have past and when POs for most items will have been written and released.

c. Ignores completely items that are not ordered during a given year such as where the quantity on hand exceeds your use for that entire year.

Criteria: Only cycle count items at zero or negative balance

Benefits:

1. Negative balances should always trigger a count

2. Items at zero should be easy to verify.

Problems:

a. Neither of these is statistically significant and both fail to represent a cross-section of all items.

Using the Diminishing Population Technique with Product Categories

- Define the criteria by which each SKU will be placed into a category.

- Decide sequence in which categories will be counted: all manufacturer X's products this week, all of manufacturer Y's products next week.
- Divide the number of SKUs in the category by the number of days to determine how many must be counted per day. See Exhibit 6–7.
- Move to the next category.

The product categories method of cycle counting involves a great deal of administration but provides you with more detailed information and audit trails as to what you have actually done during a cycle count.

A-B-C Analysis Cycle Counting Method

The most sophisticated method of cycle counting, and the one preferred by most accountants, is to break your inventory up into A-B-C classifications. Items **are not** treated equally. Based on classification, the A items will be counted more frequently than the B items, and the B items will be counted more frequently than the C.

The classifications are based on "Pareto's Law"—the 80–20 Rule. See Chapter 3, pages 66–75 for a discussion of Pareto's Law and of how to determine which SKUs go into which categories.

For cycle counting purposes, classifications are determined by "value." Value could be based on money, usage rate, or a combination of the two.

Step-By-Step Implementation of the A-B-C Cycle Count Method

- Perform Pareto analysis of SKUs utilizing desired criteria. See Chapter 3.
- Assign SKUs into A-B-C categories

- Decide count frequency of each category. See Determining A-B-C Count Frequency below.

- Multiply respective number of SKUs per category by desired frequency to establish total counts. Cycle is assumed to be one year. See Exhibit 6–8.

- Divide total counts by the number of count days, (for example, 200 days per year,) to determine number of items to be counted each day. See Exhibit 6–8.

- Ask yourself, Is this a reasonable number of daily items? If "Yes," proceed. If "No," then change the frequencies and recalculate until a reasonable daily total is established.

- Determine how many items from each category will be counted each day: (See Exhibit 6–9)

  —Divide the number of annual counts within each category by the total (annual) number of counts. This establishes the percentage of counts represented by the respective categories when compared to the total counts.

  —Multiply the A, B, and C percent of total by the number of items to be counted daily. This establishes the quantity of each category to be counted each day.

- Count each category the desired number of times using the diminishing population technique.

Determining A-B-C Count Frequency

Determine count frequency by:

- Decide count frequency of each category. You can count the respective categories the number of times you desire. There is no rule-of-thumb. You may want to count "A"

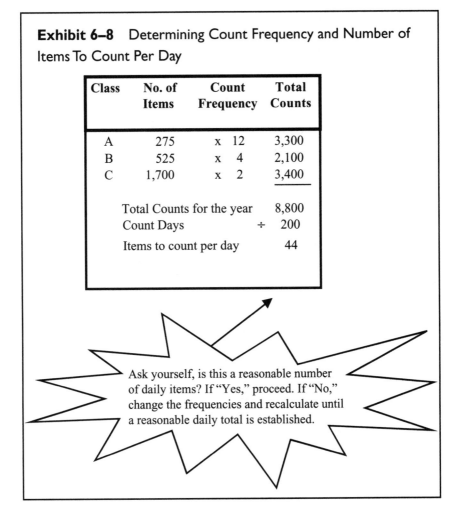

Exhibit 6–8 Determining Count Frequency and Number of Items To Count Per Day

Class	No. of Items	Count Frequency	Total Counts
A	275	x 12	3,300
B	525	x 4	2,100
C	1,700	x 2	3,400

Total Counts for the year		8,800
Count Days	÷	200
Items to count per day		44

Ask yourself, is this a reasonable number of daily items? If "Yes," proceed. If "No," change the frequencies and recalculate until a reasonable daily total is established.

items 12 times per year, "B" items 4 times per year, and "C" items 2 times per year. See Appendix A.

- Multiply the respective number of SKUs per category by the desired frequency to establish total counts. Cycle is assumed to be one year.

- Divide the total counts by the number of count days, (for example, 200 days per year) to determine the number of items to be counted each day.

Exhibit 6–9 Determining How Many Items from Each Category Will Be Counted Each Day

Number of counts per year taken from Exhibit 6–8.

Category	Annual Counts		Total Annual Counts		Percent of All Counts
A	3,300	÷	8,800	=	.375 > 38%
B	2,100	÷	8,800	=	.238 > 24%
C	3,400	÷	8,800	=	.386 > 39%

Category	Total Daily Counts		Percent of All Counts		Number of SKUs To Be Counted Daily
A	3,300	x	38%	=	16.72 > 17 A SKUs per day
B	2,100	x	24%	=	10.56 > 11 B SKUs per day
C	3,400	x	39%	=	17 C SKUs per day

Count each category the desired number of times using the diminishing population technique.

Determine How Many Items from Each Category Will Be Counted Each Day

- Divide the number of annual counts within each category by the total (annual) number of counts. This establishes the percentage of counts represented by the

respective categories when compared to the total counts. See Exhibit 6–9.

- Multiply the A, B, and C percent of total by the number of items to be counted daily. This establishes the quantity of each category to be counted each day. See Exhibit 6–9.

When To Count

The ideal time during the day to cycle count would be when there is no movement of paper or product. You may, therefore, want to count:

- at end of business day
- prior to start of day
- over the weekend
- during slowest shift

Another alternative is to creating a cycle counting cut-off during a regular business day by using time-of-day.

To use this approach you would:

1. Create a list of items to be cycle counted the next day.

2. Distribute the list to Shipping, Receiving, the stock put-away workers, order fillers, and data entry clerks.

3. Have Receiving, Shipping, the stock put-away workers, order fillers, and data entry clerks all note the time of day they interacted and actually dealt with any of the items on your list.

4. You now have the ability to audit back into any time frame during the day. For example:

- You cycle count widgets at 1:00 P.M. using a stock status report generated by data entry at 11:30 A.M.

- You find that there are 10 less widgets on the shelves than the stock status shows.
- You review all of the paper work from these different departments.
- The receiving paperwork shows that 10 widgets were received at 10:30 A.M.
- There is no paperwork from the stock put-away workers indicating that the widgets were ever moved into stock.
- The missing widgets are sitting out in the dock area. Your record count matches what you have in house.

Who Should Count

If there are 4 hours of counting involved in cycle counting all items on any given day, should you have a single person count for four hours and then begin any necessary reconciliations—or—does it make more sense to have 4 people count for one hour each and then let the inventory control clerk have the rest of the day to correct any problems? It makes sense to spread the raw counting portion of the cycle count among a group of people. This will allow the inventory control clerk to devote more hours of each day to actually fixing the system as opposed to spending each day counting boxes.

recap The objective of this chapter was to provide you with insights as to why many inventory control systems fail.

Often failure is due to individuals in different departments simply not understanding the unintended consequences of their own actions.

A review of who is supposed to write something down, what they are supposed to write down, who they are to give the information to, what that person is supposed to do with the information, and the sequencing and overall timing of these events often reveals that respective departments are using different units of measure to define inventory. Some use dollars, while others use actual physical units. In addition, seemingly simple issues like the timing of when an item is entered into the computer system or who is allowed to actually see various items of information can cause severe misunderstandings and inventory inaccuracies.

In analyzing "what is going on," metrics should be used, with the old management phrase, "you can't control what you don't measure," being a constant guiding principle.

By documenting the who, what, when, where, why, and how of how the system is actually working you can demonstrate to yourself and others where changes might be necessary.

? REVIEW QUESTIONS

1. Cycle counting is: 1. (a)

(a) counting a statistically significant cross-section of your inventory frequently.

(b) counting everything in your facility at least twice per calendar or fiscal year.

(c) determining a fair valuation of your inventory value at least once per fiscal year.

(d) counting all of the bicycle parts in your facility.

2. Flow charts allow you to: 2. (a)

(a) analyze the sequential sequence of a set of events.

(b) determine trends.

(c) compare a projected value against an actual one.

(d) create a report that identifies the number of items per level and number of tiers of product on a flow-through rack.

3. Run charts allow you to: 3. (b)

    (a) analyze the sequential sequence of a set of events.

    (b) determine trends.

    (c) compare a projected value against an actual one.

    (d) create a report that identifies the number of items per level and number of tiers of product on a flow-through rack.

4. **True or False**   4. (b)

The diminishing population method of cycle counting involves counting items when that SKU'S stock level reaches zero.

    (a) True

    (b) False

5. Fill rates indicate: 5. (c)

    (a) how much of a particular SKU you have in stock at the end of a calendar month.

    (b) the quantitative nature of your inventory.

    (c) if you had what you needed when you needed it.

    (d) the ratio of accurate shelf counts to record counts.

NOTES

1. *Backflushing* refers to a software technique where raw materials and other components going into a particular sub-assembly or final product are relieved from stock when that sub-assembly/product is completed. If there were a seat and a leg assembly that goes into making up a stool, then upon completion of the stool these items would be deleted from inventory.

Until the backflush occurs the respective parts, sub-assemblies, and so on remain in the record count. Contrast this to having each item relieved from stock as it is removed from the shelf for production purposes. Backflushing reduces the time and effort involved in tracking individual inventory transactions.

2. *Work in process* is used to describe raw materials, parts, and sub-assemblies as they are being used to produce the next higher level component or finished item in a bill of materials (the recipe of materials going into an assembly of some type).

3. *Allocation* refers to an item being tied to a specific order. "Relieving" an item refers to it actually being removed from stock in terms of both its paper life and its real life.

4. Based on four days per week, fifty weeks per year.

5. It is a rule-of-thumb that cycle counting should be done four days per week, fifty weeks per year, 200 days per year.

6. Issues like who will count, when should they count, how many people should count, and so on will be covered as part of the cycle count discussion.

CHAPTER 7

Protecting Inventory

Introduction

The objective of this chapter is to provide you with a basic understanding of how to approach emergency/disaster and business continuation planning for the storekeeping portion of your operation. You must decide what an "emergency" is for your organization. An event that would be viewed as an irritant by one company, for example, a 48-hour power outage, might be a disaster to a different organization.

What would the department managers, supervisors, and team leaders of your organization actually do within the first thirty minutes of any of the following emergencies?

- Area wide power outage
- Significant workplace violence incident
- Major theft incident
- Earthquake
- Tornado
- Major fire within your space

What *would* everyone do? What incremental steps, policies, procedures, and internal training presently exist within your organization to prevent or mitigate these types of major disruptions?

Many organizations aren't sure what the answer would be. In fact, many companies are not fully prepared to react to a *natural, technological* or *incited* emergency. Consider these recent Federal Emergency Management Agency statistics:

- Most businesses do not have an emergency or recovery plan.
- Forty-seven percent of businesses that experience fire or major theft go out of business within two years.
- Forty-four percent of companies that lose records in a disaster never resume business.
- Ninety-three percent of companies that experience a significant data loss are out of business within five years.
- Most businesses spend less than three percent of their total budget on business recovery planning.

Organizations that do have some form of plan unfortunately only concentrate on protecting data files with no consideration being given to other aspects of the business. A disaster plan is more than having daily data file backups taken offsite. Offsite data doesn't do much good if there is no recovery site from which to operate and no equipment or application software to run it on.

Another example of the broad range of topic areas you must consider when assessing the impact of a crisis is: Assume that other than serial number and descriptive information contained in its data files, your company has no offsite records related to powered industrial trucks or other equipment used in

your stock keeping operations. There is an area wide disaster, a tornado, and your building and its contents are lost. Your insurance carrier states that it cannot process a claim on the equipment unless you can provide not only descriptions and serial numbers of lost equipment but also copies of the relevant purchase orders. It's simply too late to think about critical records retention after a tornado has destroyed the building.

Legal Duties

Under the Uniform Commercial Code, as well as the common law (effective in all states except Louisiana), if you are storing goods for a third party the degree of care you must show toward the items is that of a reasonably prudent owner. In other words, how would you care for the items if you owned them? Basically, then, if you don't take reasonable precautions to protect items, your organization becomes legally liable for their loss.

If you are storing items for your own organization, you must legally act in the best interests of the company's shareholders. Once again the question will be: Did you act in a reasonable manner?

Emergency planning helps you fulfil your legal obligations of care.

The Plan

There are three sections that make up an emergency/disaster and business continuation plan (the Plan): **preparation**—including steps toward disaster avoidance and mitigation; **execution**—including handling the crisis as it unfolds; and **recovery**—initiating business continuation.

Preparation

The first step toward protecting the product is assessing your vulnerability to *natural*, *technological*, or *incited* emergencies.

Natural Emergencies

- Earthquakes
- Coastal Erosion
- Tornadoes
- Droughts
- Hailstorms
- Extreme Heat
- Severe Winter Storms
- Volcanoes
- Tsunamis
- Hurricanes
- Storm Surges
- Wildfires
- Landslides
- Windstorms
- Freezing
- Severe Thunder and Lightning
- Flooding
- Hailstorms

A good deal of information regarding specific measures to prepare for specific natural disasters may be obtained from the Federal Emergency Management Agency (FEMA).

Technological Emergencies

- Power Outage
- Power Surge or Spike
- Hardware Error
- Software Error
- Software Virus
- Loss of Natural Gas
- Loss of Water
- Loss of Hydraulics
- Loss of Elevators
- Loss of Communications Equipment
- Loss of Compressed Air
- Loss of Municipal and Internal Sewage Systems
- Loss of Waste Water Treatment Services
- Fire Alarms
- Security Alarms
- HVAC Systems (Heating, Ventilating, and Air Conditioning Systems)
- Manufacturing Equipment Failure

Incited Emergencies

- Workplace Violence
- Arson
- Internal Theft
- Mass Theft

- Bomb Threat
- Sabotage
- Area-wide Terrorism Incident
- Labor Stoppage (strike)

Planning Team

Although the objective of this chapter is to focus on that portion of the organization charged with protecting inventory, any planning team formed to assess vulnerabilities should include individuals from several departments. Contingency planning is a business issue and not just an inventory or information technology or accounting issue. Each department is dependent on the others: operations supports sales, the computer department supports many functions, the facility manager supports the computer department, and so forth.

A multi-functional contingency planning team allows:

- a comprehensive understanding of the total company effort required;
- broad-based commitment to the effort;
- a definition of recovery requirements from the perspective of the business units being impacted;
- a definition of each department's "pain threshold." One department may be devastated by a 24-hour event, while another department may only be inconvenienced; and,
- for a plan comprehensible to each impacted group.

The Assessment

The team should assess each type of risk—natural, technological, and incited—and determine the probability of each event occurring and its potential impact on each department if it did happen.

Potential threats should be broken down into two groupings:

1. Threats likely to occur within the facility
2. Threats likely to occur in the surrounding area

Probability should be based on such factors as:

- **Historical**—What types of emergencies have occurred at this facility, this community, this region?
- **Geographical**—Is the facility close to a flood plain; seismic faults; dams; controversial organizations such as research institutions or abortion clinics; or nuclear power plants?
- **Technological**—What could result from a process or systems failure caused by fire, explosion, release of toxic fumes, loss of communications, or power failure?
- **Human Error**—What could result from poor training, poor maintenance, poor safety practices, misconduct, substance abuse, or fatigue?
- **Physical**—What is the building made of? What and how much is stored in the facility?
- **Regulatory**—What emergencies or hazards (such as hazardous material spills) are you regulated to deal with?

Exhibit 7–1 Self-Assessment Worksheet

Business component or function _____

Assessment prepared by: _____ Date: _____

1. List all business processes performed by this business unit.
   a. Check ☑ processes required to maintain business functions.
   b. Rank, as follows:

   C for Critical This ranking denotes operations we cannot do without or a function that is vital to the operation and/or poses the risk of serious injury or death (life safety risk).

   E for Essential This ranking denotes operations that are difficult to operate without, but the organization could function for a period of time without them.

   NE for Nonessential Disruption would be an inconvenience.

   c. Prioritize as to maximum allowable recovery or down time, as follows:

   Imm for Immediate 0 to 24 hours
   Del for delayed 24 hours to 7 days
   Def for deferred Beyond 7 days

   d. Categorize as to vulnerability, as follows:

   H for Highly Vulnerable Business functions with a great risk of experiencing a threat or hazard
   V for Vulnerable May experience a threat or hazard
   NV for Not Vulnerable Threat or hazard not likely to occur

Business Process	Required to maintain business function ☑	Ranking C, E, or NE	Priority Imm, Del, or Def	Vulnerability H, V, or NV

Cont. on page 204

Cont. from page 203

2. Prioritize all critical processes.
   a. List plans for process recovery.
   b. List resources required to maintain the business function.

Priority	Critical Processes	Recovery Plan(s)	Required Resources
1			
2			
3			
4			

3. List duties and tasks needed to recover the critical process.
   a. If an alternate site is required
      (1) List needed resources.
      (2) Explain what must be accomplished at that location.
         A. _____
         B. _____
         C. _____

4. Where will recovery resources be obtained?
   a. List resources from within business unit.
   b. List resources from other business units.
   c. List resources required from contractors, vendors, or other outside sources.
         A. _____
         B. _____
         C. _____

5. Identification of persons responsible for the above recovery process:

Employee	Home Phone	Work Phone	Pager

6. Identify customers, suppliers, and other operations affected by the disruption.
   A. _____
   B. _____
   C. _____

Break down your assessment of impact in the following areas:

- **Human Impact**—death or injury
- **Property Impact**—cost to replace, cost of temporary arrangements, cost to repair
- **Business Impact**—interruption, loss of customers, employees unable to report to work, violations of contractual arrangements, fines and penalties.

Whenever possible, the team should be assisted in its efforts through the use of worksheets, checklists, and other job aids. An example of an assessment worksheet is contained in Exhibit 7–1.

The assessment should allow you to (a) develop plans for preventing or mitigating the threat, (b) assign duties to be carried out during and immediately after an emergency, and (c) plan for business continuity.

Theft

A particular danger of inventory loss comes from theft. All too often a stockkeeper almost invites the problem. Consider the situations in Exhibits 7–2 and 7–3.

Types of Theft Threats

Generally stockroom or warehouse thefts fall into the categories of mass theft and pilferage.

Mass theft would involve a major break-in and removal of significant amounts of product or the hijacking of a truck or trailer. Pilferage covers a wide range of activities from the removal of small amounts of merchandise on a continuous basis

resulting in significant losses to collusion between employees or between employees and shippers or customers involving either shipping or receiving.

Assessing the Threat

Just as you did in preparing to counter a natural or technological emergency, to prevent or mitigate a theft you must first assess the probability of a loss occurring and its expected impact if it did happen. To accomplish this, do a crime pattern analysis:

1. Write down each activity engaged in as part of your direct stockkeeping operation. For example:

Receiving Activities

- Check-in loads against bills-of-lading, purchase orders, or packing slips
  —Inspect goods
  —Count items
  —Check count against paperwork
  —If items are damaged
    - Stop unpacking
    - Alert driver
    - Make appropriate notations on paperwork
    - Photograph
    - Notify shipper's claims department
    - Refuse load or isolate damaged product for inspection by shipper's representatives

---

2. Write down the sequential steps involved in each activity.

3. Review the physical layout of your facility.

4. Using the information gained through steps 1 through 3, apply the following crime pattern analysis:

- *Type of crime*—What type of crime could occur during any of the activities or sequential steps you listed? What type of crime could occur because of your physical layout?
- *Attack methods*—Given the type of crime identified, what methods would an attacker use to "pull it off"?
- *Times of Attack*—Given the type of crime identified and attack methods likely to be used, what time periods (seasons of the year, particular days of the week, particular hours of the day) seem the most logical for the attack to occur?
- *Suspect Characteristics*—Who is most likely to engage in the particular crime you have identified? Is a worker acting alone the danger? Are two workers acting in concert the danger?
- *Typical Types and Amounts of Loss or Injuries Suffered*—The amount of money, time, and effort you will use to deter one type of loss will certainly be different from the resources devoted to a different, lesser danger.

Countering the Threats

Countering theft threats involves developing physical barriers and deterrents such as lighting, fences, security cameras, intrusion sensors and alarms, as well as thoroughly checking the background of people you hire.

Crime Prevention Through Environmental Design (CPTED)

CPTED is a modern approach to crime prevention that seeks to balance a facility's layout (design) with the processes (human

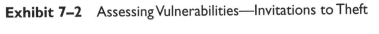

Exhibit 7–2   Assessing Vulnerabilities—Invitations to Theft

INSTRUCTIONS: Review the photographs below. What vulnerabilities do you see?

circulation, product flow, and information flow) taking place within it. This concept employs strategies of access control, natural surveillance, territoriality ("Why are you in this part of the building?"), management, and maintenance to support legitimate activity. It strives to create an environment where:

- suspicious behavior will be observed, caught, and punished.
- it takes a lot of extra effort to commit a crime.
- there is a reduction in the reward for attempting the crime: target items are sheltered, distanced, reduced in quantity.
- there is a removal of excuses for improper behavior through clear work rules and policies, signage, and border definition.

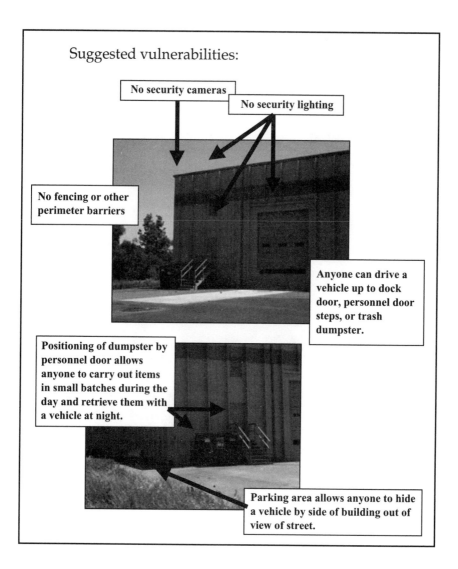

Suggested vulnerabilities:

No security cameras

No security lighting

No fencing or other perimeter barriers

Anyone can drive a vehicle up to dock door, personnel door steps, or trash dumpster.

Positioning of dumpster by personnel door allows anyone to carry out items in small batches during the day and retrieve them with a vehicle at night.

Parking area allows anyone to hide a vehicle by side of building out of view of street.

CPTED uses three strategies:

1. Organizational—staff and perhaps outside security personnel both overt and covert.

2. Mechanical—technology and hardware.

3. Natural—architectural and circulation flow patterns

Use CPTED to plan an overall approach to preventing or at least lessening the opportunity for crime to occur. Exhibit

Exhibit 7–3   Assessing Vulnerabilities—Invitations to Assault

INSTRUCTIONS: Review the photograph below. What major vulnerabilities to assault are identifiable in the picture?

7–4 contains a list of CPTED-related action items you should consider.

Collusion Theft

Collusion theft occurring through the partnership of a truck driver and a warehouse worker is difficult to actually "catch." However, there are effective techniques aimed toward prevention through increasing the possibility of detection. Consider the following:

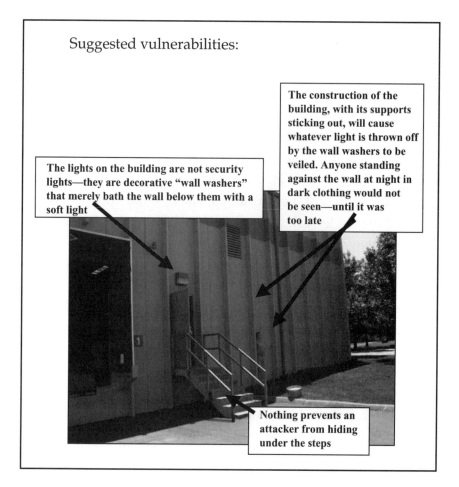

Suggested vulnerabilities:

The construction of the building, with its supports sticking out, will cause whatever light is thrown off by the wall washers to be veiled. Anyone standing against the wall at night in dark clothing would not be seen—until it was too late

The lights on the building are not security lights—they are decorative "wall washers" that merely bath the wall below them with a soft light

Nothing prevents an attacker from hiding under the steps

- Random, detailed checking of loads on outbound trucks at the dock.

- At least twice each month, call a driver back in after she has left the facility. Thoroughly check the load. Check drivers on a random basis.

- Receiving by appointment coupled with random detailed checking of incoming loads.

- Using cycle counting. See pages 176–193 in chapter 6. Once employees understand that there is an ongoing effort to discover and hunt down the causes of inventory discrep-

ancies, they will also understand that management is watching.

Background Checks

No discussion of deterring crime would be complete without considering that the most effective method of avoiding both pilferage and collusion theft is to hire honest people. Since many people misrepresent their history, a background check is a must.

A reasonable background check will help you hire qualified workers, avoid hiring the dishonest, and assist you in avoiding claims for negligent hiring if a worker commits a crime against a customer, the public, or another employee.

It is not the objective of this text to serve as a guide to all human resource procedures that need to be followed in the hiring process. Therefore, no attempt is made to address issues such as discrimination, immigration, equal employment recordkeeping, and so on. However, since you may personally be involved in reference checking, it is important to use techniques calculated to encourage former employers and others to actually provide you with useful information.

An unfortunate fact of life is that many employers will either provide you with no information or will limit it to the following:

- They will confirm or deny that an individual worked for them.

- They will confirm or deny a length of employment.

- They will confirm or deny a job title or brief job description of their former employee.

- They will confirm or deny what you tell them the former employee says she was compensated.

Exhibit 7–4 CPTED-Related Action Items

- Control facility parking
  —Fencing
  —Gates
  —Card activated gates or barrier arms
  —Signage
- Control adjacent parking
- Provide a waiting area for outside supplier truck drivers. These areas may include vending machines, pay telephones, and restrooms. Remove reasons for a driver to leave the waiting area. Restrict access. Do not let outside drivers wander around.
- 24-hour CCTV surveillance and recording of all desired locations
  —Parking lots
  —Doorways
  —Valuable stock areas
  —Docks
  —Infrared LED lighting with low light cameras to observe dark areas either within or outside of the facility
- Lighting with emergency backup
  —Security lighting should be overlapping with tamperproof housings

Cont. on page 214

When you follow-up with questions such as, "Would you rehire the worker?" a former employer's response could well be, "Sorry, I've given you all of the information I can. Don't take my lack of information as either a positive or negative recommendation. I hope I've helped. Good bye."

Cont. from page 213

- Extend the physical perimeter with barriers
- Receiving and shipping procedures should be thoroughly examined for vulnerabilities to theft
  —Employees responsible for ordering items should not be the same individuals responsible for receiving them or paying for them
- Trash removal containers and procedures should be reviewed for vulnerabilities to theft
- Determine security guard requirements
- Consider undercover detectives periodically working within the workforce
- Install intrusion detection equipment and monitoring
- Provide employee and visitor identification systems
- Display employee identification at all times
- Prevent unauthorized access to utility areas
- Install mylar film on all exterior windows for shatter protection
- Control keys
  —Issue as few keys as possible
  —Establish specific rules regarding "loaning out" keys
  —Have keys stamped "Do Not Duplicate"
  —Control who can make duplicate keys
  —Periodically inventory keys
  —Institute an electronic access card system

To overcome the fear of liability and litigation that many organizations have in providing background information regarding a job applicant, you should use release forms. An example of a reference/background release form is contained in Exhibit 7–5.

Exhibit 7–5 Background Check Release Form

Use this in conjunction with your application form

RELEASE FORM

I understand that, in connection with my application for employment with _____ , investigative inquiries are to be made on myself including, but not limited to, consumer credit, criminal convictions, motor vehicle history, educational transcripts, and other reports of any nature and type. These reports will include information as to my character, work, habits, performance, and experience together with reasons for termination of past employment.

Further, I understand that you will be requesting information from various federal, state, and other agencies that maintain records concerning my past activities related to my driving, credit, criminal, education, and other experiences.

I authorize without reservation all corporations, companies, credit agencies, persons, educational institutions, law enforcement agencies, and former employers to release information they may have about me, and I release them from any liability and responsibility for doing so; further, I authorize the procurement of an investigative consumer report related to me and acknowledge my understanding that such report may contain information as to my background, mode of living, character, and personal reputation.

This authorization, in original and copy form, shall be valid for this and any future reports that may be requested.

I hereby authorize investigation of all statements made by me either in writing or verbally with no liability arising therefrom.

I willingly provide the following personal information as an aid in the proper identification of my file or records.

PRINT NAME: _____

SOCIAL SECURITY NUMBER: _____

CURRENT ADDRESS: _____

FORMER ADDRESS: _____

APPLICANT SIGNATURE: _____ DATE: _____

The form in Exhibit 7–5 releases both the provider of information and your organization from liability.

It is important that you follow your organization's guidelines regarding what you may or may not ask during reference checking or interviews. Generally, prospective employers are allowed to check criminal conviction records when the type of position being filled justifies the inquiry. Some state laws only allow you to deny someone a job if they were convicted of a crime reasonably related to the position for which you are considering the applicant for.

Do not ask about arrest records. Many state laws (a) do not permit inquiry into or (b) at least restrict information regarding arrests. An arrest record does not prove that the applicant committed any crime.

recap Business emergencies are a question of "when," not "if." Therefore, to fulfill your legal obligations of care you must assess any reasonably foreseeable circumstances that might cause harm to or loss of the inventory you are storing and handling.

Each organization should methodically assess its vulnerability to natural, technological, and incited emergencies. That assessment must involve a determination of not only how likely an event is, but also what impact it might have on the inventory or the business as a whole.

The vulnerability assessment should lead to an action plan that includes specific procedures, responsibilities, and resources to be used to (a) prevent or mitigate a crisis, (b) to handle the crisis as it unfolds, and (c) to allow for business continuation.

❓ REVIEW QUESTIONS

1. Which of the following is not an incited crisis?   1. (c)
   (a) Terrorism
   (b) Arson fire
   (c) Work stoppage due to an employee refusing to use a
piece of equipment
   (d) Work stoppage during a labor dispute

2. List three potential technological threats.

   (a) _____

   (b) _____

   (c) _____

- Power Outage
- Power Surge or Spike
- Hardware Error
- Software Error
- Software Virus
- Loss of Natural Gas
- Loss of Water
- Loss of Hydraulics
- Loss of Elevators

3. Duty of care you owe under the Uniform Commercial
Code is: 3. (d)
   (a) each item you store must be fully insured at its replacement value.
   (b) each item you store must be fully insured at its depreciated value.
   (c) you may not store items without a written contract.
   (d) you must act as a reasonably prudent owner.

4. When can you inquire into an applicant's criminal history?
    4. (b)
   (a) Always
   (b) Convictions for offenses related to the job applied for
   (c) After an arrest for an offense related to the job applied for
   (d) Never

Appendix A—
Inventory

A	B	C	D	E	F	G
Line No.	Part No.	Description	Annual Usage	Cumulative Usage	% Total Usage	% Total Items
1	Part 79	Product A	8,673	8,673	6.3%	0.3%
2	Part 133	Product B	6,970	15,643	11.3%	0.7%
3	Part 290	Product C	5,788	21,431	15.5%	1.0%
4	Part 65	Product D	5,690	27,121	19.6%	1.3%
5	Part 111	Product E	4,899	32,020	23.2%	1.7%
6	Part 195	Product F	3,669	35,689	25.8%	2.0%
7	Part 139	Product G	3,364	39,053	28.3%	2.3%
8	Part 131	Product H	3,250	42,303	30.6%	2.7%
9	Part 132	Product I	3,022	45,325	32.8%	3.0%
10	Part 175	Product J	2,864	48,189	34.9%	3.3%
11	Part 255	Product K	2,844	51,033	36.9%	3.7%
12	Part 101	Product L	2,670	53,703	38.9%	4.0%
13	Part 265	Product M	2,665	56,368	40.8%	4.3%
14	Part 48	Product N	2,453	58,821	42.6%	4.7%
15	Part 2	Product O	2,222	61,043	44.2%	5.0%
16	Part 14	Product P	1,976	63,019	45.6%	5.3%
17	Part 70	Product Q	1,896	64,915	47.0%	5.7%
18	Part 117	Product R	1,888	66,803	48.4%	6.0%
19	Part 134	Product S	1,872	68,675	49.7%	6.3%
20	Part 170	Product T	1,687	70,362	50.9%	6.7%
21	Part 182	Product U	1,666	72,028	52.1%	7.0%
22	Part 28	Product V	1,646	73,674	53.3%	7.3%
23	Part 138	Product W	1,566	75,240	54.5%	7.7%
24	Part 23	Product X	1,530	76,770	55.6%	8.0%
25	Part 300	Product Y	1,057	77,827	56.3%	8.3%
26	Part 9	Product Z	1,050	78,877	57.1%	8.7%
27	Part 241	Product AA	1,022	79,899	57.8%	9.0%

A	B	C	D	E	F	G
Line No.	Part No.	Description	Annual Usage	Cumulative Usage	% Total Usage	% Total Items
28	Part 219	Product AB	1,022	80,921	58.6%	9.3%
29	Part 51	Product AC	1,001	81,922	59.3%	9.7%
30	Part 278	Product AD	997	82,919	60.0%	10.0%
31	Part 222	Product AE	991	83,910	60.7%	10.3%
32	Part 154	Product AF	986	84,896	61.5%	10.7%
33	Part 184	Product AG	972	85,868	62.2%	11.0%
34	Part 190	Product AH	968	86,836	62.9%	11.3%
35	Part 87	Product AI	964	87,800	63.6%	11.7%
36	Part 95	Product AJ	943	88,743	64.2%	12.0%
37	Part 6	Product AK	894	89,637	64.9%	12.3%
38	Part 142	Product AL	889	90,526	65.5%	12.7%
39	Part 210	Product AM	889	91,415	66.2%	13.0%
40	Part 13	Product AN	888	92,303	66.8%	13.3%
41	Part 121	Product AO	888	93,191	67.5%	13.7%
42	Part 3	Product AP	875	94,066	68.1%	14.0%
43	Part 235	Product AQ	867	94,933	68.7%	14.3%
44	Part 297	Product AR	861	95,794	69.3%	14.7%
45	Part 266	Product AS	856	96,650	70.0%	15.0%
46	Part 239	Product AT	846	97,496	70.6%	15.3%
47	Part 233	Product AU	843	98,339	71.2%	15.7%
48	Part 77	Product AV	800	99,139	71.8%	16.0%
49	Part 188	Product AW	795	99,934	72.3%	16.3%
50	Part 240	Product AX	788	100,722	72.9%	16.7%
51	Part 103	Product AY	779	101,501	73.5%	17.0%
52	Part 160	Product AZ	766	102,267	74.0%	17.3%
53	Part 211	Product BA	764	103,031	74.6%	17.7%
54	Part 243	Product BB	761	103,792	75.1%	18.0%
55	Part 201	Product BC	754	104,546	75.7%	18.3%
56	Part 202	Product BD	712	105,258	76.2%	18.7%
57	Part 75	Product BE	698	105,956	76.7%	19.0%
58	Part 206	Product BF	697	106,653	77.2%	19.3%
59	Part 200	Product BG	697	107,350	77.7%	19.7%
60	Part 124	Product BH	689	108,039	78.2%	20.0%
61	Part 208	Product BI	662	108,701	78.7%	20.3%
62	Part 253	Product BJ	644	109,345	79.2%	20.7%
63	Part 264	Product BK	640	109,985	79.6%	21.0%
64	Part 230	Product BL	614	110,599	80.1%	21.3%
65	Part 53	Product BM	590	111,189	80.5%	21.7%
66	Part 33	Product BN	587	111,776	80.9%	22.0%
67	Part 104	Product BO	566	112,342	81.3%	22.3%
68	Part 207	Product BK	564	112,906	81.7%	22.7%
69	Part 63	Product BL	544	113,450	82.1%	23.0%
70	Part 275	Product BM	533	113,983	82.5%	23.3%

A	B	C	D	E	F	G
Line No.	Part No.	Description	Annual Usage	Cumulative Usage	% Total Usage	% Total Items
71	Part 155	Product BN	530	114,513	82.9%	23.7%
72	Part 7	Product BO	512	115,025	83.3%	24.0%
73	Part 90	Product BP	499	115,524	83.6%	24.3%
74	Part 59	Product BQ	468	115,992	84.0%	24.7%
75	Part 122	Product BR	467	116,459	84.3%	25.0%
76	Part 35	Product BS	456	116,915	84.6%	25.3%
77	Part 67	Product BT	450	117,365	85.0%	25.7%
78	Part 92	Product BU	444	117,809	85.3%	26.0%
79	Part 83	Product BV	443	118,252	85.6%	26.3%
80	Part 287	Product BW	433	118,685	85.9%	26.7%
81	Part 162	Product BX	420	119,105	86.2%	27.0%
82	Part 189	Product BY	420	119,525	86.5%	27.3%
83	Part 245	Product BZ	398	119,923	86.8%	27.7%
84	Part 274	Product CA	382	120,305	87.1%	28.0%
85	Part 242	Product CB	355	120,660	87.3%	28.3%
86	Part 258	Product CC	354	121,014	87.6%	28.7%
87	Part 136	Product CD	353	121,367	87.9%	29.0%
88	Part 238	Product CE	334	121,701	88.1%	29.3%
89	Part 115	Product CF	333	122,034	88.3%	29.7%
90	Part 94	Product CG	333	122,367	88.6%	30.0%
91	Part 64	Product CH	332	122,699	88.8%	30.3%
92	Part 298	Product CI	326	123,025	89.1%	30.7%
93	Part 295	Product CJ	325	123,350	89.3%	31.0%
94	Part 30	Product CK	325	123,675	89.5%	31.3%
95	Part 11	Product CL	323	123,998	89.8%	31.7%
96	Part 192	Product CM	321	124,319	90.0%	32.0%
97	Part 96	Product CN	321	124,640	90.2%	32.3%
98	Part 40	Product CO	298	124,938	90.4%	32.7%
99	Part 47	Product CP	285	125,223	90.7%	33.0%
100	Part 125	Product CQ	269	125,492	90.8%	33.3%
101	Part 198	Product CR	260	125,752	91.0%	33.7%
102	Part 135	Product CS	258	126,010	91.2%	34.0%
103	Part 130	Product CT	256	126,266	91.4%	34.3%
104	Part 85	Product CU	255	126,521	91.6%	34.7%
105	Part 216	Product CV	223	126,744	91.8%	35.0%
106	Part 193	Product CW	222	126,966	91.9%	35.3%
107	Part 285	Product CX	220	127,186	92.1%	35.7%
108	Part 288	Product CY	200	127,386	92.2%	36.0%
109	Part 26	Product CZ	199	127,585	92.4%	36.3%
110	Part 176	Product DA	199	127,784	92.5%	36.7%
111	Part 186	Product DB	194	127,978	92.6%	37.0%
112	Part 173	Product DC	189	128,167	92.8%	37.3%
113	Part 81	Product DD	188	128,355	92.9%	37.7%

A	B	C	D	E	F	G
Line No.	Part No.	Description	Annual Usage	Cumulative Usage	% Total Usage	% Total Items
114	Part 172	Product DE	188	128,543	93.1%	38.0%
115	Part 144	Product DF	186	128,729	93.2%	38.3%
116	Part 12	Product DG	186	128,915	93.3%	38.7%
117	Part 141	Product DH	186	129,101	93.5%	39.0%
118	Part 15	Product DI	185	129,286	93.6%	39.3%
119	Part 227	Product DJ	185	129,471	93.7%	39.7%
120	Part 191	Product DK	184	129,655	93.9%	40.0%
121	Part 272	Product DL	178	129,833	94.0%	40.3%
122	Part 279	Product DM	156	129,989	94.1%	40.7%
123	Part 247	Product DN	150	130,139	94.2%	41.0%
124	Part 89	Product DO	144	130,283	94.3%	41.3%
125	Part 174	Product DP	143	130,426	94.4%	41.7%
126	Part 118	Product DQ	133	130,559	94.5%	42.0%
127	Part 27	Product DR	116	130,675	94.6%	42.3%
128	Part 34	Product DS	116	130,791	94.7%	42.7%
129	Part 169	Product DT	116	130,907	94.8%	43.0%
130	Part 178	Product DU	113	131,020	94.8%	43.3%
131	Part 84	Product DV	105	131,125	94.9%	43.7%
132	Part 204	Product DW	103	131,228	95.0%	44.0%
133	Part 273	Product DX	102	131,330	95.1%	44.3%
134	Part 24	Product DY	101	131,431	95.1%	44.7%
135	Part 114	Product DZ	100	131,531	95.2%	45.0%
136	Part 57	Product EA	100	131,631	95.3%	45.3%
137	Part 168	Product EB	99	131,730	95.4%	45.7%
138	Part 187	Product EC	99	131,829	95.4%	46.0%
139	Part 214	Product ED	99	131,928	95.5%	46.3%
140	Part 220	Product EE	98	132,026	95.6%	46.7%
141	Part 29	Product EF	98	132,124	95.6%	47.0%
142	Part 98	Product EG	98	132,222	95.7%	47.3%
143	Part 261	Product EH	97	132,319	95.8%	47.7%
144	Part 180	Product EI	97	132,416	95.9%	48.0%
145	Part 289	Product EJ	96	132,512	95.9%	48.3%
146	Part 146	Product EK	96	132,608	96.0%	48.7%
147	Part 299	Product EL	94	132,702	96.1%	49.0%
148	Part 68	Product EM	92	132,794	96.1%	49.3%
149	Part 41	Product EN	91	132,885	96.2%	49.7%
150	Part 38	Product EO	90	132,975	96.3%	50.0%
151	Part 140	Product EP	89	133,064	96.3%	50.3%
152	Part 16	Product EQ	89	133,153	96.4%	50.7%
153	Part 128	Product ER	88	133,241	96.5%	51.0%
154	Part 25	Product ES	88	133,329	96.5%	51.3%
155	Part 45	Product ET	87	133,416	96.6%	51.7%
156	Part 1	Product EU	86	133,502	96.6%	52.0%

A	B	C	D	E	F	G
Line No.	Part No.	Description	Annual Usage	Cumulative Usage	% Total Usage	% Total Items
157	Part 246	Product EV	85	133,587	96.7%	52.3%
158	Part 108	Product EW	85	133,672	96.8%	52.7%
159	Part 231	Product EX	85	133,757	96.8%	53.0%
160	Part 21	Product EY	84	133,841	96.9%	53.3%
161	Part 183	Product EZ	84	133,925	97.0%	53.7%
162	Part 248	Product FA	84	134,009	97.0%	54.0%
163	Part 199	Product FB	84	134,093	97.1%	54.3%
164	Part 120	Product FC	80	134,173	97.1%	54.7%
165	Part 224	Product FD	80	134,253	97.2%	55.0%
166	Part 256	Product FE	76	134,329	97.2%	55.3%
167	Part 281	Product FF	76	134,405	97.3%	55.7%
168	Part 157	Product FG	76	134,481	97.4%	56.0%
169	Part 5	Product FH	75	134,556	97.4%	56.3%
170	Part 56	Product FI	75	134,631	97.5%	56.7%
171	Part 44	Product FJ	74	134,705	97.5%	57.0%
172	Part 76	Product FK	74	134,779	97.6%	57.3%
173	Part 267	Product FL	74	134,853	97.6%	57.7%
174	Part 262	Product FM	72	134,925	97.7%	58.0%
175	Part 225	Product FN	68	134,993	97.7%	58.3%
176	Part 276	Product FO	67	135,060	97.8%	58.7%
177	Part 43	Product FP	66	135,126	97.8%	59.0%
178	Part 10	Product FQ	66	135,192	97.9%	59.3%
179	Part 126	Product FR	65	135,257	97.9%	59.7%
180	Part 296	Product FS	64	135,321	98.0%	60.0%
181	Part 277	Product FT	63	135,384	98.0%	60.3%
182	Part 42	Product FU	63	135,447	98.1%	60.7%
183	Part 197	Product FV	62	135,509	98.1%	61.0%
184	Part 284	Product FW	61	135,570	98.1%	61.3%
185	Part 22	Product FX	61	135,631	98.2%	61.7%
186	Part 39	Product FY	61	135,692	98.2%	62.0%
187	Part 82	Product FZ	58	135,750	98.3%	62.3%
188	Part 237	Product GA	56	135,806	98.3%	62.7%
189	Part 69	Product GB	56	135,862	98.4%	63.0%
190	Part 62	Product GC	56	135,918	98.4%	63.3%
191	Part 213	Product GD	56	135,974	98.4%	63.7%
192	Part 109	Product GE	55	136,029	98.5%	64.0%
193	Part 149	Product GF	55	136,084	98.5%	64.3%
194	Part 159	Product GG	55	136,139	98.6%	64.7%
195	Part 113	Product GH	54	136,193	98.6%	65.0%
196	Part 110	Product GI	54	136,247	98.6%	65.3%
197	Part 218	Product GJ	54	136,301	98.7%	65.7%
198	Part 46	Product GK	53	136,354	98.7%	66.0%
199	Part 112	Product GL	52	136,406	98.7%	66.3%

A	B	C	D	E	F	G
Line No.	Part No.	Description	Annual Usage	Cumulative Usage	% Total Usage	% Total Items
200	Part 179	Product GM	52	136,458	98.8%	66.7%
201	Part 100	Product GN	52	136,510	98.8%	67.0%
202	Part 37	Product GO	52	136,562	98.9%	67.3%
203	Part 282	Product GP	50	136,612	98.9%	67.7%
204	Part 116	Product GQ	48	136,660	98.9%	68.0%
205	Part 8	Product GR	46	136,706	99.0%	68.3%
206	Part 254	Product GS	45	136,751	99.0%	68.7%
207	Part 148	Product GT	45	136,796	99.0%	69.0%
208	Part 66	Product GU	44	136,840	99.1%	69.3%
209	Part 18	Product GV	43	136,883	99.1%	69.7%
210	Part 119	Product GW	43	136,926	99.1%	70.0%
211	Part 52	Product GX	42	136,968	99.2%	70.3%
212	Part 123	Product GY	41	137,009	99.2%	70.7%
213	Part 55	Product GZ	41	137,050	99.2%	71.0%
214	Part 147	Product HA	37	137,087	99.2%	71.3%
215	Part 161	Product HB	36	137,123	99.3%	71.7%
216	Part 127	Product HC	34	137,157	99.3%	72.0%
217	Part 74	Product HD	34	137,191	99.3%	72.3%
218	Part 250	Product HE	33	137,224	99.3%	72.7%
219	Part 260	Product HF	32	137,256	99.4%	73.0%
220	Part 263	Product HG	32	137,288	99.4%	73.3%
221	Part 20	Product HH	28	137,316	99.4%	73.7%
222	Part 229	Product HI	26	137,342	99.4%	74.0%
223	Part 58	Product HJ	25	137,367	99.4%	74.3%
224	Part 31	Product HK	25	137,392	99.5%	74.7%
225	Part 50	Product HL	24	137,416	99.5%	75.0%
226	Part 217	Product HM	24	137,440	99.5%	75.3%
227	Part 232	Product HN	23	137,463	99.5%	75.7%
228	Part 234	Product HO	23	137,486	99.5%	76.0%
229	Part 257	Product HP	22	137,508	99.5%	76.3%
230	Part 280	Product HQ	21	137,529	99.6%	76.7%
231	Part 80	Product HR	21	137,550	99.6%	77.0%
232	Part 88	Product HS	20	137,570	99.6%	77.3%
233	Part 49	Product HT	19	137,589	99.6%	77.7%
234	Part 212	Product HU	18	137,607	99.6%	78.0%
235	Part 226	Product HV	18	137,625	99.6%	78.3%
236	Part 97	Product HW	18	137,643	99.6%	78.7%
237	Part 166	Product HX	18	137,661	99.7%	79.0%
238	Part 293	Product HY	18	137,679	99.7%	79.3%
239	Part 36	Product HZ	18	137,697	99.7%	79.7%
240	Part 249	Product IA	17	137,714	99.7%	80.0%
241	Part 143	Product IB	16	137,730	99.7%	80.3%
242	Part 145	Product IC	16	137,746	99.7%	80.7%

A	B	C	D	E	F	G
Line No.	Part No.	Description	Annual Usage	Cumulative Usage	% Total Usage	% Total Items
243	Part 167	Product ID	15	137,761	99.7%	81.0%
244	Part 268	Product IE	15	137,776	99.7%	81.3%
245	Part 181	Product IF	14	137,790	99.8%	81.7%
246	Part 292	Product IG	14	137,804	99.8%	82.0%
247	Part 19	Product IH	14	137,818	99.8%	82.3%
248	Part 185	Product II	14	137,832	99.8%	82.7%
249	Part 102	Product IJ	13	137,845	99.8%	83.0%
250	Part 269	Product IK	12	137,857	99.8%	83.3%
251	Part 270	Product IL	12	137,869	99.8%	83.7%
252	Part 158	Product IM	12	137,881	99.8%	84.0%
253	Part 228	Product IN	12	137,893	99.8%	84.3%
254	Part 205	Product IO	11	137,904	99.8%	84.7%
255	Part 223	Product IP	11	137,915	99.8%	85.0%
256	Part 17	Product IQ	10	137,925	99.8%	85.3%
257	Part 156	Product IR	10	137,935	99.9%	85.7%
258	Part 171	Product IS	10	137,945	99.9%	86.0%
259	Part 137	Product IT	9	137,954	99.9%	86.3%
260	Part 203	Product IU	9	137,963	99.9%	86.7%
261	Part 106	Product IV	9	137,972	99.9%	87.0%
262	Part 209	Product IW	8	137,980	99.9%	87.3%
263	Part 244	Product IX	8	137,988	99.9%	87.7%
264	Part 99	Product IY	8	137,996	99.9%	88.0%
265	Part 60	Product IZ	8	138,004	99.9%	88.3%
266	Part 71	Product JA	8	138,012	99.9%	88.7%
267	Part 93	Product JB	8	138,020	99.9%	89.0%
268	Part 150	Product JC	7	138,027	99.9%	89.3%
269	Part 215	Product JD	7	138,034	99.9%	89.7%
270	Part 294	Product JE	7	138,041	99.9%	90.0%
271	Part 236	Product JF	6	138,047	99.9%	90.3%
272	Part 86	Product JG	6	138,053	99.9%	90.7%
273	Part 32	Product JH	6	138,059	99.9%	91.0%
274	Part 129	Product JI	5	138,064	99.9%	91.3%
275	Part 164	Product JJ	5	138,069	100.0%	91.7%
276	Part 283	Product JK	5	138,074	100.0%	92.0%
277	Part 252	Product JL	5	138,079	100.0%	92.3%
278	Part 259	Product JM	5	138,084	100.0%	92.7%
279	Part 152	Product JN	5	138,089	100.0%	93.0%
280	Part 78	Product JO	4	138,093	100.0%	93.3%
281	Part 251	Product JP	4	138,097	100.0%	93.7%
282	Part 73	Product JQ	4	138,101	100.0%	94.0%
283	Part 194	Product JR	4	138,105	100.0%	94.3%
284	Part 107	Product JS	3	138,108	100.0%	94.7%
285	Part 196	Product JT	3	138,111	100.0%	95.0%

A	B	C	D	E	F	G
Line No.	Part No.	Description	Annual Usage	Cumulative Usage	% Total Usage	% Total Items
286	Part 177	Product JU	3	138,114	100.0%	95.3%
287	Part 221	Product JV	3	138,117	100.0%	95.7%
288	Part 105	Product JW	3	138,120	100.0%	96.0%
289	Part 72	Product JX	2	138,122	100.0%	96.3%
290	Part 286	Product JY	2	138,124	100.0%	96.7%
291	Part 291	Product JZ	2	138,126	100.0%	97.0%
292	Part 54	Product KA	2	138,128	100.0%	97.3%
293	Part 163	Product KB	2	138,130	100.0%	97.7%
294	Part 271	Product KC	1	138,131	100.0%	98.0%
295	Part 4	Product KD	1	138,132	100.0%	98.3%
296	Part 153	Product KE	1	138,133	100.0%	98.7%
297	Part 91	Product KF	1	138,134	100.0%	99.0%
298	Part 151	Product KG	—	138,134	100.0%	99.3%
299	Part 61	Product KH	—	138,134	100.0%	99.7%
300	Part 165	Product KI	—	138,134	100.0%	100.0%

Appendix B—Formulae

A	B	C	D	E	F	G
Line No.	Part No.	Description	Annual Usage	Cumulative Usage	% Total Usage	% Total Items
1	79	Product A	8673	=0+D1	=E1/$E$300	=A1/$A$300
2	133	Product B	6970	=E1+D2	=E2/$E$300	=A2/$A$300
3	290	Product C	5788	=E2+D3	=E3/$E$300	=A3/$A$300
4	65	Product D	5690	=E3+D4	=E4/$E$300	=A4/$A$300
5	111	Product E	4899	=E4+D5	=E5/$E$300	=A5/$A$300
6	195	Product F	3669	=E5+D6	=E6/$E$300	=A6/$A$300
7	139	Product G	3364	=E6+D7	=E7/$E$300	=A7/$A$300
8	131	Product H	3250	=E7+D8	=E8/$E$300	=A8/$A$300
9	132	Product I	3022	=E8+D9	=E9/$E$300	=A9/$A$300
10	175	Product J	2864	=E9+D10	=E10/$E$300	=A10/$A$300
11	255	Product K	2844	=E10+D11	=E11/$E$300	=A11/$A$300
12	101	Product L	2670	=E11+D12	=E12/$E$300	=A12/$A$300
13	265	Product M	2665	=E12+D13	=E13/$E$300	=A13/$A$300
14	48	Product N	2453	=E13+D14	=E14/$E$300	=A14/$A$300
15	2	Product O	2222	=E14+D15	=E15/$E$300	=A15/$A$300
16	14	Product P	1976	=E15+D16	=E16/$E$300	=A16/$A$300
17	70	Product Q	1896	=E16+D17	=E17/$E$300	=A17/$A$300
18	117	Product R	1888	=E17+D18	=E18/$E$300	=A18/$A$300
19	134	Product S	1872	=E18+D19	=E19/$E$300	=A19/$A$300
20	170	Product T	1687	=E19+D20	=E20/$E$300	=A20/$A$300
21	182	Product U	1666	=E20+D21	=E21/$E$300	=A21/$A$300
22	28	Product V	1646	=E21+D22	=E22/$E$300	=A22/$A$300
23	138	Product W	1566	=E22+D23	=E23/$E$300	=A23/$A$300
24	23	Product X	1530	=E23+D24	=E24/$E$300	=A24/$A$300
25	300	Product Y	1057	=E24+D25	=E25/$E$300	=A25/$A$300
26	9	Product Z	1050	=E25+D26	=E26/$E$300	=A26/$A$300
27	241	Product AA	1022	=E26+D27	=E27/$E$300	=A27/$A$300
28	219	Product AB	1022	=E27+D28	=E28/$E$300	=A28/$A$300
29	51	Product AC	1001	=E28+D29	=E29/$E$300	=A29/$A$300
30	278	Product AD	997	=E29+D30	=E30/$E$300	=A30/$A$300
31	222	Product AE	991	=E30+D31	=E31/$E$300	=A31/$A$300
32	154	Product AF	986	=E31+D32	=E32/$E$300	=A32/$A$300
33	184	Product AG	972	=E32+D33	=E33/$E$300	=A33/$A$300
34	190	Product AH	968	=E33+D34	=E34/$E$300	=A34/$A$300
35	87	Product AI	964	=E34+D35	=E35/$E$300	=A35/$A$300
36	95	Product AJ	943	=E35+D36	=E36/$E$300	=A36/$A$300
37	6	Product AK	894	=E36+D37	=E37/$E$300	=A37/$A$300

A	B	C	D	E	F	G
Line No.	Part No.	Description	Annual Usage	Cumulative Usage	% Total Usage	% Total Items
38	142	Product AL	889	=E37+D38	=E38/$E$300	=A38/$A$300
39	210	Product AM	889	=E38+D39	=E39/$E$300	=A39/$A$300
40	13	Product AN	888	=E39+D40	=E40/$E$300	=A40/$A$300
41	121	Product AO	888	=E40+D41	=E41/$E$300	=A41/$A$300
42	3	Product AP	875	=E41+D42	=E42/$E$300	=A42/$A$300
43	235	Product AQ	867	=E42+D43	=E43/$E$300	=A43/$A$300
44	297	Product AR	861	=E43+D44	=E44/$E$300	=A44/$A$300
45	266	Product AS	856	=E44+D45	=E45/$E$300	=A45/$A$300
46	239	Product AT	846	=E45+D46	=E46/$E$300	=A46/$A$300
47	233	Product AU	843	=E46+D47	=E47/$E$300	=A47/$A$300
48	77	Product AV	800	=E47+D48	=E48/$E$300	=A48/$A$300
49	188	Product AW	795	=E48+D49	=E49/$E$300	=A49/$A$300
50	240	Product AX	788	=E49+D50	=E50/$E$300	=A50/$A$300
51	103	Product AY	779	=E50+D51	=E51/$E$300	=A51/$A$300
52	160	Product AZ	766	=E51+D52	=E52/$E$300	=A52/$A$300
53	211	Product BA	764	=E52+D53	=E53/$E$300	=A53/$A$300
54	243	Product BB	761	=E53+D54	=E54/$E$300	=A54/$A$300
55	201	Product BC	754	=E54+D55	=E55/$E$300	=A55/$A$300
56	202	Product BD	712	=E55+D56	=E56/$E$300	=A56/$A$300
57	75	Product BE	698	=E56+D57	=E57/$E$300	=A57/$A$300
58	206	Product BF	697	=E57+D58	=E58/$E$300	=A58/$A$300
59	200	Product BG	697	=E58+D59	=E59/$E$300	=A59/$A$300
60	124	Product BH	689	=E59+D60	=E60/$E$300	=A60/$A$300
61	208	Product BI	662	=E60+D61	=E61/$E$300	=A61/$A$300
62	253	Product BJ	644	=E61+D62	=E62/$E$300	=A62/$A$300
63	264	Product BK	640	=E62+D63	=E63/$E$300	=A63/$A$300
64	230	Product BL	614	=E63+D64	=E64/$E$300	=A64/$A$300
65	53	Product BM	590	=E64+D65	=E65/$E$300	=A65/$A$300
66	33	Product BN	587	=E65+D66	=E66/$E$300	=A66/$A$300
67	104	Product BO	566	=E66+D67	=E67/$E$300	=A67/$A$300
68	207	Product BK	564	=E67+D68	=E68/$E$300	=A68/$A$300
69	63	Product BL	544	=E68+D69	=E69/$E$300	=A69/$A$300
70	275	Product BM	533	=E69+D70	=E70/$E$300	=A70/$A$300
71	155	Product BN	530	=E70+D71	=E71/$E$300	=A71/$A$300
72	7	Product BO	512	=E71+D72	=E72/$E$300	=A72/$A$300
73	90	Product BP	499	=E72+D73	=E73/$E$300	=A73/$A$300
74	59	Product BQ	468	=E73+D74	=E74/$E$300	=A74/$A$300
75	122	Product BR	467	=E74+D75	=E75/$E$300	=A75/$A$300
76	35	Product BS	456	=E75+D76	=E76/$E$300	=A76/$A$300
77	67	Product BT	450	=E76+D77	=E77/$E$300	=A77/$A$300
78	92	Product BU	444	=E77+D78	=E78/$E$300	=A78/$A$300
79	83	Product BV	443	=E78+D79	=E79/$E$300	=A79/$A$300
80	287	Product BW	433	=E79+D80	=E80/$E$300	=A80/$A$300

A	B	C	D	E	F	G
Line No.	Part No.	Description	Annual Usage	Cumulative Usage	% Total Usage	% Total Items
81	162	Product BX	420	=E80+D81	=E81/$E$300	=A81/$A$300
82	189	Product BY	420	=E81+D82	=E82/$E$300	=A82/$A$300
83	245	Product BZ	398	=E82+D83	=E83/$E$300	=A83/$A$300
84	274	Product CA	382	=E83+D84	=E84/$E$300	=A84/$A$300
85	242	Product CB	355	=E84+D85	=E85/$E$300	=A85/$A$300
86	258	Product CC	354	=E85+D86	=E86/$E$300	=A86/$A$300
87	136	Product CD	353	=E86+D87	=E87/$E$300	=A87/$A$300
88	238	Product CE	334	=E87+D88	=E88/$E$300	=A88/$A$300
89	115	Product CF	333	=E88+D89	=E89/$E$300	=A89/$A$300
90	94	Product CG	333	=E89+D90	=E90/$E$300	=A90/$A$300
91	64	Product CH	332	=E90+D91	=E91/$E$300	=A91/$A$300
92	298	Product CI	326	=E91+D92	=E92/$E$300	=A92/$A$300
93	295	Product CJ	325	=E92+D93	=E93/$E$300	=A93/$A$300
94	30	Product CK	325	=E93+D94	=E94/$E$300	=A94/$A$300
95	11	Product CL	323	=E94+D95	=E95/$E$300	=A95/$A$300
96	192	Product CM	321	=E95+D96	=E96/$E$300	=A96/$A$300
97	96	Product CN	321	=E96+D97	=E97/$E$300	=A97/$A$300
98	40	Product CO	298	=E97+D98	=E98/$E$300	=A98/$A$300
99	47	Product CP	285	=E98+D99	=E99/$E$300	=A99/$A$300
100	125	Product CQ	269	=E99+D100	=E100/$E$300	=A100/$A$300
101	198	Product CR	260	=E100+D101	=E101/$E$300	=A101/$A$300
102	135	Product CS	258	=E101+D102	=E102/$E$300	=A102/$A$300
103	130	Product CT	256	=E102+D103	=E103/$E$300	=A103/$A$300
104	85	Product CU	255	=E103+D104	=E104/$E$300	=A104/$A$300
105	216	Product CV	223	=E104+D105	=E105/$E$300	=A105/$A$300
106	193	Product CW	222	=E105+D106	=E106/$E$300	=A106/$A$300
107	285	Product CX	220	=E106+D107	=E107/$E$300	=A107/$A$300
108	288	Product CY	200	=E107+D108	=E108/$E$300	=A108/$A$300
109	26	Product CZ	199	=E108+D109	=E109/$E$300	=A109/$A$300
110	176	Product DA	199	=E109+D110	=E110/$E$300	=A110/$A$300
111	186	Product DB	194	=E110+D111	=E111/$E$300	=A111/$A$300
112	173	Product DC	189	=E111+D112	=E112/$E$300	=A112/$A$300
113	81	Product DD	188	=E112+D113	=E113/$E$300	=A113/$A$300
114	172	Product DE	188	=E113+D114	=E114/$E$300	=A114/$A$300
115	144	Product DF	186	=E114+D115	=E115/$E$300	=A115/$A$300
116	12	Product DG	186	=E115+D116	=E116/$E$300	=A116/$A$300
117	141	Product DH	186	=E116+D117	=E117/$E$300	=A117/$A$300
118	15	Product DI	185	=E117+D118	=E118/$E$300	=A118/$A$300
119	227	Product DJ	185	=E118+D119	=E119/$E$300	=A119/$A$300
120	191	Product DK	184	=E119+D120	=E120/$E$300	=A120/$A$300
121	272	Product DL	178	=E120+D121	=E121/$E$300	=A121/$A$300
122	279	Product DM	156	=E121+D122	=E122/$E$300	=A122/$A$300
123	247	Product DN	150	=E122+D123	=E123/$E$300	=A123/$A$300

A	B	C	D	E	F	G
Line No.	Part No.	Description	Annual Usage	Cumulative Usage	% Total Usage	% Total Items
124	89	Product DO	144	=E123+D124	=E124/$E$300	=A124/$A$300
125	174	Product DP	143	=E124+D125	=E125/$E$300	=A125/$A$300
126	118	Product DQ	133	=E125+D126	=E126/$E$300	=A126/$A$300
127	27	Product DR	116	=E126+D127	=E127/$E$300	=A127/$A$300
128	34	Product DS	116	=E127+D128	=E128/$E$300	=A128/$A$300
129	169	Product DT	116	=E128+D129	=E129/$E$300	=A129/$A$300
130	178	Product DU	113	=E129+D130	=E130/$E$300	=A130/$A$300
131	84	Product DV	105	=E130+D131	=E131/$E$300	=A131/$A$300
132	204	Product DW	103	=E131+D132	=E132/$E$300	=A132/$A$300
133	273	Product DX	102	=E132+D133	=E133/$E$300	=A133/$A$300
134	24	Product DY	101	=E133+D134	=E134/$E$300	=A134/$A$300
135	114	Product DZ	100	=E134+D135	=E135/$E$300	=A135/$A$300
136	57	Product EA	100	=E135+D136	=E136/$E$300	=A136/$A$300
137	168	Product EB	99	=E136+D137	=E137/$E$300	=A137/$A$300
138	187	Product EC	99	=E137+D138	=E138/$E$300	=A138/$A$300
139	214	Product ED	99	=E138+D139	=E139/$E$300	=A139/$A$300
140	220	Product EE	98	=E139+D140	=E140/$E$300	=A140/$A$300
141	29	Product EF	98	=E140+D141	=E141/$E$300	=A141/$A$300
142	98	Product EG	98	=E141+D142	=E142/$E$300	=A142/$A$300
143	261	Product EH	97	=E142+D143	=E143/$E$300	=A143/$A$300
144	180	Product EI	97	=E143+D144	=E144/$E$300	=A144/$A$300
145	289	Product EJ	96	=E144+D145	=E145/$E$300	=A145/$A$300
146	146	Product EK	96	=E145+D146	=E146/$E$300	=A146/$A$300
147	299	Product EL	94	=E146+D147	=E147/$E$300	=A147/$A$300
148	68	Product EM	92	=E147+D148	=E148/$E$300	=A148/$A$300
149	41	Product EN	91	=E148+D149	=E149/$E$300	=A149/$A$300
150	38	Product EO	90	=E149+D150	=E150/$E$300	=A150/$A$300
151	140	Product EP	89	=E150+D151	=E151/$E$300	=A151/$A$300
152	16	Product EQ	89	=E151+D152	=E152/$E$300	=A152/$A$300
153	128	Product ER	88	=E152+D153	=E153/$E$300	=A153/$A$300
154	25	Product ES	88	=E153+D154	=E154/$E$300	=A154/$A$300
155	45	Product ET	87	=E154+D155	=E155/$E$300	=A155/$A$300
156	1	Product EU	86	=E155+D156	=E156/$E$300	=A156/$A$300
157	246	Product EV	85	=E156+D157	=E157/$E$300	=A157/$A$300
158	108	Product EW	85	=E157+D158	=E158/$E$300	=A158/$A$300
159	231	Product EX	85	=E158+D159	=E159/$E$300	=A159/$A$300
160	21	Product EY	84	=E159+D160	=E160/$E$300	=A160/$A$300
161	183	Product EZ	84	=E160+D161	=E161/$E$300	=A161/$A$300
162	248	Product FA	84	=E161+D162	=E162/$E$300	=A162/$A$300
163	199	Product FB	84	=E162+D163	=E163/$E$300	=A163/$A$300
164	120	Product FC	80	=E163+D164	=E164/$E$300	=A164/$A$300
165	224	Product FD	80	=E164+D165	=E165/$E$300	=A165/$A$300
166	256	Product FE	76	=E165+D166	=E166/$E$300	=A166/$A$300

A	B	C	D	E	F	G
Line No.	Part No.	Description	Annual Usage	Cumulative Usage	% Total Usage	% Total Items
167	281	Product FF	76	=E166+D167	=E167/$E$300	=A167/$A$300
168	157	Product FG	76	=E167+D168	=E168/$E$300	=A168/$A$300
169	5	Product FH	75	=E168+D169	=E169/$E$300	=A169/$A$300
170	56	Product FI	75	=E169+D170	=E170/$E$300	=A170/$A$300
171	44	Product FJ	74	=E170+D171	=E171/$E$300	=A171/$A$300
172	76	Product FK	74	=E171+D172	=E172/$E$300	=A172/$A$300
173	267	Product FL	74	=E172+D173	=E173/$E$300	=A173/$A$300
174	262	Product FM	72	=E173+D174	=E174/$E$300	=A174/$A$300
175	225	Product FN	68	=E174+D175	=E175/$E$300	=A175/$A$300
176	276	Product FO	67	=E175+D176	=E176/$E$300	=A176/$A$300
177	43	Product FP	66	=E176+D177	=E177/$E$300	=A177/$A$300
178	10	Product FQ	66	=E177+D178	=E178/$E$300	=A178/$A$300
179	126	Product FR	65	=E178+D179	=E179/$E$300	=A179/$A$300
180	296	Product FS	64	=E179+D180	=E180/$E$300	=A180/$A$300
181	277	Product FT	63	=E180+D181	=E181/$E$300	=A181/$A$300
182	42	Product FU	63	=E181+D182	=E182/$E$300	=A182/$A$300
183	197	Product FV	62	=E182+D183	=E183/$E$300	=A183/$A$300
184	284	Product FW	61	=E183+D184	=E184/$E$300	=A184/$A$300
185	22	Product FX	61	=E184+D185	=E185/$E$300	=A185/$A$300
186	39	Product FY	61	=E185+D186	=E186/$E$300	=A186/$A$300
187	82	Product FZ	58	=E186+D187	=E187/$E$300	=A187/$A$300
188	237	Product GA	56	=E187+D188	=E188/$E$300	=A188/$A$300
189	69	Product GB	56	=E188+D189	=E189/$E$300	=A189/$A$300
190	62	Product GC	56	=E189+D190	=E190/$E$300	=A190/$A$300
191	213	Product GD	56	=E190+D191	=E191/$E$300	=A191/$A$300
192	109	Product GE	55	=E191+D192	=E192/$E$300	=A192/$A$300
193	149	Product GF	55	=E192+D193	=E193/$E$300	=A193/$A$300
194	159	Product GG	55	=E193+D194	=E194/$E$300	=A194/$A$300
195	113	Product GH	54	=E194+D195	=E195/$E$300	=A195/$A$300
196	110	Product GI	54	=E195+D196	=E196/$E$300	=A196/$A$300
197	218	Product GJ	54	=E196+D197	=E197/$E$300	=A197/$A$300
198	46	Product GK	53	=E197+D198	=E198/$E$300	=A198/$A$300
199	112	Product GL	52	=E198+D199	=E199/$E$300	=A199/$A$300
200	179	Product GM	52	=E199+D200	=E200/$E$300	=A200/$A$300
201	100	Product GN	52	=E200+D201	=E201/$E$300	=A201/$A$300
202	37	Product GO	52	=E201+D202	=E202/$E$300	=A202/$A$300
203	282	Product GP	50	=E202+D203	=E203/$E$300	=A203/$A$300
204	116	Product GQ	48	=E203+D204	=E204/$E$300	=A204/$A$300
205	8	Product GR	46	=E204+D205	=E205/$E$300	=A205/$A$300
206	254	Product GS	45	=E205+D206	=E206/$E$300	=A206/$A$300
207	148	Product GT	45	=E206+D207	=E207/$E$300	=A207/$A$300
208	66	Product GU	44	=E207+D208	=E208/$E$300	=A208/$A$300
209	18	Product GV	43	=E208+D209	=E209/$E$300	=A209/$A$300

A	B	C	D	E	F	G
Line No.	Part No.	Description	Annual Usage	Cumulative Usage	% Total Usage	% Total Items
210	119	Product GW	43	=E209+D210	=E210/$E$300	=A210/$A$300
211	52	Product GX	42	=E210+D211	=E211/$E$300	=A211/$A$300
212	123	Product GY	41	=E211+D212	=E212/$E$300	=A212/$A$300
213	55	Product GZ	41	=E212+D213	=E213/$E$300	=A213/$A$300
214	147	Product HA	37	=E213+D214	=E214/$E$300	=A214/$A$300
215	161	Product HB	36	=E214+D215	=E215/$E$300	=A215/$A$300
216	127	Product HC	34	=E215+D216	=E216/$E$300	=A216/$A$300
217	74	Product HD	34	=E216+D217	=E217/$E$300	=A217/$A$300
218	250	Product HE	33	=E217+D218	=E218/$E$300	=A218/$A$300
219	260	Product HF	32	=E218+D219	=E219/$E$300	=A219/$A$300
220	263	Product HG	32	=E219+D220	=E220/$E$300	=A220/$A$300
221	20	Product HH	28	=E220+D221	=E221/$E$300	=A221/$A$300
222	229	Product HI	26	=E221+D222	=E222/$E$300	=A222/$A$300
223	58	Product HJ	25	=E222+D223	=E223/$E$300	=A223/$A$300
224	31	Product HK	25	=E223+D224	=E224/$E$300	=A224/$A$300
225	50	Product HL	24	=E224+D225	=E225/$E$300	=A225/$A$300
226	217	Product HM	24	=E225+D226	=E226/$E$300	=A226/$A$300
227	232	Product HN	23	=E226+D227	=E227/$E$300	=A227/$A$300
228	234	Product HO	23	=E227+D228	=E228/$E$300	=A228/$A$300
229	257	Product HP	22	=E228+D229	=E229/$E$300	=A229/$A$300
230	280	Product HQ	21	=E229+D230	=E230/$E$300	=A230/$A$300
231	80	Product HR	21	=E230+D231	=E231/$E$300	=A231/$A$300
232	88	Product HS	20	=E231+D232	=E232/$E$300	=A232/$A$300
233	49	Product HT	19	=E232+D233	=E233/$E$300	=A233/$A$300
234	212	Product HU	18	=E233+D234	=E234/$E$300	=A234/$A$300
235	226	Product HV	18	=E234+D235	=E235/$E$300	=A235/$A$300
236	97	Product HW	18	=E235+D236	=E236/$E$300	=A236/$A$300
237	166	Product HX	18	=E236+D237	=E237/$E$300	=A237/$A$300
238	293	Product HY	18	=E237+D238	=E238/$E$300	=A238/$A$300
239	36	Product HZ	18	=E238+D239	=E239/$E$300	=A239/$A$300
240	249	Product IA	17	=E239+D240	=E240/$E$300	=A240/$A$300
241	143	Product IB	16	=E240+D241	=E241/$E$300	=A241/$A$300
242	145	Product IC	16	=E241+D242	=E242/$E$300	=A242/$A$300
243	167	Product ID	15	=E242+D243	=E243/$E$300	=A243/$A$300
244	268	Product IE	15	=E243+D244	=E244/$E$300	=A244/$A$300
245	181	Product IF	14	=E244+D245	=E245/$E$300	=A245/$A$300
246	292	Product IG	14	=E245+D246	=E246/$E$300	=A246/$A$300
247	19	Product IH	14	=E246+D247	=E247/$E$300	=A247/$A$300
248	185	Product II	14	=E247+D248	=E248/$E$300	=A248/$A$300
249	102	Product IJ	13	=E248+D249	=E249/$E$300	=A249/$A$300
250	269	Product IK	12	=E249+D250	=E250/$E$300	=A250/$A$300
251	270	Product IL	12	=E250+D251	=E251/$E$300	=A251/$A$300
252	158	Product IM	12	=E251+D252	=E252/$E$300	=A252/$A$300

A	B	C	D	E	F	G
Line No.	Part No.	Description	Annual Usage	Cumulative Usage	% Total Usage	% Total Items
253	228	Product IN	12	=E252+D253	=E253/$E$300	=A253/$A$300
254	205	Product IO	11	=E253+D254	=E254/$E$300	=A254/$A$300
255	223	Product IP	11	=E254+D255	=E255/$E$300	=A255/$A$300
256	17	Product IQ	10	=E255+D256	=E256/$E$300	=A256/$A$300
257	156	Product IR	10	=E256+D257	=E257/$E$300	=A257/$A$300
258	171	Product IS	10	=E257+D258	=E258/$E$300	=A258/$A$300
259	137	Product IT	9	=E258+D259	=E259/$E$300	=A259/$A$300
260	203	Product IU	9	=E259+D260	=E260/$E$300	=A260/$A$300
261	106	Product IV	9	=E260+D261	=E261/$E$300	=A261/$A$300
262	209	Product IW	8	=E261+D262	=E262/$E$300	=A262/$A$300
263	244	Product IX	8	=E262+D263	=E263/$E$300	=A263/$A$300
264	99	Product IY	8	=E263+D264	=E264/$E$300	=A264/$A$300
265	60	Product IZ	8	=E264+D265	=E265/$E$300	=A265/$A$300
266	71	Product JA	8	=E265+D266	=E266/$E$300	=A266/$A$300
267	93	Product JB	8	=E266+D267	=E267/$E$300	=A267/$A$300
268	150	Product JC	7	=E267+D268	=E268/$E$300	=A268/$A$300
269	215	Product JD	7	=E268+D269	=E269/$E$300	=A269/$A$300
270	294	Product JE	7	=E269+D270	=E270/$E$300	=A270/$A$300
271	236	Product JF	6	=E270+D271	=E271/$E$300	=A271/$A$300
272	86	Product JG	6	=E271+D272	=E272/$E$300	=A272/$A$300
273	32	Product JH	6	=E272+D273	=E273/$E$300	=A273/$A$300
274	129	Product JI	5	=E273+D274	=E274/$E$300	=A274/$A$300
275	164	Product JJ	5	=E274+D275	=E275/$E$300	=A275/$A$300
276	283	Product JK	5	=E275+D276	=E276/$E$300	=A276/$A$300
277	252	Product JL	5	=E276+D277	=E277/$E$300	=A277/$A$300
278	259	Product JM	5	=E277+D278	=E278/$E$300	=A278/$A$300
279	152	Product JN	5	=E278+D279	=E279/$E$300	=A279/$A$300
280	78	Product JO	4	=E279+D280	=E280/$E$300	=A280/$A$300
281	251	Product JP	4	=E280+D281	=E281/$E$300	=A281/$A$300
282	73	Product JQ	4	=E281+D282	=E282/$E$300	=A282/$A$300
283	194	Product JR	4	=E282+D283	=E283/$E$300	=A283/$A$300
284	107	Product JS	3	=E283+D284	=E284/$E$300	=A284/$A$300
285	196	Product JT	3	=E284+D285	=E285/$E$300	=A285/$A$300
286	177	Product JU	3	=E285+D286	=E286/$E$300	=A286/$A$300
287	221	Product JV	3	=E286+D287	=E287/$E$300	=A287/$A$300
288	105	Product JW	3	=E287+D288	=E288/$E$300	=A288/$A$300
289	72	Product JX	2	=E288+D289	=E289/$E$300	=A289/$A$300
290	286	Product JY	2	=E289+D290	=E290/$E$300	=A290/$A$300
291	291	Product JZ	2	=E290+D291	=E291/$E$300	=A291/$A$300
292	54	Product KA	2	=E291+D292	=E292/$E$300	=A292/$A$300
293	163	Product KB	2	=E292+D293	=E293/$E$300	=A293/$A$300
294	271	Product KC	1	=E293+D294	=E294/$E$300	=A294/$A$300
295	4	Product KD	1	=E294+D295	=E295/$E$300	=A295/$A$300

A	B	C	D	E	F	G
Line No.	Part No.	Description	Annual Usage	Cumulative Usage	% Total Usage	% Total Items
296	153	Product KE	1	=E295+D296	=E296/$E$300	=A296/$A$300
297	91	Product KF	1	=E296+D297	=E297/$E$300	=A297/$A$300
298	151	Product KG	0	=E297+D298	=E298/$E$300	=A298/$A$300
299	61	Product KH	0	=E298+D299	=E299/$E$300	=A299/$A$300
300	165	Product KI	0	=E299+D300	=E300/$E$300	=A300/$A$300

BIBLIOGRAPHY

Anderson, Barbara V. *The Art and Science of Computer Assisted Ordering: Methods for Management*. Westport, CT: Quorum Books, 1996.

Arnold, J. R. Tony and Stephen N. Chapman. *Introduction to Materials Management*, fourth edition. Upper Saddle River, NJ: Prentice Hall, 2001.

Bernard, Paul. *Integrated Inventory Management*. New York, NY: John Wiley & Sons, Inc., 1999.

Brooks, Roger B. and Larry W. Wilson. *Inventory Record Accuracy: Unleashing the Power of Cycle Counting*. New York, NY: John Wiley & Sons, Inc., 1995.

Collins, David Jarrett and Nancy Nasuti Whipple. *Using Bar Coding: Why It's Taking Over*, second edition. Duxbury, MA: Data Capture Institute, 1994.

Cullinane, Thomas P., James A. Tompkins, and Jerry D. Smith. *How to Plan and Manage Warehouse Operations*, second edition. Watertown, MA: American Management Association, 1994.

Delaney, Patrick R., James R. Adler, Barry J. Epstein, and Michael F. Foran. *GAAP 98: Interpretation and Application of Generally Accepted Accounting Pricinples 1998*. New York, NY: John Wiley & Sons, Inc., 1998.

Eisen, Peter J. *Accounting the Easy Way*, third edition. New York, NY: Barron's Educational Series, Inc., 1995.

Feld, William M. *Lean Manufacturing: Tools, Techniques, and How to Use Them*. Boca Raton, FL: The St. Lucie Press/APICS Series on Resource Management, 2001.

Grieco, Jr., Peter L., Michael W. Gozzo, and C. J. (Chip) Long. *Behind Bars: Bar Coding Principles and Applications.* Palm Beach Gardens, FL: PT Publications, Inc., 1989.

Harmon, Craig K. and Russ Adams. *Reading Between the Lines: An Introduction to Bar Code Technology.* Peterborough, NH: Helmers Publishing, Inc., 1989.

Landvater, Darryl. *World Class Production & Inventory Management.* New York, NY: John Wiley & Sons, Inc., 1993.

Martinich, Joseph S. *Production and Operations Management: An Applied Modern Approach.* New York, NY: John Wiley & Sons, Inc., 1997.

Melnyk, Steven and R. T. "Chris" Christensen. "Understanding the Nature of Setups, Part Two: Setups and Lot Sizing." *APICS Online Edition.* www.apics.org/magazine/apr97/basics.htm. (September 9, 2000).

Meredith, Jack R. and Scott M. Shafer. *Operations Management for MBAs.* New York, NY: John Wiley & Sons, Inc., 1999.

Palmer, Roger C. *The Bar Code Book, 3rd Ed: Reading, Printing, Specification, and Application of Bar Code and Other Machine Readable Symbols.* Peterborough, NH: Helmers Publishing, Inc., 1995.

Robeson, James F. and William C. Copacino. *The Logistics Handbook.* New York, NY: The Free Press: A Division of Macmillan, Inc., 1994.

Thomsett, Michael C. *The Little Black Book of Business Math.* New York, NY: AMACOM, 1988.

Thomsett, Michael C. *Winning Numbers: How to Use Business Facts and Figures to Make Your Point and Get Ahead.* New York, NY: AMACOM, 1990.

Tompkins, James A. and Dale Harmelink. *The Distribution Management Handbook.* New York, NY: McGraw-Hill, Inc., 1994.

Tompkins, James A. and Jerry D. Smith. *The Warehouse Management Book.* New York, NY: McGraw-Hill Inc., 1988.

Waters, C. D. J. *Inventory Control and Management.* Chichester, West Sussex, England: John Wiley & Sons Ltd., 1992.

INDEX

A

A-B-C categorization, 66–73
  cycle counting and, 188–192
accessibility, 45
accounting, 19–20
accounts receivable, obsolete stock
    and, 33–34
accuracy, inventory record,
    166–170
acid test, 29–30
acquisition/ordering costs, 2–3
actual cost method, 21
adjustments, tolerances and, 170,
    171
allocation, 196n3
American Production and
    Inventory Control Society
    (APICS), 137–138
annual inventories, 147–148,
    176–177
anticipation stock, 6
assets
  current ratio analysis of, 28–29
  definition of, 22
average cost method valuation, 21,
    24–26

B

backflushing, 132, 156, 163–164,
    165, 195n1

background checks, 212–216
balance sheets, 22
bar codes, 89–113
  applications of, 105–111
  benefits of, 89–90
  character set in, 96
  Code 39, 98–100
  Code 128, 100–101
  components of, 90
  data characters on, 94
  definition of, 90
  discrete vs. continuous, 96
  elements of, 93–95
  number of element widths in,
    96–97
  printing, 103–105
  product moves and, 84
  quiet zone on, 94
  scan boards/menu cards,
    107–108
  scanning, 101–105
  start/stop characters on, 94
  structural rules for, 95–101
  structure of, 94–95
  symbology types, 96–97
  UPC, 98
  "X" dimension on, 95
batch systems, 156, 159
bill of materials (BOM),
    132–133

buffer/safety inventory, 6–9
business impact, 205

C
capital structure, obsolete stock
    and, 33–34
carrying costs (K Factor)
    balancing with replenishment
        costs, 115–120
    demonstrating, 39
    determining, 36
    obsolete stock and, 36–37
    purchasing and, 40
    replenishment costs and,
        115–120
Cartesian coordinates, 83
case studies
    Barash Foods, 63–64
    Big Hammer, Inc., 149–164
    Carr Enterprises, 10–14
    Charmax Manufacturing, 64–65
    combination locator systems,
        63–65
    inventory failures, 149–164
    paper life tracking, 10–14
charge coupled devices (CCDs),
    104
charts, 172–175
    flow, 173, 175
    logic, 175
    run, 173, 174
    variance reports, 175
Code 39, 98–100
Code 128, 100–101
collusion theft, 210–212
combination locator systems, 62–65
consultants, 154
consumables, 5
contingency planning, 201. *See also*
    emergency/disaster
    preparedness
control group cycle counting
    method, 179–181

control systems, 43–88
    A-B-C categorization, 66–73
    addresses in, 76–86
    combination, 62–65
    fixed, 49–57
    item placement theory and,
        65–76
    locator, 44–65
    memory, 47–49
    random, 60–62
    selecting, 44–47
    SKU identifiers in, 76–86
    types of, 44
    zoning, 57–59
costs
    acquisition/ordering, 2–3
    balancing carrying and
        replenishment, 118–120
    of goods sold, 22
    holding, 2
    inventory, 2–3
    ordering, 4
    replenishment, 115–120
count frequency, determining,
    189–191
credits, issuing, 163
crime prevention through environ-
    mental design (CPTED),
    207–210, 213–214
criticality, 168–169
current assets, 22
current ratio, 28–29
cycle counting, 176–193
    A-B-C analysis method, 188–
        192
    annual inventories vs, 176–177
    bar codes in, 111
    control group method, 179–181
    diminishing population method,
        184–185
    location audit cycle method,
        181–184
    methodologies for, 177–179

objectives of, 177
product categories method,
185–192
random selection method, 184
when to count, 192–193
who should count in, 193

D
damage, costs of, 2
demand
dependent, 121–122, 130–137
fluctuations in, 3
independent, 121, 122–126
dependent demand, 121–122
materials requirements planning
in, 130–137
Descartes, René, 83
design, theft prevention through,
207–210
diminishing population cycle
counting method, 184–185
direct thermal printing, 105
distribution, demand in, 155
documentation, 157
dot matrix impact printing, 105
Drucker, Peter, 149, 165

E
economic order quantity (EOQ)
formula, 127–130
80–20 Rule, 66
Einstein, Albert, 149
electronic data interchange (EDI),
14–15
emergency/disaster preparedness,
197–217
incited emergencies, 201
legal duties in, 199
natural emergencies, 200
plan elements, 199–201
preparation in, 200–201
technological emergencies, 200
theft, 205–216

employees, background checks on,
212–216
enterprise resource planning
(ERP), 135, 138–139
equity, 22
European Article Numbering
System (EAN), 98
Excel
A-B-C classification with,
69
EOQ formulas in, 129–130

F
family grouping, 73–75
Federal Emergency Management
Agency (FEMA), 200
fill rate, 166
financial statements, ratio
analyses, 27–31
finished goods inventory, 20
finished product, 4
first-in, first-out (FIFO) valuation,
20–21, 24–26
fixed location systems, 49–57
honeycombing in, 50–53
flow charts, 173, 175
free on board (F.O.B.), 8

G
geographical threats, 202
goods
value of not sold, 23
value of sold, 22, 23–24
gross profit, calculating,
23–24

H
Harris, F. W., 127
historical threats, 202
holding costs, 2
honeycombing, 50–53
human error, 202
human impact, 205

I

identification markings, 76, 77
 tying SKUs to location addresses
   with, 78–79
incited emergencies, 201
income statements, 23–26
independent demand, 121, 122
 economic order quantity (ECQ)
   formula, 127–130
 inventory, 122–126
 order-point formulae, 122–126
information flow, 194
ink jet printing, 105
inventory
 A-B-C categorization of, 66–73
 accounting for, 19–20
 annual, 147–148
 buffer/safety, 6
 costs of, 2–3
 failures in, 147–196
 financial aspects of, 19–42
 importance of, 1–9
 objectives of, 142–143
 problem solving, 172–175
 purpose of, 3–4
 raw materials, 19–20
 types, 121–143
inventory management, 121–122.
   See also planning
inventory protection, 197–217
inventory record accuracy (IRA),
   166–170
 cycle counting and, 176–193
 test counts, 166
 tolerances in, 166–170
inventory stratification, 65–73
 family grouping with, 75
inventory turnover ratio, 30–31
item placement theory, 65–76
 family grouping, 73–75
 inventory stratification, 65–73
 special considerations in,
   75–76

J

just-in-time (JIT) systems, 135,
   137–142
 definition of, 137–138
 implementing, 140–142

K

K Factor. *See* carrying costs
   (K Factor)

L

labor costs, 2
 address systems and, 77
 dead stock and, 35
 storage considerations and, 45
lasers, bar code reading with, 104
laser (xerographic) printing, 105
last-in, first-out (LIFO) valuation,
   21, 24–26
lead times, 141
legal considerations, 199, 212–216
liabilities
 current ratio analysis of, 28–29
 definition of, 22
liability issues, 199
light pens, 104
like product grouping, 73–75
location addresses, 76–86
 considerations in, 76–78
 system selection for, 80–81
 tying SKUs to, 78–86
location audit cycle counting
   method, 181–184
locations, multiple business, 154
locator systems, 43–88
 addresses in, 76–86
 combination, 62–65
 fixed, 49–57
 item placement theory and, 65–76
 memory, 47–49
 random, 60–62
 selecting, 44–47
 SKU identifiers in, 76–86

types of, 44
zoning, 57–59
logic charts, 175
Lotus, A-B-C classification with, 69

M
machine vision, 91
magnetic stripe systems, 91
maintenance, 141
bar codes in, 110
manufacturing
bar codes in, 109–110
demand in, 155
master production schedules, 131–132
materials requirements planning (MRP), 130–137
bill of materials in, 132–133
enterprise resource planning and, 135
just-in-time (JIT) and, 135, 137–142
master production schedule in, 131–132
phasing chart for, 134
ROP compared with, 133
memory systems, 47–49
menu cards, 107
metrics, 165–172
charts in, 172–175
cycle counting, 176–193
fill rates, 170, 172
inventory record accuracy, 166–170
min-max systems, 123–126
misidentifications, 148
MRP. *See* materials requirements planning (MRP)
multiple locations, 154

N
natural emergencies, 200

O
objectives, 142–143
obsolescence, costs of, 2
obsolete stock, 31–39
disposal methods for, 38
problems with disposing of, 32–34
reasons to dispose of, 34–38
reasons to maintain, 32
Ohno, Taiichi, 137
optical character reading (OCR), 91
order fulfillment, 55, 56–57
ordering costs, 4
order-point formulae, 122–126
Orlicky, Joseph, 130

P
paper life
EDI and, 14–15
separation of real life from, 161
tracking, 9–14
Pareto, Vilfredo, 66
Pareto's Law, 66, 67, 71, 75
phantom items, 159, 161–162
physical threats, 202
pilferage, 205–207. *See also* theft
planning, 115–145
emergency/disaster, 197–217
inventory types in, 121–143
materials requirements, 130–137
replenishment costs in, 115–120
planning teams, 201
plus/minus notation, 17n2
popularity, placement by, 67, 68
predictability, 3
price protection, 4
problem solving, 172–175
cycle counting for, 176–193
product categories cycle counting method, 185–192
product positioning, 55
property impact, 205

purchase order systems, 161
purchasing, carrying costs and, 40

Q
quantity discounts, 4
quick ratio, 29–30
quiet zone, 94

R
radio frequency tags, 92
random location systems, 60–62
random selection cycle counting
　　method, 184
ratio analyses, 27–31
　　current, 28–29
　　honeycombing and, 52, 54
　　inventory turnover, 30–31
　　quick or acid test, 29–30
　　unloading/loading ratios,
　　　72–73
raw materials, 4
　　inventory, 19–20
real time systems, 155–156, 158
receiving
　　bar codes in, 108
　　marking SKUs in, 78–79
record count, 147, 157
regulatory threats, 202
release forms, background check,
　　215
reorder points (ROPs), 122–126
　　in materials requirements plan-
　　　ning, 130–131
　　MRP compared with, 133
replenishment, 115–145
　　balancing carrying costs and,
　　　118–120
　　costs, 115–120
　　inventory types in, 121–143
requirements approach, 122
review cycles, 125–126
R Factor, 115–120
risk assessment, 202–205

ROP. *See* reorder points (ROPs)
run charts, 173, 174

S
SAW systems, 92
scan boards, 107
scanners, bar code, 101–105
self-assessment worksheet,
　　203–204
service, repair, replacement and
　　spare items (S&R items), 5–6
setup times, 141
shelf count, 147, 157
shipping
　　bar codes in, 108
SKUs. *See* stock keeping units
　　(SKUs)
software systems
　　backflushing, 132, 156, 163–164,
　　　165, 195n1
　　batch, 156, 159
　　credits in, 163
　　integrating, 155
　　real time, 155–156, 158
space
　　planning, 61
　　utilizing, 46
space costs, 2
　　dead stock and, 34
　　in random location systems,
　　　60–62
　　in zoning systems, 57–59
specific cost method, 21
spreadsheets, 69–71, 129–130
square footage method, 53, 54
S&R items, 5–6
standard cost method, 21
stock
　　metrics for, 165–172
　　negative balances of, 158
　　obsolete, 31–39
　　relieving items from, 163–164
　　types of, 4–9

stock keeping units (SKUs)
    A-B-C categorization of, 66–73
    in fixed locator systems, 50–53
    location addresses with, 76–86
    marking, 78–79
    price protection and, 4
    in random location systems,
        60–62
    unloading/loading ratios, 72–73
    in zoning systems, 57–59
storage
    conflicts in, 45
    grid addressing system, 83–84
    honeycombing in, 50–53
    location addresses, 76–86
    special considerations in, 75–76
    unloading/loading ratios, 72–73
suppliers, in JIT systems, 140, 141,
    142
supply, unreliable, 3
surface acoustic wave (SAW) sys-
    tems, 92
symbologies, bar coding, 95–101
    Code 39, 98–100
    Code 128, 100–101
    discrete/continuous, 96
    popular, 97–101
    selecting, 101
    summary of, 96–97
    UPC, 98

T
technological emergencies, 200, 202
test counts, 166
theft, 205–216
    assessing for, 205–207
    background checks and, 212–216
    collusion, 210–212
    costs, 2
    countering, 207–216
    CPTED and, 207–210
    types of, 205–207

thermal transfer printing, 105
tolerances, accuracy, 166–170, 171
tracking. *See also* bar codes
    card file system for, 85–86
    location addresses, 76–77
    paper life, 9–14
    updates in location systems,
        84–86
training
    cross-, 141–142
    in JIT, 141–142
transit inventory, 6

U
Uniform Code Council (UCC), 98
Uniform Commercial Code (UCC),
    9, 199
Universal Product Code (UPC), 98
unloading/loading ratios, 72–73

V
valuation, 20–21
variance reports, 175
vulnerability assessment, 200–201,
    202–205
    self-assessment worksheet for,
        203–204
    for theft, 205–207

W
wand scanners, 104
waste
    address systems and, 77
    in JIT systems, 139–140
work in process (WIP), 5, 196n2
work-in-process (WIP) inventory,
    20
write offs, 32–33

Z
zero-tolerance policies, 142–143
zoning systems, 57–59

DATE DUE

Discussion of Example Case   154
Metrics   165
    Inventory Record Accuracy   166
        Test Counting   166
        Tolerances   166
        Impact of Tolerances on Adjustments   170
    Fill Rates   170
Tools with Which to Uncover
    System Dysfunctions   172
        Run Charts   173
        Flow Charts   173
        Logic Charts   175
        Variance Reports   175
Cycle Counting   176
    Annual Inventories   176
Cycle Counting   177
    Cycle Count Methodologies   177
    Control Group Cycle Counting Method   179
        Control Group Procedure   180
    Location Audit Cycle Counting Method   181
    Random Selection Cycle Counting Method   184
    Diminishing Population Cycle
        Counting Method   184
    Product Categories Cycle Counting Method   185
        Single Criteria   186
        Using the Diminishing Population Technique
            with Product Categories   187
    A-B-C Analysis Cycle Counting Method   188
        Step-by-Step Implementation of the
            A-B-C Cycle Counting Method   188
        Determining the A-B-C Count Frequency   189
        Determine How Many Items from Each Category
            Will Be Counted Each Day   191
    When to Count   192
    Who Should Count   193
Recap   193
Review Questions   194

Popular Symbologies Found in the
    Inventory World   97
  Universal Product Code/European
    Numbering System   98
  Code 39   98
  Code 128   100
  What Symbology Is Right for Your Organization?   101
Scanning Basics   101
  Printing Basics   103
Bar Code Applications   105
  Examples of Using Bar Codes   108
Recap   112
Review Questions   112

5. **Planning and Replenishment Concepts** **115**
Introduction   115
Replenishment Costs   115
Inventory Types   121
  Independent Demand Inventory   122
    Order-Point Formulae   122
    A Simple Min-Max Inventory System   123
  Economic Order Quantity Formula   127
    How To Set Up An EOQ Worksheet In
        Microsoft® Excel®   129
  Dependent Demand Inventory   130
    Materials Requirements Planning   130
    MRP Elements   131
    Just-In-Time (JIT) Inventory Systems   137
    Implementing JIT   140
  Inventory Objectives   142
Recap   143
Review Questions   143

6. **Why Inventory Systems Fail and
How To Fix Them** **147**
Introduction   147
Inventory System Failures—Example Case   149

A-B-C Categorization   66
What the Matrix Shows   67
Creating the Matrix   69
   Utilizing an SKU's Unloading/
      Loading Ratio   72
Family Grouping   73
   Pros—Family Grouping   74
   Cons—Family Grouping   74
   Using Inventory Stratification
      and Family Grouping Together   75
Special Considerations   75
Location Addresses and SKU Identifiers   76
Significance   76
Keys to Effectively Tying Together SKUs and
   Location Addresses   78
   Clearly Mark Items with a SKU Identifier;
      Clearly Mark Items with a Unit of Measure   78
   Clearly Mark Location Addresses On
      Bins/Slots/Shelves/Racks/
      Floor Locations/Drawers   80
   Tie SKU Numbers and Location Addresses
      Together   81
   Update Product Moves   84
Recap   86
Review Questions   87

4. The Basics of Bar Coding 89
Introduction   89
Elements of a Bar Code Symbol   93
   Structure of a Generic Bar Code Symbol   94
      Quiet Zone   94
      Start and Stop Characters   94
      Data Characters   94
      "X" Dimension   95
Symbologies—Bar Coding Structural Rules   95
   Discrete and Continuous Symbologies   96
   Symbology Summary   96

Problems with Convincing Decision Makers
That "It's Gotta Go" 32
Arguments in Favor of Disposing of
Dead Stock 34
Methods of Disposal 38
Carrying Cost And Purchasing 40
Recap 41
Review Questions 41

3. **Physical Location and Control of Inventory** **43**
Introduction 43
Common Locator Systems 44
Memory Systems 47
Basic Concept—Memory Systems 47
Impact on Physical Space—Memory Systems 48
Pros—Memory Systems 48
Cons—Memory Systems 49
Fixed Location Systems 49
Basic Concept—Fixed Location Systems 49
Impact on Physical Space—Fixed
Location Systems 49
Pros—Fixed Location Systems 53
Cons—Fixed Location Systems 55
Zoning Systems 57
Basic Concept—Zoning Systems 57
Impact on Physical Space—Zoning Systems 58
Pros—Zoning Systems 59
Cons—Zoning Systems 59
Random Location Systems 60
Basic Concept—Random Location Systems 60
Impact on Physical Space—Random
Location Systems 60
Pros—Random Location Systems 62
Cons—Random Location Systems 62
Combination Systems 62
Basic Concept—Combination Systems 62
Common Item Placement Theories 65
Inventory Stratification 65

CONTENTS

About This Book .... *xi*

1. Inventory as Both a Tangible and
   an Intangible Object **1**
   Introduction   1
   Inventory—Who Needs It?   1
      Inventory Costs   2
      The Purpose of Inventory   3
      Types of Stock   4
   Tracking the Paper Life   9
   Electronic Data Interchange   14
   Recap   15
   Review Questions   16

2. Inventory as Money **19**
   Introduction   19
   Accounting for Inventories   19
   How Inventory Is Valued   20
   Inventory on the Balance Sheet   22
   Inventory on the Income Statement   23
   Ratio Analyses and What They Mean   27
   Obsolete Stock   31
      Why You Have Been Told Not to
         Dispose of It   32

*Special discounts on bulk quantities of AMACOM books are
available to corporations, professional associations, and other
organizations. For details, contact Special Sales Department,
AMACOM, a division of American Management Association,
1601 Broadway, New York, NY 10019.
Tel.: 212-903-8316. Fax: 212-903-8083.
Web site: www.amacombooks.org*

Library of Congress Cataloging-in-Publication Data

Muller, Max.
   Essentials of inventory management / Max Muller.
       p.   cm.
     ISBN 0-8144-0751-X
     1. Inventory control.   I. Title.
   TS160 .M83   2003
   658.7'87—dc21
                                        2002014951

Printing number

10 9 8 7 6 5 4 3 2 1

ESSENTIALS OF
INVENTORY MANAGEMENT

MAX MULLER

AMACOM

American Management Association

New York • Atlanta • Brussels • Buenos Aires • Chicago • London • Mexico City
San Francisco • Shanghai • Tokyo • Toronto • Washington, D. C.

ESSENTIALS OF
INVENTORY MANAGEMENT

KOREA'S
QUIET
REVOLUTION

KOREA'S QUIET REVOLUTION

FROM GARRISON STATE TO DEMOCRACY

FRANK GIBNEY

WALKER AND COMPANY / NEW YORK

To Morgan, Nicky, and Will

First published in the United States of America in 1992 by Walker Publishing Company, Inc.

Published simultaneously in Canada by Thomas Allen & Son Canada, Limited, Markham, Ontario

Library of Congress Cataloging-in-Publication Data
Gibney, Frank, 1924–
Korea's quiet revolution: From garrison state to democracy / by Frank Gibney.
p. cm.
ISBN 0-8027-1261-4
1. Korea (South)—History—1960– 2. Korea (South)—Economic conditions—1960– 3. Korea (South)—Economic policy—1960–
I. Title.
DS922.2.G53 1992
951.9504'3—dc20   92-28683
CIP

Text design by Susan Phillips

Printed in the United States of America

2   4   6   8   10   9   7   5   3   1

CONTENTS

ACKNOWLEDGMENTS   vii

PREFACE   ix

CHAPTER I   **A Most Underrated Country**   1

CHAPTER II   **Celadon and Sea Battles**   13

CHAPTER III   **Wars and Occupations**   26

CHAPTER IV   **The Brief April Revolution**   39

CHAPTER V   **An Economy in Armor**   50

CHAPTER VI   **The High Costs of High Growth**   67

CHAPTER VII   **The "Miracle" and the Middle Class**   78

CHAPTER VIII   **The Patient President**   90

CHAPTER IX   **Northern Politics: Roh's Political
Pentathlon**   104

CHAPTER X   **The Marxist Shaman and His Hermit
Kingdom**   113

v

CHAPTER XI   **Explosive Cities and a Bomb Threat**   125

CHAPTER XII   **Korea in the World**   140

APPENDIX   159

BIBLIOGRAPHY   205

INDEX   207

ACKNOWLEDGMENTS

The idea for this book grew out of an article that I wrote for the *Los Angeles Times* in 1987, commenting on the emergence of Korean democracy, as well as further research on the Republic of Korea, made in the course of my work on *The Pacific Century* television series and my book of the same name. I am grateful to the producers and the scholarly advisers to the television series, notably Professor Mike Robinson of the University of Southern California, for sharing with me their interviews and insights on Korean matters.

Great thanks is also owed to Mr. Park Young-Gil, then chief of the cultural division of the Korean Overseas Information Service, and his colleagues at KOIS. They were unstinting of their time in helping arrange interviews and assemble research material. Without their help the book would still be far from complete.

I must also thank my friends in the Korean academic community, notably Prof. Kim Jun Yop, Professor Han Sung Joo, and Professor Lee Ki-baik, whose excellent history of Korea has been a constant resource. Over the years, in a variety of conversations with these and other Korean scholars I gained many insights about the politics and society of this country that would not otherwise have been made apparent to me. I am also indebted to Mr. Rhee Yun Sang, president of the Korea Britannica Company, for his many incisive comments on economic matters over the years, as well as Mr. Lee Dae Hoon, editor-in-chief of the *Britannica World Encyclopaedia* and former deputy managing editor of *Dong-A Ilbo,* for his advice. For many years before and since I have also relied on the counsel of my friend Hahn Changgi, Mr. Rhee's predecessor as president of the Korea Britannica Company and an authority in his own right on Korean art and folk culture.

The book would have been impossible without the collaboration of Ms. Sarah Kim, one of the senior editors of the Korean-language *Encyclopaedia Britannica* (*Britannica World Encyclopaedia*). Ms. Kim worked with me from the beginning of the project, arranging and interpreting interviews and gathering research materials for the book, as well as drawing on her own extensive research and teaching experience. By all rights she should be listed on the title page as the coauthor. Let us hope she will assume that role in producing an expanded Korean edition.

It goes without saying, however, that all the judgments, inferences, and conclusions made in this book are mine alone. I take full responsibility for them. In preparation of the book I am grateful for the assistance of my agent, Leona Schecter, and Ramsey Walker, president of Walker and Company, and his able staff.

PREFACE

Located some fifty miles west of Seoul, its beaches encircled by a barrier of high hills, Kanghwa Island first offers to the visitor's eye little change from the scenery he has left behind. Driving over the bridge from the mainland we find the same complex of tightly packed fields punctuated by an untidy mix of small factories and village business centers. New construction—houses, stores, apartments—sprouts everywhere. Fancy new hotels, vacation housing developments, and billboard ads for future golf courses and sports centers serve notice that South Korea's newly affluent society is spreading its tentacles.

Driving further, past the souvenir stores and real-estate ads, the visitor meets an older history. The restored battlements at Yongdu Fort and the mid-nineteenth-century guns of the Namjang battery recall the day when the Hermit Kingdom, still dead set against Western-style modernization, temporarily fought off the landings of French and American marines eager to open Korea as Commodore Perry's gunboats had opened Japan a decade or two before. Ironically, it was new Japanese gunboats that forced modernization and foreign trade on Korea just a few years later, in a treaty signed on Kanghwa Island in 1876.

On Kanghwa, relics of the nineteenth century barely scratch the surface. Walking through the graceful gates of Kanghwa Castle, one can look north and east to the old capital of Kaesong, now part of Communist North Korea, and find remains of the stronghold of the Koryo kings who held the island for decades against the thirteenth century Mongol invaders. Fortunately for Korea, the Mongols were poor swimmers and bad sailors. Other Buddhist monuments on the island date back to the fourth century.

In the seventeenth century, Kanghwa was beleaguered again, this time by the Manchus sweeping into Korea from Manchuria on their way to conquer China. More relics, more burnings, more restorations—few peoples in history have had to sweep up the rubble and put the pieces back together again so often as the Koreans. They are survivors. Against all manner of conquest and oppression—from thirteenth-century Mongol raids to twentieth-century Japanese colonialism—a stubborn cultural and ethnic togetherness has pulled them through.

This book is about modern Korea—a post World War II economic miracle of skyscrapers and steel mills and export-oriented conglomerates. But it is useful to begin at this old island, wrapped in history, still physically guarding the sea approaches to the Han River, Seoul, and the land and people that are part of them. Americans tend to be imprisoned in a contemporary time frame. That is, in a sense, our big stock in trade. Naturally enough, we think of other countries and peoples in relation to ourselves. Here we have occupied. There we have modernized. Here we have educated. There we have bought and sold. All of these things happened over the past half century as the United States and Korea developed their close relationship. Inevitably, we have come to think of Koreans as learners, apprentices, allies, or even clients. It is useful for us to recall, however, that the five decades of Korea's interaction with America—prefaced though it was by strong if intermittent contacts in the half century previous—are barely a speck on the nation's long history. Thus a visit to Kanghwa Island serves as a starting point to put what follows in better perspective.

I do not pretend to be an authority on Korea. Aside from the painful decipherment of *Hangul* signs, my knowledge of the language is almost nil. Ironically, Koreans' emancipation from the enforced Japanese of the colonial era cut off my own communication with them. As the Chinese characters went out of the signs and newspapers, I could no longer read them. Belatedly, I have taken up the study of the language, but in my work in Korea I have been powerfully helped by the linguistic talent of Koreans, who learn English and other languages quickly.

I have spent a great deal of time in the Republic of Korea—first as a journalist and later as a businessman, when I founded and briefly led a Korean company before turning management over to my more skilled Korean colleagues. I first visited Korea in May, 1950, on the eve of the Korean War. I later reported the war—in fact, I was one of the first American casualties. Through the sixties and seventies and up to the present, I managed to return to the country regularly and renew and expand my acquaintanceships there. A journalist by trade, I have continued to write about Korea. In recent years, despite the extraordinary advances of the South Korean economy, I have been troubled to find that most Americans seem to know so little about the country and the people behind the growth statistics. Hence this book.

The title, *Korea's Quiet Revolution*, deserves some explanation. Not much that happens in Korea is quiet. Koreans, as much in the following chapters suggests, are all too quick to demonstrate their concerns, congratulations, and complaints. I use the word *quiet* to indicate something that is relatively undetected and unnoticed. Over the past five years, after decades of hard-as-nails authoritarian government masquerading as democracy, the Republic of Korea has made extraordinary forward strides in the direction of a real democratic society. This fact has not really penetrated the American political consciousness. People's images of Korea are still formed by quick television sound-bites of riots in Seoul and flashbacks to the Korean War.

The growth of a newly stable democracy is the most significant development in Korea in the past decade. It holds great meaning, not only for its effect on ultimate Korean unification, but as an example to other economically developing Asian countries. Yet it continues to be obscured by business sections reporting on the ups and downs of the Korean "economic miracle." I think this imbalance needs to be addressed and corrected.

Kangwha-Do/Santa Barbara
August/September, 1992

I

A MOST UNDERRATED COUNTRY

By now the Korean miracle has become part of current economic history. Along with Japan's march toward superpowerdom and the GNP growth figures of Singapore, Hong Kong, and Taiwan, serious American newspaper readers have acquired at least a nodding acquaintance with the soaring statistics in *Business Week* or *The Wall St. Journal* for the Republic of Korea's industries. The figures themselves sound almost too good to be true. In the forty years since 1952 Korea's per capita GNP has risen from less than $70 to more than $6,000. Exports have increased from about $60 million to $70 billion, with total trade estimated at some $150 billion in 1992. Where will it all end? Is Korea, as Alice Amsden's excellent book suggests, "Asia's New Giant?"[1]

Hyundai compacts have become commonplace on America's highways; Samsung and Lucky Goldstar electronics and computer components have made their reputations with American consumers. Korea's huge government-run steel business has even set up a joint venture in the United States, to share its engineers' brand-new know-how with their original exemplars. It is all redolent of Japan's earlier export successes. And like Japan, Korea and its export surpluses have become an obvious target for American protectionists.

The two countries are often grouped together; to many Americans, Korea seems merely a Johnny-come-lately imitator of the original export-driven Japan, Inc. At best, Korea is lumped with Taiwan, Hong Kong, and Singapore as one of the Four Little Tigers or, variously, Four Little Dragons: a complex of clever Asian managers and obedient workers toiling overtime on the assembly lines at low wages, splashing ever heavier floods of goods across the Pacific.

Television viewers—which means almost all of us—have an even more limited focus on Korea. Almost ritually, through the eighties decade, the network news programs showed thirty-second bites of riot police battling mobs of firebomb-throwing students in the streets of Seoul. Yet another Korean "antigovernment" demonstration, we were told by the anchorman, generally just before the evening sports roundup. Where editorial comment was given in any of the media, pundits generally pointed out that the "authoritarian" government of South Korea was only slightly (if at all) better than the Communist regime of Kim Il Sung in North Korea. Discussing the problems of unifying the Korean peninsula, most editorialists were content to criticize equally the intransigence of North and South.

Almost a half-century after it ended in 1953, the Korean War remained the central fact about Korea in the American experience. For every American who had been to Korea, there were at least 100 who got most of their Korean impressions from TV reruns of M*A*S*H. The 40,000-odd Eighth Army troops in Korea were accepted as part of the nation's Cold War commitment, and the demilitarized truce zone at Panmunjom received almost obligatory visits by American statesmen, political candidates, or captains of industry touring East Asia. Seoul itself, a capital metropolis of 10 million souls, for all its new high-rises and industry, rated hardly a stopover for the traveler bent on Tokyo, Hong Kong, or Shanghai.

This set of two-dimensional stereotypes—whether sweatshop export machine or grim garrison state—was only slightly modified by the 1988 Olympic Games held in Seoul, successful though they were. Nor has it been materially changed for Americans by the presence of close to 1 million Koreans in the United States. Most of them first-generation immigrants, they tend to settle in clannish Koreatowns and set up businesses in small ma-and-pa-type stores—the Korean grocery is the current equivalent of the old Chinese laundry—which often become targets of resentment by blacks and other minorities. While Americans on the whole support South Korea—its "favorable" rating in a recent Potomac/Gallup poll was higher than that of either China or Japan[2]—there are few signs that the average American has an impression of Korea and Koreans, as they are today, that remotely resembles his relatively definite images of Chinese or Japanese.

It is time we brought Korea and Koreans into sharper focus. Their national character, their culture, and their postwar achievement are unique; and the international role they play can be impressive. The South Koreans are 43 million strong; some 22 million more Koreans live across the locked borders of North Korea. Historically sandwiched between China and Japan, with Russia, both in its Czarist and Soviet incarnations, looming on the north, they have spent most of their history alternately fighting or compromising with their large neighbors. Now with the global Cold War at an end and North Korea virtually deserted by its old Communist allies, Seoul is a bit closer to its long-term goal of unifying the peninsula. It is a difficult task, which has barely begun. It will require a remarkable further effort from a people that throughout this century has faced problems whose intensity was matched only by the frequency of their occurrence.

On the face of things Korea, like Taiwan and the Singapore city-state, exemplifies a new type of economy, the so-called capitalist developmental state. Capitalist its economy is. Its businesses compete often bitterly among themselves; they are driven by the profit motive; like all free enterprisers Koreans are set on building the ever-better mousetrap and if possible gaining market share for it with smart selling. But their overall growth has been managed, after the Japanese example, by strong guidance from an economic bureaucracy, driven by a demanding and autocratic government.

Yet Korea has enjoyed—or, equally, suffered from—special circumstances that set it apart. Desperate and defeated as the Japanese were in 1945, they were able to build for recovery on a well-educated population, a considerable industrial base, an experienced bureaucracy, and a modern political and economic infrastructure; these were the legacy of seventy-five years as a nation-state and two centuries before that as a regulated feudal society.

·

The Koreans had no such legacy. Since 1910 they had been cruelly colonized and exploited by the Japanese, who were also, it must be admitted, responsible for much of Korea's economic modernization. Far more than their counterparts in Taiwan or Singapore, they had suffered during World War II. An estimated 2 million had been drafted as forced laborers or soldiers in the Japanese war effort. After the war they were divided into United States and Soviet occupation zones. The division gave rise to the Korean War, which cost the lives of almost 1.5 million Koreans and left millions separated from their families, after the final truce in 1953.

When Korea's dictatorial president Park Chung Hee started his series of five-year plans in 1961, he followed in the path of Japan by building up heavy industry along with electronics and textiles as the base for export strategies. In this Korea differed sharply from the light or service industry emphasis of the other Little Dragons. Another distinguishing mark of Korea's development was Park's reliance on the large *chaebol* conglomerates, reminiscent of the Japanese *zaibatsu* or later *keiretsu* models. Unlike the Japanese, however, the Koreans relied heavily on foreign loans to keep their expansion going. And government, rather than private banking, directly doled out the money for capital investment.

Against the warnings of Western economists—the World Bank's experts among them—Park's headlong drive to economic expansion proved in the end a brilliant success, despite a variety of problems and detours on the way. "The OIG-oriented strategy, that is, outward-, industry- and growth-oriented," as the Korean economist Song Byung-Nak put it, depended not merely on the industry of Korean workers and the leadership of the chaebol bosses but equally on the skills of a new generation of technocrats who staffed Park's economic ministries and planning boards. These were in turn products of an unprecedented surge in secondary and higher education.

During the thirty-five years of Japanese colonialism, barely a thousand Koreans had been able to obtain university educations. Between the 1945 liberation and 1959, however, the number of graduates had reached 70,000.[3] Expenditures on education quickly reached 10 percent of GNP and have remained there—just about the largest such percentage in the world. By 1991 fully 1.5 million

Korean students were attending universities and other higher-education institutions.

Korea's high-risk road to economic recovery was underwritten by Park's iron control of the country's politics. Under Park and the even more tyrannical Chun Doo Hwan, Korea's military leadership more than justified the accusation of authoritarianism. Although twice legitimately elected president, in 1963 and 1971, Park ran roughshod over any political opposition, real or suspected, and his supporters in the National Assembly passed a law making any criticism of the president a criminal offense. In 1973 the Korean Central Intelligence Agency, a barely disguised secret police under Park's direction, abducted Kim Dae Jung, the leading opposition leader, from his refuge in Japan to put him under arrest in Korea. Chun, then a major-general, who seized power after Park's death, put the country under martial law in 1980. In May of that year, troops under his orders shot down hundreds of civilians while suppressing a popular revolt in the southern city of Kwangju.

Despite the rigors of Park's dictatorial rule the average Korean, through the sixties and the seventies, was not all that dissatisfied with his lot. He was too busy working. Discretionary income was up; people were beginning to enjoy creature comforts. And economic priorities came first. Most of the country accepted Park's own candid statement of this in 1970: "My chief concern was economic revolution. One must eat and breathe before concerning himself with politics, social affairs and culture." Those disturbed by crude police tactics or the KCIA's constant surveillance[4] could only reflect that the "soft authoritarianism" of the South was still better than Kim Il Sung's totalitarian North.

Yet with increased prosperity and wider education came the beginnings of popular questioning. Chun and his clique not only lacked Park's standing but their corruption was becoming all too obvious. Although Korea's economic growth machine kept on its course, with GNP growth statistics hitting 12 percent annually, the new wealth was not being shared. The revolution of rising expectations began to go political, as an increasingly well-educated urban electorate began to demand more return for their labor and more legitimacy for their vote.

In short, a new middle class was growing, urbanized and

broadly based. Technological advance was an increasing factor in its development. For all the crude attempts of Chun's government at political censorship, Korea had become a well-communicated modern society. The very dependence of the fast-growth economy on exports forced businessman and bureaucrat alike to look outside the country, to internationalize. Large numbers of Koreans— teachers, officials, and profesional people—had gone overseas, mostly to the United States, for their graduate or professional education. Such people would no longer fit into the tight society of authoritarian mandarins and obedient economic gnomes that Park Chung Hee and his generals had originally planned.

The cumulative effect of mass higher education—by 1987 almost half of the male population and one-quarter of Korean women had received a university or other post-secondary education—was showing in the intensity of students' antigovernment demonstrations. The tone of the student protests grew increasingly radical. After the mid-eighties the protest marchers were joined by discontented workers and, finally, were supported by numbers of ordinary citizens.

In 1987 the ferment within the nation boiled over. The opposition party in the National Assembly, gathering strength, had demanded direct popular election of the president, a move that Chun resisted for obvious reasons. In April, Chun's refusal to continue debate on this question touched off demonstrations across the country. They were fueled by recent instances of police brutality, during which one student had been killed under interrogation. By June the whole country, it would seem, was taking to the streets. Widespread military repression, however congenial to Chun, now seemed out of the question. Not only were the demonstrations difficult to contain but any "get-tough" policy would have lost Korea the chance to hold the 1988 Olympic Games in Seoul—an event that represented to government and people alike a long-wished-for assertion of the country's international stature.

On June 29, 1987, Roh Tae Woo, the government candidate to succeed Chun as president, took matters into his own hands and made a memorable public statement. He not only promised to revise the constitution, allowing direct presidential election, but added his pledge, as chairman of the ruling Democratic Justice

Party, to permit free political debate, give amnesty to political pri-soners—among them the opposition party leader Kim Dae Jung—and offer new guarantees for civil rights. Although a former gen-eral himself (and Chun's hand-picked candidate) Roh saw with clarity that the time for political repression was over. "The people are the masters of the country," he said, "and the people's will must come before everything else."

On February 25, 1988, Roh was inaugurated president. He won the election with less than 40 percent of the vote, thanks to a fatal division of the opposition into two opposing parties. Were it not for this, the opposition would have won, for it *was* a free elec-tion. The election was in fact the first free vote in Korea since Park's victory in 1971, and it marked a watershed in Korean politics.

In the five years between 1988 and 1992, essentially the term of Roh's Sixth Republic, the country changed itself from an au-thoritarian economic growth machine (to have called it a police state would not have been much exaggeration) into a working de-mocracy. The term, however, must be qualified. Police and bureau-crats continued to act dictatorially in a variety of matters. The human rights of some dissidents remained hostage to the whims of the security organs. Corruption in the public sector, if diminished, was far from eradicated. But by and large the government held true to candidate Roh's guarantees. The press was largely freed. It was becoming difficult, if not impossible, for officials to sweep unpleas-ant disclosures under the rug. Local elections were run fairly, as they had not been for many years past. And in the National Assem-bly the debate of national politics became a fact of life.

The public's reaction was one of intense relief. For most Kore-ans Roh's reforms amounted to both *glasnost* and *perestroika*. It is fair to say that Roh did for Korea what Mikhail Gorbachev did for the Soviet Union. There was some similarity between the two men's approaches to political liberalization: decisive in basic prin-ciple but very cautious around the political fringes. It is probably no accident that they got along quite well at their three meetings in 1990 and 1991.

Gorbachev's reform policy in the Soviet Union, along with the echoing reforms in eastern Europe, could not have been better timed for Roh. His patient spade work lobbying internationally for the 1988 Seoul Olympics had resulted in participation by the then Soviet Union, China, and all the other Communist countries except for the recalcitrant neighbor, North Korea. Building on this, South Korea established first trade, then political relations with all the former eastern bloc except China—and here political rapprochement was clearly in the cards. This served to isolate the North Korean dictatorship from its old partners and economic supporters. Pressing now for peaceful reunification with the North, Seoul knew that Pyongyang, on the verge of bankruptcy, was gradually being impelled to restore at least an economic relationship with its prosperous southern neighbor. Here, too, Roh's patient diplomacy was useful. For one thing, he worked to defuse the explosive polemics from South Korea that had for so long nullified any real gestures toward a dialogue with the North. Gradually, if slowly, the North in turn began to adjust its confrontational stance somewhat.

Such successes in foreign policy, however, could not disguise the serious domestic problems that the Republic of Korea's democratization set in train. Released from years of government repression, Korea's labor unions began a wave of strikes and walkouts. There were fully 7,000 cases of labor trouble in the two years following democratization, as workers, long dismissed as a collective "given" in Park Chung Hee's low-wage export competitiveness, began to demand their share of the economic action. The losses in productivity were predictably heavy. They were magnified by the forced appreciation of the *won,* under heavy American pressure, as protectionist reaction increased against Korean low-cost exports. Another problem was posed by Korea's newly acquisitive consumer society. Heavy demand for foreign goods, added to Korean companies' need for imported technology and machine tools, had begun by 1990 to pile up heavy unfavorable trade balances.

Like his new colleague Gorbachev, Roh Tae Woo had released a horde of economic problems by cutting the fetters of his predecessors' economic garrison state. Unlike Gorbachev or the new leaders of freed eastern Europe, however, Roh could count on a structure of competent management, skilled labor, and supportive bureaucracy already in place. As we shall see, Korea's economy rallied to become competitive again on a more complex but far more socially secure base. By the end of 1991 Korea's per capita income had reached a new high of $6,498; export volume had grown to $72 billion. This was roughly double the respective figures of $3,110 and $46.2 billion for 1987.

For some years Western economists had been dining out on their theories that the Little Dragons, Tigers, or whatever "Oriental" symbol they could conjure had been able to push up their GNP so spectacularly in large part because of cheap labor, home-grown protectionism, and authoritarian political governance. Here now was Korea, about to show them that a newly emerging middle-class democracy could handle a newly industrialized economy and make it run, so to speak, on time. For the rest of East Asia, the whole complex of countries along the west side of the Pacific Rim, the implications were enormous.

Massive "people-power" demonstrations in the Philippines had toppled the dictatorship of Ferdinand Marcos in 1986. They had a powerful effect on the middle-class demonstrators in Seoul the following year. But the promised new-broom politics of President Cory Aquino did little, as it turned out, to disturb the economic torpor of the Philippines, with its structure of entrenched land-owning capitalists and heavily exploited lower orders. The Korean changes were different. They restored—most would say instituted—democracy on the structure of a going economy. Despite the staggering problems raised, the Koreans ultimately made the package work. That put Korea ahead of Singapore, Taiwan, and Hong Kong, not to mention the emerging boom economies in southern China. In the Sinic states—Lee Kuan Yew's Orwellian Singapore excepted—crowds were demonstrating and demanding a greater measure of self-government to go with their increased pay packets. In Indonesia, Malaysia, and Thailand semidictatorial regimes continued; they remained havens of cheap labor and increasingly successful labor-intensive economies. Among generally docile electorates authoritarian politics continued to flourish. There too, however, the spread of technology and education was changing things. In time their developing middle classes would have to be reckoned with. For the past two decades, at least, Thai voters have been notably tolerant of coups d'état in their governments. The fact that Thais in the tens of thousands took to the streets in April 1992 to denounce (and ultimately oust) General Suchinda, their military prime minister, was an interesting straw in the wind.

For almost all the Asia-Pacific peoples Roh Tae Woo's Korea offered a new political paradigm. As fully as Japan had once offered its economic model as an example, Korea was providing a political one. With unification a stronger possibility than ever before, a united Korea could well emerge as one of the strongest political and economic factors in the Pacific Basin. For the past ten years Korean representatives have played a leading role in Pacific Basin economic organizations. In 1991, thanks to Roh's persevering diplomacy, the Republic of Korea was admitted to the United Nations, bringing a reluctant North Korea along with it.[5]

At home the March 1992 elections for the National Assembly proved a personal disappointment for President Roh and his ruling Democratic Liberal party, which lost heavily. Yet their fairness and the discriminating split-preference vote, as *The New York Times* editorialized, "testifies to the impressive success of Mr. Roh's democratic endeavor." *The Los Angeles Times's* editorial comment was more specific. In sending a "wake-up call" to their rulers, the paper said, Korean voters

> took a long step toward creating a competitive political system, something that no other Asian democracy has managed to do. . . .
> This is yet another sign that the country is evolving toward a more mature and responsive political system. Much of the credit for this constructive turn must go to President Roh. At various times the target of abuse from radicals, unions, businessmen, farmers, activists and cranks, he has kept the transition to democracy on course. Democracy has become normal, the natural state of things for Koreans. That's a remarkable achievement for a country that was a dictatorship not five years ago.

Such a perceptive comment suggests that the American media, after years of serving readers and viewers a diet of fragmentary coverage of student riots, broken-off unification talks, trade imbalances, and U.S. troop commitments, are coming to appreciate the realities of modern Korea. They are impressive. Korea's road to a working democracy has been a hard one, with more than its share of disappointments and disasters. It is a long road as well. For behind Korea's modernity and its accompanying economic successes lies an extraordinary mixture of traditions and influences, played out over a history that goes back almost five thousand years.

NOTES

[1] Alice Amsden, *Asia's Next Giant* (New York: Oxford University Press, 1989), p. 8.

[2] This survey sampling of American attitudes toward Korea, prepared by Potomac Associates of Washington, D.C., was taken by the Gallup Organization in February, 1992.

[3] As noted by Song Byung Nak in his book *The Rise of the Korean Economy* (New York: Oxford University Press, 1990); he quotes the economist Ahn Byung Jik as well.

[4] The Korean Central Intelligence Agency was far more than a carbon copy of its eponymous American model. Its investigations, arrests, and intrigues often more closely resembled the behavior of the Soviet KGB and similar organizations.

[5] Kim Il Sung's Democratic Peoples Republic of Korea had consistently opposed South or North joining the U.N. unless as a unified country, but unified on the North's terms. By 1991, however, both Russia and China, once Kim's strongest supporters, had agreed to South Korea's admission, thus forcing Kim to seek separate admission as well.

CELADON AND SEA BATTLES

For all the later talk of tigers and dragons, the legendary founder of Korea was a garlic-loving bear. In the year 2333 B.C., as the tradition has it, Tangun, the first Korean, was born of a union between a female bear and the son of the creator god. According to the legend a bear and a tiger met on a mountainside and lamented the fact they were not humans. The Creator heard them. If they each ate a quantity of garlic and mugwort, he promised, then retired to a cave and fasted for twenty-one days, their wish would be granted. After ten hungry days the tiger grew impatient and went off to hunt. The bear remained in the cave. At the end of the twenty-one days, the bear was transformed into a beautiful woman and was espoused by the Creator's son. Their offspring, Tangun, was acclaimed as king by the humans around him.

The timing of the myth, at least, tells us something of the unity and antiquity of the Korean people, not to mention their traditional fondness for spicy food. Of Altaic or Tungusic stock, the first Koreans migrated east and south from Central Asia and Manchuria to settle, finally, in the fertile peninsula. By Neolithic times, some five thousand years ago, the invaders had coalesced into a fairly homogeneous race. These "eastern barbarians" were well known to their Chinese neighbors over the centuries. By the fifth century B.C. Confucius, praising the discipline of their tribal society, said he would like to cross the sea from Shandong and live there.[1] Three centuries after Confucius's death Han Dynasty armies moved into Korea in force, establishing military commanderies in the north and west. Theirs was only the first of what would be continuing assaults on the peninsula by its two powerful neighbors, China and Japan.

The Koreans learned much from their Chinese opponents, however. By the fourth century A.D. Chinese Buddhism had crossed over into Korea, and Koreans had adapted Chinese characters to write their unique language. Many from the south of the peninsula migrated to Japan. They probably exercised a decisive influence on early Japanese culture, religion, and language; although Korean bears some vague resemblance to Altaic languages (i.e., Turkic, Mongolian, and Manchu), Japanese and Korean have strong structural similarities. The importation of Korean culture apparently whetted Japanese appetites for a more direct relationship. The first large-scale Japanese invasion of Korea took place in A.D. 399.

By that time three distinct kingdoms had been established on the Korean peninsula: Paekche in the southwest, Silla in the south and east, and Koguryo in the north. Each had a strong local character. Koguryo, stretching from Manchuria to the Han River, was border state to China—alternately enemy and friend but heavily influenced by northern Chinese culture. The Paekche people were sailors and traders, keeping up a busy traffic in goods and art with both Japan and the southern Chinese states, easily reachable by sea. Silla had perhaps the best-developed political institutions, and its potters and goldsmiths displayed a marvelously imaginative art. In a sense these local divisions in an otherwise homogeneous people persist to this day. While North Korea occupies much the same area as Koguryo and echoes Koguryo in its militancy, the southeast provinces in the old Silla territory have supplied most of the Republic of Korea's political leaders, Park Chung Hee and Roh Tae Woo included. People from the Cholla provinces of old Paekche—clannish, artistic, and independent-minded—remain cast in the role of outsiders.

In the seventh century, after years of inconclusive warring, the rulers of Silla invoked the aid of Tang Dynasty China to overcome their neighbors and unify the peninsula. The unified Silla kingdom developed a brilliant court civilization heavily dependent on Buddhist art and religious values. As a contemporary of Tang China's Changan (Xian) and early Heian Japan's newly founded Kyoto, the Silla capital of Kyongju, with a population estimated at 1 million, was one of the world's great cities. It was the site of libraries, a Confucian university, and the first observatory in East Asia. Some of its monuments, like the great eighth-century Buddha in the Sokkuram grotto, are still preserved, as are the low mound-tombs of the Silla kings.

After its two centuries in the sun Silla collapsed, its authority undermined by conflicts between the old feudal nobility and imported Chinese Confucian ideas of governance. It was succeeded by a revived Koryo (an abbreviated form of Koguryo) state, its capital moved to the central city of Kaesong. Here again, with the blessings of a centralized monarchy, the arts and culture flourished.

The above is a simple enough statement, the like of which is often found in history books. This may be the time to consider just what kind of art and culture "flourished" in this country. To begin with, Korean art, like Japanese, Chinese, and European art of that day, was a product of a kingly court civilization; the artists were paid by the court or high dignitaries. Other than that, there was no market for their work. Among the principal northern Asian national art forms—Chinese, Japanese, and Korean—Korean is surely the least known. For this reason it has been easy for connoisseurs of Chinese and Japanese art to dismiss the Korean variety as "derivative." It is certainly undervalued, but derivative it is not.

In the room where I am writing I can see several pieces of Korean celadon. They are from the Koryo period, simple to the point of plainness, the glaze still unspoiled after eight hundred years, their pure greens and bluish greens arresting in their simplicity of line and form. They are natural and unaffected, classic examples of the principle, codified by the architect Mies van der Rohe, "less is more." Korean potters turned to celadon with an eye on their contemporaries in Sung dynasty China. Their work has often been judged better. For many, Korean celadon is the summit of the potter's art.

In sculpture and painting, from the *bodhisattva maitreya* figures of Silla through the ink scrolls and drawings of the later Yi Dynasty, Korean art displays a kind of naturalness. It lacks the stylized discipline of the Chinese, and compared to Japanese art it tends to be bolder and rougher. In painting and certainly ceramics, however, it has had a strong influence on Japan. And while borrowing inevitably from the Chinese, Korean artists managed to make their work less formal, less ornate. Its tone tends to be more relaxed and not without humor. This is of course particularly true of the folk painting that has come to be valued only in recent times. But even in classic painting one can detect a bit of a smile. And the distinctive blue-and-white porcelains of the Yi Dynasty, which followed the work of the Koryo potters, managed to retain their simplicity of line and color.

For the Koryo kings and their people the time of gracious living came to a jarring end with the Mongol invasions of the mid-thirteenth century. Through two centuries their armies had been able to fend off various incursions by the Khitan or Jurchen tribesmen from the north, while Korean seamen and coast watchers dealt as best they could with Japanese pirate forays against the coastal cities. The Mongols were irresistible, however. After several years of fighting, during which an estimated 200,000 Koreans—civilians as well as soldiers—were killed, a peace was concluded. The Koryo kings became vassals of the Mongol khans, who by this time had also conquered China.

Kublai Khan, now head of the Yuan dynasty, had a bitter surprise in store for his new Korean subjects. He ordered Korean troops and seamen to join the armada he was preparing for the invasion of Japan. As it turned out, Koreans manned a great portion of his ships. Twice he attempted to land his soldiery and overpower the Japanese. Twice he failed, his ships scattered on both occasions by what the Japanese understandably regarded as providential typhoons (*kamikaze* or "the wind of the gods"). The losses to Korea were great, not merely from battle and shipwreck but from the systematic looting of the Korean countryside by the Mongol troops.

In the fourteenth century, shortly after the Mings chased the Mongols out of China, a Korean general named Yi Song-gye put an end to the Koryo rule and established a dynasty of his own. The Yi or Chosun Dynasty was to last for almost five hundred years. It opened auspiciously. With strong leadership and a working alliance with Ming China, the country began to recover from the disasters of Mongol rule. The ever-troublesome Japanese pirates were defeated in several major sea actions, and the Chosun kings, their capital now moved to the present Seoul, could rule in relative peace. Korea's Confucian intelligentsia busied themselves with technological improvement. Moveable metal type, first invented in Korea in 1234—some centuries before Mr. Gutenberg worked his magic—was improved and standardized, with an official government printing bureau established. A water clock, a spinning wheel, and the world's first scientific rain guage were also devised. King Sejong, probably the most enlightened of Korea's monarchs, worked hard to alleviate the lot of the perennially downtrodden peasantry, hundreds of thousands of them serfs under a form of virtual slavery. To further popular education he and his scholars devised the *Hangul* alphabet in the early fifteenth century. An intricately simple combination of vowel and consonant sounds, it was designed to free the common people from the necessity of learning complex Chinese characters in order to read. It is now used by all Koreans, North and South.

After Sejong the government became divided by factional disputes—a familiar Korean syndrome—this time among the Confucian literati in Seoul and their kinsmen among the *yangban* provincial gentry. At this point, in 1592, Japan's regent, Toyotomi Hideyoshi, having just won out in the feudal civil wars of his own country, conceived the idea of invading Ming China through Korea. In a sense, he was reviving Kublai Khan's old project of invading Japan, in reverse. Hideyoshi's samurai soldiery at first swept through the peninsula, from Pusan to Pyongyang. Stopped finally by Korean troops, reinforced by an allied army of 50,000 from Ming China, Hideyoshi retreated, then went on the attack again. His supply lines were cut by the naval victories of Korean Admiral Yi Sun-shin. The cannon of Yi's ironclad turtle ships—another Korean technological first—dominated the sea lanes; but when Yi was temporarily removed from office in a palace intrigue, Hideyoshi's commanders renewed the campaign, continuing to range over the southern part of the country.

The Japanese finally left Korea in 1598, following Hideyoshi's death, but they had done terrible damage. Farms and cities were laid waste. Most of Korea's historical monuments went up in flames. The serious modern tourist in Korea, visiting old temples, palaces, or monuments, soon becomes familiar with the notation that the original painting or building was "destroyed" in the Japanese invasion. To Koreans the name Hideyoshi holds the same legacy of opprobrium as the name Oliver Cromwell in Ireland.

After the resumption of normal relations with Japan—Tokugawa Ieyasu, Hideyoshi's successor as shogun, wanted no part of overseas adventuring—peace seemed assured. Yet barely a generation later, when a Korean king mistakenly backed the Ming losers in China's latest dynastic changeover, invaders came again. This time it was the Manchu bannermen of the new Qing regime who led their armies into northern Korea. They retraced their steps only after the Yi king had pledged total submission to the new regime in Peking.

Nineteenth-century modernization movements in East Asia brought for Korea only an intensification of the old Chinese-Japanese rivalry for hegemony in the peninsula. Just as Japan's sweeping Meiji Restoration started its successful modernization, Korea's regent, the Taewongun, holding power on behalf of the young King Kojong, decided on a reverse course. Emboldened by his troops' repulse of landing parties from U.S. and French warships,[2] the regent adopted a policy of anti-Westernization. He refused even to receive any foreign embassies. Korean Christians were again fiercely persecuted, as representatives of an alien philosophy. So were Korean reformers who wished to modernize, following Meiji's example, by using Western teachers and Western technology. There was no mistaking the virulence of the regent's hostility to foreigners. Earlier, after publicly executing French missionaries, he had thousands of Korean Catholic converts killed.

Here was a classic anachronism, a historical anomaly. Japan's Meiji Restoration, accomplished in 1868, was actually a national cultural revolution, which used the prestige of a revived imperial institution to transform the country into a modern nation-state. A small but broadly based group of modernizers, drawn from the ranks of the lower samurai military bureaucracy, had mobilized great popular support for their reforms. Similar reform currents were swirling through China under the guidance of scholars like

Yan Fu and innovative bureaucrats like Li Hongzhang, although they were in the end less successful. How was it that modernization and reform were so strenuously opposed in Korea?

For a partial answer we need to review the singularity of Korean history. For five centuries, since the beginning of the Yi Dynasty, the country had been ruled by a tight Confucian bureaucracy around the throne. More stratified than Chinese Confucianism, the Korean system combined the worst features of aristocracy and Confucianism, since only members of the yangban aristocracy were eligible to take the examinations on which all advancement was based. All power was concentrated at the center, the focus of constant familial and factional intrigues. By contrast, the very delegation and dispersal of authority under Japanese Tokugawa feudalism engendered a new class of low-ranking samurai administrators who ultimately became the civil service of modern Meiji society. Similarly, an active bourgeois merchant class had developed in Tokugawa Japan, the first forerunners of a new urban society. In Korea these factors were lacking. Nor was there any intellectual stimulus comparable to the steady infiltration of Western learning into Japan over more than a century. Here Japan's enforced isolation served as an incubator of ideas.

Koreans enjoyed no such luxury. Always, there was pressure or interference from the two neighbors on either side. From the 1870s to the close of the century, Korean efforts to modernize were smothered in a patchwork melodrama of palace coups, mutinies, popular uprisings, assassinations, and reform proclamations—almost always with a Japanese or Chinese military force camping just behind the scenery.

Korea was officially "opened" in 1876, when a Japanese ambassador, backed by warships and a landing force, imposed the Treaty of Friendship on the Koreans, after disembarking the troops on Kanghwa Island, the same island, just off the coast from Seoul, where the Americans and the French had earlier been repulsed. With the antiforeign Taewongun removed from power, the Korean "enlightenment" faction backed by the young King Kojong organized two missions to Japan, to see how a modernizing program worked. (Kojong, incidentally, was the Taewongun's son.)

When Kojong tried to modernize his palace guard, however,

army conservatives mutinied and shot the Japanese military advisor, among others. Chinese and Japanese troops quickly arrived to help the king suppress the mutineers, and the Japanese forced indemnities and another treaty on the Koreans. In 1884 Kim Ok Kyun and other pro-Japanese modernizers staged a coup d'état on the king's behalf to oust pro-Chinese conservatives from the government. Chinese troops broke up the Kapsin Coup, as it was called, with superior force, which led to Japanese demands for further indemnities and construction of a one-thousand-man barracks in Seoul for *their* troops.

In 1894 a series of populist uprisings swept the country. Under the banner of *Tonghak* or "Eastern Learning," a new religion which combined Confucianist, Taoist, and Buddhist beliefs—with a good bit of shamanist superstition thrown in—bands of angry peasants mobilized to protest pro-Western "enlightenment" movements. They were above all anti-Japanese, angered not only at Tokyo's political aggrandizement but also at the galloping prosperity of Japanese businessmen, who were quickly taking over most of Korea's trade. In some ways the Tonghak resembled the Boxers who would soon appear in China. Their xenophobic, traditionalist appeal drew hundreds of thousands of followers in what became the largest uprising in Korea's history.

True to form, both Japan and China despatched troops to help King Kojong's hard-pressed government. Their arrival led to the Sino-Japanese war, waged on Korean soil and in Korean waters. Japan's victory established that country as a world power; and in 1895, after more than two thousand years of suzerainty, China gave up all claims to its old Korean vassal.

During and after the war Korea's reformers were finally able to make the broad changes they had long advocated. A series of royal edicts and decrees provided for a modern monetary and taxation system, a national school system, an independent judiciary, and a modern army and abolished the web of class distinctions that had so long hobbled Korean society. The yangban aristocracy and commoners were now declared equal before the law. Serfdom was abolished, along with the practice of buying and selling serfs as chattels, which had so long disfigured Korean society. Both socially and administratively, the Reform of 1894, as it became known, authorized a transformation of Korean society fully as drastic as that of Japan's Meiji Restoration a generation before. The Korean modernizers were assisted by Japanese representatives in Seoul, now more powerful than ever after the defeat of China. With reformers brought back from exile in Japan now in charge of the government, King Kojong formally pledged court support for the reorganization.

Unfortunately, the reform remained little more than a set of edicts. The identification of reform with Japan aroused nationwide opposition among a people whose traditionalist sentiments were already shocked by the threat of enforced modernization. ("Cut off my head," conservatives cried out after the royal edict banning the characteristic topknot, "but my hair—never.")[3] When traditionalists rose up in revolt, in common cause with the Tonghak rebels, they were suppressed by Japanese occupying troops. There ensued a bewildering time of popular unrest and palace intrigue, of which both modernization and Korean independence were casualties.

The old Taewongun, ever resilient, had come back from exile to plot and lead the anti-Japanese opposition, along with Kojong's Queen Min. When Min was assassinated by pro-Japanese in the capital, loyalists smuggled Kojong out of the palace to the safety of the Russian legation. When he returned to the Doksu Palace, after almost a year in the legation, he declared himself emperor of the Great Han Empire (Han is the traditional name for Korea) and surrounded himself with a new group of pro-Russian advisers. For Russia, too powerful to ignore, had now taken the place of China in the uneasy balance of power among Korea's rapacious neighbors.

The balance tipped decisively in 1905, with Russia's defeat in the Russo-Japanese War. Japan's occupation of Korea, which ensued, was sanctioned by the United States as well as Russia at the Treaty of Portsmouth; Britain gave its approval in a codicil added to the Anglo-Japanese Treaty of Alliance. In 1905 Japan declared Korea a protectorate and the following year appointed Prince Ito, Japan's Meiji constitution maker, as the first resident-general. Japan formally annexed Korea as a colony in 1910.

Korea's last kings, Kojong and his son, Sunjong, are buried

with their queens in a quiet, spacious park at Kumgok, just a few miles northeast of Seoul. (The body of Kojong's wife, Queen Min, was burned after her assassination by the Japanese; apparently only a finger bone remained to be interred in Kojong's tomb.) Each tomb is surrounded by a wall (since, thanks to Kojong's 1897 proclamation, they are imperial, not merely kingly). A path lined with two rows of statues in the classic Chinese manner (horse, camel, lion, civil official, etc.) leads to a rather austere-looking stone shrine. Behind each shrine lies a low, grassy mound, which looks very much like the old Silla mound-tombs in Kyongju. The park is not crowded. Although parties of schoolchildren come for dutiful sight-seeing, it is essentially a park, a nice place for a short walk and a rest—with only an occasional memorial ceremony.

Born in 1852, Kojong was just a year younger than Japan's Meiji; but unlike Meiji's his hopes for an Age of Enlightenment were never realized; they were destroyed by Meiji's oversuccessful reformers. A weak-willed person, he was dominated first by his father, the Taewongun, then by successive councillors. Adversity increased his natural timidity. When he moved to the Doksu Palace (then called Kyongun) he had special gates prepared leading to the Russian, American, and British legations in case a hasty exit was necessary. In the last decade of his reign he grew arbitrary and reactionary, imprisoning young members of the Independence Club and other reformers. But he fought for independence as best he could. He secretly sent a mission to the World Peace Conference at The Hague in 1907, to make a public if unavailing protest against Japan's occupation. For this he was forced to abdicate, in favor of his son, who in turn had to give up his kingship three years later.

He made his last protest after his death. On March 1, 1919, two days before the scheduled memorial service for Kojong, several thousand Korean activists, mostly students and young intellectuals, gathered in Seoul's Pagoda Park to read a declaration of independence from Japanese rule. The demonstration had been planned for months, along with similar public meetings throughout the country. It was then and remains one of the modern world's memorable campaigns of passive resistance. Over the next three months more than 2 million Koreans turned out to protest.

Through the first decade of their colonial stewardship the Japanese had behaved badly but purposefully. Their aim was to integrate Korea into the Japanese empire economically as well as politically—and to the extent possible, socially. For the Japanese colonizers believed that Koreans, although doubtless of a lesser breed than themselves, were closely enough related for ultimate acceptance as good second-class citizens.

Here was a new variant on the old Western-style colonialism: absorption through oppression. Assimilation was the goal of the government-general in Korea. The national language was to be Japanese. Regulations, laws, and even folkways were to be changed to fit Japanese patterns, indistinguishable from the original. Resistance to this policy was to be rooted out by force. In the first few years of the occupation the Japanese authorities reckoned that their police and military had killed almost 18,000 Korean guerillas, putting a stop to organized resistance, at least for a time.

The March 1st demonstrations were Ghandian in their nonviolence. The Korean underground organization had circulated warnings among its members: "Whatever you do, do not insult the Japanese. . . ." The Japanese police, however, taken by surprise, reacted with almost total violence. Demonstrators were arrested, beaten, and sometimes executed. Although estimates vary, it is safe to assume some 45,000 to 50,000 were arrested and 7,000 killed. Schools and homes believed to be used as revolutionary centers were destroyed. Almost fifty churches were burned, since the Japanese, accurately enough, assumed that Korean Christians were leaders of the resistance. Of the thirty-three prominent Koreans signing the original March 1st manifesto, seventeen were Christians.

Naively, the Korean independence leaders had allowed themselves to be inspired by the noble words of Woodrow Wilson at Versailles about the "self-determination of nations." (In fact Syngman Rhee, chosen by the exiled leaders as Prime Minister of the Provisional Government organized in Shanghai in April, 1919, had been a Ph.D. student at Princeton during Wilson's presidency there.) Neither Rhee nor his fellows could have realized how much Wilson was a prisoner of the harsh realities of European power-politics and his own preconceptions. Yet they and the March 1st protesters had made a noble, shining statement, which Koreans would remember for a long time through the night that Japan had imposed on their country.

NOTES

[1] As noted in *The History of Korea* by Sohn Pow-key, Kim Chol-Choon, and Hong Yi-Sup (Seoul: UNESCO, 1970).

[2] In 1866 a Korean mob burned an American steamer, the *General Sherman,* which had run aground near Pyongyang and killed its crew. Not long afterward, nine French Catholic missionaries were arrested and beheaded. To avenge these incidents French and American squadrons landed marines and captured some fortifications on Kanghwa island, in two separate actions; but they met stiff resistance and retreated.

[3] For this incident, as well as the general background of the reform movement, I am indebted to Li Ki-baik's *A New History of Korea* (Harvard: 1984).

III

WARS AND OCCUPATIONS

"When two whales fight, the shrimp's bones are broken" is an of-
ten-quoted Korean proverb. Its applicability is not much of a mys-
tery. For more than a thousand years, as we have noted, the Korean
nation was alternately invaded and protected by its two powerful
neighbors. Both China and Japan were territorialists. If the Chinese were generally content with holding Korea as a vassal, the
Japanese, once their early pirate days were over, were bent on outright acquisition. (Munmu, Silla's seventh-century king, very pre-
sciently had his ashes buried on an offshore island so he could
guard the eastern sea approaches against Japanese invaders.) Korea
suffered badly from both its neighbors' ambitions. Having begun
the millennial period as a vassal of China, it came into the twentieth century as a colony of Japan.

From the early 1930s, when Korea was used as the base for
Japan's incursions into China and Manchuria, until the conclusion
of the Korean War armistice in 1953, the country lived through an
almost continuous state of war. Already serving both as the rice
granary for Japan and the industrial-communications nexus for
Japanese expansion in Manchuria and China, Korea was turned
into a manpower reservoir as well by the wartime army–dominated
government. Korean men were drafted, first as military civilian
(*gunzoku*) laborers to work in Japanese possessions throughout
East Asia, then in the army itself. Some 4 million Koreans were

thus uprooted from their homes and sent to work as pick-and-shovel men, essentially, on Japanese bases throughout the area. Tens of thousands of Korean women were drafted to serve as "comfort girls" in Japanese military brothels, part of the infamous Comfort Bureau *(ianbu)*. Hundreds of thousands of Korean people were killed or reported missing during the Pacific War.

In 1945 the Korean people, exhausted but exhilarated, flocked to the streets of their cities expecting liberation and a restored nationhood. Instead they found themselves, once more, in the middle of a collision between two whales: the Soviet Union and the United States. This time, however, the old rules of aggrandizement and conquest had changed. The Soviet Union, restored to the role Russia had lost in 1905, was interested in ideology more than territory. Its policy aim was to engender a brotherly (little brotherly, that is) Communist state in Korea—a vassal state in the old Chinese manner. The American objective, on its face simpler, was to bring democracy to the Koreans, while at the same time making sure that their new government would be anti-Communist. Hence there was ideology here as well, since the winds of the Cold War had begun to blow. To attain the Americans' dual objective, however, would prove exceedingly difficult.

A U.S.-Soviet joint commission was convened in March, 1946, to prepare for the eventual unification of Korea. After talks had broken down, a United Nations commission offered a plan for Korea-wide elections. Meanwhile the lines began to harden on both sides. After a brief but bloody period of shootings, rape, and robbery, the Soviet troops returned to their barracks in the North, to be replaced by a locally raised Communist soldiery. (This included both Soviet-trained partisans and several divisions of Koreans who had been released from Mao Zedong's Chinese Communist armies.) Kim Il Sung, a Soviet-trained survivor of anti-Japanese partisan warfare in Manchuria, was brought back to Pyongyang from Siberia late in 1945 to become the paramount North Korean leader. Korean Communists and their collaborators began purging landowners and other "reactionary" elements in their territory.

Syngman Rhee, who emerged as the top Korean leader in the South, was as much of a hard liner in his way as Kim Il Sung. The Americans were ill-prepared for the occupation of Korea, having lavished most of their planning on Douglas MacArthur's occupation of Japan. When Soviet troops began pouring south into Korea in the closing days of the war, alarmed Washington strategists, fearful that the Russians would overrun the entire peninsula, quickly proposed that the country be divided into two occupation zones north and south of the 38th parallel. The Russians accepted, halting their advance at the new demarcation line. Despite a variety of personality clashes—a seventy-year-old patriot returned from exile is not one for ready compromise—Rhee managed to secure increasing American support after he was flown back to Korea in October 1945. He and other right-wing leaders urged the American military government to conduct in the South a purge of Communists, real or fancied, that was almost a mirror image of Kim's attack on right-wing elements in the North.

Violence was inevitable, despite the efforts of the U.S. military occupation to prevent it. South Korea was ultimately faced with full-scale guerilla warfare. Between the end of World War II and the outbreak of the Korean War in 1950 it is estimated that 100,000 Koreans lost their lives.

These losses of course pale before the wholesale killing and destruction of the war that followed. In the three years of warfare that ended in July, 1953, some 230,000 South Korean soldiers were killed, along with 300,000 from the North. The death toll of Korean civilians on both sides of the parallel came close to 1 million. Add to these numbers 37,000 Allied dead, 34,000 of them Americans, and at least 180,000 Chinese soldiers—some estimates go as high as 500,000. Some 3.7 million people were left homeless in the South alone and more than 100,000 children orphaned. The dislocation of Korean families was tremendous. Almost half a million people managed to flee from North to South during the fighting, while an estimated 300,000 went from South to North, either on their own or forcibly drafted into the North Korean forces.

Viewed in their totality the losses sustained by the Korean people over the fifteen years ending in 1953 were staggering. The hardships and dislocations of those years were almost a continuum, a nightmare that never ended. Even to recount or summarize the history of the Korean War, therefore, we must start in August 1945. And what happened at that time also had its roots deep within

Japan's colonial occupation of Korea, which the rest of the world largely ignored.

After the bloody suppression of the March 1st demonstrations in 1919, Korean nationalist leaders met in Shanghai and elected Syngman Rhee president of a provisional government. For the next quarter-century Rhee and his colleagues continued to work for their country's independence, albeit in different ways. Rhee had been in exile since 1904; before that time, as an early member of the Independence Club, he had been jailed by King Kojong's police. A veteran propagandist by the twenties, he worked the diplomatic circuit, delivering proindependence manifestoes at the League of Nations headquarters in Geneva, talking to congressmen in Washington, and keeping up a steady stream of books and articles attacking the Japanese occupation. Kim Ku, another leader of the provisional government, remained in China; he and his group worked with the Chinese nationalists, organizing military formations and keeping up contacts with underground elements in Korea. Like Rhee he was a rightist.

An active leftist resistance—Communist and non-Communist—also continued operations. Supported by the Soviet Union and China, partisan units staged guerilla raids on Japanese positions in Manchuria and along the Korean border. Many Koreans fled across the border to the Russian Maritime Provinces, from where they would return in 1945. (During World War II Stalin, always suspicious of non-Russian ethnic groups, moved several hundred thousand of these Soviet citizens to Central Asia.) Others moved to China, where they made common cause with Communist guerillas there.

The various resistance groups, right and left, were united only by their hatred of the Japanese. By the late 1930s they were hopelessly fragmented, warring among themselves as much as against the Japanese occupation. Meanwhile the Japanese had revised their original repressive policy. From 1920 to 1931 a new governor-general, Admiral Saito Makoto, began an era of "cultural politics" *(bunka seiji)*, a soft-sell approach that allowed Koreans to develop their own cultural and educational institutions as long as they did not directly oppose Japanese rule. Even after the Japanese military hard-liners returned to power, their huge military-industrial buildup in Korea inevitably gave jobs and business opportunities to Koreans as well as Japanese. And the Japanese increasingly relied on Korean police to do the occupation's dirty work. In this way they developed a constituency of sorts among Koreans, particularly the more affluent. Against this, however, ran a wave of popular resentment at the roughshod rule of the Japanese military. By 1945 the situation within Korea could only be described as explosive.

Into it marched Lieutenant General John R. Hodge and his Twenty-fourth Army Corps, fresh from victory in the battle of Okinawa. Hodge's orders were to take the Japanese surrender of Japanese armed forces in Korea and thereafter to "establish orderly government in Korea below the 38th parallel." He and his troops were ill equipped for the task. Hodge had few detailed directives and only the sketchiest Washington staff planning available to him. His own staff had little knowledge of the country and included only a few Korean linguists.

Predictably, Hodge made mistakes. At first he relied on the Japanese-led police to keep order; at one point they fired on crowds turning out to welcome the Americans. Later he ignored various political groups who had combined to set up a provisional "people's" government, and he did little to deal with a storm of complaints from newly formed labor groups. Although he hoped to put a moderate democratic coalition in place, Hodge seemed unable to head off the rise of Rhee, Kim Ku, and other rightists to power. Rhee, who had taken charge of the Society for Rapid Realization of Independence shortly after his return, attracted popular support because of his reputation as a patriot, and he ruthlessly used police power to consolidate his position.

In the North, by contrast, Kim Il Sung and his Soviet backers enacted a sweeping land reform and dealt harshly with landowners, businesspeople, and others they denounced as collaborationists with the Japanese. All industry was nationalized, on the Stalinist model. As in eastern Europe, Soviet representatives themselves could assume an attitude of lofty neutrality, while the organizing work was done for them by Korean Communist cadres recently imported from China and the Soviet Union. They were quick to organize the women's committees, youth committees, and other normal appurtenances of classic "people's government" takeovers. It took awhile for farmers and workers to realize that they were all laboring for an increasingly totalitarian government. Certainly, Kim's decrees were all too effective in dividing Koreans into hostile groupings of extreme right and extreme left.

At the Moscow summit meeting in December, 1945, the United States, Great Britain, and the Soviet Union had agreed to put Korea under a four-power trusteeship for five years; then independence would be granted. After direct U.S.-Soviet negotiations for a unified country had broken down, the United Nations in 1947 tried to resolve the issue by nationwide elections. The North rejected this plan, in the process turning the long-planned North-South conference into little more than a propaganda forum. With the country effectively polarized, U.N.-supervised elections were held in 1948 in the South alone.

On August 15, 1948, the Republic of Korea was officially called into existence, with Rhee elected as its first president. The North followed suit with its own form of elections, in which no U.N. supervision was permitted. On September 9, 1948, the Supreme People's Assembly in Pyongyang declared the establishment of the Democratic People's Republic of Korea, with Kim Il Sung as its first prime minister. By the middle of the following year both Soviet and American garrisons were withdrawn, although they left behind sizable advisory missions to train the armies of North and South. The object of the Americans in this was defensive, as indeed was the Russians'. (Having made his territorial gains in eastern Europe, Stalin was content to hold in East Asia.) But given the expressed desires of Kim and Rhee to unify the country—each on his own terms—war seemed a foregone conclusion.

In the South, Rhee's dictatorial ways, plus his dependence on police and unruly right-wing "youth" organizations, had alienated a good proportion of the population. A faltering economy did not help. Partition had given most of Korea's natural resources to the North; the power grid lines that stopped at the parallel symbolized the South's plight. Largely agricultural, the South had little industry. It was for the time almost totally dependent on U.S. aid. Discontent blossomed, therefore, for a complex of political and economic reasons.

In 1948, led by young leftist officers, two regiments of the new Republic of Korea army mutinied at the southwestern city of Yosu; and more trouble started at Cheju Island. The incidents developed into large-scale guerilla warfare throughout South Korea, which loyal ROK troops suppressed only after an intensive, bloody struggle. Encouraged by the dissidents' early successes, Pyongyang organized the Democratic Front for the Unification of the Fatherland in 1949 and sent thousands of Kim Il Sung partisans to infiltrate the South. But they were ultimately contained and largely destroyed by Rhee's security forces. Meanwhile both sides stepped up their forays across the demarcation line, to the point of almost continuous border warfare.

During visits to Moscow in 1949 and early 1950, Kim Il Sung finally persuaded Josef Stalin to give him the wherewithal for a full-dress invasion of South Korea. Thus he was able to march across the 38th parallel with 250 T-34 tanks and 180 Soviet airplanes. His 150,000-man army, its new recruits stiffened by Korean veterans of the Soviet and Chinese armies, was assured of continuing Soviet support for its weaponry, which included 122mm heavy guns.

Although the ROK army's numerical strength was roughly equal to the North's, it had no air power, no tanks, and a relatively small quantity of 105mm artillery. Justly worried about Rhee's constant threats to invade the North, his American suppliers deliberately withheld obviously "offensive" weapons from his arsenal. In the first few days of fighting, this lack would prove critical.

At 4:00 A.M. on June 25, 1950, North Korean tanks and infantry drove southward in two columns. They achieved almost total surprise. In particular their monopoly of air and armor had a disastrous effect on the South Korean troops. Some ROK units, notably Paik Sun Yup's First Division, put up a stubborn resistance. But the premature destruction of the Han River bridge by ROK engineers cut off communications and supply lines to the defenders north of the Han, turning an orderly fallback into a rout. By June 28, when President Harry Truman ordered U.S. forces to retaliate, Seoul was already overrun. (For my eyewitness account of the war's beginning, see Appendix, "The North Korean Invasion: June 1950".)

The first U.S. Army formation to deploy in the Korean war was a reinforced battalion of the Twenty-fourth Division, Task Force Smith (named after its commander), which took up positions at Osan, south of Seoul, on July 5. The battalion was quickly overrun but in a sense achieved its objective. The very injection of an American formation on the battlefield prompted the North Koreans to hold up and regroup. It doubtless did not occur to them that the United States would commit troops in such small numbers. Since that time, when I served as a correspondent in Korea, I have always believed that this hesitation cost the North Koreans the chance to continue southward as far as Pusan and the sea.

As it happened, the U.S. occupation forces in Japan were in a deplorable state of readiness for combat; training troops was not one of MacArthur's strong points, as the Eighth Army commander once pointed out.[1] By mobilizing units elsewhere, and only after a supreme logistical effort, the Americans were able to have the greater part of three divisions and a marine brigade in place along the Naktong River line between Taegu and Pusan; they were joined by ROK units, regrouped and reequipped since the North Korean breakthrough. The infantry line held, and the supply lines strengthened, while now overwhelming U.S. airpower interfered with North Korean supply lines in turn. Thanks to the Security Council's early condemnation of the invasion, the U.S. and ROK war effort had become a U.N. war effort. British, French, Dutch, Turkish, and other national detachments were added to the Eighth Army strength.

On September 15, 1950, U.S. Army and Marine units landed at Inchon, Seoul's port, far north of the Naktong battle lines. Attacking through Inchon they recaptured Seoul, catching the bulk of Kim Il Sung's army in a pincer between them and the U.N. and ROK forces, which now broke out of the Naktong-Pusan perimeter. On September 28 MacArthur and Syngman Rhee made their formal entry into the badly battered capital, while their armies pursued the enemy northward.

At this point the war could have ended, with the lines restored at the 38th parallel or, more probably, a new boundary set to the north, just south of Pyongyang, across the still-narrow waist of the peninsula. The Democratic People's Republic of Korea would have survived as a weak, truncated buffer state. Neither Rhee nor Mac-

Arthur, however, had any intention of stopping. "The Kremlin leaders," Rhee summarized, "have destroyed the thirty-eighth parallel by their invasion. There is no reason why the U.S. and the U.N. should observe it any longer."[2] For his part MacArthur wanted to unify the Korean peninsula as totally as he had recaptured the Philippines in the last year of World War II. In a memorable meeting with President Truman at Wake Island, on October 15, MacArthur assured him that the war would soon be over. A few weeks before, he had been told by Washington that the U.N. army could move north of the 38th parallel as long as Chinese or Soviet troops did not enter North Korea or show signs of so doing.

The Soviets obliged MacArthur and Rhee by staying out of Korea. The Chinese did not. Barely two weeks before MacArthur assured Truman of the war's imminent end, Mao Zedong had made the decision to prolong it. Suspicious that the Americans now planned an invasion of China, the Chinese Communist leadership, after some discussion, had backed Mao's decision to stop the Americans before they went any further.[3] By mid-October advance parties of several Chinese armies had moved across the Yalu River boundary. On October 26 ROK units, advancing to the border, were hit by Chinese spearheads. By early November, one U.S. First Cavalry Division unit had been virtually annihilated in a Chinese "human wave" assault and other scattered U.N. units were under attack. MacArthur's headquarters in Tokyo still refused to admit there was any serious Chinese intervention so that by late November several U.S. divisions were fighting for survival. By January the Communists were back in Seoul, with the U.N. forces in full retreat.

The disaster was due to MacArthur's arrogant refusal to accept the evidence of Chinese intervention, despite a long record of intelligence to the contrary. This strategic error was compounded by his disastrous mistake in splitting the U.N. command between the Eighth Army and Tenth Corps, which reported directly to Tokyo. (It was commanded by MacArthur's former chief of staff.) As General Matthew B. Ridgeway later wrote, the example of "Custer at the Little Big Horn" constantly came to mind.[4] The supreme commander just refused to believe that the Sioux, so to speak, were out there—in the case of the Chinese, some 300,000 of them, disciplined and well led.

Ridgeway, then a lieutenant general, was put in command of the U.N. forces shortly afterward. Under his strong and skillful leadership, the Eighth Army regrouped and headed north once more, this time driving Marshal Peng De Huai's armies back. Seoul was recaptured in March. The following month U.N. lines were stabilized somewhat north of the 38th parallel. On July 10, 1951, armistice talks began at Panmunjom.

For two years thereafter fighting continued. It often escalated from positional warfare to full-dress battles, principally because Mao Zedong, in the face of increasing U.S. tactical superiority, continued to feel that somehow Peng De Huai's dogged infantry could achieve a spectacular breakthrough. His belief in his own intuition—oddly like MacArthur's—would soon be disastrously confirmed by the Great Leap Forward and other disasters in China.

Belatedly MacArthur was removed from his command, because of his vocal belief that the war should be fought through and enlarged, if necessary, by bombing Chinese cities. Truman's successor, Dwight D. Eisenhower, had already promised the American people to bring hostilities to a close. So he did, in the end, despite the Communists' continuing use of the truce talks (and the fighting) for propaganda purposes. As Ridgeway wrote later in his book: "We could have pushed right on to the Yalu in the spring of 1951, had we been ordered to do so. The price for such a drive would have been far too high for what we would have gained, however." To a democracy, lives are precious—or should be.

From the American point of view Korea, unlike Vietnam, was a war that had to be fought. However much provocation revisionist historians may claim for the North Koreans, the aggression was Kim Il Sung's. Stalin and Mao (whom Stalin consulted) had sanctioned it. Had the aggression succeeded, the consequences for Japan and Taiwan alone would have been severe, not to mention the extinction of the Republic of Korea. Considering the Cold War climate of that time, Hong Kong, Singapore, and the Southeast Asian countries would doubtless have been affected. Aftershocks would have been felt in Europe as well, for the international political balance there was precarious. Here, long before Vietnam, was a domino theory which might well have proved correct.

The effect of the war on Korea itself went beyond the deaths and separations, the hardships and destruction. Two generations of Koreans were directly scarred by it. Moderates and middle-of-the-roaders—the reasonable and temperate people—were put at risk. In the North Kim Il Sung, bailed out of disaster by his Chinese and Soviet comrades, was able to consolidate his power after the war's end. His intraparty foes proved convenient scapegoats for his military reverses. While maintaining his balancing act between his two fraternal supporters, he froze wartime hostilities into a permanent state of mind, which he riveted on his servile population. Nowhere in the Communist world was there such an inflexible hatred of "the enemy." For Kim the war never stopped. For thirty-five years—until the worldwide Communist collapses of the late eighties and the concurrent success of Roh Tae Woo's "northern politics"—he kept up a program of assassinations, spying, and tunnel building, and a variety of public atrocities as part of his continuing war.

The excesses of Kim's police state in the North offered a constant excuse for dictatorial rule in the South. Syngman Rhee proved as ruthless as Kim Il Sung in eliminating political opposition by fair means or foul. Locking up recalcitrant legislators or assassinating political opponents all seemed to be fair game.[5] The people of the Republic of Korea, the wartime experience still etched on their souls, grew tolerant of authoritarian rule. For one thing the acceptance of the central government's authority as the natural order of things was part of the Confucian tradition, deeply engrained in that country. As the historian Kim Dong Gil once noted:

> "When Japan was a feudal society, the Japanese enjoyed some advantages of decentralization. Leaders developed in local areas. There, as in medieval Europe, feudalism educated people, at least to the meaning of contracts. By contrast Korea has always been a centralized country. The king alone was able to do something for the people. No really great leaders were able to emerge."[6]

A sense of helplessness before authority had of course intensified during the long Japanese occupation. It was further deepened by the rigors of the war, where civilians seemed little more than the pawns of the military, their only protection against total disaster. Under Rhee and, later, under Park Chung Hee the mind-set of a garrison state was nurtured and preserved. For many, in the early stages of Korea's industrialization, the threat from the North was enough to justify the long hours, the low salaries, the poor living conditions. After all, since the war things *were* better. In a way the memory of past disasters helped fuel the prosperity of the future.

Yet a reaction was developing against this kind of public resignation. Pent-up anger and frustration would erupt in violent demonstrations, the first of which occurred in 1960, as ordinary people made their protest against the abuses of the authority over them. These happened over a long period. Most of them were repressed by force, often with great cruelty. But over the years the protests would grow more widespread, and more broadly based, before they culminated in success in 1987.

NOTES

[1] In a long conversation with me, during a series of interviews in July, 1950, General Walton Walker expressed the strongest criticism of the poor fighting condition of the command he had inherited.

[2] The statement was made during an interview I had with Rhee in July.

[3] Recent researches and publications by Chinese and American historians have undermined the view, once widely held, that the Chinese intervened in the war only because ROK and U.S. forces advanced too close to the Chinese-Korean border. The article "China's Changing Aims During the Korean War" by Jian Chen in *The Journal of American East Asian Relations* (Spring; 1992) summarizes recent findings in this matter.

[4] Ridgeway's short book *The Korean War* (New York: Doubleday, 1967) remains the most concise and best history of that conflict.

[5] In April, 1992, the newspaper *Dong-A Ilbo* revealed information that Rhee's old sparring partner, Kim Ku, had been assassinated in 1949 on the secret order of highly placed military officers close to the government at that time.

[6] From an interview with the author in 1990.

IV

THE BRIEF APRIL REVOLUTION

An ironic by-product of the North Korean invasion in 1950 was the rescue of Syngman Rhee's increasingly corrupt government from almost certain overthrow. Other Korean political and business leaders, notably those in the new Democratic Party, had grown increasingly angry at Rhee's high-handed ways of governance and his dependence on the police, who were still suspect for their collaboration with the Japanese. While originally Rhee had enjoyed great prestige as a revered national leader, his behavior in power squandered this asset. Increasingly obvious money politics and the vendettas and extortions of various right-wing "youth groups" cost his regime most of its popular support. Amid the hardship and devastation of the war years, however, the president once again began to look like the George Washington of his country—not surprisingly, one of Rhee's own favorite phrases. (See Appendix, "Syngman Rhee: The Free Man's Burden.")

He was an uncompromising anti-Communist. Almost to the last he had opposed accepting the armistice agreement, hoping at whatever cost to continue the war. ("The Cold War and all that," he had said, "are a waste of time. Finally, force is the only argument.") This attitude endeared him to many right-wing Americans, particularly at a time when the United States was being shaken by the mindless "anti-Communism" of the McCarthy era. As a seasoned lobbyist, Rhee was able for some years after the war to manipulate American public (and congressional) opinion so as to ensure a continuing stream of U.S. aid.

The aid was an absolute necessity. Rebuilding South Korea's industries was a staggering task in itself; and there had been relatively little industry to begin with. Two-thirds of the population was engaged in agriculture, but much of this labor force was unnecessary—the miracle rice and other productivity advances far in the future. As a result the country underwent a mass migration from rural areas to the cities, which were ill-prepared to receive more people. Capital was scarce and managerial talent very limited. The inflation rate surged. And the meager increases in GNP were barely able to keep up with an annual 3 percent population growth.

Economic policy was made on a hit-or-miss basis. It was largely a matter of import substitution, with high protectionist barriers to protect fledgling domestic industries. A great deal of the U.S. aid—which until the 1960s came mostly in grants, not loans—had to be spent on importing consumer products, as well as the rehabilitation of the country's damaged infrastructure. Out of the $4.3 billion in U.S. aid given between 1953 and 1961, much was siphoned off in the form of kickbacks—that is to say, Korean firms favored with U.S. aid contracts would be forced to make heavy contributions to Rhee's Liberal party.

This was part of a general climate of fraud, which grew sultrier with the passage of time. As political corruption spread through the government, Rhee's administration tightened its police control. The Home Ministry instituted a system of neighborhood associations *(kungminban)*, which all households had to join, on the pretext of ferreting out Communists (real or fancied). They were all too reminiscent of the Japanese *tonarigumi* (neighborhood groups) organized by the prewar militarists to mobilize support for government policies and spy on dissidents in the process.

Rhee himself, eighty-five years old in 1960, was growing ever more remote, with his work done through an almost impenetrable "human curtain" of aides.[1] Yet in 1960 he ran again for a fourth term. He won the March election unopposed, his Democratic party opponent having died during the campaign. But his henchman and presumed successor, Yi Ki-bung, defeated the incumbent vice president, Chang Myon, in the separate vice-presidential election only after the most flagrant vote rigging and police interference at the polls.

Protest demonstrations broke out in almost all of Korea's cities. They escalated after the body of a sixteen-year-old student was washed up at the southern port city of Masan on April 11. Killed during a demonstration, he had apparently been thrown into the bay there by police, afraid that this incident of brutality would be discovered. Enraged, Masan's students began three days of violent antigovernment rioting. On April 19 a student protest march on Kyongmudae, the presidential mansion in Seoul, was stopped by police bullets. More than one hundred students were killed, almost one thousand wounded. Several days later some three hundred university professors, meeting in front of the National Assembly, called for the government's resignation. With a storm of press and public anger rising, plus an official demand from Washington for his resignation, Rhee had to go.

The army refused to intervene to save him. As the then chief of staff, General Song Yo-chan, recalled later: "Personally, I respect Dr. Rhee. But history has turned him down, has scorned him and lost its trust in him. I, who saw the march of events, am sick inside about it."[2]

Shortly afterward Rhee resigned the presidency and returned to the exile he had left so hopefully in 1945. A true patriot in his way, he had outlived his time. To complete his personal tragedy, his vice president–elect, Yi Ki-bung, committed suicide with his family (including Yi's eldest son, whom Rhee himself had formally adopted).

In July, after an interim government had drafted a new constitution, elections were held again. The opposition Democratic party swept the polls, electing Yun Po-sun, the former mayor of Seoul, president. With the Assembly's consent, he appointed Chang Myon prime minister, the new constitution having provided for a parliamentary form of government. On a note of congratulations from the newly liberated national press, the country relaxed in a mood of democratic euphoria. It was to last less than a year.

It might be well here to examine three major forces that had emerged from the April revolution and that would continue to play leading if sometimes contradictory roles in Korea's evolution towards democracy: the students, the Christian churchpeople, and the ROK army.

Since the days of the fifteenth- and sixteenth-century Confucian academies Korean students had the sense of belonging to a tiny elite, with their own responsibility to criticize, if not to change, society. With the beginnings of mass education, the sense of student privilege widened. The March 1, 1919 movement enlisted thousands of students, male and female, from the high schools, private academies, and the beginnings of colleges that Korea then possessed. Throughout the Japanese occupation students continued to cherish the idea of Korean independence, for which many suffered. (Interestingly, not a few Korean students learned their revolutionary ideology from left-wing Japanese teachers.) After independence came a great national emphasis on education. By 1959 the number of university students, as we have noted, had reached 70,000; and within the next few years exceeded 100,000. By the end of 1960 the country's basic literacy rate, kept down under the Japanese occupation, had jumped from 22 percent to 72 percent. (By the 1990s it had reached virtually 100 percent.)

Thanks to the war years the students of 1960 were even more politically conscious than might have been expected. They were also worried about the dim prospects of finding jobs in a rudderless economy dependent on foreign aid and under a political regime appallingly scarred by corruption and cronyism. Borne on the high tide of new nationalism, they expected far more from their country than they were getting. They saw themselves as the vanguard of reform; and their society tended to support that view.

The success of the April Revolution—and, equally, the collapse of democracy that followed—established a tradition of student activism that each succeeding generation wished to emulate and expand upon. In succeeding demonstrations and protest movements over the years, it was almost always student activists who started things. Often they went too far. But in general the greater the grievance, the more students there were to demand redress. While similar student movements existed in China and Japan, in Korea they tended to be more focused, better coordinated, and far more violent.

The impact of Christianity in modern Korea is unique. Although the history of Christian belief in China and Japan is far older—in the sixteenth and seventeenth centuries the Jesuits made several hundred thousand converts in each country—in neither country has Christianity played a significant modern *religious* role, despite strong influences in education and modernization. In Korea Christian thinking has entered the national bloodstream. Here the strongest influence has been Protestant and American. It is recent. The first Protestant missionary, the Rev. Dr. Horace Allen, arrived in 1884. A medical missionary, he was called to attend to a Korean prince badly wounded in the attempted Kapsin Coup. He cured the prince, with gratifying consequences for his mission.

Others followed him, mainly Presbyterians. They established schools, hospitals, and, ultimately, Yonsei and Ewha universities. It was during the Japanese colonial period that the Americans began to make converts in the mass. The Japanese were nervous about interfering with mission activities, because of their overseas connections. So it fell out that to be a Christian was one way not only to get a non-Japanese international education but to demonstrate some independence from the Japanese rulers.

Beyond this there was something that appealed strongly to Koreans about the individual self-reliance and commitment so prominent in traditional American Protestantism. Soon Christians were playing a prominent role in the independence movement. The importance given by the Christian missionaries to women's education, also, was in large part responsible for the many female student activists in the independence movement—far more numerous than in Japan and China.

The once-flourishing Catholic community in Korea, first established by seventeenth-century converts from China, was almost wiped out in the Taewongun's persecutions during the late 1900s. But Catholic converts began to increase in modern times, most spectacularly in the 1950s and 1960s. During the Japanese colonial period Catholics tended to stay out of politics, adopting a neutral stance. But over the past quarter century this attitude has changed. Contemporary Catholics, led by Stephen Cardinal Kim, have played leading roles in the democracy movement. And Myongdong Cathedral in Seoul has come to be a stronghold for protestors and other dissidents.

There are now more than 9 million Protestants and 2 million Catholics in the Republic of Korea, something over 20 percent of the population. But they probably make up a far larger percentage of the actual religious believers in the country. Conservative in doctrinal matters, most Korean Christians are pious churchgoers, generally active in church organizations. Sunday morning in Korea is a busy time. One of the sights that most surprises first-time visitors to Seoul is the proliferation of crosses and church steeples—ranging from very grand churches to back-alley chapels—that dominate the skyline. Inspired by their faith to put great stress on democracy, equality, and human rights, Christian activists have been in the forefront of almost all the protest movements against authoritarian government. They have also played leading roles in labor unions and rural improvement groups. Their emphasis on individual responsibility has done much to break down the traditional Korean Confucian subservience to authority; although in matters such as family solidarity and education-consciousness they tend to be as Confucian as their neighbors.

The military has been the third major factor in Korea's modernization, as well as its ascent to democracy. It has played both a negative and a positive role. The negative side is obvious; enough has been mentioned already about the authoritarian side of Park Chung Hee and, after him, Chun Doo Hwan to use the term "military rule" as an easy pejorative. But there are also positive factors, which bear some explanation. A little history here would be useful.

The first officer corps of the ROK Army were a scratch team. Some seventy-odd among them had graduated from Japanese military academies, either in Tokyo or Manchuria. They had received a fairly sound professional education, with the strengths and limitations of the old Imperial Army. Another larger group had served with the Chinese nationalists. Although a few of these had attended military school in China, their knowledge of tactics and military technology was to say the least spotty. Some had been noncommissioned officers under the Japanese or served with the police. The American military advisors who had to pass on their qualifications, as they tried to build a Korean army in the late forties, did not have the luxury of much choice. Yet out of this group came the generals and colonels who had to take the army into battle after the North Korean invasion.

Many simply could not pass muster professionally. Their deficiencies had to be discovered under the pressures of battle. Unfortunately, given the cronyism endemic to Syngman Rhee's regime, selections of top commanders were too often made on the basis of political loyalty or malleability rather than competence. Meanwhile, as the war lengthened, thousands of noncommissioned officers, draftees, and new recruits were swept up into the armed services. Many became competent officers, learning their new trade the hard way. The more competent they grew, the less respect they had for the political appointees among their generals.

The gulf between professionals and political appointees widened after the U.S. Army command set up a proper system of military education, under the guidance of General James Van Fleet, then Eighth Army commander. The Korean Military Academy, a four-year institution modeled on West Point, set up shop on January 1, 1952. Its first class was graduated in 1955. Roh Tae Woo and Chun Doo Hwan were among its members. They and the classes who followed them received the same kind of professional engineering-oriented education as their contemporaries at West Point. As organization improved, university graduates taken into the army were given the chance to gain commissions in the reserve. Thanks to conscription, most of the country's manpower passed through the army or the other services to do their compulsory time. Increasingly, staff officers were sent to advanced schools in the United States.

Under pressure the new officers in this army were put in the vanguard of their country's modernization—the first to learn technology and apply it, albeit constricted by military usage. President Roh Tae Woo himself, on being asked about the role of the military in Korea[3], stated the situation quite well. "It's true," he said, "that people think of the military as being very regimented, apart from the mainstream of civilian life. That's not necessarily so in Korea's case. When our Military Academy was founded, our textbooks were translations of West Point textbooks. At first many of the faculty were American officers. Our cadets were one of the first groups in Korea to study Western institutions this thoroughly. Indeed, it was the army which led the modernization of the civilian sector in this country. Outsiders may think of military organizations as intrinsically nondemocratic in nature, but we received many democratic elements as part of our education."

As events showed, military officers proved an invaluable human resource in the headlong industrialization of Korea, which began in the early 1960s. And it would be wrong to dismiss them all as would-be dictators. Nonetheless the professionals among them, while on the whole competent, were impatient with the give-and-take of parliamentarians and politicians. If modernization had a high priority with them, democracy generally ran a poor second. Not every general had Roh Tae Woo's practical reasoning packed in his knapsack. As it happened, the first showdown between the military and civilian politicians came rather swiftly, in the new administration of Chang Myon.

Chang, the newly elected prime minister, had excellent credentials on the democracy side of the ledger. An American-educated Catholic, he was a teacher by profession, who had spent some years as principal of Tongsong High School in Seoul. Later he had served as first Korean ambassador to the United States. Although possessed of great integrity, he lacked the toughness of a decision maker; and neither his party nor the public gave him much of a chance to become one.

On the one hand, he was pressured by student leaders and other activists, whose political naïveté ran as deep as their indignation, to make immediate plans for reunification with the North, disband the hated police, fire most of the Rhee political appointees, and eradicate the huge, half-visible edifice of business and bureaucratic corruption. Against this he had a law-and-order faction that wanted nothing so much as political stability. Not a very decisive man, Chang temporized and vacillated between the two extremes. He made one sweeping reform when he disbanded Rhee's hated police force. This not only led to immediate problems in public order but it appeared as a single act, not related to any plan or consistent policy.

Chang had come to power as the result of the revolution, that is, a loose coalition of students, urban intellectuals, and some politicians. All of them, along with many young officers in the military, were united in their opposition to the corrupt politics of the Rhee government. They demanded immediate and drastic punishment for the oligarchy of privilege that had grown up around Rhee. Yet not all the Rhee regime people were corrupt and inefficient. Many party leaders and bureaucrats argued that some continuity was necessary. They advocated a gradual changing of the guard, in effect. In addition some of Rhee's closest supporters remained in positions of considerable power. Should they be punished or placated?

Chang could never really decide, and in the end his desire to be fair to everyone resulted in his being thought weak by almost everyone. He committed the fatal error of a democratic politician—neglecting to build up a nucleus of parliamentary support in the new National Assembly while he had the chance. He was, as the political commentator Han Sung Joo, later summarized, "caught in the middle." Han wrote: "Chang's concessions were invariably too little and too late. . . . He would systematically alienate the political forces around him without making any new allies. Chang's failure to perceive his own role as a cultivator of power in the chaotic and uncertain days of the post-revolutionary period was also evident in areas outside of party politics as well as within it."[4]

Chang and Korea were soon to receive a lesson in the proper cultivation of power from another source. Park Chung Hee, then a major general in the ROK Army, was a leader of the young officers in the "Clean Up the Military" (*chonggun*) movement. Immediately after the 1960 revolution, backed by young reformist officers, he had demanded that the ROK Army chief of staff resign for complicity in the vote-rigging processes of the Rhee administration. His request was refused, and in the months that followed most of the old and corrupt military hierarchy continued in their jobs.

This was too much for the new Military Academy graduates— as we have suggested above, a very different breed. Apart from army politics, they were also disturbed by Chang's indecisive political course. On May 16, 1961, some 250 reformist officers, led by Lieutenant Colonel Kim Jong Pil, took over the army in a bloodless coup. Although the chief of staff, Lt. Gen. Chang To Yong, was their nominal leader, he acted under coercion. The real authority in the Supreme Council for National Reconstruction, as the junta called itself, came to be held by Park Chung Hee. He would remain the boss of the country, as dictator, president, and economic czar, for the next eighteen years.

NOTES

[1] His detached behavior at that time recalls the situation of Germany's similarly venerable President Paul von Hindenburg, the World War I hero of the Battle of Tannenburg, who on viewing thousands of Hitler's Nazi storm-troopers parading beneath his palace windows in 1933, was heard to mutter, "Ach, more Russian prisoners."

[2] As quoted in *Divided Korea* by Joungwon A. Kim (Cambridge: Harvard University Press, 1976).

[3] In an interview with the author in 1991.

[4] Han's excellent book, *The Failure of Democracy in South Korea* (Berkeley: University of California, 1974), from which the excerpts above were taken, treats the April Revolution and its aftermath in some detail.

V

AN ECONOMY IN ARMOR

"In May 1961, when I took over power as the leader of the revolutionary group, I honestly felt as if I had been given a pilfered household or a bankrupt firm to manage. Around me I could find little hope of encouragement. The outlook was bleak. But I had to rise above this pessimism to rehabilitate the household. I had to destroy, once and for all, the vicious circle of poverty and economic stagnation. Only by reforming the economic structure would we lay a foundation for decent living standards."

Park Chung Hee wrote these words ten years after the fact.[1] By that time he had been president of the Republic of Korea for almost eight years. The country was at the midpoint of the extraordinary surge that Park inspired and led; and the president was by no means bashful in discussing his exploits. The GNP had doubled, from 3,071 billion won in 1962 to 6,962 billion won in 1971.[2] Exports had soared from slightly over $60 million worth in 1962 — the year Park's first five-year plan started — to exceed $1 billion in 1970; and Park had declared a national holiday to mark the event. By 1971, exports were up to $1.4 billion. The annual growth rate for the post-1962 decade averaged 9.2 percent.

For all the PR bluster in government statements of that time, it is fair to say that without Park this growth era would never have happened. It took this dour military man, who combined elements of teacher, populist, and dictator, to power his country into an extraordinary economic revolution, albeit a revolution led from above. His ideas on management and growth—in some ways quite primitive, in others highly sophisticated—gave the so-called Miracle on the Han much of its special character.

At the time of the 1961 coup, the Korean economy was not in such hopeless shape as Park declared. With the help of heavy U.S. aid, things were gradually improving, despite government inefficiency and corruption. A substantial land reform had finally been achieved. This put an end to the demeaning (and notably uneconomical) tenant-farm system. The increased incentives for the farmers laid the groundwork for improved agricultural production. (At that point in history two-thirds of South Korea's population remained on the land.) But there was no real overarching economic policy, other than continued plans for import substitution. A combination of subsidy and protectionism helped a variety of light industries to develop—textiles, cement, sugar refineries, flour mills, and the like. But the small size of the domestic market and the country's constant need for raw materials were trapping the economy in what Walt W. Rostow has termed "a vicious circle of low economic growth, low income, low savings and low investments."

The first actions of Park's military government were punitive and predictable. Some two thousand military officers, most of them quite senior, were summarily retired. Mass arrests of politicians took place, although many were later released. Existing political parties were shut down and a tight press censorship instituted, with a new security organization, the infamous Korean Central Intelligence Agency, set up for internal policing. A national campaign began against fraud, corruption, prostitution, and "hooliganism." It understandably received considerable popular support. In general, the new "law-and-order" policy of the reformers, despite their antidemocratic behavior, found favor among a public disillusioned by the weak temporizing of Chang's Second Republic. One frequently heard the phrase, "We Koreans need a strong government." When presidential elections were finally held in 1963, Park and his new Democratic Republican party won them fairly, albeit by a narrow margin.

Well before he became president, however, Park began to move on economic policy. The son of a poor family in south central

Korea, he graduated from teacher's college in 1937. He taught briefly in a primary school before accepting an appointment to Japan's prewar Manchurian military academy. He emerged from the war an odd combination of militarist and Korean patriot. But he never lost his deep feeling of solidarity with the poor country people with whom he grew up. As Chung Ju Yung, the founder of the Hyundai conglomerate and one of Park's old friends, once told me: "He hated corruption—so much so that many people for a time thought him a Communist. But it was his concern for the poorness of this country that left him obsessed with economic growth."[3]

As early as 1961 Park and his colleagues announced an overall economic plan for the country. They were agreed that the Korean domestic market was too small for industry to grow quickly there. Japan's high-growth policy might succeed because of its large domestic market, which offered exporters a good chance to realize economies of scale. By contrast Korea needed some forced feeding. An export-oriented policy was the only way to earn money for capital improvement and a buildup of heavy industry—which was Park's goal from the first.

Not the least of the reasons for industrial development was the threat from North Korea. Blessed by abundant supplies of power and most of the peninsula's raw-material resources, as well as steel mills and other factories inherited from the prewar Japanese occupiers, Kim Il Sung's Communist satrapy in the North had begun its own variety of forced-draft industrialization. With considerable help from the Soviet Union, the North Korean People's Republic had some early success in building up a Stalinist-type military-industrial complex. Given Kim's past record of aggression, this posed a direct threat to the South, whose borders began less than forty miles north of Seoul.

By contrast South Korea suffered from an almost total lack of natural resources. Almost all of its energy and raw materials had to be imported. A basic premise of the new "outward-looking" development strategy, therefore, was a large volume of exports. In the long run this was the only way to earn money for the purchase of raw materials and capital goods necessary to develop Korean industry. Here began a bold, high-risk policy that constantly courted the danger of falling into a vicious circle. To earn money in international markets for the needed capital improvements at home, the government took to subsidizing industries—textiles, plywood, and footwear were among the first—where South Korea's low wage scales gave it a large comparative advantage. Such labor-intensive industries did not require vast amounts of capital to build up, and their gestation period is relatively short. Thus Park's first five-year plan (from 1962 to 1967) began with the development of light industry.

Even to prime the pump for this effort, however, the Koreans needed large amounts of foreign loans. Thanks to the recent war and the failures of past government policies, the rate of personal and corporate savings was low, particularly in contrast, for example, to the high savings rate in Japan or Taiwan. Since Park's government was nervous about too much foreign investment, international borrowing seemed the only way to go. The risks here were obvious, as many Third World countries were already demonstrating. But they had to be taken. In some ways Park's economic strategy was like a massive leveraged buyout, where a corporate management gambles that steadily increased production will permit the servicing and gradual repayment of the heavy debt it is piling up. And in Korea's case there were no assets to sell off— nothing but the skill and industry of its people.

One of the first acts of the military reformers was to revise the Bank of Korea law, giving the government virtually total power over the central bank. This enabled the government to use the central bank and, through its leverage of equity shares, the commercial banks to support the new industrial expansion, in whatever direction the government chose to lead it. Through the sixties and seventies, at least, the private financial sector was hardly to be reckoned with. The government, broadly speaking, set the interest rates, controlled the flow of money, and approved loans to suit its policies. This kind of control obviously played hob with the price mechanism. While bigger firms prospered, smaller companies were driven into bankruptcy. Inflationary pressures began to grow.

Undeterred by conventional economic danger signals, General Park ran his economy like a military operation. If the Japanese high-growth era was primarily the work of bureaucrats, South Korea's was the work of the military. The young officers of the ROK, however, as we have noted above, were a different breed from the impacted social and professional clique that the words "military government" normally connote. They and their men had been trained in a tough war of massed armies, in which they learned progressively more about high technology. Many had undergone additional professional training in the United States. They provided a pool of relatively skilled talent, well accustomed to systematic planning and staff work.

At the outset ex-officers made up about 70 percent of the new Korean bureaucracy. In turning from military to economic pursuits, they evoked comparisons not so much with modern Japanese or American bureaucrats as with the samurai-bureaucrats who had executed Japan's Meiji Restoration a century before. The parallel was not lost on the Japanese-trained Park, who compared the two modernizations in his writings. In fact, the word *yushin,* which he later used to describe his authoritarian rule of the seventies, uses the same Chinese characters as the Japanese word *ishin,* "restoration."

Besides the officers Park gathered about him a new group of technocrats—engineers and economists—to act as a kind of general staff for the national mobilization he had in mind. Many of them had been officers themselves. Some had come back from graduate work in the United States. Thanks to Korea's intense postwar education program there was no dearth of bright college graduates to work on economic development. Indeed, the lack of enough jobs for the swelling numbers of graduates in recent years had been a factor in the popular discontent with the government of Syngman Rhee.

Park formalized his economic general staff by setting up an Economic Planning Board. Unlike the similarly named Economic Planning Agency in Japan, however, Korea's Economic Planning Board was an executive organ, not merely an advisory one. Through this board—and at the monthly meetings of the Export Planning Committee, which he personally directed—Park presided over a national mobilization. His first five-year plan gave priority to developing energy industries, expanding the economic infrastructure, export promotion, and the development of science and technology. Sacrifices were demanded of the population. Under Park this was to be a producer's economy, not a consumer's. "Success of the first Five Year Plan," he later wrote, "could not easily bring about a self-reliant economy, but it was a landmark that the people had to pass on their long, painful journey toward this goal."

With direct American aid phasing out by the mid-sixties, Park realized the obvious possibilities of obtaining both technology and capital investment from Japan. In 1965, in the face of considerable popular outcry, Park normalized relations with Japan. He thus set the stage for a mass importation of capital, as well as the heavy industry and machine tools needed to expand Korea's own industrial infrastructure. Japanese loans and reparations money were heavily utilized. The vast new Korean steel facility at Pohang, for example, was built with heavy technological support from Japanese steelmakers, who by the mid-sixties were fast becoming the world's most efficient producers. It was symptomatic of the Japanese-Korean economic relationship—a devil's bargain for both sides, in a sense—that within a decade Japanese steelmakers would refuse further technological assistance. The Koreans had by then become serious international competitors in that industry, as well as in shipbuilding (discussed in this chapter), where Japan's postwar lead in development and marketing was equally threatened.

Park's dazzling export successes concealed some growing economic problems, however. Industrial development had taken badly needed capital away from agriculture. To help the farmers the *Saemaul Undong* (New Community Development Movement) was organized in 1971. Government workers organized rural self-help programs, taught improved farming methods, and in general worked to narrow the widening gap in living standards between city and country. A new two-tiered system of rice and barley prices protected farmers while keeping prices down for urban consumers. This resulted in dramatic production increases, made all the greater by the introduction of high-yield rice strains. (By the 1970s South Korea's rice output per acre was one of the world's highest.) Government subsidies, however, also meant government deficits; consequent borrowings from the central bank added to inflationary pressures.

Worse yet, the huge export gains in textiles, shoes, and other ﬁght industries began to level off. Other developing countries were now playing the same game, pushing exports of labor-intensive products. Korea's comparative advantage in these manufactures diminished accordingly. It was time for Park's board of strategy to switch the country's emphasis toward heavy and chemical industry. Capital-intensive and dependent on technology, this new level of development would drastically change both economy and demographics. (While agriculture's, forestry's, and fisheries' share of the nation's Gross Domestic Product dropped from almost 27 percent to 19 percent during the seventies, heavy industry's contribution rose from 22.5 percent to almost 30 percent within the same period.) It would also put a severe strain on Korea's financial resources, as well as the supply of trained manpower—engineering graduates in particular. Most significantly of all, the switch to heavy industrial growth, with its need for skilled layers of management, deep corporate pockets, and economies of scale, made inevitable the rise of that unique Korean corporate phenomenon, the diversified, export-driven conglomerate company called the chaebol.

The rise of the chaebol conglomerate was an inevitable by-product of Park Chung Hee's economy in armor. Park did not make the mistake of other Third World authoritarian governments by nationalizing his country's industry. He needed the skills of the entrepreneur, and he knew it. In the course of planning his "economic revolution" for Korea he had spent a great deal of time studying the postwar economic "miracles" of Japan and Germany. In each case government had assisted the private sector but had refrained from invading it. The same was true of the Meiji reformers a century before; they had moved quickly to privatize Japan's fledgling heavy industry, divesting government of its direct responsibility for making products and profits.

At the same time he wanted Korean entrepreneurs to fit into the grand economic plan he and his technocrats were devising. Any development plan for his country, he once wrote, ". . . must rely on the creativity and initiative of private industry. We hoped to encourage businessmen who could play leading roles in planning. On the other hand rigid restrictions were placed on business activities that ran against these efforts."

The solution to this free-enterprise paradox, it seemed, was to scout out Korean companies that looked like winners, assist them with preferential loans, tax breaks, import licenses, and other forms of government subsidy if need be, and integrate them into the government's grand plan for export earnings and industrial growth. As Hyundai's honorary chairman and founder, Chung Ju Yung told me, recalling those early days: "At that time we were short on capital and management. We had very little in the way of technology. Park pointed us toward international markets. He motivated businessmen to borrow money from the government, so we could turn a profit. Of course the government guaranteed the loans. If an entrepreneur failed—well, he might even be imprisoned. So everyone worked hard. Most of us did well."

Not surprisingly, the companies that responded most readily to Park's high-risk, high-growth exhortations were led by aggressive and supremely self-confident businessmen whose single-minded drive very much resembled Park's. Hyundai is a case in point. Chung Ju Yung like a striking Japanese counterpart, the electronics tycoon, Matsushita Konosuke, went to work with only a grammar school education. He started a small auto repair shop in the early forties. He founded the first Hyundai company—the Korean word means "modern age"—in 1947 to do construction work. Working first with the U.S. Army engineers on a variety of projects, his cement and construction companies dealt heavily in Korea's postwar reconstruction. Urged on by the government's export policy, Hyundai's engineers began bidding on overseas projects. In 1976, in what company chronicles recall as "the deal of the century," Hyundai landed a $931 million project to build a huge harbor complex for Saudi Arabia at the port of Jubail, thereby setting off a boom in overseas construction projects.

In 1967 Chung founded Hyundai Motors, which at first assembled Ford cars in Korea but in 1974 was turning out the first models of the Pony, Korea's prototypical homemade car. That same year the Korean government set in motion a long-range promotion plan for the automobile industry. By the early eighties, driven by more government aid and a ten-year program of heavy technological transfer (mostly from Mitsubishi in Japan) Hyundai Motors was exporting cars across the Pacific.

For Chung's shipbuilders the learning curve was even steeper. In 1973 Hyundai Shipbuilding started work on its first dry dock at Ulsan on Korea's southeastern coast, after a logical but notably unorthodox management decision by its founder. With his construction company on solid ground and branching out into the energy business, Chung had began to think of ships. What, after all, he reasoned, is a ship but a turbine powering a considerable amount of machinery inside a metal skin? If his companies could make the components, why should he not turn out the finished product?

While his construction people were building the shipyard at Mipo Bay, Chung picked out some forty engineers and naval architects and sent them to Scotland—the historic Clydeside district outside Glasgow, to learn the business. Before they had finished their half-year course, Chung had successfully bid on two 230,000 VLCCs (Very Large Crude Carriers) for a Greek shipping firm. When the Hyundai group returned to Ulsan, armed with a small library of charts and blueprints and the memories of Clydeside culture shock, they went to work immediately on the ships. The first one, the *Atlantic Baron,* went down the ways in August 1974, just four months after the shipyard itself was finished.

Within ten years Hyundai Heavy Industries had become the world's largest shipbuilder. The Korean industry as a whole accounted for 18 percent of the world's ship orders by 1986, which can be contrasted with Japan's front-running 37 percent (in 1974 the figures had been 2.8 percent and 38 percent, respectively). How did they do it? "Strong leadership, a good bit of engineering talent and a well-educated labor force," Hyundai's shipbuilding sales director Cho Tae Yearn explained. "Past experience was not necessary. We got it on the job."

Samsung, with $42 billion worldwide sales in 1991, is almost as large as Hyundai, whose totals for the same period topped $47 billion. The thirty-odd companies in the Samsung group include makers of consumer electronic products, pharmaceuticals, textiles, and paper. A major exporter, Samsung has overseas factories in the United States, Europe, and elsewhere in Asia. Famous for its disciplined, internationally oriented management, Samsung has built up a forest of joint-venture arrangements, part of Korea's unending drive for technological transfer; among them are G.E. and Corning Glass in the United States and Seiko in Japan.

Like Hyundai, Samsung was the creature of a dynamic entrepreneur, Lee Byung Chull, who died in 1987. (In the chaebol tradition, his son, Lee Kun Hee, is the present chairman.) The elder Lee started out with a small trading company in Taegu and Seoul during the Japanese colonial period. Driven out by the Korean War, he set up Samsung Trading Company in Pusan and began to rebuild, spectacularly; heavy profits were made on a variety of postwar reconstruction projects. In 1964, with Japanese technological assistance—this time from Mitsui—and Korean government encouragement, Lee set out to build the world's largest fertilizer plant. Hanguk Fertilizer Company's plant at Ulsan, in the newly industrializing South, began operations less than three years after the ground-breaking—an extraordinary performance. Lee himself moved to the construction site and supervised work there for more than a year. The company later branched out into finance and entertainment. Of all the chaebol Samsung was most closely connected to Japanese business interests. Lee, like many wealthy Koreans of his generation, had gone to a Japanese university, and he kept a residence in Tokyo until his death.[4]

Lucky Goldstar, an amalgam of two companies, went into the consumer electronic business, like Samsung, but by a different route. The chairman of Lucky Goldstar, Koo Cha Kyung, described his group's evolution in this way:

> My father and I started a cosmetic cream factory in the late 1940s. At the time no company could supply us with plastic caps of adequate quality for cream jars, so we had to start a plastics business. Plastic caps alone were not sufficient to run the plastic-molding plant, so we added combs, toothbrushes and soap boxes. This plastics business also led us to manufacture electrical and electronic products and telecommunication equipment. The plastics business also took us into oil refining, which needed a tanker-shipping company. The oil-refining company alone was paying an insurance premium amounting to more than half the total revenue of the then largest insurance company in Korea. Thus, an insurance company was started. The natural step-by-step evolution through related businesses resulted in the Lucky Goldstar group

as we see it today. For the future, we will base our growth primarily on chemicals, energy and electronics. Our chemical business would continue to expand toward fine chemicals and genetic engineering, while the electronics business will grow in the direction of semiconductor manufacturing, fiber optic telecommunications and, eventually, satellite telecommunications.[5]

This industrial success story, which sounds in the telling like a Korean version of The House That Jack Built, represented an interactive combination of scarcities, ingenuity, and iron determination. Like the other chaebol the companies of the Lucky Goldstar group took quite a few bumps on the way to their present annual sales of $25 billion. But in greater or lesser degree, all the chaebol people were development capitalists. Without a government behind them, with the financial clout this implied, their pell-mell pace would have been impossible.

In some cases government directed what business chaebol should enter. In the late seventies, for example, President Park suggested to Kim Woo Choong, the chairman of the Daewoo group, that he take control of two tottering enterprises—one of them a shipyard and the other a government-owned machinery plant. (A suggestion coming from Park was hard to refuse.) Both takeovers worked. The machinery plant, renamed Daewoo Heavy Industries, began to show a profit after two years; as a state-run factory, it had lost money steadily for thirty. Daewoo Shipbuilding soon did as well, its sweeping overhaul made smoother by preferential government loans. By 1980 Daewoo was also into the automobile business. Its nicely designed cars made it the chief rival to Hyundai.

Kim Woo Choong saw himself as a "turnaround expert." As he wrote in his autobiographical book, *It's a Big World and There's Lots to be Done:* "If there is only a one percent chance of success, a true businessman sees that one percent as the spark to light a fire. The business world is not a matter of putting one and one together to get two, but one where you see one turning into ten and ten into fifty."

A workaholic with a keen analytical mind, Kim started his business in 1967 as a textiles exporter, making goods for sale by Sears Roebuck. Delivering fabrics to foreign firms led to the start-up of electronics, aerospace, chemicals, oil, and securities corporations. Possibly the most internationalist-minded of the chaebol bosses, Kim also downplayed the family element in his company, setting great store in the development of nonfamily top managers. The Daewoo Foundation, which he established, has as its goal Kim's stated idea of "returning corporate profits to society"; and over the past fifteen years it has made significant grants to medicine, education, and scientific research. His stated aims of curbing conspicuous consumption and restoring "the ethic of public prosperity" have struck a responsive chord. His book—in which he comes across as a combination of Horatio Alger, Benjamin Franklin, and General Motors' Alfred P. Sloan—sold some two million copies.

The extraordinary international growth of the Korean construction industry in the seventies and early eighties was a chaebol success story. In the ten years beginning in 1973 overseas orders for Korean companies rose from $170 million to almost $14 billion annually. Starting with road building and similar pick-and-shovel projects, Korean builders moved on to put up factories, shipyards, power plants, and petrochemical complexes in more than twenty countries. Their greatest profits came from the Middle East oil producers, temporarily awash in the boom resulting from the 1973 OPEC price rises. And not so incidentally, revenues from overseas construction handily served to balance Korea's heavy dollar outflows from oil price increases in the "oil shock" years of 1973 and 1979.

Most Korean construction companies learned their business repairing the devastation from the Korean War years. In fact, much of their expertise was gained working with U.S. Army engineers on war and postwar rehabilitation projects. In the middle sixties Korean builders took their first tentative steps into the overseas market, with work in Vietnam and elsewhere in Southeast Asia.

By the beginning of the seventies they were looking further afield. Urged on by the government, whose economic technocrats were sorely distressed by oil price hikes, the big conglomerates led a kind of oil rush in reverse to bid on huge construction jobs in the Middle East. The symbiosis was obvious. Countries like Saudi Arabia and Libya, oil-rich but technologically poor, wanted a lot done in a hurry, but lacked the home-grown engineering talent for it.

Koreans could provide trained engineers, in increasing numbers. Thanks to a government-prompted emphasis on the practical side of university education, engineering graduates rose from some 5,000 in 1971 to 15,000 in 1982.[6] Korean companies could also field trained and at the time disciplined work forces, who were only too happy to sign on for one or two years at double the wages they would receive at home.

The large chaebol were well equipped to deploy their troops. With a trading company to make bulk purchases and help with sales, an engineering company for specialized technical assistance and other units specializing in shipbuilding, steel, or concrete, the construction arm of a conglomerate had a lot in its favor—not to mention preferred loans from the government. As opportunities offered themselves, the builders expanded. When I interviewed him some years ago, at the height of the construction boom, Hong Sung Eun, president of Lucky Development Company, summed up the conglomerate's case:

> Our construction business actually started as an organization for acquiring land and building up properties to use as recreation hotels for company employees in the Lucky group. Thus we found ourselves with a construction capacity. In 1977 we set up operations in Saudi Arabia, where we had been recommended by the Korean government. We started doing a joint venture with a Dutch company on a project where all we did was furnish the workers and their managers. We finished six months ahead of schedule—so we were off and running. We did another job working with an American company, actually Bechtel, also in Saudi Arabia. Then we turned to jobs on our own.
>
> The strength of being part of the Lucky group is that we could exploit both the skills and services of our fellow group members. We also run joint ventures with a lot of people—Siemens, Hitachi, G.E. When we go into an area, we can mobilize our resources.

Where a company like Lucky Goldstar merely added construction to its existing portfolio, other chaebol expanded organically. The cornerstone of the Ssangyong Group was the Ssangyong ("twin dragons") Cement Company. Founded in 1962 as part of Park's first five-year plan, the cement company's annual production soon rose to half of Korea's total. Ssangyong Construction was originally a small appendage of Ssangyong Cement, but after entering the overseas market in 1977 it grew prodigiously, climaxing its expansion with a contract for building the huge new Raffles City Complex in Singapore. By the eighties Ssangyong Cement had diversified into paper manufacture, oil refineries, diesel engines, and textile machinery, later branching out to make a popular truck and minivan. Other Ssangyong properties included two nonprofit foundations and its own university.

The construction boom only served to highlight the singular characteristics of the Korean chaebol: 1) export-oriented—until the eighties exports represented almost 60 percent of the fifty chaebol total sales; 2) family-owned and run—far more than the Japanese keiretsu chains of companies or even their prewar zaibatsu progenitors (chaebol and zaibatsu use the same Chinese characters) the chaebol were led by individual entrepreneur-owners, who tended to regard their holdings as family fiefs; 3) government-dominated—Park's iron control of the economy, the nation's banking system in particular, resulted in a kind of symbiosis between the big conglomerates and the government, with increasing dangers of corruption and favoritism; 4) production-driven—in that there was a national obsession, starting at the offices in the Blue House, with increasing GNP at all costs, with a corollary reliance on foreign loans and imported technology and capital goods, mainly Japanese.

By letting competitive private industry do the job, Park and his economic general staff had avoided the pitfalls of the Marxist command economy and developed, with the help of ever-rising education levels, an economic machine led by military technocrats and officered by great numbers of apolitical engineers. Its arena of combat was the production floor. Other considerations were sacrificed to this economic war effort.

From the mid-seventies on, the government had ordered up vast investment projects to develop heavy and chemical industries. All the country's resources were mobilized under newly enacted laws like the Shipbuilding Industry Development Act and the Electronics Industry Development Act in this dramatic "catch-up" effort. Broadly speaking, it worked. Korea's international competitiveness soared. Slowly but definitely, like one of the huge new cargo carriers changing course, the country's industrial structure shifted. Thus led by heavy industry and chemicals, the manufacturing sector's share of Gross Domestic Product jumped from 22.5 percent in 1970 to 29.5 percent in 1979, with agriculture dropping correspondingly.

By the beginning of the eighties, heavy industry was dominant in the manufacturing sector, while Korean ships and electronics gear were becoming factors in international markets. It was just in time, since by the early seventies the rise of low-priced Korean textiles—hitherto the country's major dollar-earner—was already arousing protectionist sentiment in the United States.

But all this progress exacted a heavy toll. Inflation became a disturbing fact of life. The whole price mechanism was badly skewed. The country's financial resources were strained to the breaking point by the heavy capital investment. Bankers and economists were making ominous clucking noises about high risks and wasteful duplication. Overcapacity in some areas was matched by underinvestment in others; the economy grew lopsided, as development in light industry was neglected. Quality standards also suffered in the headlong advance toward heavy industrialization.

With government giving its support to big firms and their big projects, economic power was concentrated in the chaebol. Many small or medium-sized firms were driven to the wall. As the big grew yet bigger, Koreans began to wonder about such concentration of economic power, particularly when concentrated in the hands of so few people.

Most ominous of all, Korea's people were showing signs of strain and discontent. Education and improved infrastructure had raised people's level of expectation, but it was still very much a producer's society and little was done to satisfy consumer concerns. The infantry of Park's economic army was just beginning to grumble. Families of workers who poured into Seoul and other cities were living in virtual slums. Inflation's costs fell heaviest on workers whose wages were kept low, to keep their products internationally competitive.

Through the end of the seventies, while the country pushed to meet the goals of Park's third five-year plan (for developing heavy industry) public protest was muted. Even Park's new Yushin Constitution in 1972, which codified his de facto dictatorship, was ratified by the voters, under the watchful eye of police and the KCIA. Living standards continued to improve, after all. And Kim Il Sung's persistent saber-rattling from the North remained a powerful deterrent to antigovernment activity in Seoul. "Better the devil one knew . . ." was a fairly general attitude at that time. But discontent was growing, and it would not stop.

NOTES

[1] In an article written for the *Encyclopaedia Britannica Book of the Year* for 1971.

[2] At that time the exchange rate was 484 won to the dollar.

[3] As quoted in my book *The Pacific Century* (New York: Scribners, 1992).

[4] For some of this information on the chaebol I am indebted to Alice Amsden's excellent book *Asia's Next Giant* (New York: Oxford, 1989) and *The Chaebol* (New York: HarperCollins, 1989) by Richard M. Steers, Yoo Keun Shin, and Gerardo R. Ungson.

[5] From a Harvard Business School case study.

[6] The statistics and other material on the Korean construction industry are taken from a supplement "Korea's Master Builders" which I wrote for *Time* in May, 1983.

VI

THE HIGH COSTS OF HIGH GROWTH

Marching his economic troops for the "modernization of the fatherland," Park Chung Hee seemingly turned the Republic of Korea into a model of "developmental dictatorship," in the process offering a useful example to later Asian authoritarians, from Suharto on the right to Deng Xiaoping on the left. Under the slogans "Building a Self-Reliant National Economy" and "Growth First, Unification Later," he combined the appeal of anti-Communism and economic betterment. Kim Il Sung's regime in Pyongyang, with its program of intermittent infiltration raids and crude propaganda offensives, obligingly kept the red menace alive. In 1968, the same year that the North Koreans captured the U.S.S. *Pueblo* off their coast, one team of infiltrators managed to cross the border undetected and made an assault on the presidential residence in Seoul.

At the same time obvious signs of growth and prosperity—the shipyards, the Pohang steel complex, and infrastructure improvements like the new expressway between Seoul and Pusan—gave the Koreans the same kind of lift that Ikeda Hayato's successful "Double Your Income" policy had offered the Japanese just a few years before. Jobs were available, with better prospects on the way. The swift growth of educational facilities was giving many Koreans a far greater chance of advancement than they had ever contemplated.

At least through the mid-seventies Park was by no means unpopular, despite the murmurs of discontent. An emerging middle class in the cities was experiencing a kind of boom-times psychology. Strong business support and conservative thinking in the countryside had helped Park win a conclusive 55 percent majority in the 1971 elections—although the opposition candidate, Kim Dae Jung, gained a majority in the cities and his New Democratic party increased its strength in the National Assembly. The elections could be accounted free.

Foreign visitors enjoyed their trips to South Korea. After their routine inspections of the truce area at Panmunjom, American congressmen or other touring VIPs could put down their field glasses, return their borrowed combat jackets, and issue statements about preserving the bastion of the free world south of the old 38th parallel boundary. Businessmen would readily catch the enthusiasm of the capitalist-development society and laud the obvious free enterprise of their hosts. Equipped with newspapers, department stores, hardworking bureaucrats, and democratic assembly debates, the Republic of Korea offered a heartening contrast to the memories of Korean War days.

The ugly political underside of Park's high-growth era was not readily visible. A few weeks' stay, however, and some acquaintance with Koreans would make any traveler aware of an undercurrent of repression and the tensions it caused, which ran through the entire society. Marching to the general-president's drum was not difficult, as long as the troops stayed in close formation and did not question their orders. Public dissent from the established order was dangerous, however. Even private complaint could be difficult, for the KCIA—operating with virtually unlimited government funds—had managed to set up a network of informers and agents throughout the country.

Repression was justified by law, wherever possible; Park kept up the appearances of a constitutional democracy. From the severe Anti-Communism Law (1961), however, to the Special Law for Safeguarding the Nation (1971) a network of ordinances and administrative measures kept almost all political activity, labor unions, and popular movements of any sort under tight control.

Park had made it clear that he would not allow democratization to interfere with his grand plans for economic growth.

Where he had to maintain a facade of democratic practice—if for no other reason than to keep up American economic and military support—his soldiers and technocrats used often ingenious methods to frustrate or destroy opposition. Since the days of Syngman Rhee's overthrow an increasingly vigorous press had tried to criticize government's high-handed tactics. Park imposed varieties of open or behind-the-scenes censorship, which effectively muzzled the media. In 1975, for example, when Seoul's most respected daily, *Dong-A Ilbo,* proved obstreperous, Park sent out the word that corporations advertising in *Dong-A Ilbo* would be regarded by the government as unfriendly. The resultant antiadvertising campaign virtually emptied *Dong-A Ilbo*'s pages and brought the newspaper to the edge of bankruptcy before the owners capitulated. Editors and reporters hostile to the government were then dismissed.

Although Park had won the 1971 elections, the increasing success of the political opposition made his regime nervous. Led by Kim Dae Jung and others, opposition rallies drew responsive crowds—at least when they were permitted. Korean workers were growing angry and disillusioned, victims of the government's reliance on low wages and high exports. Park's continued support of the chaebol, backed by the government's preferential loan system, had already unbalanced the economy. Prices were volatile, and inflation and excessively high interest rates became unpleasant facts of life.

To keep his political control tight, Park first issued a body of emergency decrees, followed in 1972 by the Yushin ("Reform") Constitution previously mentioned. This amounted to little more than a codified form of martial law. Among other things it provided for presidential election by a National Council for Unification, a "nonparty" group with several thousand members whom Park could easily control. In addition, the president was empowered to appoint one-third of the National Assembly. In effect, this made Park president for life.

Armed wtih this new authority, the government put out a new set of restrictive decrees. Measures like the Law for Assembly and

Demonstration (1973) and the Special Law for Punishment of Anti-State Acts (1977) were worthy of a totalitarian state. Any criticism of the president was declared illegal. As if to underline the new legalized lawlessness, KCIA chief Lee Hu Rak sent his henchmen to Japan in 1973 and forcibly abducted Kim Dae Jung from his Tokyo hotel room. Dragged back to Seoul, Kim was later sentenced to death on the usual faked charges; only American pressure kept Lee's minions from executing the sentence.

As the Yushin severities intensified, public resentment began to simmer, at least among the urban intelligentsia. With the Army and the KCIA reaffirmed in power, protest became ever more dangerous. Predictably, however, some students began to demonstrate; and there were isolated but bitterly fought wildcat strikes at the new Hyundai shipyard in Ulsan and the Dong Il Textile Company. Women workers at the big textile mills, at that time still Korea's biggest export earners, were the worst paid and worst treated in Park's Confucian labor force. At Dong Il and other labor-management confrontations the women generally led the way. Still, labor unrest was generally kept down by a combination of antiunion law and police action.

Throughout the troubled seventies, however, it was Christian church groups and the Christian clergy that constituted the bulk of Park's visible opposition. This was in their tradition. For the greater part of a century, in fact, Christians—generally better educated than the bulk of the population and made by their faith and Western connections more conscious of individual rights and responsibilities—had played a leading role in expanding a sense of democratic values in this Confucian society. Now, vocally recalling the Christian leadership of the 1919 independence movement, Catholics and Protestants joined in denouncing Park's antidemocratic actions.

In 1972, in a sermon at midnight mass in Myongdong Cathedral in Seoul, Cardinal Kim (Kim Su Hwan) made one of the few direct challenges to the president. Speaking of the new Yushin Constitution, he said: "Your action will help widen the already existing gap between the people and the government and will eventually lead to a government without people and a people without a leader."

Before the sermon ended the government broadcasting station cut it off. But Kim was not so easily silenced. A political liberal and a firm believer in the *aggiornamento* of Pope John's Vatican Council II, the cardinal soon moved to the forefront of the Christian opposition. Park gave him ample grounds for complaint. In April 1974, reacting to several university demonstrations, Park's KCIA arrested several hundred activists, many of them Christians. Later, in summary trials, a military court sentenced several prominent Catholic and Protestant leaders to stiff jail terms, including a death sentence for the Catholic poet Kim Chi Ha (which was later commuted after international protests). Kim Dong Gil, the respected dean of the Presbyterian Yonsei University, and the Catholic Bishop Daniel Tji Hak Sun were given fifteen-year jail sentences. Ironically, Tji, who came from North Korea, had previously been jailed and tortured by Kim Il Sung's Communists.[1]

Throughout 1974 Korean Christians continued to organize prayer meetings and demonstrations against government repression. Catholics cooperated with the Protestant National Council of Churches in appeals for the release of political prisoners. When Bishop Tji was finally let out of his cell in 1975—his sentence had been commuted—he was met by a crowd of twenty thousand. The year before, which coincided with the Catholic Holy Year, the Cardinal and other prelates had organized a series of outdoor masses and mass meetings, generally with overtones of political protest. On one occasion a procession of five bishops, one hundred priests and three hundred nuns, and thousands of Catholic worshipers was broken up by riot police.

On March 1, 1976, an ecumenical service at Myongdong Cathedral commemorated the anniversary of the 1919 Declaration of Independence with a demand for the restoration of human rights in Korea. The KCIA's answer was more mass arrests of church leaders. Two weeks later Cardinal Kim led a large crowd of Catholic and Protestant believers in prayers for their release.

There was a significant parallel between the two March 1st demonstrations almost sixty years apart. The impetus for the original 1919 declaration had come from Christian churchpeople— almost all of them Protestants. Products of American missionary teaching, they combined Korean nationalism with a Christian activist respect for individual human rights. While their protests were a source of extreme irritation to the Japanese colonial government, they could not be so easily suppressed. Their strong ties with American ministers and teachers attracted attention in the United States—a government that the Japan of those days did not wish to offend. Although Catholics generally took the lead in the demonstrations against Park Chung Hee's Yushin autocracy (by the eighties Myongdong Cathedral had become a kind of protesters' sanctuary), the generally Christian protest found the same kind of sympathy in Jimmy Carter's America as the earlier protests had found in Woodrow Wilson's. Just as the Christians in Korea provided the leavening force that drove a traditionally Confucian society toward an ideal of individual human rights, their very presence evoked a sympathetic American political response. It was no mere coincidence that the 1976 arrests brought a public denunciation of Park's human rights abuses from his American ally.

While the protest gathered, Park himself had grown progressively more self-centered and aloof. The indignant populist of 1961 was giving way to the secluded despot of the seventies. Although at heart a decent man, Park—like Syngman Rhee before him—became yet another example of power's ultimate corruption. Unlike Rhee, Park continued to use power effectively. He was a good judge of people—and their usefulness. Until his last years he retained a faculty of knowing how far people could be pushed. His sense of mission remained, as always, strong; but dedication gave way to self-righteousness.

In the manner of all authoritarian regimes, a palace guard had grown up around Park, whose courtiers shrank from the slightest criticism. In 1970, when I visited the Blue House to edit Park's article for *Encyclopaedia Britannica's Book of the Year,* I pointed out some serious mistakes in the writing. No one in the entourage had the courage to mention it. "But the president wrote that out in his own hand—we can't touch that," I was told. They might have been yangban courtiers in the heyday of Korea's Confucian kings.

Inevitably, plots and counterplots began to surface among the leadership. Their principals were handled ruthlessly, when discovered. The case of Yoon Pil Yong is worth recalling. A two-star general, Yoon had started out in 1961 as Park's secretary; by the seventies he was commander of the Capital Garrison Command, Park's version of the Praetorian Guard and, in a sense, Park's executive officer in government. Unfortunately for Yoon, he made some unguarded remarks about Park's advancing age and the need for a successor.

Retribution was swift. In April, 1973, Yoon and a dozen other highly placed army officers were court-martialed and given jail sentences. Thirty other officers were retired and some thirty of Yoon's cohorts in the KCIA were dismissed. Other Yoon friends were equally harshly dealt with. Kim Yeon Joon, president of Hanyang University—and concurrently president of a large Seoul daily—was arrested for alleged misappropriation of a charity fund; his newspaper was shut down. Yoon himself was released after two years' imprisonment after another of Park's close associates pleaded his case. "I feel sorry for him," Park apparently said. "I told my boys to teach him a bit of a lesson, but things got out of hand."

In August 1974 North Korean agents attempted to assassinate Park, but the assassin, tragically, killed Park's wife instead. Yook Yung-Su was by all accounts an impressive woman, kind and understanding, who represented the only real leavening influence on Park. After her death he became increasingly bitter and despotic. Now convinced that he was in reality the savior of his country, he surrounded himself with an ever-tighter coterie of retainers. Although until the end, through his monthly export conferences and economic meetings, he gave ear to the advice of the technocrats and the chaebol leaders who were building what he liked to call "national capitalism," politically speaking he was a despot, acting out the final stages of Lord Acton's gloomy certitudes about absolute power. Access to the president, except on economic matters, was controlled by a zealous Army *tae kwon do* expert named Cha Ji Chul, a personal protégé who was in charge of the presidential security guard. Park had other favorites, among them a rising young general (and security guard graduate) named Chun Doo Hwan.

As Park's Yushin decade of the seventies neared its end, people were growing increasingly restive. Although the students remained relatively cowed, thanks to massive police and KCIA surveillance, the Christian protesters were now joined by low-paid workers, the first casualties of an economic downturn. In addition, the opposition New Democratic party, led by Kim Young Sam, became more outspoken in its criticism of the government. When the government majority expelled Kim from the National Assembly, his party walked out with him. In the popular demonstrations that followed, protesters called on Park to resign. The government's response was to order martial law in the south, where public protest was loudest. (Interestingly enough, Masan, a focal point of the demonstrations, had also been the starting point of the riots which brought down Syngman Rhee in 1960.)

On the evening of October 26, 1979, Park and his closest colleagues were arguing whether the uprisings, which seemed likely to spread, should be put down by armed force. Park and his protégé Cha Ji Chul thought it was time to go in with the troops. Kim Jae Kyu, Park's KCIA director, felt the government should be conciliatory this time. Kim, younger than Park but also a graduate of the Manchurian military academy, had a mind of his own. When the discussion grew heated, he settled it by shooting both Park and Cha.

Park's death shocked the country. Revered, respected, or hated, his rule had been a fact of life for a whole generation. He had remade Korea. However much people complained about the manner of his rule, he was and remains respected as the architect of his country's post-war economy. "The miracle on the Han," so-called, was Park's miracle. Park's legal successor, Prime Minister Choe Kyu Ha, was a senior bureaucrat who quickly showed signs of moderation. Early in 1980 Kim Dae Jung and hundreds of other political prisoners were released; and Choe promised an early referendum on restoring popular election to the presidency. With the Yushin decrees relaxed, though not repealed, it seemed to many that democracy was returning. Post-Park political rule, however, was characterized mostly by bitter partisan infighting. In many ways 1980 seemed a replay of 1960, when democracy protesters had toppled the autocratic rule of Syngman Rhee. Once more, as it turned out, a military dictator was waiting in the wings.

First, Chun Doo Hwan used his powers as chief investigator of Park's assassination to purge the army. In December 1979 the chief of staff had been removed, accused of plotting Park's killing. Chun's cohorts—most of them members of the *Hanawehi* clique of Military Academy graduates, took over the army leadership, although not without a bloody seven-hour firefight at ROK army headquarters. (The American Eighth Army Command, which might well have intervened to stop Chun's well-advertised coup, did nothing but acquiesce.) A mass turnout of some 100,000 student demonstrators in Seoul, demanding an end to martial law, gave Chun the excuse he had been waiting for. In a second-string reenactment of Park's original 1961 takeover, he intensified martial law, closed down Korea's universities, and banned all political activity, the National Assembly included. Kim Dae Jung and other opposition activists found themselves back in jail.

The day after the university shutdown, student demonstrations in the southern city of Kwangju, Kim Dae Jung's political power base, were brutally dispersed by Chun's Special Forces soldiery. The people of Kwangju and the surrounding Cholla provinces in the southwest, had been generally given short shrift in Park's economic development plans, which generally favored Park's own base in the southeast. They were hostile to the government in a modern political as well as an ancient traditional sense—Paekche versus Shilla. So they did not take repression lying down.

In a show of "people power" that foreshadowed later events in the Asian eighties, Kwangju people—students, workers, and police—took up weapons and drove out Chun's troops. For three days they held the city. Some thought that resistance might make Chun back off. Others hoped for American intervention, since most Koreans knew that, because of the North Korean threat, the bulk of their army remained under a unified American command.

Instead Chun sent in more troops. Despite the efforts of Kwangju citizens to work out a truce, the Twentieth Division, released from the American command, charged into the city shooting. By official estimates some 198 were killed. Korean and international human rights groups estimate the toll as many hundreds higher. Hundreds more were arrested.

The Kwangju bloodletting was the Korean equivalent of China's Tiananmen massacre—no less ruthless for having been perpetrated by an American ally. Chun told U.S. officials that his prompt military action had foiled a "Communist" plot. There was no official protest from Washington. On the contrary, President Chun, newly elected by the rubber-stamp National Council for Unification (Choe having obligingly stepped down), was cheerfully received at the White House in February 1981 by President Ronald Reagan. With his usual thoughtlessness in Pacific Basin diplomacy (he was also one of Ferdinand Marcos's firmest supporters), Reagan told Chun: "Our special bond of friendship is as strong today as it was twenty years ago."

The memory of Kwangju did not go away, however. Even today it is faithfully commemorated, as Kwangju people honor the graves of those killed. It embittered not only the people of the Cholla provinces but most of the Korean intelligentsia against Chun's government; and the stigma continued for the next decade to embarrass Roh, Chun's military academy classmate and successor. More than any other factor or event, it set in motion an undercurrent of anti-American feeling, which persists among Korean students to this day, for America's passive acquiescence in the massacre was held by many Koreans to mean active support.

Chun, a stubborn and notably insensitive man, was undisturbed by such signs of opposition. As far as he was concerned, he was to be Park Chung Hee redivivus. It soon developed that Park's boots were much too big for him.

NOTES

[1] For much of this information I am indebted to Eric Hanson's *Catholic Politics in China and Korea* (Orbis; 1988).

VII

THE "MIRACLE" AND THE MIDDLE CLASS

The year of Chun's takeover was a difficult one for the Korean economy. With growth registering a negative 4.5 percent for 1980, the vaunted "miracle on the Han" showed signs of grounding. The political time of troubles after Park's assassination affected the entire country. The rising prices of the second 1979 "oil shock" hit Korea at the same time, with an international recession putting a crimp in the export boom. Park Chung Hee's single-minded buildup of heavy and chemical industry, with his government's emphasis on export market share over profitability, had created serious imbalances in the Korean economy. Headlong investment in heavy industry had produced duplication, wastage, and, in some cases, overcapacity. In 1980, for example, electric generating manufacture was operating at 10 percent of capacity and the marine diesel industry at 7 percent. The fledgling automobile industry was running at about 30 percent of capacity.

By contrast, some sectors were starved for investment. Small and medium-sized businesses suffered, in particular, while the huge chaebol, as we have seen, grew ever huger. Inflation was running wild. Thanks to heavy-handed, if effective, government support of selective industries (and companies in them), the whole pricing system remained in disarray. Taken as a whole, the economy was badly winded, like a desperately coached long-distance runner who had done the mile in a series of frantic 100-yard dashes.

The technocrats who ran the economy were well aware of these problems. From their bureaucratic strongholds in the economic ministries—Finance, Trade and Industry, and the powerful Economic Planning Board, whose director also served as deputy prime minister—they had already started spinning the dials and tugging at the levers of their various control mechanisms. In this they received the full support of Chun Doo Hwan. His presidency revalidated by a new constitution and a well-controlled election in early 1981, Chun now felt politically secure. Seeing himself as the legatee of Park's early successes, Chun was more anxious than anyone to keep the economy moving. Without Park's vision and dynamism, however, he was content at least at first to leave economic guidance and leadership to the bureaucrats.

The new five-year plan, the country's fifth (1982–1986) was the work of the technocrats. It aimed at economic stability rather than exponential growth. Its immediate target was price stabilization. Through the seventies the impact of inflation had worked to weaken the competitiveness of Korean exports, but the government kept them internationally competitive by periodic devaluations of the Korean currency. This practice obviously could not continue. The rise of low-priced textiles exports, in particular, was evoking angry rumblings from across the Pacific. And competition from other low-wage Asian economies was intensifying.

The first order of economic business, therefore, in Chun's Fifth Republic was to cut back on fiscal spending and tighten monetary policy. The government worked hard to keep down growing consumer demand and encourage savings, which had hitherto been rather low. Unlike their Japanese cousins, Koreans have not been conspicuously heavy savers. Partly because of their stormy postwar history, they tended to save for the short term rather than the long. Although most Korean households belonged to a private *kay*—a kind of homespun but effective credit union, run by its participants, whose actual worth is rather hard to track statistically—the country's savings ratio through the sixties was far less than that of Japan or Taiwan, the NIC (newly industrialized country) most comparable to Korea. Government policies of stable but higher interest rates, among other things, helped raise the level of private as well as corporate savings. By the mid-eighties, bank savings had increased, and the national savings rate had climbed to almost 35 percent of GNP, in contrast to the low 20 percent level maintained during the decade preceding.

In addition, heavy spending on education—what the economist Song Byung-Nak calls "Koreans' massive investment in human capital"—helped give the Republic of Korea the world's highest economic growth rate by 1986–87.[1] As we have already noted, the high-growth era would have been impossible without tremendous increases in educational opportunities for Koreans in almost all walks of life.

The heavy price controls of an earlier day, when increases in the price of major manufactures required prior government approval, were now removed. It was generally recognized that price controls were counterproductive. Thanks to the long time involved in justifying price changes to the relevant government agency, it too often fell out that cost-push factors had cancelled out a price increase by the time it was approved. The government now retreated to a policy of watching and monitoring prices. Inevitably, the distorted price mechanism had led to much wasteful allocation of resources. The technocrats in the Seoul ministries now took steps to promote market competition, in an economy where government-aided oligopolies had tended to freeze out their smaller competitors.

In 1981 a greatly strengthened fair trade law was put on the books. Called the Anti-Monopoly and Fair Trade Act, it provided the framework, at least, for an economic order based on free market competition—a major step away from the old garrison-state economy.

Next came import liberalization. This was partly in response to increasing pressures from their overseas customers to open Korea's domestic markets. It was also commonsense economics to do so. Korea had long ago forsworn the early postwar policies of import substitution. Unless Korean producers could hold their own against foreign competition in the domestic market, where foreign goods were handicapped by tariffs and transportation costs, the bureaucrats reasoned, it would be impossible to compete effectively overseas.

Another sector in need of liberalization was Korea's banking system. Tight government controls had made Korean banks something of a financial basket case. The Finance Ministry now prepared to loosen the bonds, allowing the banks some degree of independence in budgeting and personnel management, as well as allowing them a decent level of profitability. It was during the eighties that the government began to sell off its equity shares in commercial banks. In 1982, in another major move, the interest differential between preferential (policy) loans and general loans was abolished—at a time when the ratio of interest-subsidized preferential loans to other loans was fully eight to two. Of course, given the limited supply of loan capital, favored corporations could still count on having money made available to them, through not-so-hidden government pressure. Later in the decade banks were allowed to introduce a prime lending rate system, with some spread permitted in their interest rates.

Finally, the government set out to reduce waste growth in heavy industry by enforcing a series of reorganizations and mergers among the big firms. This policy—a far more drastic version of what Japan's MITI (Ministry for International Trade and Industry) already had done in that economy—fell heavily on industries like automobiles, construction equipment, diesel engines, and heavy electrical equipment. It evoked predictable hardships and complaints. But in the end this policy, its effects cushioned by heavy financial support, resulted in greatly improved competitive efficiency for the corporate survivors.

On the whole financial stabilization had a quickening if unpleasantly medicinal effect on the Korean economy. By the mid-eighties inflation increase had dropped to a single-digit level. And the heavy industry sector, forcibly streamlined, was in good competitive shape. In 1985 the fabled "three lows"—lowered oil prices, lower interest rates, and a lowered U.S. dollar (with the resultantly high Japanese yen)—combined to produce a great economic boom. In the three years beginning with 1986 GNP soared at an annual increase of 12 percent annually. Meanwhile the balance of payments picture improved, with greatly widening surpluses. As the country reduced its foreign debt, increased investment funds were made available for Korean manufacturers.

To an extent public benefits were increased as well. A national pension system was established. Medical insurance coverage was expanded. A minimum-wage system was introduced, with increased government support for the urban poor and some aid to Korea's embattled farmers.

These gains were not accidental. They were accomplished under Chun's idea of *sunjin choguk changjo*—"creating an advanced fatherland"—which became the watchword of his administration. Chun was bright enough to realize that the single-minded emphasis on heavy industry and exports of Park's era had to be subsumed into a general drive for national growth, in which all segments of the society would participate. According to his timetable for the year 2000, Korea by that time would be one of the developed countries, with incomes and an infrastructure to match.

But this admirable economic blueprint was not enough, for the sweeping advances in GNP had been accompanied by the grimmest kind of political repression. Nor had the profits of export success been at all equitably shared. A growing gap between the haves and the have-nots in Korea's industrializing society was made worse by flagrant corruption and influence peddling, which soon became a virtual trademark of Chun's governance. On top of this, the character of the population had sharply changed. The level of rising expectation had soared as high as the ballooning GNP figures. The emerging middle class, which we have mentioned, was now an accomplished fact. There were real people out there, increasingly better educated, increasingly aware of the human rights and democratic share in government that Chun Doo Hwan and his capable technocrats had, variously, overlooked, denied, and trampled upon.

The statistics on income distribution for Korea in the eighties were quite reasonable—while less equitable than neighboring Japan and Taiwan, the percentages of income for the upper-bracket 20 percent of the population (42.2) and the lower 20 percent (19.7) were roughly comparable to Sweden's and vastly better than other developing countries like Brazil or Turkey. Capital gains were not included in these figures, however, and it was the growing concentration of property ownership and financial assets that set Korean salaried workers to grumbling. Sporadically, the government took steps to curb real estate speculation, as well as the soaring prices of the most elemental housing. They were ineffective. In 1988 one government report conceded that the total supply of housing was some 40 percent short of the number of households.

While government held down general consumption—until 1980 Koreans were not allowed to buy the color TV sets their factories were busy making for export—a new class of rich had begun to appear. Chun and his relatives were conspicuous members. Contributions to the president were channeled through the notorious Ilhae Foundation, which levied heavy tribute on the chaebol, which in turn continued to find favor with the government. Increasingly, Chun played favorites with business. The resulting climate of corruption—a sharp contrast to the severe but Spartan rule of Park Chung Hee—cast its miasma over the country.

The most obvious inequities of income were evident on the farm. Park's *Saemaul Undong* movement for agricultural help under Chun was turned into yet another control (and enrichment) device of his administration—his brother was put in charge. In general, farm income, if we subtract extra income transferred from other sources, was less than 80 percent of urban income. Despite the use of a new strain of "miracle" rice and other improvements, rural Korea, which still accounted for 20 percent of the work force, lagged far behind the cities in conveniences, education, medical care, and transportation. In the process of heavy industrialization the people in the agricultural sector—both as producers and potential consumers—had been seriously neglected.

Not that urban labor was all that much better off. In Chun's Fifth Republic wages were kept down for the sake of export competitiveness. Before 1987 the hourly pay of workers in Korean manufacturing industries was only 11 percent of American wages and 14 percent of Japan's; in Taiwan and Singapore, also, the pay was considerably higher. Yet the working hours were almost the world's longest, having actually increased to the level of 54.3 weekly between 1975 and 1983.[2] It was small wonder that union activity, assisted and often led by idealistic Christian activists, had increased in the late seventies, despite the severities of Park's Yushin era.

Chun Doo Hwan's solution to the gathering labor problem was characteristically simplistic. He was determined to perpetuate—

and indeed expand—a high-growth economy that demanded increased productivity, based on low-cost labor. He saw the maintenance of industrial peace as purely a matter of labor control, by police repression where necessary. Existing labor laws were revised early in the 1980s, ostensibly to stabilize labor-management relations by improved consultation and arbitration procedures. In fact, they served to strengthen the position of employers. Unions, already hindered in their organizing, found that consultation requirements further restricted them. The right to strike was effectively denied, while union leaders and organizers were periodically investigated and questioned by the KCIA—renamed the Agency for National Security Planning after the Park assassination. A Committee to Counteract Labor Insurgency was set up by the Commission for this purpose. Most employers seemed quite happy with its activities.

Throughout Chun's repressive regime the labor situation polarized. When Christian social workers and other intellectuals tried to better bad and unsafe working conditions—the safety record of Korean industry throughout this period was notably poor—the Chun government redoubled its already tight controls, conveniently lumping together angry workers and protesting activists as "pro-Communist" enemies, set on destroying the South Korean economy in the interests, it was assumed, of Kim Il Sung. In turn supporters of labor rights became total opponents of the Chun regime. Labor leaders became increasingly political and radicalized, so that Chun's denunciations of them as extremists became a self-fulfilling prophecy. Admittedly, labor's cooperation was necessary to avoid costly disruptions of the high-growth, export-oriented economy. By bottling up labor's justified resentments and grievances, Chun's repression made inevitable the explosion of labor strikes and unrest under the presidency of Roh Tae Woo, his democratically inclined successor.

Much the same thing resulted from Chun's repressive treatment of the students and the political opposition. In the 1985 parliamentary elections the moderate opposition Democratic Party was pushed aside by the New Korean Democratic Party, which gained heavy majorities in Seoul and other urban districts—although losing in the end to the government's Democratic Justice

Party, thanks to the heavy support Chun mobilized in rural areas and a proportional representation system favoring the government. (In any case, there was little hope that Chun's government would allow itself to lose a national election.) But the mobility of the political opposition was heavily circumscribed. There was little doubt of Chun's unpopularity. Even secret polls conducted by the government had turned up a national average of 65 percent opposed to his government—among college graduates the figure was 85 percent.[3] But with so much other potential criticism muzzled, the student activists became the visible center of opposition to Chun's rule.

From the outset Chun's government attempted to control the universities through a combination of threat and surveillance. When Kim Jun Yeop, one of Korea's outstanding political scientists, was selected as president of Korea University, he found the anteroom of his office occupied by various agents of the police and the Education Ministry. (His chief secretary had been ordered to report daily on all the president's activities.) At that time eighty-six professors had been dismissed, by official pressure, since they were regarded as "antigovernment" in their attitude. Unable to reinstate them, Kim had their research salaries paid for the next four years. All were finally restored in 1984—just before the 1985 elections— when the Education Ministry relaxed its prohibition.

Professor Kim stayed in his job for just under three years, during which time he consistently resisted government pressures to expel students suspected of dissident activity. Most other university presidents were relatively complaisant. Government instructions of that day, he recalls, were arbitrary and often unpredictable. One day they would order various students expelled, the next day they might order the same people reinstated. As Kim recalls it, "To them there were no laws or school regulations—no consistency either. It was like dealing with a madman wielding a knife."[4] He finally resigned, under government pressure, in 1985.

If its dealings with university professors and administrators were at least half-polite, the Chun regime used a crude bare-knuckles approach on its students. Police habitually moved in on the university campuses at the least sign of demonstrations. Tens of thousands of new army recruits, also, had been put into mobile formations for police and riot control work. In October 1986, almost 20,000 police charged into Seoul's Konguk University to put down a mass meeting of student delegates from 26 of Korea's 114 colleges and universities. More than 2,000 students were taken into custody—about half of them were eventually formally arrested.

Chun's efforts to solve the student problem by police suppression served to radicalize the students more thoroughly than he had radicalized the labor unions. From prodemocracy they became antigovernment. The government's understandable resistance to various naive proposals for immediate unification of the country—on Kim Il Sung's terms—ultimately led them to demand some form of instant reunification. Activists performed various forms of verbal gymnastics to show their cohorts that North Korea's Communist state was at least as good as Chun's government, for which words like "fascist" and "dictatorship" were readily used.

Taking off from the alleged U.S. support of the military's 1980 Kwangju killings, activists turned sharply anti-American. As late as 1990 intensive polling showed that a majority of students believed that the United States was responsible for Kwangju, the partition of Korea, and, in fact, most of Korea's problems.[5] This was of course a new generation, to whom the Korean War—and American participation in it—was not even a memory. In their lack of historical sense the Korean students of the late eighties resembled no group so much as their radical Japanese counterparts of the sixties a generation before.

They were nonetheless effective. And Chun gave them a popular issue to demonstrate for. By refusing to amend the constitution to allow direct election of the president, he alienated not merely student activists but the majority of the country—most particularly the urban middle class. The example of the Philippines, where Corazon Aquino's "people power" had toppled Ferdinand Marcos's army-backed dictatorship in 1986, had received wide publicity throughout Korea. In January 1987, as it happened, a student activist from Seoul National University named Park Chong Chol died under police torture. This sort of thing had happened before. But this time public indignation over the incident forced Chun to ask for the resignation of both the home affairs minister and the head of the national police.

When Chun refused to yield on the issue of direct presidential elections—after having at first indicated some concession—mass demonstrations flooded the streets of Seoul, Pusan, and other cities. This time the students were joined by businessmen, housewives, and workers. As in Manila the year before, it seemed as if the whole country was taking to the streets. With the 1988 Olympic Games hanging in the balance, Chun found himself unable to resort to the use of suppressive force.

It was at this point in time, in June 1987, that Gaston Sigur, assistant secretary of state for Asia/Pacific affairs, arrived to tell President Chun, as Marcos had been told the year before, that the United States would not take any military intervention lightly. Sigur's recollection of that time is worth quoting, as a pithy summary of the situation. "Korea by 1987," he said, "had irrevocably changed. The middle class had become a power. And it could no longer be disregarded. The government wasn't dealing with a handful of left-wing students. They may have been out front, but it was plain you had strong middle-class support for the demonstrations.

"As one cabinet member said to me—a man not known for his leniency on human rights, 'There is a storm in this country. And the right word for it is democracy.' "⁶

A few days later, on June 29, Roh Tae Woo, the majority party's candidate for president, made his memorable statement pledging the establishment of democratic rights. As he later said in his inaugural address the next year: "The era when human rights and freedom were neglected in the name of economic growth and security has now ended."

Chun Doo Hwan went along with this. Shortly thereafter he publicly accepted his classmate Roh Tae Woo's proposals and prepared to make his own quiet political exit. Everything in his makeup argued for calling out the troops to suppress the demonstrations by force. But to do so would risk an indefinite period of martial law. This could easily provoke an international boycott of the 1988 Olympic Games in Seoul, which had become a major political goal of Chun's regime. For once a sense of political realism arrested his normal impulse toward military repression. In his way Chun was a patriot. Perhaps his greatest contribution to Korea's future was to refrain from calling out the troops to quell the protests.

As I shall detail in the chapters to follow, Chun's annointed successor, Roh, was true to his word. He became the middle-class president—the first in his country's history. But it would require all his leadership skills and every ounce of patience he possessed to channel the pent-up frustrations and deep-rooted political concerns of the Korean people, so badly suppressed and polarized after six bruising years of Chun Doo Hwan's grim Fifth Republic.

NOTES

[1] Here I have relied heavily on the chapter "Savings and Investment" in Song's *The Rise of the Korean Economy* (New York: Oxford University Press, 1990).

[2] Walden Bello and Stephanie Rosenfield, *Dragons in Distress: Asia's Miracle Economies in Crisis* (Food First, 1990).

[3] According to Dong Wonmo, in an article on student activism in *Political Change in South Korea* (New York: Paragon, 1988) Ilpyong J. Kim and Young Whan Kihl, eds. The newspaper that conducted the poll was cited as *Kyunghyuan Shinmun*.

[4] As noted in Kim's autobiography, *Long March* (Seoul: Nanam Publishers, 1989).

[5] As reported by R. A. Brown in an article in the *Journal of Northeast Asian Studies* (Winter 1990).

[6] Gibney, *The Pacific Century* (Scribners, 1992).

VIII

THE PATIENT PRESIDENT

Shortly after his election as president in December 1987, Roh Tae Woo called on a variety of prominent Koreans to seek their counsel. Some were close friends. Others he knew less well. Their common denominator was the possession of interesting or provocative opinions. He is a good listener—unlike so many of his political contemporaries—but he also likes to test out his own ideas on others. In one such conversation, after hearing out his visitor, a distinguished Korean clergyman, for several hours, Roh talked quite candidly of his own objectives in office.

"Park Chung Hee built Korea's high-growth economy. That is accomplished. He will go down in history for that. It is left to me to bring Koreans democracy. That, I hope, will be my monument."

Roh had sketched the outlines of his monument in the Declaration of Democratic Reform, which he issued on June 29, 1987. The time was a crisis point in modern Korean history. Following a spring of angry antigovernment demonstrations—climaxed by a violent "Peace March" of firebomb-wielding students on June 26—politicians of the government's majority Democratic Justice party had been conferring about possible concessions or countermeasures. The statement of Roh, the party's chairman and presidential candidate, went further down the path of reform than any of them had contemplated. Its eight points dealt with virtually all of the nation's democratic discontents. They were, in summary:

1. Revise the constitution, through consensus between the governing party and the opposition, in order to adopt, among other things, a direct presidential election system favored by the public so that there could be a peaceful change of government in February 1988, when the term of the incumbent president was to end.
2. Revise without delay the Presidential Election Law to ensure fair management of elections.
3. Release those imprisoned or detained for political dissent and restore their civil rights.
4. Institutionalize respect for human dignity and the protection of basic rights.
5. Promote freedom of the press by abolishing all manner of overt and covert censorship.
6. Guarantee private initiative and self-regulation and reinstate local autonomy to build a vibrant democratic society.
7. Create a political climate conducive to dialogue and compromise and guarantee sound political party activities.
8. Carry out bold ethical reforms to build a clean and honest society.

Having made his statement, Roh added that he would present it to President Chun for approval. He was prepared to resign, if Chun did not accept it. Chun did accept it, publicly, in a televised speech to the nation two days later. Just a week later more than 500 political prisoners were released, and pardons, with restoration of civil rights, were granted to 2,300 others. Conspicuously included in this number was the opposition leader Kim Dae Jung, whose name Roh had mentioned in his statement. A working committee was set up to implement the reforms he promised, specifically in the area of labor rights, election laws, and freedom of the press. Roh himself began a series of talks with opposition party leaders — an act virtually without precedent at that time in Korean politics.

He won the December election with 36.6 percent of the vote, thanks largely to a split between the opposition party leaders Kim Dae Jung and Kim Young Sam, neither of whom proposed to play second fiddle to the other. At his inauguration Roh proclaimed that the "era of the common man" had come to Korea, thus canonizing the new dominance of Korea's middle class. In the Jimmy Carter tradition, he broke with past presidential precedent by refusing to be called "excellency" *(kakha)*, instituting a series of round table meetings and carrying his own briefcase—the last activity no idle gesture, as any longtime visitor to a Confucian society could attest. The country breathed a collective sigh of relief at the first peaceful transfer of power since the Republic of Korea was established in 1948.

The euphoria did not last long. The release of dissidents did not necessarily decrease the high decibel level of their complaints against the established order. Press criticism grew stronger—and considerably more varied—as it was freed of censorship. (The thirty daily newspapers in Korea at the time of Roh's 1987 declaration had grown to more than ninety by 1991; and there are now more than 6,000 magazines in circulation.) And with restrictions on union activity largely removed, the labor front exploded.

Some 3,600 labor-management disputes broke out in the six months following Roh's declaration—more than double the incidence of labor disputes recorded over the ten years previous. In two years the number of unions doubled, shooting up to almost 7,400 by the end of 1989. Strikes and walkouts were the order of the day, not merely among traditional blue-collar workers but by white-collar office employees in finance and other service sectors. Frustrated by years of low pay and iron-fisted paternalism, angry employees made huge demands of their companies, enforcing them with mass "struggle" tactics—"sit-ins first, negotiations later," as the saying went. Employers reacted by lockouts and shutdowns. These were supported on the whole by police and security forces who found the new democratization measures hard to get used to.

Not surprisingly, heavy-industry plants were the scenes of the most bitter labor warfare, reflecting the long suppression of union activities during the all-out export drives. In December, 1988 workers at Hyundai Heavy Industries shipyards in Ulsan began what turned into a 109-day strike against a company that was traditionally antiunion. Demanding heavy wage increases and the reinstatement of various fired union officials, the workers fought off company security guards and were subdued in the end when the government sent 14,000 riot police in to clear the plant.

The Hyundai battle was an extreme case, for in general Roh's government tried to back away from labor-management disputes. Ingrained institutional attitudes do not change overnight, however. On the one hand labor wanted big gains *now*. Union leaders contended, with some justice, that the workers had been cheated of a fair share of profits during two decades of all-out, determinedly low-cost production. They were not easily appeased. Against them both management and the bureaucracy argued that sudden wage hikes could destroy national competitiveness in Korea's chronic "export-or-die" situation.

The problem was real. After years living under a garrison-state economy, the Korean people were understandably anxious to improve their quality of life. Many managers, the chaebol leaders in particular, were fearful that pay raises would cripple their competitiveness. Union leaders wanted the raises at all costs. More farsighted economic planners saw the Korean middle class developing into the kind of big consumer economy the country needed, if it was ever to escape excessive and ultimately dangerous reliance on its overseas customers. (As Japan's example indicated, a strong domestic market also helped keep export products competitive.) Roh's reform administration, caught on the horns of this dilemma, was in a difficult position.

"Going back to 1987," Roh told me once in an interview, "you must realize that the public's demands began to erupt like a volcano. Everybody wanted something he hadn't had before. And inevitably, all the critics concentrated on the president. We have an old Korean saying, 'The drum in the middle of the village is beaten by everyone who passes.' So *that* one must expect. I have endured the criticism for some years and tried to persevere in the course I set.

"When I went to the United Nations, in 1988, after the Olympics, one thing interested and encouraged me. Countries with bitter domestic conflicts and internal discord were actually heading towards democracy. The countries with no apparent internal problems were generally autocracies or dictatorships. Therefore, I felt that our course was not at all wrong."

Roh's 1987 decision, as he pointed out to me in a conversation we had some years later,[1] "was not something that happened overnight. Of course, my thinking was influenced by outside events, but I had been pondering this kind of thing for a long time. The decision could not have come by accident."

What qualities did Roh possess, one might ask, that made him reflect (and act) so drastically? His background and early life were not that different from many of his military contemporaries. Born in Taegu in southeastern Korea in 1932, he was in high school when the Korean War broke out. Still wearing his school uniform, he joined the army as a student soldier. In 1951 he was chosen as a cadet in the new Korean Military Academy and was graduated in 1955, along with Chun Doo Hwan and others, in the Academy's first four-year class. As a major-general and a divisional commander, he had supported Chun in his seizure of power. But he was a far more thoughtful and patient personality. He is the only patient man in Korean politics, it is said. In a country whose explosive politicians have traditionally short fuses, he is a planner who can wait for things to happen. In addition, thanks to years of international travel working out Korea's hosting of the Olympic games, he had developed something of an international perspective, beyond the Command and Staff school education of his army colleagues.

In sharp contrast to his predecessors, Roh's idea of leadership emphasizes harmony and adaption over top-down command. "The role of my presidency," he once explained, "is to serve as a kind of large furnace in which all extremes of controversy are melted. In the end we can make stronger steel out of the mixture."

This change in leadership style came at a most opportune moment, for by 1988 the Republic of Korea's version of the command-developmental economy had become the prisoner of its own success. A new consumer society, vastly better educated than the generation preceding, wanted less regulation and more creature comforts. "Democracy is a rather noisy thing," Roh was wont to observe—and his loyal citizenry was quick to demonstrate. His management style, given a variety of problems and pleadings, was to avoid direct government interference as much as possible, while people worked off steam in protests, demonstrations, and strikes.

Koreans being a highly volatile people, there was considerable risk that the economy, as well as the politics of the country, would fragment in the process. For economic change had brought with it a social revolution, which was now working its way through the country at the same frenetic pace. The transformation from an agricultural to an urban society, with corresponding pressures on the remaining farm families, a rash of environmental pollution problems—the accumulated legacy of pell-mell industrialization—punishing housing shortages compounded by wholesale land speculation: all these long-standing problems had by 1988 assumed crisis proportions. They had been so long neglected.

"I can't think of another country, at least in recent history, that went so swiftly from an authoritarian system to democracy on its own," one of Roh's cabinet members told me. "We did, however, pay a heavy economic price for it. By 1990 the economy was getting into trouble. Exports were off and the balance of payments took a sharp turn for the worse. The wage increases workers demanded were huge. Thank God for Gorbachev—with Communism fading away, the ideology had gone out of the union movement, at least.

"By the next year the anarchy had spent itself—and the country had really been close to anarchy. People realized that they had to pull together. They needed community spirit. And they began to realize that Roh was a lot better than they had thought."

From the moment Roh's June 1987 declaration was issued, workers' demands for increased pay skyrocketed. Between 1987 and 1992 basic salary levels in Korea almost doubled. And beneath the turmoil of wage demands and new special-interest pleading, other societal changes were enforcing themselves. Increased international economic competition now mandated a new emphasis on the research and technology needed for high-tech industry and invention. Graduate students and technicians at the post-graduate level were still in short supply, however. Women, now accounting for one-third of all university degrees, were becoming increasingly more important in the workplace and throughout Korean society. Yet in this land of Confucian tradition, it was not until 1989 that, following intense political pressure from women's groups, the government amended the archaic family laws under which women could neither inherit money nor have legal custody of their children. Similarly, for many years political commentators had fretted over the lack of strong local self-government, in a country where traditional Confucian centralization of authority had intensified under modern military rule. In 1991, under Roh's administration, elections for local assemblies were held throughout the country for the first time in thirty years—that is, since Park Chung Hee's coup abolished them in 1961.

On assuming the presidency, therefore, Roh Tae Woo faced a staggering task. While the din of newly liberated groups and organizations grew oppressively, he had the obligation, as the "democracy" president, of supporting them. He was faced with mounting public grievances against the chaebol, whose heavy-handed land speculation had helped drive up the prices of urban land and housing to a point far beyond the reach of most private citizens. In addition the competitive power of the chaebol, backed by years of preferential government financing and export subsidy, was enough to make life rocky for new, smaller enterprises. Yet it was here that the entrepreneurial spirit needed to be fostered.

The country's infrastructure was in some disrepair. The pressure for economic liberalization continued, as Korea was becoming recognized as a rather big player in international trade. The farming sector, by 1988 shrunk to 17 percent of the total, was in trouble. Increasingly farmers' groups began to demonstrate, arguing for price increases and protection against agricultural imports from abroad. Meanwhile increasingly radicalized student groups kept up their warfare with the riot police. Demanding reunification of Korea at all costs, they became willing dupes of North Korean propaganda in their demands for unilateral South Korean concessions.

Buoyed by its success in hosting the 1988 Olympics, which became a time of national pride and stock-taking (see chapter 9), Roh's government set itself some broad objectives for the Sixth Republic. The overarching goal was to move toward reunification. Here Roh made a sharp break with his predecessors, abandoning a confrontational policy for one of accommodation with the North wherever possible. (See chapters 9 and 10.) Other international goals included an increase of trade with Russia, China, and other former Communist bloc countries, as well as increased liberalization of trade with the United States and other leading international customers—in which respect the Koreans succeeded in liberalizing far beyond Japan's trade liberalization at a comparable stage in Japan's development.

Most immediate were the demands of the infrastructure. While expanding welfare and pension programs and subsidies to the needy, Roh made housing the centerpiece of his policy here. "I feel pain in my heart," he said at a May 1991 meeting, ". . . at the prices of apartments, houses, and land that have been soaring at a runaway speed during the last three years." He promised to construct an additional 2 million units of affordable housing during his administration. The promise was kept.

Roh's pledges to curb the power of the chaebol, although popular with most of the citizenry, met with less success. Legislation was passed barring further land speculation by the chaebol, but this was tantamount to locking the barn door after several generations of horses had galloped out. Nonetheless the government managed to cut back severely on the traditionally preferential treatment the chaebol had received, in some cases subjecting selected conglomerates and their owners to tax investigations and penalties. Chung Ju Yung, Hyundai's founder and honorary chairman, was among those most affected. In 1991, despite the past close relationships between Hyundai and the government,[2] Roh's government slapped him with a $180 million bill for allegedly unpaid personal income taxes. In retaliation Chung formed a new political party, which would draw an embarrassing 10 percent of the vote in the 1992 National Assembly elections.

The long-developed symbiosis between the chaebol and the Korean government would be mutually destructive to terminate. Most of the chaebol have grown mightily over the years. In 1991, for example, the four largest of the thirty-odd chaebol, Hyundai, Samsung, Lucky Goldstar, and Daewoo amassed estimated sales of $135.3 billion altogether, slightly more than half of the country's $264.8 billion GNP.[3] Originally family owned and managed, they are gradually moving to a professional management system and, in many cases, divesting themselves of various subsidiaries. Conversely, smaller entrepreneurial companies are increasingly coming to the fore.

It is in the area of political democratization, however, that Roh Tae Woo's administration will be most critically judged. On the whole, the record is good. While labor unions have been given ever wider latitude in organizing and representing their workers—by 1990 eight thousand unions were in place—and restrictions removed on a wide variety of business activities, the government has been most active in the human rights sector. Some 1,600 statutes and administrative decrees were revised or repealed to eliminate human rights abuses that proliferated under past governments. This included the infamous National Security law, which, under the guise of curtailing pro–North Korean political activity, provided a handy excuse for arrests or surveillance of a wide variety of "suspects."

Democratization is far from complete. Changing laws is merely a first, albeit essential, step. The judiciary needs additional strengthening. Although Roh has restored the authority of the constitutional court, for example, its judgments need more consistent enforcement. The legacy of four decades of authoritarian governments has left its mark on the bureaucracy that administers the laws, not to mention the host of administrators, from university presidents to broadcasting executives, who grew all too accustomed to having decisions made for them. The tendency to play it safe and steer clear of the politically "controversial" and wait for the next government directive has been implanted in several generations of officials as deeply as the tendency to follow a kind of outmoded knee-jerk leftism—pro–Kim Il Sung, antigovernment, anti-American—has fastened itself on successive generations of student radicals who in this respect continue to resemble the professionally wild-eyed student "radicals" of Japan in the mid-sixties. Each extreme is dangerous.

Roh's great contribution here has been to defang the entrenched opposition of past governments to the give-and-take of the democratic process. He has done this principally by reviving—establishing is probably a better word—the authority of the National Assembly to make laws and conduct audits and investigations in support of its laws. (Its new privileges include the right to televise sessions and hearings.)

In past years the Assembly functioned mostly as window dressing for the executive branch, any possibility of really independent action being canceled by the automatic government party majorities. When the Thirteenth National Assembly met in April 1988, Roh's government party was in a minority. The three opposition parties controlled 55 percent of the votes. Roh pledged himself to work with the opposition—the first time this had happened in recent Korean history—but he did not find it easy. One of the Assembly's first votes was to turn down Roh's candidate for chief justice of the Supreme Court. Next, the Assembly formed several special committees for public investigations of what abuses had been allowed in Chun Doo Hwan's Fifth Republic. For the first two years of Roh's governance, executive and Assembly lived in a kind of perpetual stalemate. Roh could veto legislation, but he lacked the power to put through new laws. The three opposition parties, in turn, fought among themselves. In a delicate period of national transformation lawmaking was severely restricted, apart from obvious cases of agreement about repealing old security regulations.

Roh is quite sincerely a democrat. "There is an old Korean saying," he once told me, "that the wishes of the people are the wishes of God." At the same time he holds a firm if unstated belief in the old adage that politics is the art of the possible. And in a most delicate political and economic situation he badly needed an Assembly majority to carry out his program. Almost from the moment of his inauguration he set about contriving a merger of convenience between his minority Democratic Justice party and two of his election opponents—the Reunification Democratic party of the longtime reformer Kim Young Sam and the right-wing New Democratic Republican party of Park Chung Hee's old henchman Kim Jong Pil. For two years trusted staff members carried out negotiations with both parties, neither of whom knew that the other was in on the deal.

"We came to him from time to time," one of his close political aides recalled, "and said the outlook was hopeless. He would only say, 'Go back and keep at it. Just call them up again.' Once he has set his objective, he never deviates from it."

The result of the merger was the Democratic Liberal party, announced by the president to a surprised nation in January 1990. The reaction in the country was by no means favorable. There were predictable denunciations of under-the-counter tactics, most particularly from Kim Dae Jung, the veteran opposition leader whose party had been left out. But Roh and his people were happy. With a legislative majority he could now govern. His tactics may have been embarrassingly covert, but they won for him. The merger was not popular with the populace; cries of "sellout" predominated. At least it ended a frustrating time of political stalemate, which neither Roh nor the country could afford.

Whatever the flaws in his tactics and however many abuses remained from an earlier day, the patient president had brought democracy back to Korea. Others had tried to do this before, but their efforts had faded along with their brief hopes. Roh's democratization was successful because he institutionalized it. However strong the holdovers from the authoritarian past—and censors, police power, and industrial despots have by no means vanished from the scene—the Sixth Republic established and made firm for the first time a solid structure of democratic law and practice, supported by the vast majority of its citizens. The norms, guidelines, and safeguards of a working democracy are in place. Noisy, unruly, and contentious though it be, the Korean polity is governed by the give-and-take of democracy at work. That is the legacy Roh Tae Woo will turn over to his successor in 1993. It is a great achievement, one that Roh hopes will stay untarnished by favoritism or military coup. "The next president," he has announced, "should come neither from the army nor from my family circle."

Two and a half cheers for democracy, one might say, but what was the price? What has the infusion of democratic values done to Park Chung Hee's ironclad economic miracle? At this point it might be worth evaluating how the country's economy has fared in the process of democratization.

From 1987 through 1991 the economy grew at an annual rate of slightly more than 9 percent. Per capita income doubled during this time in U.S. dollar terms from $3,110 in 1987 to $6,498 in 1991—a tremendous increase, even allowing for some won depreciation. Inflation, tightly held at less than a 5 percent annual increase during the early 1980s, has grown. But the consumer price index rise has been kept under 8 percent. This is no mean national achievement, particularly when we factor in annual national wage increases of 20 percent each year.

Since 1990 the country's international balance of payments has worsened, with substantial deficits. Yet thanks to surpluses accumulated in preceding years — the not-inconsiderable legacy of Chun Doo Hwan's expanded export economy — the net foreign debt went down by $10 billion, from $22.4 billion in 1987 to $12.5 billion in 1991. This is not a bad performance for a country whose high-risk borrowing policies (foreign debt once exceeded $40 billion) gave so many extra gray hairs to international banking authorities.

The bad news came in the form of sagging exports and increased imports. In 1991 South Korea's trade balance was unfavorable, to the tune of almost $10 billion. (Most of this was owing to Japan, symptomatic of Korean industry's continuing dependence on Japanese products and technology for its own industry.) High labor costs inevitably slowed the pace of export growth. Corporate bankruptcies multiplied. Another factor was the transition time needed to switch to more advanced and high-tech products — even after the investment in new plants and technology has been made.

There was some good news to offset the imbalances. The savings rate, that is, domestic gross capital formation, once cause for concern, has reached a level of 34 percent. Korea's skilled engineers, technocrats, and work force are fully capable of shifting to higher technology and higher-quality products; universities, ministries, and technology institutes are working out a new philosophy of innovation. As Shim Shang Chul of the Korea Advanced Institute of Science and Technology, puts it: "We must invent and invent. That is the challenge that faces us now."

While land speculation continues, the worst of the housing shortage is over. Roh has made good on his promise to build 2 million new houses and apartment units by 1992. Partly government built, but more than half the work of private construction companies, the new housing was all sold off by the end of September 1991. Even before that, housing prices had begun to slide.

Beneath the figures lies the sweeping change in consumer habits and buying power. The Republic of Korea is now a consumer society. Domestic demand has become a powerful engine of growth. The boom in consumer spending has been explosive. Imports, many of them luxury items, went up by almost 20 percent annually over the past four years. The number of private cars, for example, soared from some 556,000 in 1985 to 850,000 in 1987 to 2,816,000 in February 1992. This growth has been hard to manage. With imports of foreign goods now largely liberalized and a whole new generation of consumers flooding department stores and discos alike, government planners have done their best to discourage excess consumption with every fiscal and monetary tool they possess. To an extent they have succeeded. Wage increases, for one thing, are coming down to reasonable levels. For all the short-term rips and bulges in the economy, the new Korean consumer society is in itself living proof of democracy at work.

NOTES

[1] The interview, as well as a later conversation with President Roh, was given in connection with an article I wrote about him and his own comments in a leading article which he wrote for the *Encyclopaedia Britannica's Book of the Year* for 1992.

[2] Some $30 million worth of Hyundai money, it was said, was "loaned" to the government for construction of the new Presidential office and reception building at the Blue House.

[3] Hyundai's share of this figure was $47.4 billion, Samsung's $42.4 billion, Lucky Goldstar's $25 billion, and Daewoo's $20.5 billion. These figures, taken from the Business Yearbook of *Maeil Kyungje,* include all the chaebol subsidiaries.

IX

NORTHERN POLITICS: ROH'S POLITICAL PENTATHLON

With 106 nations sending 13,000 athletes to Seoul, the 1988 Summer Olympics—part of the twenty-fourth Olympiad—proved to be the largest Olympic games in history. For the first time since 1972, everyone in the world participated—everyone that is, but the Democratic People's Republic of North Korea, which boycotted the games for obvious reasons. The South Korean government breathed a collective sigh of relief as the entire Communist world— athletes from China, the Soviet Union, and eastern Europe, as well as the uncommitted nations of the Third World—trooped happily into the Olympic village in the capital city of a nation that for the past four decades had been a constant on almost every socialist country's blacklist. The visitor's impression was generally good. Barring occasional unpleasantnesses caused by partisan spectators, which every Olympic Games Committee has had to live with, Koreans turned out by the tens of thousands to welcome their Olympic guests. Not the least part of the welcome was a totally new subway system, a new highway network, and a complex of spacious parks along the Han River. All of them had been put up in record time by Korean construction companies, who this time used the best of their international experience and technology on their home grounds.

The analogy with 1964 was clear to most Koreans. That year, the Tokyo Olympics had signaled Japan's real return to the community of nations, after war and occupation. The spacious Olympic buildings, the new gymnasiums and playing fields, as well as the network of belt expressways seemed the culmination of Prime Minister Ikeda Hayato's new "Double Your Income" policy. The psychological lift for the Japanese was predictably tremendous. In 1988 much the same thing happened in Seoul. Hosting the Olympics meant for most South Koreans world recognition of their republic's dramatic postwar economic resurgence.

For the Republic of Korea's president, the Olympics represented only the first milestone, if an all-important one, on a political course he had been pursuing for almost seven years — and would continue throughout his Sixth Republic. In a sense, the Olympics were part of Roh Tae Woo's political pentathlon. The pentathlon, a hallowed Olympic event for military men, involves sustained performances in riding, running, swimming, fencing, and target shooting. Fittingly enough for a former four-star general, Roh's pursuit of "northern politics" — both before and after 1988 — was a classic exercise in the political version of such diverse skills. It also represented something of a turning point in modern Korea's history.

Roh's efforts at "northern politics" fell in naturally with what other Korean statesmen had begun to discuss. The word *Ostpolitik* — eastern politics — was of course coined by Germany's then Prime Minister Willy Brandt in the 1970s. Although at first he had very little to show for his efforts, Brandt kept extending the hand of reconciliation to East Germany, subsidizing a variety of aid and trade relationships with West Germany's well-heeled economy. Nor did he neglect to cultivate Communist Poland and the Soviet Union. His work was instrumental in breaking down the worst of the barriers between East and West and paving the way for Germany's ultimate unification.

The impact of Brandt's work was not lost on the Koreans. As early as 1973, in a June 23 declaration on peaceful unification, the Korean government of Park Chung Hee officially opened its door to Communist countries and proposed a new groundwork for inter-Korean relations to its hostile opposite number in Pyongyang. Yet throughout the garrison-state seventies — characterized as they were by continual North Korean acts of subversion and military muscle-flexing—few really substantive gestures were made toward harmony in the peninsula.

It was in the early eighties that some political leaders in Seoul began to think of taking a leaf from Brandt's book. If North Korea itself remained unresponsive, their reasoning ran, why not try to develop good relations with Korea's northern neighbors, the People's Republic of China and Soviet Union, as a prelude to realizing some sort of détente, at least, with North Korea itself. Former Prime Minister Lee Bum Suk probably used the term northern policy for the first time. In a lecture at the National Defense College in June 1983, Lee had said: "The supreme goal of our diplomacy in the future lies in realizing a northern policy. By normalizing relations with the Soviet Union and China. . . . It is desirable to pursue this Northern strategy to prevent recurrence of a war."

After Roh Tae Woo retired from the army in 1981, he was given a job as the minister of state for national security and foreign affairs in Chun Doo Hwan's government. This was a cabinet post without portfolio, but his responsibility was clear: to nail down Seoul's hosting of the 1988 Summer Games. The Olympic Committee had awarded the games to Seoul at its Baden-Baden meeting in 1981, but that was only the beginning. Through the mid-eighties the Cold War was very much with us. The United States had after all boycotted the Moscow Olympics. There was now considerable doubt as to whether the USSR, the People's Republic of China, and other Communist countries would send their athletes to Seoul against the loud and vociferous opposition of their brethren in Kim Il Sung's North Korea.

In 1982 Roh became Korea's first minister of sports. His ministry was created largely to support the Olympic games. At the same time, as the president of the Seoul Olympic Organizing Committee, it fell to him to travel worldwide for the next five years, attempting to talk up the Olympics and persuade all concerned that the Republic of Korea was going to be an open and impartial host.

This was not an easy job. One of the by-products of Korean partition was the garrison-state mentality implanted in the leadership of South Korea, as well as the North. The very word Communism had long been anathema. In fact, until Roh's Sixth

Republic's democratization policy, articles on Communism and Marxism in such respected publications as the *Encyclopaedia Britannica* had to be erased or censored before they could be sold in South Korea. Rigid security laws against Communists or Communist sympathizers were on the books. According to a strict interpretation of those laws, in fact, a large portion of the Communist countries' Olympic athletes, not to mention their coaches and security handlers, would have been banned as subversives from entering the country.

Roh spent a great deal of time talking to people around the world, in an attempt to dispel the widespread impression that the Republic of Korea was imprisoned in a hopeless Cold War mindset. In the course of so doing, he shed a good bit of that mind-set himself. As he later said, "One thing that I learned from my work with the Olympics was that harmony is the most important political need. It doesn't really do much good to try to keep old ideological hatreds alive. For almost ten years, I traveled around the world talking to people in every kind of country. I found that most people everywhere were as persuaded as I was that the world must strive to harmonize different systems."

The fact that so many Communist countries even considered showing up at Seoul was a tribute to the salesmanship of Roh's political pentathlon. Of course there were two powerful factors working in his favor. Politically speaking, the time of decommunization was almost upon us. Starting with Gorbachev's reforms in the Soviet Union and Polish President Jaruzelski's devolution of political power to the Solidarity unionists and their allies, the bonds of ideology in eastern European were clearly loosening. Roh took every possible advantage of this fact. His first target was Hungary. He followed this with the visits to the Soviet Union and other countries in eastern Europe, as a prelude to the Olympics itself.

After Roh Tae Woo's famous 1987 statement promising democracy to the Koreans, it logically followed that he would set an active northern politics in motion as president. He made some public statements on this matter in 1988. In a break with past presidential behavior in Seoul, he deliberately tried to set aside the polemics with which South Koreans referred to their northern neighbor and began to talk in terms of unification and reconciliation. He refrained from further harsh words about Kim Il Sung's ideology.

There was little positive reaction to this from the North; as late as 1985 North Korean agents had assassinated several members of the South Korean government in an infamous incident in Burma. But a lot of people were listening. For the first time, the South was talking about the North, not primarily as a competitor but as a partner. This certainly fell in with the peaceful overtures being made by Moscow and, to a great extent, by the People's Republic of China. With Deng Xiaoping modernizing China on the west and Gorbachev's Soviet Union to the north, Kim Il Sung's hard-line regime was increasingly isolated. It was also, more and more, the prisoner of its own increasing economic failures.

As the thaw in Eastern Europe became a veritable torrent, the Republic of Korea began to expand its "northern politics." Diplomatic relations were established with Hungary in February 1989. Relations were normalized with Poland in November 1989, with Yugoslavia in December 1989, and with Czechoslovakia and Bulgaria in March 1990. Ceauşescu's dictatorship in Romania— which had been closest to Kim Il Sung's in spirit and operating methods—was the last holdout. After Ceauşescu himself was overthrown and a new government set up, a Romanian ambassador traveled to Seoul in 1990.

The alacrity with which the eastern European countries set up relations with Korea was not prompted solely by good fellowship. South Korea's economic progress by this time was well known. With the Japanese reluctant to deal heavily in East Europe, partly because of their lasting antipathy to Russia, South Korea seemed a likely economic partner. In fact, as an emerging Third World country itself, it was easier for Korea to work on development projects with eastern European countries. Although its technology was not nearly so sophisticated as that of Japan or the United States, there was a spirit of "catch-up" and improvisation in Korean companies that appealed to the East Europeans.

Russia itself was by no means immune to the contagion. After Gorbachev made his famous Vladivostok speech in 1986, emphasizing the importance of the Asia Pacific region, conversations began to multiply. It was still a matter of surprise when Roh Tae Woo met Gorbachev in San Francisco in June 1990, but they got along famously. Indeed, as it turned out, each was playing roughly the same historical role in his country, that of breaking an old mold and setting the groundwork for a new kind of democratic politics.

Roh made it quite clear to Gorbachev that South Korea wanted to deal with North Korea on the basis of dialogue, not confrontation. His emphasis on inter-Korean relations went down well. Later, after diplomatic relations were set up, he paid an official visit to Moscow, the first South Korean president to do so. He was in fact the first Korean head of state to visit Moscow, since Kim Il Sung had wangled permission from Stalin to invade South Korea some forty years before.

With him in 1990 Roh brought a $3 billion loan package for helping development in Siberia and elsewhere in what was then still the Soviet Union. Korean chaebol tycoons like Chung Ju Yung began to make the pilgrimage to Moscow as well, and Soviet scholars, academics, and trade officials began tramping into Seoul. After so many decades of thinking of the Soviet Union as the basic enemy, the evil empire that stood behind Kim Il Sung, South Koreans were at first nonplussed to find that the Russians were in their midst. But relations grew and continued to get stronger. In April 1991, Gorbachev stopped off at Cheju Island after his visit to Japan for the third meeting with his opposite number, Roh Tae Woo.

With the Soviet part of the northern policy secured, what was happening to relations with China? Here the economic interest was paramount. The Chinese had kept up relations with Kim Il Sung's satrapy rather more intensively than Moscow had. They were, of course, closer, with a very large border between them. When one visited Beijing, the North Koreans were a familiar sight, although not a very pleasant one. Unlike the Chinese, who by the mid-eighties were talking freely about politics as well as economics with foreigners, the North Koreans stuck to themselves. Their habit of dining at the same table in the Peking Hotel and elsewhere was symbolic. They remained as seclusive as their reputation.

North Korea's economy, however, was getting progressively worse. It was becoming a liability to both China and the Soviet Union. By contrast, the Chinese had taken full notice of South Korea's economic progress and were anxious to trade. By the late eighties, unofficial visitors were trekking back and forth in a steady stream between Seoul and Beijing—as unobtrusively as possible, since the Chinese were reluctant to offend their old running mate and wartime ally, Kim Il Sung. But money talked. By 1989, the annual trade between the People's Republic of China and the Republic of South Korea had passed the $3 billion mark. Chinese were talking about a steamer ferry service between the Shandong peninsula and the west coast of Korea, and economic officials of both countries were waxing enthusiastic about mutual development projects involving Shandong and the Korean west coast.

Again, Korea could offer exactly the middle-level technology that China needed—and on considerably more favorable terms than Japan. From where Beijing sat, also, expanding economic relations with Korea would be a good competitive stimulant to encourage Japan and Taiwan to invest and trade more in the P.R.C.

By 1991, the two-way trade was up to $5.8 billion. On February 1992, a bilateral trade agreement went into force, granting a "most favored nation" status to both. Following this agreement Korea's exports to China were expected to increase appreciably. Similarly, Korean industrialists hoped to boost sales of petrochemical products and some varieties of steel 30 to 40 percent by eliminating the old discriminatory tariff barriers.

Now in contact with Beijing and Moscow, Roh Tae Woo continued lobbying, this time to secure a joint entry to the United Nations for both Koreas. Since 1973, Kim Il Sung had totally opposed this, wanting the Koreas to join the United Nations only under the guise of a single membership, with both countries participating. This was seen in the South as an obvious attempt to infiltrate the South Korean government and bring the whole peninsula under Kim's Communist rule. (Interestingly enough, however, the South had proposed a single membership for both countries during the sixties, only to be opposed by the North.) Since 1949 South Korea filed for U.N. membership eight times; the North had filed four. Each was vetoed by the other's proponents on the Security Council.

Ultimately the Chinese and the Russians agreed with the South's view that the best way to encourage unification was to have simultaneous entry of both nations into the United Nations. Russia announced that it would support this. The Chinese leadership, in informal talks with Kim Il Sung, made it increasingly clear that he could expect no veto from China to keep South Korea out.

With this the last barrier went down. In May 1991, North Korea accepted South Korea's call for joint entry. In September of that year, South and North joined the United Nations.

The "northern politics" were fortuitously timed. South Korea's obvious advantages as an economic trading partner bulked large, as the ideological ties of the old Communist bloc had begun to dissolve. But without the Olympics and the bridge-building approach Roh had used, it is doubtful that things would have happened so fast. As it is, "northern politics" stands as the great success of postwar Korean diplomacy. By persuading just about everyone to welcome Korea as a useful partner, the Republic of Korea for the first time broke out of its isolation.

Even during the long centuries of its independence, Korea lived in a constant forced symbiosis with China and Japan—a prisoner of its peninsular geography. For almost three decades after 1945, South Korea was a virtual client-state of the United States. Now neither a Japanese nor an American client—and positioned at a more secure economic, political, and social level than Taiwan, the city-states of Hong Kong and Singapore, or the emergent Southeast Asian NICs—Korea was equipped to play an independent role in Pacific and world politics.

On August 24, 1992, this new independence was spectacularly confirmed when Roh Tae Woo announced the establishment of full diplomatic relations between South Korea and the Peoples Republic of China—perhaps the ultimate expression of joint national interests' triumph over fading ideology. The declaration was not unexpected. Over the past two years communications between the two countries had intensified; more than 40,000 Koreans had visited China in 1991. Various chaebol had already announced plans for major investments and joint ventures in the PRC. Roh's prediction of $10 billion in bilateral trade for 1992—with imports and exports virtually in balance—seemed realistic. The United States and Japan looked on approvingly.

Taiwan, long Korea's political ally (and business competitor) reacted indignantly and prepared to move its diplomats out of their expensive Seoul embassy, a sacrifice to Beijing's "one China" policy. But a prospering Taiwan, possessor of the world's largest hard-currency reserves ($80 billion plus) suffered only facial bruises from the slight. For struggling North Korea the defection of its last strong supporter amounted to a disaster. There was no comment from Pyongyang.

". . . the last external constraint for a peaceful unification of the Korean peninsula," Roh said in his statement, "is now removed. . . . Normalization of relations between Korea and China will greatly contribute to the resolution of various pending issues between South and North Korea. . . ."

Ideally, yes. But for the time being the ultimate answer to unification remained inside the battered, but still unbowed satrapy of Kim Il Sung.

X

THE MARXIST SHAMAN AND HIS HERMIT KINGDOM

It was quite a birthday party. There were massed formations of 100,000 uniformly dressed students—no demonstrators allowed here—waving and switching their sector cards to form human mosaics on parade grounds or inside huge stadiums, 8 million flowers woven into massive tribute wreaths, a special blanket made of feathers from 700,000 birds, 5,000 frogs trapped by army detachments to produce stamina-building elixirs, 1,300 snapping turtles sacrificed for the same purpose, incessant parades attended by 3,600 international VIPs and five obliging Third World presidents, rhapsodic editorials, televised pageants, new revisions of the 35-book shelf of the birthday boy's collected works, newly cast additions to the 35,000 pieces of statuary already in place to honor the Great Leader. All this was in honor of Kim Il Sung's eightieth, memorialized with much éclat on April 15, 1992.

The price tag for the weeks of celebration in the Democratic People's Republic of North Korea was estimated at $1 billion, almost one-twentieth of North Korea's estimated GNP. This was seen by the country's ruling circles as no more than fair congratulation for President Kim Il Sung, "peerless patriot," "savior of humanity," "ever-victorious, iron-willed military commander," "the greatest philosopher-politician in the annals of human history," "the sun of the nation"—as North Korea's obedient press reports had it—"the most profound revolutionary genius of all time." As

113

in past years, celebrants were mobilized around the 23-meter-high bronze statue of Great Leader in his antiseptic capital of Pyongyang. Kim is looking south, presumably awaiting the day of unification, his idealized expression mirroring the "lofty, virtuous Communist character which no one has ever had before."

Kim, born Kim Sung Jo, was, like his original counterpart Syngman Rhee, an exile. He grew up in Manchuria and the Soviet Union. After making a modest reputation in partisan border warfare against the Japanese, Major Kim was brought back to Korea, uniformed and trained by his Soviet sponsors. He was installed as the chairman of the then North Korean Communist Party late in 1945, after Soviet troops had marched in to occupy the northern portion of Korea. He was then thirty-three. Forty-seven years later, he remains the supreme dictator of North Korea, having survived two generations of war, invasion, economic disaster, intraparty warfare, ideological infighting by big power sponsors, and, ultimately, the collapse of world Communism.

Starting as an obedient pro-Soviet Communist, he gradually abridged, then threw out the conventional Marxist-Leninist scriptures to develop his home-grown ideology of *juche*—roughly translated as "national self-reliance." This is, as the master himself defined it, "an independent, self-reliant policy of solving one's affairs by oneself under all circumstances." Practically speaking, *juche* means that over the years Kim managed to shake off traditional Communist subservience to both the Soviet Union and the People's Republic of China, his two ideological, military, and economic supporters, and set up North Korea as a personal satrapy ruled by himself and members of his family.

His eldest son, Kim Jong Il, a.k.a. Beloved Leader, is as of this writing the number two man in the country. Long since ticketed to succeed his father as president of the People's Republic and secretary general of the Korean Workers' Party—he is already supreme commander of the People's Army—he has become the subject of the same hagiography as his parent. His birth fifty years ago is now piously commemorated by the regime's spokesmen as the appearance of a "guiding star" atop Mt. Paekdu, Korea's traditional sacred mountain.[1] Saddam Hussein, Sese Seko Mobutu, Fidel Castro, and the shades of Josef Stalin, Mao Zedong, and Nicolae Ceauşescu, take note. For all their conspicuously successful consolidations of power, Kim's is the name which must take priority in the modern despots' Book of Records.

Without due attention to Great Leader Kim and his hold on power, it is quite impossible to understand the curious and unique situation of the Democratic People's Republic of North Korea, the gulf that separates the North Korean people from their relatives in the South—and the problems in the way of Korean reunification. Although constantly compared to the former East and West Germany, the Korean case is different. The two postwar Germanys did not fight a three-year civil war. Before their final unification in 1990, they had, thanks to the Ostpolitik of the Federal German Republic in the seventies, almost twenty years of practical, if uneasy, coexistence behind them. By contrast, Kim has kept the North Korean people almost totally sealed from the outside world, fraternal Communist allies included, at least since the late fifties. The modern isolation of North Korea resembles nothing so much as the Hermit Kingdom which all Korea was, almost until the close of the nineteenth century.

Kim's ascendancy cannot be dismissed as the result of an outside Soviet power grab. The Soviet armies who occupied the northern half of the Korean peninsula, it is true, had at first a great deal going for them. With the Soviet troops—in fact among them, in many cases—came some 30,000 Soviet Koreans, people whose families had fled across the border years before to escape the Japanese colonial regime. Many other Koreans had fought with the Chinese Communists through World War II and the anti-Guomindang civil war in China that followed. Trained men from these two groups provided the nucleus of the North Korean Army.

Yet there already existed in North Korea a considerable underground of Communist and other leftist sympathizers, who had kept up connections with guerillas like Kim Il Sung fighting the Japanese in border areas. The Soviets and their Korean supporters were quick to proclaim and effect a sweeping land reform in their occupation zone north of the 38th parallel—in contrast to the ill-informed American occupiers in the South, who unwisely made common cause at first with pro-Japanese police and other collaborationists from the colonial days. The land reform was popular, as was the prompt nationalization of all property formerly owned or occupied by the Japanese. Instead of organizing a military government, as the Americans had in the South, the Soviet authorities kept in the background, leaving the apparent governance of the country to the Korean peoples' committees that had sprung up after the Japanese surrender. The anti-Communist opposition was pushed aside with the usual roughness, and many fled to the South. This left North Korea, however, with at least the appearance of a unified "people's" and "liberation" government, which enjoyed a great deal of popular support. Most of Korea's large property owners and business leaders were in the South. To the poorer farmers and townspeople of the North, many of them barely eking out a subsistence living, the coming of the Soviet troops and the apparent egalitarianism of the peoples' committees at first seemed like a real "liberation."

Young and dynamic, his wartime guerilla activities skillfully magnified by local Communist propagandists, Kim seemed a perfect candidate for the leadership of a Soviet satellite. He proved, however, to be far from the obedient puppet his Soviet sponsors hoped for. An adept organizer and manipulator, in the Marxist sense of the word almost a perfect "political," Kim set out from the start to build his personal power base. He did not have an easy time of it. Within the Korean Communist leadership there were three factions. Kim led the Soviet faction, composed of Koreans from the USSR, many of them Soviet citizens and Red Army veterans; it was this group that first seized the levers of power, thanks to the support of the Russian occupiers.

There was a second strong group of Yanan Koreans, that is, Koreans who had worked and fought with the Chinese Communists. They kept up close contacts with Mao Zedong and other party leaders across the border. A third group comprised various distinguished members of the Korean Communist underground. Some of them, like Park Hun Young, were well known throughout the country. Park, for one, had far better party credentials than Kim. An older man, he was one of the founders of the Korean Communist party in 1921. He had worked as an organizer in Seoul and elsewhere in the South, studied in Moscow, and been captured by the Japanese police when he returned to Korea. (He was released

STUDENT DEMONSTRATORS IN SEOUL, APRIL 4, 1990. *(Yon Hap News Agency)*

PRESIDENT ROH TAE WOO (RIGHT) WELCOMING PRESIDENT MIKHAIL GORBACHEV TO CHEJU ISLAND. THEIR INFORMAL SUMMIT CONFERENCE WAS HELD ON APRIL 19 AND 20, 1990. *(KOIS)*

PRESIDENT ROH ADDRESSING THE HUNGARIAN PEOPLE'S COUNCIL (PAR-
LIAMENT) ON NOVEMBER 23, 1989. ROH'S TRIP TO HUNGARY WAS THE
FIRST KOREAN STATE VISIT TO A SOCIALIST COUNTRY. *(KOIS)*

PRESIDENT ROH TAE WOO (RIGHT) WELCOMING PRESIDENT
VACLAV HAVEL OF THE CZECH AND SLOVAK FEDERAL REPUBLIC TO
CHONG WA DAE (THE PRESIDENTIAL RESIDENCE) ON APRIL 27, 1992.
THEIR WIVES ARE BEHIND THEM. *(KOIS)*

FORMER PRIME MINISTER KANG YOUNG HOON (RIGHT) OF SOUTH KO-
REA GREETING PRIME MINISTER YON HYONG MUK OF NORTH KOREA
UPON HIS ARRIVAL IN SEOUL FOR THE FIRST ROUND OF SOUTH-NORTH
HIGH-LEVEL TALKS (SEPTEMBER 4, 1990). *(Yon Hap News Agency)*

NORTH KOREAN CLASSICAL ARTISTS AND MUSICIANS CAME TO SEOUL FOR
YEAR-END SOUTH-NORTH UNIFICATION CONCERTS IN DECEMBER 1990.
(KOIS)

THE FIRST SOUTH-NORTH JOINT TEAM TO PARTICIPATE IN INTERNA-
TIONAL COMPETITION WON THE WOMEN'S TEAM TITLE IN THE 41ST
WORLD TABLE TENNIS CHAMPIONSHIPS IN CHIBA, JAPAN, FROM APRIL 24
TO MAY 6, 1991. *(Yon Hap News Agency)*

BISHOP TJI HAK SOUN OF SOUTH KOREA HAS AN EMOTIONAL REUNION
WITH HIS NORTH KOREAN SISTER DURING THE FIRST AND ONLY EX-
CHANGE OF HOMETOWN VISITING GROUPS FROM SEPTEMBER 20–23,
1985. *(Yon Hap News Agency)*

OPENING CEREMONY OF THE SEOUL OLYMPIC GAMES, SEPTEMBER 17, 1988. *(Song Ki Yup)*

SEOUL, SHOWING TOKSUGUNG PALACE IN THE CENTER FOREGROUND, CITY HALL TO THE LEFT, AND NAMSAN MOUNTAIN TO THE RIGHT. *(KOIS)*

TAE KWON DO, THE TRADITIONAL MARTIAL ART OF KOREA, WAS DEVEL-
OPED OVER TWO THOUSAND YEARS AGO. *(KOIS)*

THE OLYMPIC PARK IN SEOUL, SCENE OF THE 1988 GAMES. *(KOIS)*

PRESIDENTS ROH AND BUSH PRESIDE AT A ROK-U.S. MINISTERIAL CON-
FERENCE ON JANUARY 5, 1992. *(KOIS)*

President Roh transplanting rice seedlings on May 10, 1992, in Umsong, Chungchongbuk province, in commemoration of Farmers' Day. *(KOIS)*

Rev. Moon Sun Myung meeting with North Korean President Kim Il Sung in Pyongyang on December 7, 1991. *(Segye Times)*

after feigning insanity.) When he fled north after the U.S. military government ordered prominent Communists' arrests, he and other old Communists had to be brought into the leadership of the new Korean Workers' Party in Pyongyang. Their alliance with Kim Il Sung was an uneasy one, however, and it took some time before he consolidated his power.

In 1950 Kim Il Sung made a bad miscalculation in assuming that the Americans would not intervene in the Korean War. By the time the armistice was finally signed in 1953, North Korea had been as badly devastated as the South—saved only by Chinese intervention from total defeat. Although himself responsible for the war, Kim now used the defeat as a pretext for eliminating leaders of the rival Communist factions. Park Hun Young, then the foreign minister, was arrested even before the July armistice as an "American imperialist spy." He was later executed, along with other prominent old Communists. Thousands more were purged. Next, despite the presence of Chinese Communist troops in Korea, Kim went to work on the Yanan faction, dismissing and imprisoning many. (Everyone, it seemed, was responsible for wartime mistakes except Kim.)

Throughout the fifties Kim cleverly played off his Soviet sponsors against the Chinese, using each "big brother" to support various measures unpalatable to the other. (For example, he used Mao's adoption of agricultural communes as a pretext for collectivizing Korean agriculture, a move the Khrushchev Russians opposed.) By the sixties he had worked out his juche program, while managing to extract aid from both Moscow and Beijing, and the mystique of the Great Leader began to grow, promoted by consistent propaganda campaigns. (Those old Communists who had warned against "the cult of personality" in Korea were no longer around.)

Now politically supreme, Great Leader presided over an economic modernization drive that at first yielded impressive results. Aided by China and the Soviet Union, the North Koreans pushed steel, machinery, and other heavy industry in the old Stalinist tradition. At first the achievement was impressive; education and health facilities were vastly better than before the war and for a time the lot of the average family improved. Until 1965, at least, per capita GNP in the North was higher than in the South.

But where Park Chung Hee in the South was wise enough to diversify, import new technology, and continue to produce consumer goods—despite his growing emphasis on heavy industry—Kim Il Sung stuck to an old-fashioned Marxist command economy. Scorning foreign technology and restricting trade generally to countries of the then-Soviet bloc, the North Koreans in fact combined the worst features of the Soviet and Chinese systems. While keeping a centralized Stalinist-type industry, they based production increases on the Stakhanovite system. Hoping through constant pressure and exhortation to get ever more work out of each worker, Kim repeated the mistakes of Mao Zedong in his Great Leap Forward. In addition, his emphasis on weapons production and underground defenses—part of his plan "to convert the country into a military fortress"—left the economy hopelessly unbalanced.[2]

Unlike Park, Kim Il Sung did not have to worry about student dissidents, restless workers, or quality-conscious international customers. By the beginning of the seventies North Korea was riveted into a continuing war economy; and Kim's publicly aggressive attitude left little doubt but that he contemplated a second invasion of the South, when and if the chance offered itself. "Great Leader's" domination of the country had become total. There were no Korean Liu Shaoqis or Deng Xiaopings to urge a more rational approach to the economy. And the frenzied adulation that Mao needed a stormy Cultural Revolution to invoke in China had in Korea turned into a virtual religion, complete with hagiography and even miracles.

From 1980 his son-successor, Kim Jong Il, was pushed to the fore. By all accounts a spoiled, weak, and sybaritic character who at one point had abducted South Korean movie personalities to advise him on film matters,[3] Kim was first lauded by the propaganda machine as "Comrade Leader," who epitomized the nation's "unlimited" loyalty to his father. By the early eighties, now upgraded to the status of "Dear" or "Beloved Leader", he was being heralded as the parent's logical successor to continue the dynasty. Despite increasing official adulation, he has yet to make a public speech on his own. His apparent instability has allegedly provoked some criticism among the army hierarchy, in particular. But no real dissent has surfaced.

Under the eyes of a ubiquitous security police and a national network of informers, the entire North Korean population was marched to the elder Kim's beat. No country was more rigorously secluded from the outside world. The capital of Pyongyang, as foreign visitors testified, was turned into a huge Potemkin village—type showcase, with only a certain number of favored citizens allowed to live there and all communication with foreign visitors sedulously policed. Its massive triumphal arch dedicated to the Great Leader, a complex of stadiums erected in the expectation that Pyongyang would be cohost of the 1988 Olympics (Seoul offered to share them, but the North Koreans demanded impossible terms), and a giant 105-story hotel, for years unfinished, stand as barren monuments to Kim's Napoleonic ambitions. When foreigners visit, local inhabitants point to them with apparently unrehearsed pride.

Almost two generations of Koreans have grown up within the confines of "Kim Il Sung thought," the idea of Great Leader's infallibility dinned into them at school, in the workplace, and through the media. "Thank you, Great Leader, Kim Il Sung" is the phrase North Korean children are taught as a kind of grace before meals. From government day-care centers to totally regimented schools—the leading college is of course Kim Il Sung University—from compulsory military service to working for Stakhanovite goals in farms and factories, North Koreans are rigidly organized. Wages are minimal. Economists in Seoul estimate that personal consumption makes up less than 30 percent of the country's GNP! Basic clothes and comestibles are rationed—or handed out to the populace as gifts from the Great Leader. Nowhere even in the old Communist world had ideological regimentation seemed so complete.

So tightly did Kim Il Sung enclose his modern Hermit Kingdom that accurate accounts of what goes on there remain difficult to find, still more to assess. One thing is sure. The North Korean economy is a crumbling museum piece. Industrial plant has not been replaced; it is simply running down. There was a temporary rash of foreign technological imports in the 1970s—for which North Korea, now an international bankrupt, was unable to pay. Since that time foreign banks and businesses have been understandably unwilling to advance any more credit. Without any prospect of technological transfer, there has been no technological change. And the few foreign joint ventures are mostly small factories supported by a surprisingly loyal group of North Korean sympathizers among Koreans living in Japan.

Most of the country's Research and Development seems to have been lavished on producing and developing weaponry originally imported from Russia and China (Kim's impressive, single-minded drive to acquire nuclear weapons capability, originally based on Soviet technology, has borrowed from many sources). (See chapter 11.) Factories are running at about 45 percent of capacity. Consumer goods are in desperately short supply—except for the well-stocked showcase stores in Pyongyang.

The political disintegration of the old Soviet Union and eastern Europe's decommunization removed North Korea's major source of oil and capital goods, for which the North Koreans could once pay in barter or on favorable reduced terms. (The Russians now demand hard currency or, at the least, delivery of barter goods on very favorable terms.) The Chinese, busy working up their burgeoning trade relationship with South Korea, have not been forthcoming with lavish aid or trade offers. While Kim's ideological stance for a time gratified the hard-line stalwarts of Beijing's post-Tiananmen leadership, he cannot match the obvious economic advantages of Chinese trade with Seoul. Chinese aid shipments of foodstuffs and oil, amounting to something under $200 million, were sent to North Korea in 1991; but from 1992 Chinese trade with Pyongyang will apparently be done at market prices.

Reliable statistics on the North's economy are hard to come by, but most appraisals agree that the GNP in 1991 was something under $25 billion. Chinese and Russian estimates peg the per capita GNP lower than $500. Total foreign trade amounts to less than $5 billion, by most estimates; products are low-grade and not competitively priced, thanks to four decades of autarkic import-substitution policies. Food now is in short supply. Except for Seoul-subsidized rice and other commodities—the South Korean government funds "exporters" to the North much the way the West Germans used to fund trade with the East—there is little hope of importing from overseas. Kim Il Sung's "workers' paradise"—the term is frequently used—already owes almost $8 billion for past technology imports which it cannot pay.

Despite such conditions little visible discontent seems to have surfaced. According to *Asia Watch* estimates, there are about 150,000 prisoners in political concentration camps, but police surveillance—reported by foreign visitors as ubiquitous—is difficult to quantify. Defectors have been few, although the stories they tell of Kim's closed society are harrowing. It is possible that continued privation may blow the lid off his police state, but we cannot be sure, since the blackout of news from the outside, except for government announcements, has been total. Except for relatively highly placed officials—Pyongyang has its own well-cared-for *nomenklatura*—the North Korean population knows only what the government tells them. The rule of Kim Il Sung is all most North Koreans can remember. The effect of his constant messianic buildup, among people whose historical memory is bounded by the Korean War, Japanese colonialism, and the crumbling Confucian autocracy of the Yi dynasty, can only be conjectured. It would seem to have assumed the status of a state religion, literally. "People of the world," an official newspaper once editorialized, "if you are looking for miracles, come to [North] Korea. Christians, do not go to Jerusalem. Instead, come to [North] Korea. Do not believe in God. Believe in the great man."[4]

In 1991, during the course of a reporting trip in Seoul, I received some interesting insight on this matter from a distinguished Korean Christian leader. The Rev. Kang Won Yong, a Presbyterian clergyman for the past forty years, has a distinguished record as an educator and advocate of human rights in South Korea. To explain the strange hold Kim Il Sung may have fastened on the North Koreans, he looked for an analogy.

> As you know, we Koreans have always been fascinated by shamanism. Shamanism is the cult of the seer *(wudang)* who speaks with the voice of the gods; it has always been a part of the Korean society and life. Even now, in the countryside and to an extent in the cities, you will find shamans who are religiously sought by

people to bless anniversaries, solve problems, or suggest ways out of difficulties. Like the Greeks who believed in the oracles of Delphi, even well-educated Koreans south of the 38th parallel — though they may have been freethinkers in every other respect — have a kind of weak spot for the shaman in their society.

Take a look at Kim Il Sung. What inspires this loyalty to him? First you have shamanism, the idea of the infallible seer which has been implanted in his people. Next you have Confucianism. The Korean is traditionally a Confucianist. This Confucian tradition of obedience to authority is a state of mind that has grown up among us over the centuries; and it persists. So does the mind-set that identifies virtue with authority, putting it all in one package.

Finally, you have Communism. Communism, in its Korean dispensation, has exploited very well the ideas of shamanism and Confucianism. It intensified these traditional feelings, developed and codified them through the normal regimentations of the Communist state. Thus it was that Kim Il Sung came to power and stayed there. There was perhaps enough rooted Korean tradition to fasten his hold on the twenty million people living north of the truce line. So we have there shamanism and Confucianism — plus Kim's style of Marxism.

Then let's take another prominent Korean, the Reverend Moon, the founder of the Unification Church, with its thousands of fanatic "moonie" believers.[5] Moon Sung Myung offers us a case of shamanism and Confucianism — plus Christianity. All the same devices, the same appeal to authority, the same sense of communion with the divine which characterized the Korean mystic are observed at work among the followers of the Reverend Moon. It was no coincidence that Moon and Kim Il Sung got along so well, when Moon made his unauthorized visit to Pyongyang in 1991.

It is high irony that the Rev. Moon, whose multibillion-dollar messianic activity, through his Unification Church, has not been deterred by his 1984 conviction for income tax law violation in the United States, began his "divine" mission as a crusade against Communism, which he identified with Satan. Conversely, one of Kim Il Sung's first political tasks was to eliminate his Christian rivals from the scene in North Korea, which before the war was a Christian stronghold.

The Great Leader in Pyongyang has shown a Moon-like flexibility in regard to established doctrine. What is left of actual Marxist-Leninism in his juche dominion is barely visible. But like the Rev. Moon, he has combined the roles of shaman-seer and people-leader with great talent. All observers of North Korea agree that his Dear Leader son lacks the capability to succeed him. But whether the world of juche will break up if the father dies is a matter of conjecture.

In extending his northern politics toward the goal of re-unification, Roh Tae Woo has done almost everything possible to arrange a gradual coming together of Korea's sundered halves. Few politicians or businessmen in the South would welcome a sudden North Korean disintegration—almost as bad as the threat of nuclear armament which Kim Il Sung still implicitly makes. To rehabilitate the economically retrograde North would probably require an impossibly high expenditure of $300 to $400 billion.

In the chapters to follow we shall take a final look at the present condition of the Republic of Korea and the chances for unification with Kim Il Sung's kingdom in the North.

NOTES

[1] By a happy coincidence, the same mountain where Tangun, the legendary founder of the Korean nation, first appeared some 5,000 years back.

[2] I am indebted for this quotation and other comments on the economy to Tai Sung An's *North Korea in Transition: From Dictatorship to Dynasty* (Westport, Conn.: Greenwood, 1983).

[3] In 1973 Kim's agents kidnapped a leading film director, Shin Sang Ok, and his wife, the actress Choi Eun Hee, in Paris and brought them to Pyongyang, where they were installed as film advisers to assist him in appraising and improving the quality of North Korean movies. As research material they had access to Kim's international film collection, which reputedly runs to 15,000 titles. After eight years of this bizarre captivity, they escaped. Shin later wrote a book about their experience.

[4] As quoted in An's *North Korea in Transition.*

[5] A one-time Presbyterian clergyman — at least until his excommunication from the church in 1948 — Moon founded his "Church," officially known as the Holy Spirit Association for the Unification of World Christianity, in 1954. With funds available from a network of factories and other businesses in Korea and Japan, he set up a world-wide missionary operation in the 1970s. Later he moved his activities to the United States, where he and his zealous followers acquired a variety of enterprises, including magazines, at least one newspaper, and, most recently, a university.

XI

EXPLOSIVE CITIES AND A BOMB THREAT

A business-minded visitor to Korea might do well to come in from the south rather than expose himself immediately to the heavy traffic, vehicular and political, in the capital city of Seoul. Flying in from Pusan, a long car ride north brings you to Ulsan and beyond that to the city of Pohang. These two cities on Korea's southeastern coast epitomize the explosive growth of the South's economy and society over the past quarter-century. They straddle the sedate city of Kyongju, the historic capital of Korea's unified Silla kingdom of more than one thousand years past. But the old Silla kings sleeping under their grassy burial mounds would scarcely have comprehended the kind of growth that has taken place so close around them.

Ulsan is almost the ultimate company town. Now a city of about 730,000 souls, it grew up spectacularly in the past two decades, almost solely because of Korea's hugest conglomerate, Hyundai. Some 23,000 workers are employed at Hyundai Heavy Industries, a messy complex of shipyards and feverish construction on the shores of what was once an exceedingly tranquil Mipo Bay. Some 39,000 others work at Hyundai Motors, not far away. Hyundai Heavy Industries is one of the world's largest shipbuilders. Hyundai Motors is Korea's largest car maker and the first one to make its mark in the international market. More than half of Ulsan's population is dependent on Hyundai in one way or another.

Besides the actual employment of Hyundai workers there is a host of suppliers, subcontractors, and other companies that depend on the big ones. It is estimated that almost five hundred of Hyundai's suppliers and subcontractors do business in a small radius, close to the automobile assembly lines.

Ulsan is an attractive city in many ways. Surrounded by the low hills of a farming region, which stretches out to the west, it can boast of reasonable cultural facilities and an excellent school system, as good as Seoul's, made so to fit the standards of the thousands of engineers, technicians, business bureaucrats, and other highly skilled people and their families who have come there to work and, necessarily, to live.

Barely twenty-five years ago Ulsan was little more than an asterisk on the map of Korea. There were only a few fishing villages along the beach at Mipo, which had been memorable principally as a place where King Munmu of the old Silla monarchy enjoyed a couple of very good dinners. In 1967 Hyundai started a small factory there, which some years after began to make small cars under license to General Motors. In 1972 the ground was broken for the shipbuilding works. Just three years afterward its first products rolled down the ways.

In many ways the atmosphere at Ulsan resembles that of Toyota City in Japan. There is the same oppressive clubbiness of "working for the company" and the same tight sense of community among its people. The community, like the corporate community at Toyota, is by no means wholly peaceful. It was symptomatic that the most violent strikes and labor demonstrations in modern Korean history took place at Hyundai, when workers of the shipbuilding plant, at last free to demonstrate after the democratization of 1987, took out their long-suppressed rage against their paternalistic employer in a strike that had to be broken by police action. Toyota, too, has had its ups and downs, including a very unpleasant strike in the early fifties that resulted in the resignation of most of Toyota's management at the time.

But there is one significant difference. Toyota City, once named Koromo, was a going business concern almost half a century ago, when the first Mr. Toyoda built a new automobile factory there, near his original Toyota Loom Works. By contrast, Ulsan has grown up suddenly and explosively in the last twenty-five years. It is obviously fresh. It is also rough and appallingly vigorous. Looking over the yards, talking to the highly-skilled engineering talent assembled there, watching the robots doing their thing at the car company on the other side of town, and noting the handy "just-in-time" warehousing system—"Much the same as Toyota's, yes" said our Hyundai guide, "but a bit different"—you have a feeling of production, progress, and regimentation.

The Hyundai work jackets are almost ubiquitous. Hyundai people are happy to wear them. With the jacket come the lapel buttons and other signs of the company man. Such identification is still a big factor in this Confucian-oriented country. At Hyundai Motors, also, there are some nice homey touches. Musical chimes, reminiscent of the background accompaniment on a pinball machine, signify different processes taking place. There is a folksy painted backdrop of a forest scene on the side of the brick headquarters in the shipbuilding area. More businesslike are the workplace posters advising everyone just how much money is lost whenever the assembly line shuts down.

The 1989 strike at Hyundai Heavy Industries lasted 128 days. Management and labor were at each other's throats. The "family" spirit, which Hyundai's founder, Chung Ju Yung, had strenuously fostered, seemed to disappear in the fumes of tear gas and smashed gasoline bombs. Now labor and management have more or less made peace. They recognize—just as labor and management did in Japan some years before—that they have to work together. After the 1992 union "spring struggle," the new wage increase ended up at about 10 percent. This represented a compromise between the union bosses, who wanted much more, and management's (and the government's) desire, spurred by inflation, to keep wage increases down to one digit. It was still a far cry from the raises of the immediate postdemocratization era, which ran about 30 percent annually. But, of course, wages were very low to begin with.

It is significant, however, that at the National Assembly elections in April 1992, Ulsan delivered a resounding majority for the candidates put up by the Unification Democratic Party, the new political organization led by Mr. Chung, now Hyundai's honorary chairman—but still the boss. (One of his sons, not so incidentally, was one of the candidates.) Strikes or no strikes, loyal Hyundai workers and their families turned out massively to vote for him.

Some miles up the coast, on the other side of Kyungju, a second industrial center has risen from the quiet wilderness of Youngil Bay. The Pohang Iron and Steel Company (POSCO) was founded in 1968 by Park Tae Joon, a general turned industrialist on Park Chung Hee's orders. Construction began in 1970. Park recruited engineers and experienced workers from Korea's existing small mills, and used the best of Japanese technology then available and funding from Japanese reparations. He proceeded to build a steel company that is now the world's third-largest producer. Economic experts at the International Monetary Fund and other foreign observers all warned against it. For a government to build its own huge steel mill had ominous overtones, recalling the disastrous efforts of so many Third World countries in Africa and Latin America to put up steel mills as a sign of national economic sovereignty. Most failed.

The mill at Pohang did not fail. It was organized by the government, since the scale of investment—by Park Chung Hee's reckoning—was simply too large even for the big chaebol that had sprouted up by that time. Therefore, it seemed best to set it up as a government-run institution. It has remained so. POSCO's plant at Pohang has a production capacity of 9.4 million tons a year. Its new plant at Kwangyang on the south coast, probably the world's most modern, can produce an additional 8.1 million. Besides a wide variety of steel products its managers are not afraid to diversify. The technicians at the new plant, in response to South Korea's dwindling farm production, have set up a kind of special greenhouse farming system, borrowed from Holland, which may have revolutionary applications. The basic business, however, is steel. As at Ulsan, the visitor gets the impression of raw power but power very purposefully coordinated. The mills are spotless, heavily automated, and very, very well run. They are complemented by a bureaucracy and a public relations administration that is ever ready to point out the greatness of the achievement.

One of the most interesting features of POSCO is the technology and research establishment that has grown up along with the steel mill. The Research Institute of Industrial Science and Technology—RIST in the familiar acronym—is, as its prospectus indicates, an "integrated research" group established by the Pohang Iron and Steel Company. Situated on a high bluff overlooking the city, RIST was reorganized as an independent research institute in 1987. Its technology, of course, directly relates to steel and other industries. As its founders pointed out, it was increasingly apparent that, given technological advances, Korea had to work constantly to develop new ideas and applications to remain competitive.

Even more interesting is a brand-new university, the Pohang Institute of Science and Technology, which shares a campus with RIST. Here a select group of students from all over the country, with abundant scholarship help—taken, I was told, from the top 2 percent of the nation's high school graduates—work on a curriculum largely devoted to science, technology, engineering, and economics. The Institute awards graduate as well as undergraduate degrees. The graduate student body is expected to grow to about one thousand in the next five years, while the faculty of about two hundred are estimated to reach a total of three hundred by that time.

The Institute is of course by no means an unselfish effort. The pick of the graduates are offered jobs at POSCO, and it is a rare person who refuses. In a sense, the existence of what is in effect a company science university, suggests an interesting compromise between the American system of educating skilled workers at independent universities and the Japanese idea of having people take most of their postgraduate training after they enter the company. Nothing, however, better symbolizes Koreans' awareness that the entire country has to undertake a massive research and development effort if it wants to hold its head up in the high-tech business.

To the northwest of Pohang, on the road to Seoul, stands the city of Taejon, the site of the Korean Advanced Institute of Science and Technology. KAIST now has five thousand students—two thousand undergraduates and three thousand graduates. Again, they concentrate on science, engineering, and technology. The directors and senior faculty of KAIST spend a good deal of their time developing a cooperative relationship between Korean corporations and university research. Most Korean engineers and scientists either took their postgraduate education in the United States or are heavily influenced by American—rather than Japanese—standards. Thus they are more comfortable with university work. Nonetheless, the Korean corporation tends to like company education. The people at KAIST, as at Pohang, are doing their best to develop a middle ground where R & D can be done with corporate cooperation, but at a university level and with the detachment afforded by the university.

As we noted before, the Koreans have fought their way up from success in labor-intensive industries like textiles onto the high ground of high-tech, where they now compete with Japanese, Americans, and Europeans possessing far longer backgrounds of scientific research and development. Koreans make good scientists. But for many years, particularly during Park Chung Hee's politically oppressive regime, promising Korean graduate students tended to stay in the United States, once they arrived, and do their work there. One of the government's major tasks over the years has been to talk these students back to Korea, as well as to persuade a new crop that conditions in the new democratic Korea no longer make a brain drain necessary.

Much of this effort is coordinated by the Korean Ministry of Science and Technology, which uses all the leverage it has to promote research and development in industry. In a sense the present government is trying to use the Ministry of Science and Technology the way Park Chung Hee used government control over banks. The Ministry's funding and planning programs can act as a lever to push industry ever faster into the twenty-first century.

Korea plays catch-up ball with a vengeance. From a stand-up start in the late sixties, the Korean electronics industry has come up to fourth place in the world, just behind Japan, the United States, and Germany. In the output of DRAM semiconductors, the Republic of Korea is already in third place. Television production of 13 million units puts the Koreans just behind Japan in this category. Helped by a continuing massive government education effort, the big chaebol—Samsung, Lucky Goldstar, Daewoo, and Hyundai—are out to capture as much of the world market as they can.

Pohang and Ulsan typify the explosive growth of this economy and South Korea's new middle-class society. Japan's Meiji Revolution of 1868 has been justly acclaimed, as condensing a century and a half of the Industrial Revolution into the space of less than fifty years. The Koreans, with very little start on the modernization process, have made this transition even more quickly. Although their achievement is spectacular, its consequences, real and unintended, are also heavy. In a sense, the Republic of Korea is the prisoner of its own success. The very speed of the business miracle caused massive environmental problems, left the country's infrastructure perilously neglected, and helped create a stormy political situation. It is in Seoul, the capital, that all these problems come home to roost.

With its population of almost 10 million, still expanding, Seoul is the world's fifth-largest city. An additional 8 million live in the Seoul metropolitan area. The total comprises more than 40 percent of Korea's population. More than half of the nation's industry is located there, as are the headquarters of virtually all the great chaebol—vast, shining high-rise buildings, which combine to make Seoul one of the most dynamic looking of Asian cities, as well as one of the more conspicuous victims of urban sprawl.

The pollution is extraordinary. The 1.5 million cars of Seoul's new middle-class population clog the streets and make traffic a continuing nightmare. The city fathers have planned a large and elaborate subway system, with continuing extensions to the suburbs to divert traffic from the surface, but this is going to take a long time to encompass. The situation cannot get much better for the next five years.

The concentration of the government bureaucracy in Seoul is almost stifling—so much so, in fact, that huge sections of the government, including the Ministry of Trade and Industry, have now been moved out to the suburbs. Forty percent of Korea's university population study—and some demonstrate—in Seoul. The media and communications industry also hugs the capital.

When I first came to Seoul in 1950, it had the look of the dusty former Japanese colonial capital that it was. The Ducksoo Palace, the Namdaemon Gate, and other monuments recalled the past golden age of Korean independence, as did a few public buildings. The old Bank of Korea building and the capitol, once the seat of the Japanese governor-general, also remained. It is a commentary on the current state of Korean nationalism and anti-Japanese feeling that the capitol building, now the site of the National Museum, has been marked for demolition as an unpleasant reminder of Japan's occupation—despite the fact that it is one of the more graceful surviving pieces of nineteenth-century architecture in town.

Over the years I have come back many times to Seoul; in the sixties, the seventies, and up to the present day. I have done business there, as the president and later an adviser of a Korean company, and reported there as a journalist. With each visit the population seemed to have doubled. Through a good bit of the seventies and into the eighties, in fact, the city was disfigured by jerry-built shanty towns, housing poor people who had come from the country looking for work and could find no housing.

The second time I saw Seoul was in late September 1950, from a distance. I accompanied U.S. Marines from the First Division, with whom I had landed at Inchon, in the process of outflanking the North Korean armies. The city, of course, was in ruins. It would change hands again three times, before the final truce came in 1953. In the sixties, when I visited Seoul a great deal as a businessman, the reconstruction was complete, but it was on a modest level. Seoul at the time had a population of about 4 million, just about the size of Chicago. It was a rather grim town. There was a curfew at night; people were constantly aware of the danger from the North. Before the 12:00 P.M. curfew the streets were packed with people desperately scurrying to get home, by whatever means possible, for the curfew was generally rather strictly enforced by the police and the military.

Later in the seventies the atmosphere grew more relaxed, but it was still very much a military-business town. The American Eighth Army presence was almost ubiquitous. The various bargain discount stores, bars, and assorted fleshpots in the Itaewon area next to Eighth Army headquarters had begun to draw more than their share of customers and contention. But there was a bustle of change in the air.

By the eighties the city had taken on some aspects of opulence. The skyscrapers began to go up. A new National Assembly Building was built on Yoido, an island in the middle of the Han River, which was occupied by new offices, public buildings, and fairly expensive high-rise apartments. The land boom was on and very hard to turn off. The shantytowns were going as more housing went up around the city. By the late eighties there were as many people living south of the Han as there were north. Still, the city kept its classic landmarks. The vehicular tunnels under Namsan (South Mountain) grew more crowded, the department stores became flashier, and their consumer appeal was supplemented by amusement parks and a bewildering variety of boutiques. By the nineties traffic had multiplied to the point of almost continual gridlock. The ever more expensive stores, restaurants, and bars testified to the growing affluence of this consumer society. The arts flourished. Concerts and plays could be attended everywhere and Korean painters and musicians were becoming part of the world cultural conversation. Churches continued to proliferate, testifying to the continuing zeal of the Christian one-quarter of Korea's population.

The demonstrations and rallies in Seoul of course continued. They grew more intense in some ways after the democratization of 1987. Every dissident in the country seemed to head for Seoul, to plead his case. It was and is a magnet for dissent, as well as the center of authority. In the nineties it had become an exciting, stimulating place, for all the discomforts and soaring land prices. The struggling, battered, tentative capital of fifty years ago is now a world metropolis.

By 1992 the discontents had multiplied and become more intense. As we have noted earlier, Roh Tae Woo's democratization brought with it a flood of problems, as everyone tried to push his way to the next level on the spiral of rising expectations (political as well as economic). The polls now showed that most Koreans regarded themselves as middle class, with the number of those who thought of themselves as upper or lower class markedly decreasing. As such, most of their concerns were economic. The drives of a new consumer society had started strong inflationary tendencies, and contributed to a lopsided balance of payments.

The domestic construction boom had not helped the problem. While Cho Soon, the head of the Bank of Korea, did his best to throttle down the overheated economy, the complaints were rising.

As companies grew stronger they became more independent, too. The bureaucracy was losing its iron grip on business, for economic democracy was becoming a fact. Yet people could still justly complain about business and government corruption, which remained rife. In all these respects post-1987 Korea was far different from the country I had known for the thirty years before. It exhibited all the struggles, pains, and adversary screamings of a modern democratic society, whose people were not afraid to vent their discontent or, for that matter, rage at government policies.

In the March 1992 elections, 70 percent of those eligible voted. The government gained only 38.5 percent of the vote, with a good bit of that in safe country districts. While this was interpreted as a government defeat, the government, helped by some independents, managed to hang on to its plurality in the Assembly. "It is significant," President Roh Tae Woo noted, "that none of the parties fighting this election have raised any questions about democratization. This is now accepted. They are criticizing me because of economic problems and for economic reasons, but democratization stands. Nonetheless, we managed to keep a nine percent annual growth going in our GNP as we pushed toward democratic goals. Not a bad achievement."

In 1992 the Korean economy was in serious recession, like that of Japan and the United States. Inevitably, people blamed the government. What they complained about most was Roh's apparent reluctance to deal quickly with the pressing problems that had piled up. His supporters argued differently. As a senior minister said, "If you tried to move in and order people around, the way Chun used to do, you could have had a revolution. Best to let discontent rise to the surface."

In December 1992 the presidential election will take place. President Roh cannot succeed himself. There are three leading candidates. Kim Young Sam, long a minority party leader, was picked as the presidential candidate by Roh's ruling Democratic Liberal party. Kim is obviously President Roh's preference, but he is far from content with Korea's current state. While lauding the success of democratization, he has denounced the accompanying "breakdown of authority and order;" "excessive consumption;" and "deepening class, regional, and generational strife." All of this he called "the Korean disease."

Against him stands Kim Dae Jung, the perennial dissenter, who was nominated by the opposition Democratic Party. Kim Dae Jung continues to occupy a very special place in Korean politics. For all his faults—he has been accused with some justification of being excessively stubborn and single-minded—he has led the fight for human rights in his country for more than two decades. Particularly when one recalls his arrests and persecution by past governments, the parallel between Kim and the martyred Filipino dissenter Ninoy Aquino comes to mind. Indeed, Kim was lucky not to have escaped Aquino's fate. A fervent Catholic, Kim's religious faith has lent added conviction to his fight for democratic rights. At the same time he remains a sectional candidate. To many of his fellow countrymen in the neglected Cholla provinces, Kim stands as their representative in the age-old struggle of the people in Korea's southwest against the domination of the southeast and the north.

An added starter is Hyundai's founder and honorary chairman, Chung Ju Yung. At seventy-six, Chung has decided to stay in politics. In its first run at public office, his new Unification National Party managed to place thirty-two members in the National Assembly. To American observers he suggests a parallel to a "business" candidate like Ross Perot in the 1992 U.S. election campaign. The likeness is only superficial, however. Chung's stature and achievements are on a far higher level. He can be accounted one of the Korean economy's major builders.

For all three candidates, the basic issues are economic. There are also continuing accusations of corruption or high-handed behavior against the Democratic Liberal party—many of them no doubt justified, for it has been in power for a number of years. But the opposition—and a great many voters—feel that the government has not done enough to right the economy, even though there have been some gains. The Economic Planning Board's goal of the "three sevens" by 1992—GNP up by only 7 percent, inflation down to 7 percent, and the current account imbalance down to $7 billion—seems reasonable. By the summer of 1992 the current account deficit continued to decrease, but the economic depression continues.

The other constant issue, which subsumes almost all political discussion in the Republic of Korea, is the question of unification. All Koreans want it. The truncation of their country lies like a heavy load on people's minds, particularly the hundreds of thousands of South Koreans with close relatives in the North. (Each year at *Chusok,* the Korean Thanksgiving, people with relatives in the North come to the demilitarized zone at Panmunjom to celebrate the ancestor festival of Mang Hyang-Je—as close as they can come to their homes in the North.) Except for the diminishing number of hard-line radical students who advocate unification on North Korean terms, people of every political stripe are well aware of the pitfalls in uncritically accepting the North's proposals. Inevitably each party will set forth its own program for reunification, contending that theirs can succeed better than the others.

For most of the postwar period progress on unification was dismal. The Korean Red Cross first started discussions with its northern counterpart in 1971 about people exchanges, but very little happened thereafter. Finally in 1985, the first visits between separated families from the South and North were held in a series of meetings at Panmunjom; only sixty-five people were involved. After this, however, a kind of dialogue began to develop. North Korean officials have visited the South and people from the South have come north. A modest series of "interparliamentary" discussions were held in '85 and thereafter.

From the outset of Roh Tae Woo's Sixth Republic, reunification was pushed as the hoped-for culmination of Roh's northern policy. In 1990 and 1991 significant meetings were held at the prime-ministerial level between the two countries. At one such meeting, in Pyongyang, Kim Il Sung went so far as to acknowledge the South Korean prime minister as the head of an independent country, a big departure from his earlier violent denunciations of the "puppet regime" in the South. Sports exchanges have done better. Both Koreas agreed to field a unified team for the 1990 Asian games, with a kind of improvised Korean flag covering the two; but talks foundered over similar cooperation in the 1992 Olympics. A certain amount of cultural exchange has also been worked out.

In the spring of 1992, finally, a significant nonaggression agreement was signed by the prime ministers of the North and the South. A further limited exchange of visits was set and three North-South commissions established—on military affairs, economic exchange and cooperation, and social and cultural exchange. So far little has been done to implement these agreements.

Historically, the North's attitude has ranged from noncooperation to active hostility. Kim Il Sung's efforts to assassinate Park Chung Hee and others was followed in 1983 by the infamous bombing of a South Korean official delegation in Rangoon, Burma (Myanmar), where four cabinet ministers were killed. In 1987, the North Koreans blew up a South Korean airliner, killing all 150 passengers. The North's program of tunnel digging and suspected infiltration along the boundary continued through the late eighties. Only in the nineties has Pyongyang showed signs of conciliation.

While the South has not been guilty of subversion or aggression, anti-Communist security laws were often followed to the point of absurdity. A series of cultural exchanges was wrecked, for example, when the South refused to admit a "revolutionary" opera from the North—hardly a threat to democracy. Nonetheless, Roh Tae Woo's conciliatory policies have had some effect.

Several leaders of the chaebol, first Chung Ju Yung from Hyundai and later Kim Woo Choong from Daewoo, were invited to Pyongyang and began discussions about various joint venture businesses. The appeal to the bankrupt North is obvious, as is its advantage to the South. Access to cheap labor in the North would give a new lease on life to South Korea's textile and other labor-intensive industries, now hard-pressed by competition from Southeast Asia. The North, however, is understandably wary. With its allies gone and its economy in tatters, Kim Il Sung's juche kingdom is staring at the prospect of slow economic starvation, with the social disorders this would inevitably bring about. Pyongyang seems divided between hard-liners who wish to keep out any contacts with the South and others who would prefer some sort of gradual economic cooperation.

Politically, South Koreans have generally backed Roh's idea of a "Korean commonwealth," with both sides starting a program of gradual people exchanges and trade relations. The North officially continues to hold to Kim Il Sung's original formula, whereby a single nation would be declared, but with each side retaining its own systems in totality. (This is rather like Deng Xiaoping's idea of "two systems in one country" proposed for Hong Kong and Taiwan, which recent Chinese activities in Hong Kong have put into deep question.)

In the nineties the pace of communication has intensified, at least compared with the rigid past. The South hopes with some justification for a complete change on Kim Il Sung's death. It is doubtful that his son, Dear Leader, will continue to hold the loyalty of the party bosses and the military around him. The question remains, however: Would there be a palace revolt, with softer-line Communists taking over, or a total collapse of the regime, as occurred in East Germany? This latter possibility worries South Koreans almost as much as a continuation of the current Cold War atmosphere, for an effort to bail out a bankrupt North Korea, with its factories rusting and its infrastructure almost gone, would impose an incredible burden on the South.

There is one unpleasant wild card in the deck. For this we turn to a fourth city, quite different from the other three we have mentioned. Yongbyon, some ninety kilometers north of Pyongyang, is the site of North Korea's most intensive nuclear energy project. On both sides of the 38th parallel there has been intensive nuclear development. Half of South Korea's power is derived from its nuclear plants. But the North has steadily tried to make bombs. Its first nuclear hardware came in the fifties from the Soviet Union; North Korean scientists were sent to Moscow to learn advanced Soviet nuclear technology. The first nuclear research complex in North Korea was established in 1961, so there is a long history of activity.

In 1985, the North began to construct its third nuclear plant at Yongbyon. This is now the center of North Korea's nuclear facilities; the installation there is scheduled to be operational in the next one or two years. Once constructed, it is believed the North can produce a relatively large amount of plutonium, which can be used in nuclear weapons. The North joined the International Atomic Energy Agency in 1984 and in 1985 signed the Nonproliferation Treaty. In September 1991, IAEA passed a resolution urging North Korea to sign nuclear safeguards. More recently, attempts have been made for mutual inspections and one U.N. group was actually allowed in for a brief look.

To help speed the progress of these talks, the United States agreed to withdraw its nuclear weaponry from Korea. Roh Tae Woo has done everything possible to push a mutual inspection program through. But the North continues to resist, on a variety of pretexts.

The problem here is obvious. The nuclear weapon is the last card in Kim Il Sung's deck. Kim's possession of such weapons would unquestionably pose a mortal danger to the South as well as to Japan. Even a few nuclear-tipped Scud missiles would offer the prospect of disaster.

On January 30, 1992, North Korea at last signed the Nuclear Safeguard Accord, but thus far U.N. inspectors have been barred from any meaningful investigation. Even the question of what inspection might reveal, based on experience in Iraq, makes one suspicious.

Yongbyon is barely a speck on the map, a closely guarded complex at the heart of North Korea's powerful security system, but the threat it poses cannot be ignored. In the worst case it might elicit a preemptive strike by the United States and South Korea. There is reason to assume that the nuclear card might be played by Kim Il Sung's son even more radically, which puts the whole unification prospect at risk.

There is no doubt that the South has won the long struggle with the North. A good scenario for future cooperation would involve a series of special economic zones in the North, as in China, with heavy participation from the South. This would lead to more general people exchanges and parliamentary meetings pointing toward a viable form of coexistence. On the other hand, Kim Il Sung and his elderly retainers are understandably paranoid about the effect of more extensive contact with the South. It could bring about the dissolution of their entire polity. To encourage and widen contact, without causing collapse, will take great forbearance, consummate diplomatic skill, and above all, the kind of democratic consensus in the Republic of Korea's politics that would deter the North from any desperate, last-ditch adventuring.

XII

KOREA IN THE WORLD

A look through most current writings on Korea's international situation, up to the late eighties, leaves a reader with one overriding impression: however trenchant or thoughtful, they are overwhelmingly out of date. They have been overtaken by events. The Cold War has ended. Communism has collapsed as an international force. We see America's military-power preponderance coupled with its economic problems, the pending unification of Europe, the breakup of the old Soviet Union, and the United States's emergence as something of an international arbiter offset by startling increases in ethnic and religious violence throughout the world. All of this has happened within the past five years. Those same years— 1988 to 1992—have been the particular focus of this writing. No country has been more affected than the Republic of Korea by the changes of these years. Inevitably, the role Korea plays in the 1990s will be governed by a new set of circumstances.

To review the major changes:

1) The breakup of the Soviet block marvelously accelerated Roh Tae Woo's northern politics. Within a few years Kim Il Sung's Democratic People's Republic of Korea lost its primary ideological and economic supporter, the Soviet Union, thereby ensuring the crash of an already tottering economy. With Castro's Cuba virtually its last remaining friend—even Albania having defected—the

North Koreans received lukewarm comfort and hardly any economic support from the People's Republic of China, whose managers continued to promote first economic and then political ties with Seoul.

2) The possibilities of Korean reunification, so long remote, now became attainable. Also possible was the imminent collapse and consequent opening of Kim Il Sung's Hermit Kingdom, particularly if the "great leader" suddenly turned mortal. But such a collapse could have perilous results, ranging from the economic strain of supporting the bankrupt North to the danger of a desperate last-ditch military invasion from Pyongyang, backed by nuclear weapons.

3) The success of democratic reforms, over the past five years, has substantially changed the character of the South Korean polity. Despite remnants of old surveillance and censorship habits,[1] the Republic of Korea must now be classed as a working parliamentary democracy. Its government no longer deserves the pejorative designation of "authoritarian." However volatile its politics may appear, they now enjoy the underlying stability of government by law and legislature. In this respect the Republic of Korea, along with Japan and the Philippines, has distanced itself from its other East Asian neighbors.

4) The end of the Cold War has dramatically changed the military situation—and strategic politics with it. Old alliances and security treaties are wearing thin, albeit kept in place temporarily for the Republic of Korea by the threat of Kim Il Sung. Thanks to increasingly intensive economic competition and new ties forged with both Pacific Basin and European countries—Russia and eastern Europe conspicuously included—Korea's postwar relationships with other countries need to be reappraised. This holds true particularly for relations with the United States and Japan.

Historically, Korea's peninsular position has exposed it to the interplay of its two larger neighbors, China and Japan. From earliest times China has hung over the peninsula like a huge shadow. The Chinese contribution to Korea's early culture and civilization was immense. It is a tribute to Korean vitality that its culture, despite China's proximity, developed so strongly on its own. From the days of the Han dynasty Chinese armies have tramped across the country, trying to make Korea their dependency. Silla unified the ancient three kingdoms in the seventh century only with Chinese support. For a time, under the Mongols, Korea was crushed. Even afterward, its independence was kept only by periodically placating the Chinese. At least nominally, it was a client state.

In the third century A.D. the Japanese came into the picture, alternately playing the roles of traders, pirates, and, ultimately, invaders. Although Japan received a great portion of its art and culture from Korea, the political relationship was generally hostile. In the early twentieth century, three hundred years after Hideyoshi's invaders left, Korea became the first prey of Japan's modern post-Meiji imperialism. China's armies tried to protect Korea—at least from the Japanese—but failed disastrously in the Sino-Japanese War. After its subsequent defeat of Russia, Japan made Korea its colony. Here the Koreans' fate strikingly recalled the European case of Poland, another nation with strong culture and unfortunate geography, which lost its independence for almost two centuries to greedy and powerful neighbors.

With the end of World War II, Korea's big-power relationships were transformed. Japan disappeared as a politico-military factor, at least for a time. Russia and China—also, as it proved, temporarily—resumed their historic roles as hegemons with Kim Il Sung's North. In the South, however, it was the Americans who cast the big shadow. Playing the roles variously of partitioner, wartime rescuer, political ally, moralist adviser, economic supporter and protectionist adversary, the United States came also to wield a cultural—or at least civilizational—influence on the Republic of Korea quite comparable to China's role in ancient days. Over the years the American influence widened.

Militarily, this influence was decisive. Not only was the great bulk of the U.N. forces in the Korean War American; ultimately, 350,000 troops were committed; and 34,000 Americans were killed. But also, at least until recently, the major portion of the ROK Army was under American command, part of the U.S. Eighth Army's mandate to resist any further aggression from the North. In 1971 the Nixon administration pulled back a division, and in 1977 President Jimmy Carter attempted a further depletion of forces, only to call it back as unwise. (See Appendix, "The Ripple Effect in Korea," on this subject.) Since then some 40,000 troops and, until recently, a considerable arsenal of nuclear weapons, have remained in place, although some cutbacks are now to be made.

For forty-seven years the American military presence in Korea has been a fact of life. While still welcome to most Koreans—in view of Kim Il Sung's constant threat—the American troops have increasingly been resented by the younger generation, to whom the Korean War is merely a dim bit of history. Relations have hardly been improved by the notably acultural night-life activities of U.S. troops in the Itaewon area, not to mention the American military's insistence on retaining the huge Eighth Army headquarters area (with golf course attached) in the center of Seoul. (Even the Mongols generally kept their soldiery outside of the cities.)

The economic influence has been proportionally strong. U.S. aid was vital to Korea's economic survival in the fifties and sixties. The success of Korea's export-driven economic "miracle" was grounded on sales to American consumers, assisted by freedom from most tariff restrictions as a friendly developing country. American companies helped set up the first joint ventures in Korea, although their subsequent experiences have not been all that happy. Some have left. (Foreign-capital companies are apt to be caught in an unpleasant cross fire between union leaders who want to get as much as they can out of non-Korean managements and a government that, despite recent mellowing, has been chronically nervous about foreign investment—as opposed to foreign loans.)

Inevitably trade frictions resulted. Koreans complain that American government agencies—so long complaisant about elbows-out competition from Japan—began to turn protectionist just as Korean exports to the United States were becoming a major factor. On the whole, as we have noted, the Koreans have been quicker than the Japanese to respond to American pressure. They have gone a long way toward import liberalization, and at an earlier stage of the trade relationship. Continuing demands for a "level playing field" in agricultural products—a favorite arguing-point of American trade negotiators—have prompted boycotts and violent demonstrations by Korean farmers, who feel hard-pressed enough as it is. As Korea becomes a big consumer market itself, however, imports of manufactured goods are rising, and Korean-American trade problems are not a patch on the Japanese-American variety.

Korean manufacturers are diversifying. Europe and Southeast Asia are attractive prospects. A by-product of Roh Tae Woo's northern politics has been a continuing push to sell to Eastern Europe, Russia, and the other CIS (Confederation of Independent States) components of the old Soviet Union. Hard-currency problems notwithstanding, the Korean chaebol see the Russian market as ideal for Korean products that are less expensive than the Japanese, if not always so finely tooled. It is no coincidence that visitors to Moscow are greeted by a barrage of advertising signs from Samsung, Lucky Goldstar, and others.

Nonetheless, the American consumer market sets the tone for Korean production. As Yu Deuk Hwan, the Ministry of Trade and Industry's assistant minister for trade policy, explained: "I like to tell American businessmen about our thirty equals one hundred syndrome. We export roughly thirty percent of our products to you, perhaps twenty percent to Europe. But there that twenty percent is divided into twelve EEC countries—each country with different markets, different tastes. In America we have one huge market. We can aim thirty percent of our goods at that market, with all the standardization of materials and design that implies. This produces great economies of scale. In the end we base almost one hundred percent of our exports on the thirty percent aimed at the United States."

The American connection with the Republic of Korea, it must be added, is based on ties far more substantial than trade. Just as Korea's early-twentieth-century industrialization, such as it was, occurred under Japanese auspices, modernization for almost the past half-century has been largely American-style. Unlike the Japanese, who modernized Korea in the interests of colonial empire, the American influence has been altruistic and on the whole benign—bumbling, uncertain, and often wrong-headed, but well-meaning. And it has reached far beyond trade and technology transfer. It has been religious, cultural, political and in almost every sense of the word educational. Which is why the ancient preponderance of Chinese influence comes to mind.

Through several accidents of history—an ill-advised partition, an unexpected war, and a long Cold War relationship thereafter—the Republic of Korea became in effect a client-state of the United States. It is now emerging from that relationship, which no free people welcome. While many in the new generation are as anxious to become totally independent of the United States as their forefathers were to escape from the armies and cultural gravitational pull of the Chinese empire (which, too, had its beneficial results), the effects of the American connection are difficult, almost impossible, to eradicate. On the whole Korea has profited from it. Probably a majority of Koreans would agree.

The great American legacy has been democracy itself. Through four decades—despite the excessive tolerance of anti-Communist American presidents for authoritarians like Park Chung Hee and Chun Doo Hwan—steady pressure has come from Americans, public and private, to have the Republic of Korea deliver in practice the high-sounding guarantees of human rights incorporated in its various constitutions.[2] Here the influence of American education and example has been strong. While American human rights activists may deplore the low intensity of their government's advocacy, the fact remains that American political pressure braked the authoritarianism of both Syngman Rhee and Park Chung Hee and in the end helped sustain Roh Tae Woo's commitment to democracy.

American technology, ironically, became a factor in Korea through the exigencies of the Korean War. (The international Korean construction industry, for example, had its beginnings in contract work for the U.S. Army Corps of Engineers.) American aid, to the tune of almost $15 billion in the thirty-five years since 1945, primed the pump for South Korea's economic recovery; and Korean chaebol profited greatly from American offshore contracts during the Vietnam War. Large sums for military assistance, making up about half of the total aid package, freed Korean capital for economic development. The massive American contribution to Korean security speaks for itself. Even at the beginning of the nineties decade, most Koreans in the South—given Kim Il Sung's aggressive track record—would be nervous about a total pullout of U.S. troops.

Korean education has been heavily influenced by the United

States. The rapid expansion of the primary and secondary school system was at first greatly facilitated by U.S. aid and advisers. At the university level the relationship has become almost symbiotic. Roughly two-thirds of students going overseas study in the United States. More than half of the Ph.D.s in the top Korean universities gained their doctorates in American universities. Far more than their distant cousins in Japan, Korean academics have an international perspective. In general education as well as on technical levels there is a great deal of trans-Pacific intellectual cross-fertilization. South Korea's large Christian universities, like Yonsei and Ewha, have American roots that long predate World War II. Among Korean Protestants the American church connection is particularly strong.

Beyond church and academy, however, the influence of modern American culture, with its grab bag of popular literature, movies, media, TV, rock music, clothes styles, fast food, and contemporary art, has worked on Koreans powerfully. For most Koreans America is the empire next door. It is far closer, thanks to modern communications and technology, than the China of Tang or Ming was to their forefathers, and its contemporary influence is more pervasive. The ties have been considerably strengthened by immigration. There are now about 800,000 people of Korean stock living in the United States—200,000 of them in southern California. Better educated than most Americans, notably hardworking and strongly motivated, over the past two decades they have built up a successful and highly visible minority culture.

All this interchange between Koreans and Americans has resulted in something less than an international love feast. Particularly among the young student generation, as we have noted, anti-Americanism runs high. The infamous Kwangju massacre in 1980, the partition, the Korean War itself are all blamed (by many) on the Americans, whatever the facts involved. American finger wagging over Korean trading practices has also been much resented. Few Koreans would deny, however, that the American relationship is a fact of their lives—and will remain so. On the American side, also, recent public opinion polls indicate a growing appreciation of the Korean relationship. Given the end of the Cold War, Korean economic progress and a kind of healthy cultural nationalism in

South Korea—where the same jeans-and-disco younger generation shows an increasing interest in Korean music and folk art—the old client-patron relationship with America is giving way to a better one. And high time.

Not so with Japan. The historic antipathy of Koreans toward their island neighbors has diminished only somewhat with the passage of time. Essentially, the Japanese are regarded as immensely talented predators, despite the many cultural similarities between the two peoples. Korean perceptions of Japan have hardly been modified by the second-class-citizen treatment accorded Koreans resident in Japan,[3] still less by recent disclosures of past Japanese misdeeds, like the drafting of tens of thousands of Korean women to serve as "comfort girls" for the wartime Japanese army. (South Korea's famous Independence Hall near Taejon—visited daily by thousands—contains a gruesome museum of Japanese colonial atrocities.) Even an innocuous proposal like the dispatch of Japanese troops overseas on U.N. missions has evoked strong government and popular protest in Korea, as an alleged harbinger of new Japanese militarism. Although Japan has formally apologized for the "comfort bureau" and other wartime or colonial excesses, such regrets were a long time coming.

In recent years, also, Japan's attitude toward Korean unification has seemed rather ambivalent. While postwar Japanese governments have given support and heavy reparations aid to South Korea since official relations were restored in 1965, a significant lobby of Japanese politicians, in the majority Liberal Democrat Party as well as the minority Socialists, have kept putting out feelers towards Kim Il Sung. The 1990 visit of Japan's mafioso-type Liberal Democratic political boss, Kanemaru Shin, to Kim Il Sung, with his public promises of forthcoming aid, was regarded in Seoul, perhaps with some reason, as a Japanese attempt to play off North against the South, using economic aid as its bargaining counter. By strengthening Kim's hand, Kanemaru struck a blow *against* unification, and at a critical time in North-South negotiations.

Against popular political attitudes that could still be called anti-Japanese, we must weigh the continuing economic dependence of South Korea on Japan. This began in 1965, with payment of reparations and the beginnings of Japanese investment. Park Chung Hee, who was comfortable with the Japanese, welcomed this. From textiles to electronics to automobiles, technology transfer from Japan became the order of the day. While American economic aid was given on a governmental level, or in aid-related private contracts, Japanese corporations and technical consultants moved in force on the private sector. POSCO began its steelmaking with the help of Japan Steel, Daewoo began making cars based on Toyota technology, Hyundai used Mitsubishi. The list is nearly endless. On the personal-business level Japanese and Koreans can work well together. Knowledgeable and near at hand, the Japanese from the seventies on played the same preponderant role in Korean technology transfer that American patents had earlier played in Japanese.

As Korean companies began to grow more competitive, however, Japanese businesses became understandably reluctant to share their latest state-of-the-art technology with their neighbor. Meanwhile Korean industry had been riveted into a continuing dependence on Japan. Almost 90 percent of Korea's 1991 trade deficit of almost $9 billion could be credited to Japanese purchases.

"Originally," a veteran Korean bureaucrat explained, "Korean export business started as a process of assembly. That is, you bought the components, assembled them in Korea, then sold them. Most of the components came from Japan. As Korean industry got better and expanded faster, it grew beyond its capacity to create homemade components. Thus the run on Japan continued. Why didn't we buy more from the United States and western Europe? The answer is simple. Japanese products were very good. Their after-sales service was superb. If the machine broke down, you called the Japanese supplier and a new one would be on the way by air from Tokyo the next day. In the case of American or German manufacture, you might have to wait for weeks."

The result of this continuing dependence on Japan was to make Korea a kind of technological halfway house. Now too competitive for their major suppliers, Koreans sense an imperative to create, innovate, and develop at a level of technology higher than their present capability. Nowhere more than here do we find Korean industry the prisoner of its own dramatic growth. The opening certainly exists for greater interaction with American technology, if not European. (Since Japan Steel recently proved uncooperative, for example, POSCO built its new Kwangyang plant—possibly the world's most advanced—with German technology.)

The national concern over technology and education was encapsulated in a December 1991 meeting of the Science and Technology Council, with President Roh Tae Woo presiding. A new five-year plan (1992–96) was authorized "to bring Korea's level of technology in specific fields up to the level of the advanced industrialized countries by the year 2000." New technical institutes are to be created, while existing centers will be expanded. Research and development funding is to be increased—up to 5 percent of GNP by 2000—and creative work in the sciences will be emphasized, to supplement the engineering talent now available. (In 1990 Korean universities graduated 33,000 engineers, with an additional 4,700 receiving graduate degrees.)

"The government," the Council stated, "will resolutely implement a policy to develop science and technology so as to avoid Korea being subjugated to the technologies of advanced countries, becoming an industrial subcontractor, or being used as a base for 'after-sales service' for the products of more advanced countries. . . ." Technological cooperation with the United States, the statement added, interestingly enough, will be further promoted to an "alliance level."

Whereas Korea is still a learner among Japanese and Americans, to the People's Republic of China, it is a valued teacher. In an ironic reverse of its historic cultural borrowings from China, the Republic of Korea has now become a useful source of relatively low-cost manufactured imports for the Chinese. By 1991 the South's trade with China was more than ten times that of the North and the disparity will increase. The new Chinese rapprochement with the South—on both sides a pragmatic, economics-first relationship—is untroubled by the politically abrasive aspects of the PRC's dealings with Japan and the United States. By contrast, North Korea has become something of an encumbrance to Beijing, although their continuing ideological camaraderie at the top level seems to act as a strong restraining factor against either Great

Leader or Dear Leader undertaking any desperate military adventures.

The Chinese relationship is many-sided. Besides being a market for Korean manufactured goods, China is also an increasingly effective competitor. This is especially so for labor-intensive goods like textiles and very simple electronic gear, where China's low-paid work force can deliver the goods at far less cost than countries with far higher labor costs. (Korean wages are now, after Japan's, the highest in East Asia.) In a sense China in the competitive marketplace of the nineties has become what Korea was in the early days of Park Chung Hee's early industrial drive—a reservoir of abundant and cheap labor, quick to assimilate new skills.

There are 2 million people of Korean descent living in China. This minority, concentrated in the border areas north of the Democratic People's Republic of Korea, is much more prosperous than the people of Kim Il Sung's neighboring "worker's paradise"; and the Korean-Chinese, who could move in North Korea with relative freedom, have served in some cases as a bridge between North and South. Now, given the restoration of full diplomatic relations we can expect Korean companies to go into business in China, in considerable strength and, one assumes, to considerable profit. If the customer-competitor relationship between China and Korea grows more complex, it will be no different from that with most of the other countries in the Pacific Basin.

Korea's relations with the Southeast Asian countries and its fellow NICs in Taiwan and Hong Kong have the same overtones of ambivalence, but they are on the whole quite good. Since the beginnings of Pacific Basin organizations, Korea has played a very prominent role in furthering economic dialogue and some cooperation among the Pacific countries. This can be expected to grow in the future.

It is safe to estimate that by the end of this decade Korea will be unified. In the last analysis—barring an unforeseen war or a series of economic and political disasters—the nation will be unfied on South Korean terms. The result will be a country with a population approaching 70 million, an enlarged domestic market that will modulate the needs for further export drives, steadily increasing industrial power, plus a welcome supply of minerals, timber, and other natural resources from the North. The basic cultural cohesiveness of the Korean people—founded on their historic resistance to Chinese and Japanese aggrandizement—can prove a very useful solvent in combining two populations whose experiences for almost the last half century have been strikingly different. Even more than in the case of East Germany, however, the people of North Korea may prove difficult to immediately assimilate economically. They have grown thoroughly insulated in a society where the iron rice bowl is a fact of life, where private connections are all-important, and where individual initiative has been dramatically deemphasized in the face of constant repression.

It is, as we have noted, difficult in the extreme to predict how the people of North Korea would behave, once the cloak of the Great Leader's totalitarian society is removed. Uncertainty, incomprehension, and disillusionment would result, in varying degrees. Nowhere else in the world has totalitarianism been so complete. The Koreans of the North have experienced neither the trauma of a Maoist Cultural Revolution, which by its very horrors undermined the pretensions of Chinese Communism, nor the Khrushchevian exposés of Stalinism, which conditioned the Soviet peoples to accept, if not to anticipate, the attempted *perestroika* of Gorbachev a generation before it occurred. Even assuming that they would respond positively to the exposure of totalitarianism, like people awakening from a long-suffered nightmare, the experience in Russia, eastern Europe, and China has shown that the ingrained work habits and lassitude of people who have lived under a Communist command economy are harder to eradicate than the climate of political censorship.

Some argue, in fact, that a temporary military dictatorship in the North, authoritarian but pragmatic, might be the best possible successor to Kim Il Sung's one-man empire. Such a government might best be able to preside over a gradual transformation of North Korea's economy and, ultimately, as the North confronted the vastly different state and society south of its borders, its polity, without risking the explosions of an immediate political and social upheaval. A northern version of Park Chung Hee's economy in armor might simplify transition problems.

However it happens, reunification seems the strongest possibility. Once accomplished, it would leave an augmented Republic of Korea as the significant middle power of the Pacific Basin.

Smaller than Japan or Indonesia, the combined republic would be, nonetheless, far larger than the ASEAN (Association of South-East Asian Nations) countries. The Koreans are entitled by their past performance to be something of an example to their Asian Pacific neighbors, not to mention other countries in the Western hemisphere, who may gradually be drawn into the Pacific conversation. The manner of their governance also makes them a useful example for many. It is highly doubtful that Korea will ever turn into another version of democracy as it is practiced in the United States. There are many varieties of popular government, and the Koreans are finding their way toward their own. But establishing the rule of law has proved a valuable support for openness, and individualism has offered a counter in its way to the sense of hierarchy and binding personal relationships imparted to Koreans by their centuries-long Confucian heritage. The combination, in fact, is not a bad one.

Democracy in Korea is far from complete. People there are still adjusting the balance between social discipline and honest dissent, between legal decision and group consensus, between internationalism and a kind of defensive chauvinism. The passage is a painful one, but they are getting there.

For all of this Roh Tae Woo's Sixth Republic deserves a great deal of credit. Like his international colleague, Mikhail Gorbachev, Roh has had the unenviable position of being admired greatly outside Korea—he is, for example, the first Korean president who seems to have made a mark on Americans—but within the country blamed for most of its problems. This is probably inevitable. There is something to be said here for a foreign perspective. During the time of troubled change that Korea has been undergoing, it is often easier to appreciate change from the outside rather than from within. It would be foolish to conceal the problems that await Korea over the next decade. It would be equally foolish to underrate the tremendous contribution of the people who have made its current level of democracy possible. The dissidents, the technocrats, the bureaucrats, the workers, the students, all have played a part—

not least of all Roh Tae Woo himself, who has given the world an example of what patient leadership can do.

The government of the Republic of Korea cannot avoid responsibility for many problems. The rise of the vast chaebol and their disproportionate amount of economic clout has no parallel even in modern Japanese history. (The dinosaur trusts in late nineteenth-century America, in what the historian James Truslow Adams called the "Jurassic Period" of American economic history, offer one possible comparison.) A reckoning must be made with the extraordinarily unhealthy growth of land values, which the government has done little to check. And in a society where wealth has been fairly well distributed, the growing gulf between the very rich and the lower and middle classes has caused concern.

Beyond these domestic issues, there is a basic problem endemic to Korea. There is some truth to the concept of the shrimp caught between the two whales, but it has its limits. A traditional memory of outside oppression or outside dependence has made it all too easy for Koreans to blame just about everything that happens in their society on either Japan or the United States. It is time to look closer inside for this society's defects. There remains the contrast of authoritarian tendencies inside government and hopelessly fractionalizing tendencies outside. Koreans are a nation of barely suppressed rock throwers. The Japanese enforce conformity by a constant antennae rubbing. Koreans historically have tended to keep their balance by alternating repression with riots. This is not a very healthy system. But there are signs that the growth of institutional democracy, whatever its defects, will do much to cure it.

All this being said, Korea today presents the spectacle of a great and dynamic country and an ancient culture, which has made a striking comeback in reasserting its people and its values. Unique in East Asia and the world, South Korea first built up a dynamic and successful economy directed by an authoritarian government, and then brought forth a working democracy—without destroying its economic achievement.

For other East Asian nations still coping with the crosscurrents of cultural tradition and modernization, economic advances and political freedoms, the immediacy of the Republic of Korea's example is obvious. Among the NICs, Taiwan offers the closest parallels to the Korean economic success story—even though the nature of Taiwan's economy, with its concentration on small family businesses, has represented a different kind of Confucian capitalism than the Korean model. Since the repeal of martial law in 1987 and the succession of Lee Teng-hui in 1988 (following the death of Chiang Ching-kuo), as the Republic of China's first Taiwan-born president, Taiwan too has moved toward democracy. Its political problems have been complicated, however—even more so than Korea's—by its relationship with the People's Republic of China on the mainland. Until 1991 the membership of Taipei's Legislative Yuan was largely composed of ancient survivors of the Kuomintang flight from the mainland, representing provinces and districts that have been under PRC control since 1949. Now a majority of both the Legislative Yuan and the National Assembly are natives of Taiwan.[4]

The secret police structure in Taiwan has been rather thoroughly dismantled—paralleling the changes in the Korean KCIA. Minority parties are no longer harassed as they were in past years. Basic democratic guarantees are largely in place. And since 1989 the press has been virtually free of censorship. Although the average citizen of Taiwan still has somewhat less influence on the governing process than his or her counterpart in the Republic of Korea, Taiwan is moving steadily toward democracy. The example set by Roh Tae Woo's Korea may continue to influence the expansion of democracy in Taiwan—despite the unpleasantness caused by Korea's sudden recognition of mainland China.

Thailand and Indonesia suggest their own parallels to the Korean experience. Both have been run by essentially military governments for the past three decades. While Thailand's army leadership can best be compared to the rotating Latin American *juntas* of past years, the uninterrupted reign of Indonesia's president, Suharto—since the deposition of Sukarno in 1966—offers closer parallels to the Korean experience. In both Taiwan and Indonesia the path of modernization has been rockier and the pace far slower than in Korea. Indonesia and Thailand remain basically commodity-producing economies. (Indonesia, in fact, was able to put off many basic economic decisions for years because of its abundant oil resources.) Both economies have done well recently with labor-intensive exports coming to the fore. Nonetheless, there are increasing demands for democracy in both countries. The public demonstrations against the short-lived prime ministership of General Suchinda in 1992 served notice that the urban population of Thailand is actively discontented with the rule of a powerful but corrupt military elite. More disturbances can be expected, but the path toward democracy that Thailand is following seems clear.

Indonesia poses more difficult political problems. In a sense Suharto has proved a "softer" authoritarian than Park Chung Hee, although his reign has lasted for thirty-six years rather than eighteen. Like Park, Suharto has relied heavily on the economic expertise of a group of intellectuals and technocrats—most of them with Chinese backgrounds—who have played a major role in modernizing the country. In recent years Indonesia's economic progress has been impressive. Yet the army is still very much in control. One might compare it to Park Chung Hee's Korea as it existed in the seventies. The 1991 massacre in East Timor, where Indonesian troops wantonly fired on and killed scores of peaceful demonstrators, was the Indonesian Army's equivalent of Tiananmen in China and Kwangju in Korea. The Suharto regime has shown itself to be extremely rough in its treatment of dissidents and minority populations. Over the past decade and a half, the occupation of formerly Portuguese Timor bears witness to a policy of brutal assimilation.

Indonesia, moreover, faces a succession problem of no mean proportions as it goes into the nineties. It is aggravated by the complexities of army politics and the far-ranging economic adventurism of Suharto's family; in this respect Suharto has combined the worst features of Park's Korea and the regime of Chun Doo Hwan, which succeeded it. A mass prodemocracy movement has yet to emerge. The tendency is running in this direction, however, even if it is complicated by the growth of strong Muslim factions. Here again, the example of Korea is extremely meaningful. For it shows that a developing country can go from garrison-state economics to democracy without, so to speak, breaking the bank.

The Korean example holds particular meaning for both China and the Soviet Union. In a sense the South Koreans have combined economic growth with both *glasnost* and *perestroika*—albeit the high growth was achieved under a procapitalist sort of authoritarian rule. Deng Xiaoping and his economists have been deeply interested in South Korea's success story. At least until democratization began, the Chinese technocrats were quick to point out that China was going exactly the way of South Korea—emphasizing high growth rates and ever higher living standards, without retreating from the need for authoritarian rule. Of course China's surviving communism—or attempts to perpetuate it—is a far more unyielding type of autocracy than the "soft authoritarianism" of Park Chung Hee's Korea. Nonetheless the Chinese have constantly used Korea as a model in their own economic modernization program. Deng Xiaoping has frequently cited the Korean example. Along with Meiji Japan, the Korean and other Asian NIC economies were what Deng's economists set their sights on.

Interestingly, the same pressures toward democracy had been working in China as they have in Korea. The differences, of course, are great. China is still basically an agrarian country with a relatively small urban intelligentsia—and an intelligentsia that has been heavily roughed up by Mao's Cultural Revolution, not to mention the leadership's repressive measures after the Tiananmen massacre. There are vast differences in living standards between the people of South Korea and the people of China. In addition, although Park's regime could be called authoritarian, the structure of democratic rule was always kept in place. In China this was not the case. In a way, the 1989 revolution of the students and workers at Tiananmen was premature. Unlike the middle-class protest movement in South Korean in 1987, the Chinese protesters did not have anything like a majority of the country behind them. As prosperity grows, however, and the economy becomes ever freer, the same pressures toward some form of democracy will intensify.

Russians are envious of Roh Tae Woo's Korea for obvious reasons. Roh Tae Woo has given Koreans far more democracy than Gorbachev and Yeltsin have to Russians in that he has either strengthened or activated a network of strong democratic institutions. But he had the framework on which to build these institutions already in place. In Russia it must be constructed almost from the ground up. In addition Russia and the other former Soviet countries have yet to shake off the dead structure of the Soviet command economy. This gives us the unfortunate picture of Russia and the other former Soviet republics going into the nineties with free speech, free expression, and the beginnings of democratic institutions but superimposed on a chaotic economy, with vested supporters of the command economy still fighting a rear-guard action against the often inept efforts of young economic planners.

The historic Polish parallel I have already noted. Culturally and politically speaking, that country's situation is far closer to Korea's than to Russia's. Like Korea, Poland is an old, culturally intact, and assured civilization that has constantly had to fight against the gravitational pulls of two large neighbors—the Germans on the west and the Russians on the east. (Interestingly enough, Poland also was overrun by the Mongols in medieval times.) Although the trade unionists of Solidarity paved the way for a free society in Poland, it could not have been accomplished without the transition provided by the former president General Wojciech Jaruzelski. Jaruzelski, a patriotic Pole despite his Communist coloration, had realized that an invasion by the pre-Gorbachev Soviet Army was a distinct possibility. At the least the Polish army regime he established forestalled this. In the end it was he who turned the country over to Solidarity and the democratic intellectuals, paving the way for a free society. Yet Poland, like the old Soviet Union, was for so many years mired in the Marxist command economy that its effects remain. Since 1990, Poland has swallowed some bitter economic medicine in the effort to create a free-market economy. Try as they might, however, the Poles find their country has a long way to go before they can reach the level of modern capitalist society that the Republic of Korea attained some years back.

In all these countries—however disparate their political and economic circumstances—the central problem of the nineties will be to reconcile economic growth and stability with the demand for human rights and political democracy. For all of them, the transition accomplished within the Republic of Korea during Roh Tae Woo's Sixth Republic is of central importance. The rest of Asia—and the world—can learn a great deal from Korea's successful struggle.

NOTES

[1] Absurd legal penalties remain in force for South Korean citizens suspected of any dealings with the North, however innocent, for example; and foreign television programs must be censored before airing.

[2] During its forty-six years of existence the Republic of Korea has promulgated no less than six separate constitutions.

[3] Until the relevant laws were finally overturned in 1990, they had to be fingerprinted.

[4] Through years of mutual hostility, both the Beijing and Taipei governments adhered to the "one China" policy—each holding the other to be a usurper, but insisting on the unity of the country. In recent years informal relations have greatly improved. Both governments have largely done away with adversary pronouncements, and representatives from both attend many international organizations. With economic ties growing, as well as considerable travel taking place between Taiwan and the mainland, increasingly amicable coexistence seems a likely prospect.

APPENDIX

By way of background to this book, which was written in the spring of 1992, I thought it might be useful to add three magazine articles dealing with Korea, which I wrote quite a few years earlier. The first "The North Korean Invasion: June 1950," is a piece of straight reporting, written for the July 10, 1950, issue of *Time* magazine. Then *Time*'s bureau chief, I had flown into Seoul late in the afternoon of June 27, two days after the North Korean forces had begun their surprise attack on Sunday, June 25, 1950. In this article I describe the beginning of hostilities, my arrival and hasty escape from Seoul, and other personal experiences. Along with similar articles written by three fellow-correspondents, this report constituted one of the first eyewitness accounts of the Korean War. As such it faithfully records the observations of a twenty-five-year-old newsman, who had narrowly escaped death in the premature destruction of the Han River bridge and thought for a time that Kim Il Sung's Soviet-backed invasion was the beginning of World War III.

The second article, "Syngman Rhee: The Free Man's Burden," first appeared in *Harper's* magazine in April 1954. A discussion of the various problems American policymakers had been experiencing with the Republic of Korea's dictatorial first president, Syngman Rhee, it includes a summary of Rhee's life and South Korean politics during the turbulent days of Rhee's First Republic. Again, this piece of interpretive journalism was written in the context of its time, when the tensions and perspectives of the Cold War were at their height. It did outline the difficulties of the American strategic superpower in handling Cold War allies, whose obvious commitment to the anti-Communist cause was negated by their crude authoritarian politics. As such, it presaged similar problems that were to grow even worse in dealing with the Marcos dictatorship in the Philippines and successive authoritarian and ineffective governments in South Vietnam.

The third article, "The Ripple Effect in Korea," was written for *Foreign Affairs* and appeared in the October 1977 issue. It is written from the standpoint of an American political commentator criticizing the decision of President Jimmy Carter to withdraw U.S. troops from Korea in 1976. This decision was based partly on the Carter administration's evaluation of the political situation in East Asia and partly on Washington's amply justified discontent with the government of Korea's then president, Park Chung Hee, whose increasingly personal dictatorship, far more efficient than Rhee's, had consistently violated the human rights of its citizens. As the article points out, however, there were two sides to that story. Authoritarian though he was, Park had led and presided over an extraordinary economic resurgence. Korea's "Miracle on the Han" had become one of the Third World's few success stories. The average Korean's lot had been hugely improved; and Park's regime, despite its oppressive nature, had received wide public support.

The realities in the Republic of Korea were more complex than they seemed to Washington's political thinkers at the time—particularly when one considered the aggressive threat to the peace posed by Kim Il Sung's totalitarian dictatorship in the North. I had visited the Republic of Korea extensively since 1966 and kept in constant touch with a wide spectrum of the Korean people, through my work there as a businessman as well as a journalist, so I was impelled to make some critical comment. The article was widely quoted in Korea and may have had some influence on Washington opinion. Just two years later Park Chung Hee was killed and a new era in Korean politics began.

The North Korean Invasion: June 1950

The morning of Sunday, June 25, 1950, began drearily in Seoul, the drab, sprawling capital city of the Korean republic, as long-awaited summer rains drenched rutted streets and parched, drought-threatened fields of surrounding country. Like December 7, 1941, this was a typical, humdrum, lazy Sunday. Neat khakied Korean soldiers were padding into town from units stationed in the surrounding country and from the north near the 38th parallel—as on most Sundays one third of the soldiers in most Korean army units had been given weekend passes. . . .

At eight-thirty in the morning UP's Seoul correspondent, Navy veteran Jack James, left his house in a jeep and drove downtown to U.S. headquarters at the Banto building. James, who had been scheduled to go on an early picnic if weather was good, decided to run downtown anyway to take a look around the office. At the entrance to the Banto building he found a breathless U.S. Army friend running for his jeep. "What do you hear from the border?" shouted the Army man. After a brief exchange and hours worth of extra checking in telephone calls, James had got hold of his biggest story—the military invasion of South Korea.

At four-thirty Sunday morning, the North Korean Army, supported by tanks and heavy artillery, had crossed the 38th parallel. Within a few hours they were attacking South Koreans in all sectors. The timing was perfect. Recent proposals for a general election made by North Koreans had left many observers feeling that the weakened North was almost trying to come to terms with the strengthened South. Border incidents had decreased perceptibly, which strengthened the view that the North was trying a propaganda peace offensive. A few days before the attack the Chief of Staff of the South Korean Air Force, having proposed that Koreans acquire a large shipment of airplanes from private U.S. sources immediately, suggested that they "wait sixty days and see what happens first."

What happened came all too fast. When U.S. advisers, pulled out of bed with first news of the attack, rushed up to join the Korean units (from battalion upwards) to which they were attached, they confirmed that a general assault was in progress. Since the 38th parallel border itself was not generally defensible, most Korean Army units fell back to prepared positions on the main line of resistance, which had been selected with greatest care by U.S. advisers during the past year. On the first day of the assault Communist army gains were largely restricted to the territory South Koreans did not expect to hold anyway. Thus the territory west of the Imjin River, including the town of Yonan, was evacuated according to plan and fighting naturally reached the city of Kaesong, which was located almost athwart the border.

On the extreme east there was no frontal assault against the mountainous frontier held by the Eighth Division. Instead North Koreans mounted a series of amphibious attacks down the beautiful rockgirt coast south of Kangnun. In the west no one gave much hope for smart Colonel Paik In Yup's Seventeenth Regiment, which held the strategically indefensible Ongjin Peninsula—linked to the rest of South Korea only by the sea.

The aggressive, fast-thinking Paik fooled everyone. Instead of waiting for an attack he charged across the border himself and captured the big North Korean town of Haeju. Later, since communications were too tenuous, he voluntarily gave up the town and successfully evacuated his regiment by sea to the South Korean mainland.

All through the first day North Koreans avoided striking at the broad flat Uijongbu corridor, the South's most heavily defended position, which leads like a dagger into Seoul. The ruse, as U.S. advisers realized, was transparent. Early Monday morning Communists mounted a large-scale attack straight at the corridor, since the time of Genghis Khan a favorite route of invaders striking at the South. In their way stood the crack Seventh Division of the Korean Army backed up by the Second Reserve Division, with the First Division on its flank.

Fine fighting troops of these divisions ordinarily would have held. They did beat off and check infantry assaults. But the forty-odd tanks the Communists had sent over were too much. Unopposed tanks rattled on towards Uijongbu from the border. Uijongbu, the key to the Seoul defense system, was commanded by Second Division Commander General Li Hun Koon, a smarty-pants political appointee. Li did nothing about the tanks threatening the core of his defense position. They rattled on through to become the margin of victory in that sector.

U.S. advisers had rightly insisted that tanks were useless sitting ducks on Korea's network of narrow roads, mountains, and impassable rice paddies. But they reckoned without the tremendous psychological effect of tanks on Korean soldiers who had never before seen them and held them in the same superstitious awe that made Roman recruits tremble at the sight of Hannibal's elephants. Instead of shattering tank columns with AT fire, Korean soldiers and officers both either despaired or offered desperate suicide tactics in opposition. The lieutenant and four men in the First Division strapped land mines to their shoulders and rolled under enemy tanks. Each suicide netted one tank with him.

On Tuesday South Koreans counterattacked. At first they were successful. But again North Korean tanks were able to slip between the two advancing divisions, causing enough havoc—more psychological than material—to wreck the plan. By late Tuesday North Koreans had taken Uijongbu and advanced to the outskirts of Seoul. Tuesday evening I arrived in Korea.

For two days Tokyo had wallowed in rumors about Korea. With communications down and only three correspondents there, very little news had got out. SCAPS machinery, taken by surprise, was undecided whether it should be playing war under peacetime rules or playing peace under wartime rules. For once Tokyo's policymakers were worriedly and expectantly waiting for word from Washington.

Tuesday at 4:00 I landed with other correspondents in Kyushu's Itazuke air base, just an hour's flight from the nearest point in Korea. Already the runways at Itazuke were jammed with CC-54s and CC-47s from all over Japan. In the sky was the terrifying roar of jets going or returning on escort missions to Korea.

After a breakneck dash from the operations office I clambered aboard the last evacuation plane for Seoul's Kimpo airfield. With me were three other correspondents, Keyes Beech of the Chicago *Daily News*, Burton Crane of *The New York Times*, and the *New York Herald Tribune*'s Marguerite Higgins.

Under a rainy sky our aircraft hedgehopped over the broad quiet Korean countryside, whose rice paddies glistened with water and whose shallow sluggish rivers were muddied and yellowed from the new rains. Even as we approached Kimpo there was no sign of the actual war. This trip seemed little different from the last time I had flown into Seoul with Northwest Airlines.

But as the plane dipped over the field we noticed the first incongruity. Groups of American civilians were wildly waving strips of white cloth towels and flags as a signal that the airfield was safe for landing. On landing we found the field undamaged by bombs but littered with refuse and debris from past evacuations and the recent occupation by Korean troops. With the exception of evacuees and a few Korean Air Force soldiers it was deserted. The only sign of life was vicarious. Outside of the administration building and arranged in neat rows in an adjacent parking lot were thirty-odd shiny new American sedans—Dodges, Buicks, and one ironically bright blue Studebaker with white sidewalls. They all bore blue "CDA" license plates used by U.S. mission personnel. Beside them with the same kind of license plates were several new commercial jeeps . . . .

Among the quiet Korean soldiers on the field there was no panic. Guards in blue air force caps carrying MM-1s kept stolid watch over the empty hangers. Aside from a few cubs there was one silver CC-54 on the field—the same plane that had been held at Kimpo by motor trouble and later strafed by Yaks. A sharp-faced Korean air force lieutenant looked disconsolately at the few poor lanes on the field and the receding form of the CC-54 with its jet escort. "Here we are," he said, "an air force without planes. How do you Americans expect us to fight those Yaks on the ground? For a year we have asked you for planes. But you never believed us. Now perhaps it is too late."

But the lieutenant's pessimistic comment bore no relation to his will to fight. Here among the scarred half-completed buildings of what Koreans had hoped would be a great international air terminal was felt for the first time the tough strong spirit of Korean resistance. "We will win . . . we will win," they said." . . . They smiled the words with confidence. They meant them. But there was no disguising their worry. Against planes and tanks they wanted American help—and it seemed far away.

Just in front of the administration building, where four weeks ago I said good-bye to smiling groups of friends, Lieutenant Colonel Edward Scott of KMAG Headquarters, tight-lipped and haggard, was quietly burning stacks of documents on the rubble-strewn concrete. When he had finished, he said he was ready to take us into Seoul . . . .

. . . We picked out three evacuee cars, a commercial jeep piled high with rations and spare gasoline cans, a new Dodge, and the wildly incongruous baby blue Studebaker with white sidewalls. Forming a convoy behind baggage trucks and the colonel's jeep, we rattled at a sixty-miles-an-hour clip over the smooth paved road to Seoul.

First appearances were reassuring. Tokyo reports had spoken of panic and mass headlong evacuation. But the road-site vista between Kimpo and Seoul looked much as I had remembered it from more peaceful days . . . . The only touches of war were speeding military truck convoys and jeeps packed with soldiers, which sped along the roads—all vehicles covered with the inevitable Korean camouflage of twigs and branches.

Shortly after nine we rolled through the heavily guarded gates leading to Korean military headquarters . . . . Like the entire city of Seoul, headquarters was completely blacked out . . . . Less than twenty-four hours before KMAG personnel had hastily evacuated their own headquarters and billets, which were located near the headquarters of the Korean army. An hour before our arrival, when the situation on the front north of Seoul looked more stable, they had returned. But during the time they were away Korean civilians had systematically looted many of the billets and the once-spacious KMAG Officer's Club. Even KMAG's offices in the National Defense building were only shells. Before the first evacuation, officers had destroyed most of their files and papers.

The normally impeccable Chief of Staff's office of KMAG had become a frowsy litter of coffee cups, cigarette butts, carbines, and musette bags. The old commander of KMAG, Brigadier General William Roberts, a straight-thinking, leathery fighting man, had left for the U.S. a few days before and his successor had not yet arrived. A huge situation map of Korea that took up one wall of the office for so many months—static and unchanged—now told the alarming story. Blue lines indicated positions where the Korean army defenders had been dangerously pushed back to a narrow perimeter around Seoul. All along the line arrows marked in red indicated further advances of the invading army. Inside the general's office, its window blacked out with hastily strung cardboard blocks, we talked with Colonel Sterling Wright, a youngish, handsome cavalryman who, as Chief of Staff, was now KMAG's acting commander . . . .

Wright quickly explained the situation. Although Seoul had been in imminent danger of falling very early today, the situation had not bettered itself. "Fluid but hopeful" was the way he put it. Korean officers who entered the room were more pessimistic. A tall, round-faced colonel Kim Pak Il was an ex-Japanese army captain who was now generally accredited as the Korean army's smartest staffman. Tuesday night he shook hands with me warmly, but his usual cheerful manner had given way to worried tenseness. "Not very good . . . not very good," he kept saying when I questioned him about the situation.

We sat in the chief of staff's office for another hour talking about a question we had come to answer—why had the South Korean Army been driven back so precipitately? Four weeks ago in the same office Wright had mentioned obvious deficiencies in the South Korean position: lack of air power, lack of heavy artillery, and relative sluggishness in organizing themselves. Now these theoretical problems had translated themselves into the droning of

Yak fighters over the South Korean countryside and the hacking cough of the Communists' 120-millimeter mortars and field pieces. All the KMAG officers were worried. But Tuesday's stout resistance had encouraged them in thinking that this critical situation might be redeemed.

Shortly before midnight we all turned in. Crane, Beech, and I stayed at the house of Walter Greenwood, evacuated only a few days before by his wife and child. After hours of talk we got to sleep. By this time everyone had become slightly reassured about the fate of Seoul. We made plans to drive into town the next morning to set up communications at the RCA office. Perhaps we would move our headquarters into the downtown Chosun Hotel.

At 2:15 the telephone rang in Greenwood's room. Within five minutes, after a terse conversation, he had dressed and was bounding out of the door. "It looks bad. I think they've broken through," he said. "You'd better get out of here as fast as you can. Head south for Suwon."

We dressed in record time, then rushed to put extra gasoline cans and ration boxes back into our jeep. With Burton Crane at the wheel we dashed off into a blacked-out road network of military reservation. From the north, sporadic artillery fire had stepped up to the intensity of crescendo, muffled only by the steady drizzle of summer rain.

In pitch dark it was almost impossible to locate the right road to Suwon. We decided to check in at KMAG headquarters for directions. There we found Major Sedbury sitting at the general's ornate corner desk, giving quiet instructions to a Korean army staff officer. "It's bad," he confirmed. "Tanks have broken into the city and we don't know how much longer the lines will hold. Enemies at the traffic circle outside the headquarter's entrance. They will be here any minute. I have to stay here until the colonel comes, but you'd better turn left at the headquarters road and get across the bridge as soon as you can. Then make for Suwon." . . .

We half ran down the stairs of the emptying building. Outside truck motors were revving as crews and reinforcements prepared either to help stem the advance or retreat south of Seoul. As we reached the landing my eyes were struck by a bright new poster on the KMAG bulletin board. It read "Don't forget . . . Tuesday June 27 . . . Bingo."

Traffic was heavy on the road running south to the big steel Han River bridge. There were no signs of military rout. Soldiers, even those in retreat, were more apt than not to be singing. Guided by MPs, automobiles kept strictly in line. The only disorder was outside the military line of march. Thousands of poor refugees, women toting bundles on their heads, and men carrying household goods in wooden frames fastened to their backs. Early civilian composure noticed en route from Kimpo to Seoul had certainly not lasted long.

Traffic moved quickly until we reached the bridge. There the pace slowed, then stopped . . . . That traffic would never get going again. Without warning the sky was lightened by a huge sheet of sickly orange flame. There was a tremendous explosion immediately in front of us. Our jeep was picked up and smashed back fifteen feet by the blast.

We were all hurled back into our seats by the force of the explosion. My glasses were smashed. Blood began pouring down from my head over my hands and clothing. I felt strangely weak in the knees. I had no idea how badly I was hurt. At first I thought my leg was broken. Crane's face was covered with blood. I heard him say, "I can't see."

Thinking at first that the explosion was some kind of air raid, we recovered ourselves and in a split second's time raced for the grass and gullies leading off from the bridge, Beech leading Crane, whose wound looked very bad. Crane ripped off his undershirt and had me tie a crude tourniquet around his head. Beech rushed back to the jeep to retrieve our baggage. When he came back he helped me tie a towel around my head, which was still dripping blood.

At first we thought that the bridge might still be passable. We got back into the jeep and drove through a clear space on the bridge's right for about twenty-five yards. There, directly in front, we saw the remains of a truck still burning brightly. Beyond it, two blown spans had dropped thirty feet to the level of the river. Obviously, the bridge was no hope. We backed up the jeep, got out, and started walking off the bridge.

The scene that met us, lit only by the glow of the burning truck and occasional headlights, was apocalyptic in frightfulness. All the soldiers in the truck ahead of us had been killed. Bodies of dead and dying were strewn over the bridge, civilians as well as soldiers. Confusion was complete. With the cries of the wounded and dying forming the background, scores of refugees were running pell-mell off the bridge and disappearing into the night beyond. It was here that we first noticed the pathetic trust that Koreans had placed in Americans. For ten minutes as we rested on the grass, men with bloody faces would come to us, point to their wounds, and say hopefully in English, "Hospital . . . you take hospital." All we could do was point to our own bloody faces and shake our heads. . . .

Grabbing our baggage, we started off along the river banks, dimly hoping that we could find some boat that might take us across. Along the dark, crowded road we ran into two twenty-year-old cadets from the Korean artillery school, An Se Cha, baby-faced, a spectacled former engineering student and an even younger-looking friend. When we asked them in Japanese about the possibility of boats, they were pessimistic. They themselves had become separated from their unit on the burning bridge and were aimlessly working their way east along the river. Another man joined us, Mr. Ho, a tall, thin-faced, solemn young man who worked as a translator for the Korean Defense Department.

After a short council of war, we decided that it was pointless to attempt to find boats during the night and in weakened condition. We started to head back to KMAG's abandoned housing area, which we had left earlier, and wait for dawn. It was then about three o'clock. Artillerymen guided us through the black maze of the paddy fields and streams for about an hour until we came through the now unguarded gate of the military reservation. . . .

We found one house with the lights still burning inside. It was occupied by Corporal Li, a Korean army driver for a U.S. captain who had lived there, and two Korean women, evidently former servants. After a suspicious once-over they let us in. Expecting that by this time disillusioned Koreans would be beginning to turn against their erstwhile American friends, we were bowled over by the kindness they offered us. Women tore up makeshift bandages and rustled in the still-functioning kitchen for coffee and food. The corporal and I drove in his jeep to an abandoned KMAG dispensary and found some bandages and old packages of sulfanilamide powder. Back in the house, we changed to clean clothes and rebandaged our wounds.

. . . Expecting capture at any moment, Burton and I burned our old wartime identification cards in the navy and OSS. (Beech, as an old marine, didn't have identification cards.) The corporal, however, wasn't worried. "We'll stay here until morning," he said, "then General MacArthur is coming here with the Twenty-fourth Corps to push the Communists back. I know." We could only smile weakly at his optimism. . . .

Before dawn we gathered up all the available provisions and clothing and prepared to make a run for it. Corporal Li, persuaded that it might be better to wait for the Twenty-fourth Corps in the mountains to the east, said he knew a place where boats to cross the river were available. At seven-fifteen, we piled into the corporal's jeep and another we found abandoned nearby and started cautiously for the river road. . . .

There were very few soldiers in sight along the broad stretch leading out of Seoul. But already long lines of civilian refugees, packs and bundles on their backs, were walking toward escape routes. . . . We checked with a few soldiers the fact that boats were plying at ferry points. For the first time in five hours we began to have hopes of successfully escaping. At eight-thirty we drove jeeps along sandy river flats to ferrying points on the Han several miles upstream from the shattered bridge. . . . Hundreds of pathetic families lined the banks waiting for transport. Whenever a boat touched shore, there was a desperate, pathetic scramble for places inside. . . .

A few Korean soldiers were attempting to cross the river to find supplies for their units. From them we got the story of the night's action. A 2:00 A.M. alarm had been given when North Korean tanks forced their way into Seoul. (Here again the tank was most important psychologically.) After initial confusion, the army dug in on approaches to Seoul and fought off advancing North Korean infantry, establishing positions on the hills just outside of Seoul. North Koreans were pushing steadily but at last report, the South's line was holding. . . .

While fighting went on outside, North Koreans plastered Seoul with mortar barrages. This started panic among civilians, which precipitated mass evacuation to the river. "The hearts of the people are heavy," said a Seoul shopkeeper. "When will the Americans come? Why do you not come sooner?" . . .

Young An, the artillery cadet was more sanguine. "We have no equipment to fight with now, so we are being beaten. But the Republic of Korea is like a sleeping tiger. Just give the tiger some help and he will awake."

We asked another soldier, a stubbled infantryman with cluster grenades dangling from his belt, how morale was. "Morale is fine. We have the best morale in the world," he said, "but what can morale do against planes and tanks?" The sergeant with him added, "There were Russians in those tanks. Their aim was deadly." When I looked at him disbelievingly he added, "Of course they were Russians. Have you ever seen Koreans with red hair?" (No official or unofficial American confirmation thus far of Russians fighting on the front.) After half an hour of fruitless waiting I took a rowboat to the south side of the river and found a large, flat-bottomed skiff big enough to take our jeeps across. . . .

Through the entire progress we had been surprised by the staunchness and helpfulness of the Koreans, whom we had fully expected to be embittered and disgusted at the lack of American aid. As we trundled south, our jeeps slipping and miring down in narrow muddy roads and twisting through rice paddies, lines of refugees paused in flight to cheer the first Americans they'd seen that day. More often they incongruously clapped—with the fast, excited clapping of a tennis audience at Wimbledon or Forest Hills. . . .

As roads we traveled met with others we saw more and more soldiers. No one was running or in disorder. Each man had kept his weapon and equipment. They were not deserters. Some had lost contact with units in fighting, others had been ordered south as part of a planned evacuation. . . . Nearing the main road to Suwon retreating soldiers were strung out in a thin single column on both sides of the road. Gradually local country people watching the unending procession of soldiers and civilians going back began to lose some of their early faith. Finally as we passed someone said the inevitable. From a crowd at a small village intersection, out stepped a dark chunky woman. She stared at us beadily. "Why you Americans quit? Why you quit?" she shouted in English. We looked away and had no answer.

By 10:25 our original party had now swelled by ten more soldiers, and we were heading into another town along our route. Suddenly from soldiers on top of jeeps and dirty, wearied refugees alongside the roads there came shouts followed by wild cheering. People ran from houses into dusty roads and pointed at the sky. All traffic stopped. Never had I seen such a heartfelt manifestation of joy. Above us, flying northward in neat formation, were six B-26s. . . .

We ourselves were just as surprised as the Koreans. We had no idea that the U.S. government would have the guts to live up to its obligations here. At the same time we wondered whether this would be overpowering. For the first time in this long trip we felt we could hold up our heads among the Koreans. We had not failed these people, who deserved so much.

As we climbed back into the jeep, a tired artillery lieutenant traveling with us nodded contentedly. "Well, they have come. They will help. But if they had only come a little earlier what a difference it would have made."

Syngman Rhee: The Free Man's Burden

Syngman Rhee is probably the most intense overseas supporter of the American struggle against Communism. He is also one of the sharpest thorns in the fingers of the men who are trying to win that struggle on terms consistent with our national safety. He is a man of American education and some democratic instincts in the American sense of the term. His public statements sound like Fourth of July oratory, and at times his actions display an embarrassingly keen judgment of which forces can make American democracy act, and which restrain it.

Yet in his conduct of Korean domestic affairs he is, without question, a dictator, seldom reluctant to use police intimidation and force to suppress the political freedoms whose theory he defends. On the international level, he recklessly and systematically tries to undermine the foreign policy of his American ally, whenever it conflicts with his individual concept of his country's needs.

The Korean War has revealed both sides of Syngman Rhee very plainly. On the one hand, he has become an invaluable rallying point for his people. His uncompromising stand, and his courage in the war's darkest days, have made him what he could never make of himself in peacetime—the symbol of a hitherto frustrated nationalism. In making this stand, however, he has reduced his National Assembly to a rubber stamp; and he has used mob violence in support of his program as skillfully as any Communist. In 1952, while he was coercing the Assembly to reelect him president, he unhesitatingly shut down all the United States Information Service broadcasts on the Korean radio, because they were giving Koreans the only true and uncensored reports about the political situation. When Communists accuse American representatives of supporting a "Fascist" dictator in Korea, they rub a sensitive nerve.

In his dealings with the American public Rhee is a man with two faces—and few Americans choose to look at more than one. In the American tradition of moralizing our international politics, our conservatives idealize Rhee as the great spokesman of the democracies against Communism in Asia, the courageous "little man" who never gives up, the old-fashioned Oriental patriarch happily outfitted with Christian as well as "Confucian" virtues. Liberals in their turn make Rhee the incarnation of this country's failure to insure "real democracy" throughout the non-Communist world, the man who mocks the honest peace-making of the United Nations, whose "authoritarian" tactics do more damage to the cause of the United States than reinforcements to the Russian air force.

The truth about Syngman Rhee does not lie between these two extremes. It incorporates both. They, in turn, must be triangulated with a very important third factor—the history and traditions of Rhee and Korea. Backed by the implicit certainties of the Magna Carta, Protestant Christianity, and the Gettysburg Address, Americans have a tendency to judge the world's politics and politicians by sharp Anglo-Saxon standards. Unfortunately the classic Anglo-American labels of "radical," "conservative," and "middle-of-the-roader" are imprecise yardsticks for judging Asia's politics. Rhee and his country can no more easily be shoehorned into a set of Western-style definitions than a rice-eating Buddhist can be transformed into a Christian who likes bread.

Syngman Rhee and the zigzags of his political career represent a phenomenon of our time—a phenomenon partially expressed, in recent years, by that other Oriental champion of the *idée fixe*, Mohammed Mossadegh. Rhee is shrewd and wise. He is logical. But he is not "reasonable." He is the man who feels he has little to lose from all-out catastrophe, and, perhaps, everything to gain. He personifies the small nation with a grenade at its breast, threatening to blow itself—and anyone else within range—into eternity, if its demands are not met; and at the same time not fully realizing the grenade's potential for destruction.

The United States is desperately concerned with this phenomenon. There are no American satellites. But there must be American allies. And if Communism is to be defeated, a large number of these allies must be Asians. This poses a problem: how far can the United States indulge the independence and assertiveness of small allies when they thereby threaten the policy of the United States, its safety, and that of the world it leads? It is Syngman Rhee's backhanded accomplishment to have exposed the horns of this dilemma to perfect view.

The Making of a Revolutionary

Rhee came from an upper-class Korean family and received a good education, including a significant term at a Christian mission college. Like most students of his day, the more he learned the more disgusted he grew at his country's predicament. In that period, in the 1880s and '90s, Korea was ruled by the weak survivors of a once-powerful dynasty. In past centuries, Koreans had kept their independence partly through the strength of their own armies, partly because of the balance of power between their two great neighbors, China and Japan. At the time of Rhee's youth, the strength of the armies had ebbed with the corruption of the ruling classes. With China also weakened, Korea became a strategic prize in the rivalry between Russia and Japan in Northeast Asia.

In 1905 the custody of the prize was settled. Japanese domination was confirmed at the Portsmouth Peace Treaty, and none of the interested powers in Asia, including the United States, made much of a protest when Japan formally annexed Korea in 1910. Rhee never forgot this. It is what he referred to, for example, in his 1948 Inaugural Speech, when he spoke of "the fateful Korean nation, which was the first to be sacrificed in the cynical abandonment of the nineteenth-century system of security through national agreements."

As early as 1897 Rhee was a leader of student agitation against the decadent Korean government. He was thrown into jail, where he spent seven years, and repeatedly tortured and beaten. When released in 1904, he fled to the United States. Six years later, he returned to Korea as a YMCA representative. This did not prevent him from plunging into political hot water again. He left shortly afterward, just one step ahead of the Japanese police.

In March 1919, the Korean people, led by their students and intelligentsia, started a national passive revolution against the Japanese. As unarmed crowds demonstrated in the streets of Seoul, their leaders, full of the high ideals then echoing from Woodrow Wilson's statements at Versailles, drew up their Korean Declaration of Independence. "Lo!" it concluded, "a new world unfolds before our eyes. The age of force is past and the age of justice has come."

The young Korean idealists were deceived. No one in the new "age of justice" did anything to help them, while the Japanese stamped out the rebellion with efficient ruthlessness. Thousands were killed, beaten, or imprisoned. What leadership was left was driven into exile. Rhee, already overseas, had been acclaimed first president of the Provisional Government of Korea. In Shanghai, he made contact with the survivors of the Passive Revolution, and exchanged bitter reflections. The Korean government in exile was born.

Although few people ever heard of it, this odd combination of bomb throwers and shoestring diplomats kept its identity until 1945. Kim Koo, the leader of the actively resistant forces, began a program of assassination and intrigue against the Japanese from his base in Shanghai. Rhee became the "outside man" who operated in Washington, Hawaii, and Europe. He was more comfortable in his office on Colorado Avenue than Kim was in Shanghai, perhaps, but also more frustrated. He lacked even the concrete satisfaction of planning political sabotage. He was the fruitless negotiator, the little man from a place no one had heard of, who paced outside the doors of state departments, embassies, and newspaper offices, talking to anyone who would listen about the wrongs of Korea.

Not many heard him, or even bothered to give him the time of day. He made some American friends, and got some valuable financial help this way. But, even during World War II, he found no official encouragement. Korean "self-determination," said the State Department—looking fishy-eyed at Rhee's movement—would follow the peace.

On October 20, 1945, U.S. General John Hodge, addressing a mass meeting in Seoul, led a man out from behind a screen. It was Syngman Rhee. He was introduced, recognized, and cheered. He had been flown back to Korea by the U.S. Army, in the hope that he could help found a stable political situation. The exile was deeply grateful for his return, and anxious to get to work. But he was not, as the military government advisers may have hoped, an ordinary modern politician, somewhat democratic and pro-American, who could be counted on to participate in a group effort at "self-determination."

Events had long since made of Rhee a man whose life was dominated by a single idea, whose goal in 1945 was no different from his goal in 1919 or 1897: a free, unified, militant Korea. The frustrations and plottings of thirty-five years had left no room in him for any compromise except tactical compromises of expediency, at which he proved adept.

Through the years he had learned a good deal about political democracy and its American application (his doctoral thesis at Princeton, interestingly, was on "The Concept of Neutrality as Influenced by the United States"). He appreciated the significance of World War II and the tensions after it. He was not such an anachronistic nationalist as Mossadegh, who could dismiss the struggle of Communism and the democracies as just another phase of the nineteenth-century Anglo-Russian imperialist rivalry over Iran. But he was still primarily an Asian nationalist who put complete independence from foreigners first, and ideologies, parliaments, and public education systems afterward. He had a cynicism for foreign promises, which Korea's history and his own well justified.

GEORGE WASHINGTON WITH A BLACKJACK

Syngman Rhee, once back in Korea, behaved like Ulysses returned to Ithaca, sure of his rightful title and determined to square things for all time with the wicked interlopers who had been ravaging his country. The Japanese, luckily for them, were beyond his vengeance. It was the Russians and his old friends the Americans who took over the villain's role, with their postwar proposal of a ten-year Russo-American trusteeship for Korea. Rhee found considerable conservative Korean backing and put himself at the head of a large but loosely formed political bloc, the Society for the Rapid Realization of Independence. It was the lineal descendent—with an unchanged objective—of the Independence Club he and other nationalist students had joined in 1894.

American military government officers soon found Rhee and his movement embarrassing. Their orders, in the postwar Era of Good Feeling, were to negotiate with the Russians for the establishment of a unified trusteeship government, made up of Korean leaders from both sides of the 38th parallel. The Russians acted with consistency. They established a virtual Soviet state north of the parallel, while with the help of their official Korean Labor (i.e. Communist) party, they set out to stall negotiations for a union.

While the Russians made their frontal diplomatic assaults on the American position, U.S. military government advisers were smarting from a flank attack by their old friend Rhee. By various means Rhee and his old-time allies like Kim Koo had made themselves the most powerful political group in the country. Faced with trusteeship, Rhee loudly cried that he would have no part in a "chop-suey" government. His own solution was simple: Korea for the Koreans—all foreign military governors leave at the nearest exit.

For a while military government tried to find some trustworthy Korean "leftists" to balance the preponderance of Rhee and his "rightists." Unhappily most of the "leftists" or "middle-of-the-roaders" (a near-fatal path in Korean politics) were more decorative than effective. Some became prisoners or converts of the Communists. Rhee was left holding the field by default. In 1948 the Americans gave up their one-sided efforts to unite Korea by negotiation. Three years after the Russians, the United States set out to build up its half of Korea as a temporarily separate country. In 1948, by vote of a hastily elected Assembly, Rhee became the first president of the Republic of Korea.

It is still uncertain how much of a test of popular representation this election actually was. The ruthless colonialism of Japan had left Korea the most exploited country in Asia. Two generations of Koreans had been scrupulously kept away from positions of responsibility, or opportunities for higher education. The citizens of the new republic were at first easy targets for pressure from wealthy landlords, or intimidation from underground pro-Communist groups.

Leadership was almost hopelessly deficient. Corruption and mismanagement were foredestined in any independent Korean state, simply from the dearth of competent men to prevent them. There were a few good officials at the top, but the difference of their backgrounds did not make them comfortable harness-mates, and their long exile had left them with little more than a historical acquaintance with the people they had to govern.

In this democracy of form without content, Syngman Rhee was typical. His 1948 inaugural speech was packed with fine Jeffersonian phrases. Immediately after making it he began a pattern of government that has been consistently dictatorial. Few men in Korea have ever been safe from the coercion of Rhee's large police force. Opposition candidates for the Assembly have been arrested on the eve of elections, as in 1950. Assemblymen themselves have been arrested, or beaten by gangs of pro-Rhee strong-arm boys, as in the crisis of 1952. Men whose names have been mentioned as opposition leaders have found one of three courses advisable: (1) prompt disavowal of their supporters; (2) a hasty trip to the United States; (3) convenient illness demanding care in a safe hospital.

The explanation of contrast between form and content is that Rhee believes himself to be Korea's only real democrat—"the George Washington of Korea," as he likes to be called. Very sensitive to Korea's political immaturity, he feels that he alone can bring the "will of the people" to fruition, since other Korean leaders are hopelessly incompetent for the job (and they are in truth not very competent.) Through years of exile, Rhee came to identify Korea's interest with his own. Once in power, he saw any attack on him as obviously unpatriotic. Characteristically, he always refused to form a political party (Washington was not a party man); and he resents others who do.

"Why should we create anything," he said to me once, "between the president and the people?"

Neither Rhee nor Korea advanced much under his "nonpartisan" rule. The fight for an independent Korea turned into a series of involved, niggling political intrigues within a small, struggling republic. Fighting his factional political battles, Rhee's courage and consistency were transformed into arbitrariness and brute stubbornness. The old exile was swamped by desperate economic crises (as were most of his American advisers), and serious political unrest, most of it Communist-inspired.

At the same time, younger Koreans were showing an appetite for more real freedom. An exuberant nationalism was developing, and a new generation of students talked secretly of getting rid of Rhee and giving Korea its independence—quite the way Rhee had talked when he was a student plotting against the corrupt Korean emperor.

The Assembly elections of May 1950 were a defeat for Rhee. Despite the efforts of his police chiefs to control the opposition candidates, most of them were elected. (The elections, held under UN supervision, were fair ones.) The new Assembly was more anti-Rhee than ever. South Korea, helped by drastic economic reforms which the Americans had finally pushed through, began to edge out of crises in an approach, at least, to some kind of political stability. The people of the Republic, as the elections showed, were beginning to get a feel for democracy. Rhee's autocratic powers suffered, and it was clear that he would not be re-elected in 1952. Then the war came.

THE MAKING OF A HERO

On June 25, 1950, the Republic of Korea changed from a postulant democracy, bruised by past mistakes but gradually prospering, into a battlefield that killed many hopes of its early youth. The American position in Asia changed from hesitant diplomatic and economic involvement to resolute commitment, military, economic, and political. The Communists changed from a long-distance propaganda enemy into a direct military antagonist. Only Rhee did not change.

As the shady complications of Korean politics fused into war-time monochromes, the simple revolutionary took a new lease on life. Since 1945 Rhee had behaved like a man at war. Now the war had caught up with him. His early demands for a definition of joint Soviet-American trusteeship "democracy," his appeals for military aid, his reiterations that communism was not only a political threat but a military danger, all burned themselves on consciences which had argued "self-determination" and troubled little about Korean aid bills, or whether Korea was inside any defense "perimeter."

At home, Rhee set the clock back on popular democracy. The debaters and the middle-of-the-roaders were swept away in the first shock of battle; the contentious students died on the approaches to Seoul or Taejon. And the tough guys returned. Rhee's old associate Lee Bum Suk, the former Chinese Nationalist general, had been pressured out of public office by the Americans for the excesses of his bully-boy private police force, the Taehan Youth Corps. With the war, back came Lee, the Youth Corps, and other unsavory groups. (Lee has since, due to personal ambition, fallen out of favor with his chief and been expelled from his party.) Until June 1950, it was possible for public opposition to Rhee to exist in Korea. Since then, opposition is dead, and personal liberty has existed almost wholly on Rhee's sufferance.

It would be unjust, however, to place the entire blame on Rhee for what happened to the Korean republic. Korea's political polarization in a civil war for survival was partly inevitable. The tough guys were also fighters, and most of the good-willed democrats were not—some deserted to the Communists to save their lives. In war, the "stubborn, arbitrary" man of peacetime can become, again, "courageous" and "comforting." Rhee is a fighter, and he became an inspiration to many of his people.

His international stature changed similarly, especially in America. The "courageous patriot" of 1945 had become the "extreme rightist" or "reactionary Korean statesman" in 1947 when he started opposing our trusteeship efforts. In 1951 Rhee was a "patriot" again, a "courageous, anti-Communist leader," and a figure of warning to "left-wingers" that no one can compromise with communism.

As the truce talks in Korea progressed, the irreparable split between Rhee's views and American policy came into full view. Rhee sees Korea as the linchpin of the international struggle, and warns sincerely that a prolonged truce there will only be the "Munich" leading to World War III. American diplomacy sees Korea as only one part of a fluid world-wide engagement against Communist aggressors—a struggle that may parallel the centuries-long conflict, punctuated by wars and truces, between the Christian West and Islam.

One reason, for instance, that the Eighth Army lacked enough men and arms to assure a successful major offensive in Korea in 1951 was General Eisenhower's insistence that the NATO forces desperately needed reinforcements. Reinforcements were therefore diverted from a fighting force in Asia to supply an "army in being," as Mahan might have put it, in Europe. Considering the American stake in Europe this paradoxical decision was justified.

Behind the American position on Korea are two important premises. First, the heavy moral obligation of the United States—shared neither by the Russians nor by Syngman Rhee—to avoid another world war. Beyond this is an even more fundamental fact of American policy, recognized by two administrations: since 1951 it has been clear that the American people, whatever newspaper editorials say, has not been prepared to go into a world war over Korea. This is hardly to be wondered at. Americans have the most to lose and least to gain from such a war. It is, in fact, evidence of great political maturity that a people who were isolationist in the nineteen-thirties backed as resolutely as they did the limited, bloody, and wasteful war in Korea, recognizing the stake involved.

THE SEARCH FOR A TECHNIQUE

Dealing with a man like Syngman Rhee is a new problem for Americans—a problem that will doubtless be aggravated in the diplomacy of the United States for years to come.

The Republic of Korea is not a satellite. It is an independent country, allied to the United States and dependent on it for economic, political, and moral support. It is not a sister democracy of the United States, nor in any sense an equal bargainer. Yet its single-minded leader does not hesitate to throw his homemade monkey wrench into the gears of American policy, without fear or scruple.

How does the United States lay down its policy lines to Korea? By force? Force is undemocratic, and there are enemies to point out the inconsistency. By persuasion? Sweet reason is wasted on a man like Syngman Rhee.

In practice, American treatment of Rhee and Korea has oscillated between these extremes. When some of the truce negotiation terms were shown to the Communist enemies before they were shown to Syngman Rhee, the Americans were treating Korea the way the Imperial British used to treat tributary sultans. At the other pole was the spectacle of John Foster Dulles, American Secretary of State, rushing out to Seoul, hat in hand, in an only semi-successful effort to persuade Rhee to sanction American and United Nations policy, after Rhee had archly refused to commit himself to Dulles's subordinates.

American diplomacy has yet to find the tricky combination of toughness and respect that must be used in dealing with Syngman Rhee and the kind of country he represents. Certainly Rhee must be faced with a firm stand, unyielding where necessary. The American electorate can justly wonder how tough their government got with this man over the recent armistice plans, when the assistant secretary of state, back from his mission to make a tough attitude plain, gave the impression that he had been rarely privileged to have had an audience with the world's greatest living patriot.

But toughness, if it can be achieved, need not imply lack of respect. No one is more sensitive of his national dignity than an old Korean revolutionary. Yet at many times in the past, Rhee's dignity as head of a state has been slighted or ignored.

Washington has not shown much of a feeling for developing policy and counterpolicy in Korea on a continuing basis. The Truman administration seemed surprised in 1950 to find that Korea's economy had become an object of international concern, although its decay had long been apparent. The Eisenhower administration seemed painfully surprised in 1953 when Rhee would not accept an armistice, although everything he had done and said since 1947 suggested that he would take this stand.

On the tactical level, our representatives in Korea have seldom had the stature or the freedom of movement to negotiate on anything like equal terms. Instead, a succession of plenipotentiaries has been used for moments of crisis. An extraordinary example of the failings of this system was given in the summer of 1953. To press Rhee's acceptance of an armistice, General Mark Clark — previously the highest United States bargaining agent in Korea — was bypassed, and Assistant Secretary of State Walter Robertson was sent out from Washington. Robertson had scarcely begun to talk with Rhee, when Washington newspaper bureaus began (correctly) to speculate on the coming arrival of Secretary Dulles. Question: how could Rhee be expected to deal with Clark and Robertson?

Rhee's own clever appraisals of American public opinion are an additional cross for the State Department, for he constantly tries to turn the diplomats' flank by direct appeals to the American public, or to some American leaders. In his statements, he capitalizes on our sympathy for the underdog, and our traditional hankering after the blunt kind of "shirt-sleeve diplomacy" that he practices.

There have been some significant responses. Probably the most egregious was the letter from Representative Alvin O'Konski, Wisconsin Republican, to Rhee praising his illegal release of 27,000 North Korean war prisoners and suggesting that he might release the rest — in direct opposition to the stated policy of O'Konski's country.

The shaky record of American dealings with Rhee's Korea — the hasty compromises, the harried reproaches, the overgenerous praise — reflect the search for a new kind of relationship between a big power and a small ally. The Imperial British approach of the nineteenth century is the only available comparison — and it gives little help now. The British formula was the old White Man's Burden: initiate and keep order; make the country reasonably decent by raising some basic standards; with great gradualness, instruct it; and, also, profit from it. Such a system, in this revolutionary age, is scarcely realistic.

The American error, if such it is, is the opposite of the nineteenth-century British. Where they did too little for a colony or dependency, the Americans try to do too much, and the American

Free Man's Burden weighs heavily on all parties to the bargain. Where the British tried to remake the superstructure of a country in their own image, the American tendency is to start doing over the base. The drive to introduce democracy elsewhere may be the only answer to the drive to impose communism everywhere; but there is nothing more risky than introducing the forms of a democracy to a people without its experience or traditions.

The urge to introduce democracy is almost a moral compulsion for Americans; and where it has been introduced, Americans are quick to observe and make their moral judgments. This is the great difficulty in our relationship with Syngman Rhee. Helped by his mastery of American slogans, he has become virtually an American to many people in the United States, and his acts are judged almost the way we would judge those of a contemporary American politician.

In handling Rhee as an international problem, the State Department was handicapped by the corollary popular tendency to describe him in moral rather than political terms. American aspirations for Korea were at once too low and too high, and where some liberals wrote off Rhee in disgust, some conservatives prematurely canonized him. Because the war fought in his country shed American blood and touched the American conscience, it became progressively harder to judge this man by anything like objective standards.

Through these same circumstances, Rhee was able to push the foreign policy of his big ally harder and heavier than would have ordinarily been possible. He thereby brought into sharp relief the underlying difficulties of the big power-small ally relationship. It is to the credit of the United States, at least, that this relationship has not been resolved over-hastily, and has been honestly pondered. An interesting testimony to its puzzling character is the contradictory criticism coming from some of America's European allies in the United Nations. On Monday they will contemptuously accuse the Americans of developing submissive satellites in Korea and elsewhere, and on Tuesday will impatiently demand that the Americans tell Rhee what to do.

Unfortunately there is no easy formula for carrying the Free Man's Burden; it is a new relationship, and one that must be worked out by experience. It is obviously crucial to the world's future—especially in Asia.

In Syngman Rhee's case, we must recognize that this believing democrat who rules as an autocrat is a passing—and possibly a necessary—phenomenon in the history of new modern states. He may be succeeded by despotism; or he may give way to a progressively more relaxed and democratic government. He is sensitive to American pressure, and the United States without trying to sterilize the moral climate of his country, can powerfully though quietly influence the tactics of his government and the character of his successors. At the best, the United States can re-create a climate in which forces for good government can grow—the only abiding solution to a stable Korean-American relationship. The maddening thing for Americans is that the good and the stable in any country must do their own growing—and the growth is never swift.

The Ripple Effect in Korea

I believe it will be possible to withdraw our ground forces from South Korea on a phased basis over a time span to be determined after consultation with both South Korea and Japan. At the same time, it should be made clear to the South Korean government that its internal oppression is repugnant to our people and undermines the support for our commitment there.

—*Jimmy Carter, June 23, 1976*

When President Carter made this statement, he was still very much a candidate. He repeated it in the course of his campaign and had obviously given it a great deal of thought. Early this spring, after informing (if not quite "consulting") the governments of South Korea and Japan, he announced the phased withdrawal as one of the first major foreign policy moves in his administration.

On its face the withdrawal is a prudent one. It will be staged over a five-year period for the laudable purpose of getting American troops out of an exposed overseas position. Given the general and persisting American disenchantment after Vietnam, a pullout from Korea would seem logical and necessary. After thirty years of American troops manning its borders, one might say, it is time for a nation to start defending itself. President Park Chung Hee's government, in addition, is objectionable to most Americans. Park has crudely abused the freedoms of many Koreans and persecuted and jailed leaders of the political opposition. Of late his regime's monumentally ham-handed attempts to win friends and influence Congressmen in Washington have had wide notoriety in the American press. So a pullout of troops, well-advertised, should be a good warning to him and his men.

At that, the troops to be withdrawn are only the 27,000 combat soldiers of the Second Infantry Division. Air Force and logistics units will remain. The armed forces of the Republic of Korea, 625,000 strong, are generally competent and well trained, larger than the Communist armies of Kim Il Sung, the North Korean dictator, which oppose them on the truce-line border. If the South Koreans lack quantities of modern weapons—notably tanks and aircraft—these can be supplied in the form of new American equipment. And administration spokesmen pointed out at the time of the announcement that the pace of the withdrawal could be slowed or even stopped if a threat of war seemed imminent. As *The New York Times* said in an approving editorial: "So the South Koreans will begin to kick their American habit. . . . But it won't be cold turkey. . . ." Any announced withdrawal of troops, it is argued, means an automatic lessening of tensions in an area—another sign, doubtless, that the bad days of the Cold War are forever past.

So runs the persuasive logic of what we might call "The View from Here"—or at least, from Washington; and it is a perspective that many Americans would seem to share. But is the logic and rationality of this pullout announcement only superficial? Does it raise more questions than it settles? Does it, in fact, disturb a precarious *political* equilibrium far more than it solves a problem in military disposition? Even granting our national concern for human rights, now a policy matter, and a correct desire to cut foreign involvements where we can, are there not larger issues at stake here, which transcend the maintenance of one U.S. division across the invasion route north of Seoul?

I believe there are. We should consider them. We should consider Korea's position and its history. We should consider the Korean economic—and, yes—social achievement of the past fifteen years, which makes it possibly the world's most striking case of an underdeveloped country working hard and making good. We should consider also the ripple effect of a round, shiny pebble from Washington suddenly tossed into a still Asian pond, causing undulations far beyond the point of impact. No one expects that the North Korean army will now begin gassing up its tanks, prepared to head for the border tomorrow or the next day or the next year. But for a variety of reasons, the announcement of a new American pullout has increased tension instead of alleviating it. It has disturbed a balance of power which, however curious and offhand in its construction, has hitherto been quite secure in this area. That is "The View from There"—the view from Asia, where, in this case, the action is.

II

Let us start with an obvious parallel. In Western Europe the United States maintains some 300,000 troops because we believe they are a necessary shield against Soviet pressure. The Seventh Army forces are tactical troops. The basis for their commitment is that the presence of American units in the immediate path of any incursion, able to defend in force, would presumably bring on war with the United States. Even though the Soviet Union, our adversary-partner in détente and arms control negotiations, has shown a sophisticated awareness of war risk and demonstrated a desire to avoid it, the presence of U.S. troops, on the ground and ready, is regarded in Washington as the only sure guarantor of the European status quo.

A mere token force we would regard as inadequate. There is a matter of public commitment and European morale, as we Americans sense it. There are the Germans to be considered. There is NATO. There is, we believe, the integrity of all Western Europe at stake.

In Korea, the total American troop commitment is little more than one-tenth of the American divisions in Europe. Yet, there has been almost a complete consensus about their value to the security of Asia as a whole. The people of South Korea, as the party most intimately affected, want American combat troops stationed north of Seoul, the vital, bursting capital of 7 million people only thirty miles from the North Korean border. This goes for opposition partisans as well as government spokesmen. Koreans are disturbed as a people, not merely as a regime, by the pullout announcement, and in the light of past history, intensely worried by its implications.

The Japanese have always wanted an American presence in South Korea to continue, as a safeguard both against North Korean aggression, which they see as possible, and against rash political behavior on the border or within it, by the South Korean government of Park Chung Hee. If the American presence is withdrawn, the Japanese might have to think about backing up the Koreans militarily themselves. This they would be reluctant to do—Japan's military forces are small and under constant fire politically, even with their present limited defense missions. And the Koreans, still recalling vividly past Japanese rule and oppression, would surely be even more reluctant to permit it. Thus there arises the worst possible specter in the calculations of Japanese defense experts—a Republic of Korea worried, isolated, and truculent enough to produce nuclear armaments on its own, the nonproliferation treaty notwithstanding. That is the one development that would surely drive Japan to do the same.

The same extrapolation may have been made in Peking, which may partially account for several significant invitations to Japanese Self-Defense Force officials to visit Peking in recent months, where they have been entertained most handsomely by the same bureaucracy that not so many years ago was denouncing Japanese militarist revanchist tendencies. Peking has been quite happy about the presence of the Second Division and nervous at its announced withdrawal. Concern about Kim Il Sung, the unpredictable Stalinist dictator of North Korea, is a prime factor. After oscillating between Peking and Moscow for many years, Kim has, since the death of Mao Zedong, tended to favor the Soviet Union. To the Chinese, who are almost paranoid on the subject of the Soviet threat, any removal of the American presence is a temptation to their old Russian allies to break the peace.

It does not follow, however, that the Russians are pleased by the prospect of an American withdrawal in Korea. On the contrary, the Soviet Union, as a veteran Japanese Russia-watcher put it, has been "not at all unhappy" over the continued presence of American troops. In an area where Russian and Chinese influence has been so closely balanced, an active American presence in Korea has kept the whole precarious house of cards in place. The Russians were certainly satisfied. One Korean War was enough for everybody and if there is anything the Brezhnev regime dislikes it is surprises. There have been notably few cries of joy in the Moscow press about the American withdrawal.

The only voice in favor of the American pullout in Korea comes from the North Korean regime in Pyongyang—whose proven irrationality is what the American military presence was supposed to nullify. Surely this is an odd situation. It is one thing to intervene where only a few oppose intervention or to pull out when many advise a pullout. In Korea we are announcing a removal of our presence from the one spot—in the invasion corridor north of Seoul—where all the Asian neighbors of Korea, not to mention other Asian countries farther south, wish us to remain.

III

It is true that the withdrawal is a "phased" one. This spring's announcement fell short of the original crisp intention set forth in President Carter's campaign, and since then it has been decided that only 6,000 men will be withdrawn in 1978; two combat brigades and the Second Division headquarters will not leave until 1981–82. Moreover, since the announcement was first made, explanation has followed upon explanation that the "military balance" will be kept up by additional tanks, aircraft, and other useful staples for President Park's army. A program of two billion dollars' worth of arms deliveries, mostly through sales, has been put before Congress. Looking at the world from Washington, one might wonder what the fuss was all about.

Perhaps in concrete military terms President Carter's advisers are right. But, of course, the problem is only secondarily a military one. Primarily it is political. It is not so much a question of military capability, to use the old Pentagon phrase, as it is a matter of political intention, of national will.

Here Asia is suspicious of us. It is ironic that a country whose dealings with Europe show generally constant consultation and feedback has shown in its Asian diplomacy a spasmodic jump-in and pull-back syndrome, a gross parody of Toynbee's classic challenge and response. Only months before the original North Korean invasion in 1950, both Dean Acheson and Douglas MacArthur, those antipodal spokesmen for U.S. policy, had omitted the Republic of Korea when stating the perimeter of American responsibility. Yet, we wondered why Stalin let his Korean surrogate Kim Il Sung make the quick armored gamble. After so many years of commitment to the engagement in Vietnam—our own voluntary re-creation of Athens' disastrous Sicilian expedition—the final American withdrawal in 1973, and then the debacle in 1975, had the shock of both the unexpected and the irresponsible. Before that an administration led by the man who made his reputation abetting Senator Joseph McCarthy's persecution of, among others, the courageous American diplomats who had called it right on China, signaled its new relationship with the People's Republic of China by crudely bypassing its closest Asian ally, Japan, on the way to Peking. And the 1970s decade opened with the Nixon "shocks" visited on Japan and Korea in the form of sudden trade embargo threats, the hallmark of an economic adversary diplomacy. Although economic peace, with Japan at least, was declared during the Ford Administration, the image of the unpredictable American remained green.

Thus, however calm and reasoned the planning for the Carter pullback from Korea had been, to Asians the announcement was the thing. Here, at a vital point of potential trouble, the U.S. government was saying: no change in the commitment, just a few infantry troops taken out so the South Koreans can assume their own defense. But did this not really mean, in the context of past American performance: "We are getting out of Korea because we got out of Vietnam and because we don't like Park's government anyway. You had all better start working out your own arrangements"? Why else would a unilateral withdrawal be announced, with no concessions from the other side, by a country that had hitherto shown a great proclivity for tit-for-tat negotiations with the Soviet Union and its allies?

It is understandable that the Vietnam experience has colored American thinking so thoroughly that, having finally extricated ourselves from that war, a disaster almost solely of our own making, we now feel that any withdrawal of American troops anywhere in Asia is automatically a good thing. It may be, in the long run. But as I have tried to demonstrate, it is not so regarded by most Asians.

Let us look again at the Japanese, and at the roots of their reaction. In Japan today the Security Treaty with the United States, so long the focus of riots, protest marches, literary denunciations and steady opposition from the left, is now almost universally accepted as part of the local furniture—a bit unsightly in spots, but better to have than not. Discouraged, among other things, by China's evident satisfaction with the American military presence in Japan, even the hard-line Marxists in the Socialist party have ceased to use the treaty as a big campaign issue. In private, Communists too admit they are content with the status quo. Of the 46,000 members of the U.S. military stationed in Japan, 21,000 comprise the two-thirds of a Marine division, with an accompanying air wing, camping on some choice land in the crowded, poverty-ridden island of Okinawa. Agitation against removal of the American base there, once the talking-point that elected successive Socialist-Communist governors there, has died down.

To my own mind a pullback of the Marine regiments on Okinawa might have been a good substitute for withdrawal of the Second Division from Korea. A virtual division of troops is hardly necessary to provide backup for the contingency of occasional rescue operations in Asia, like that of the *Mayaguez*. I have heard very few Japanese, however, who shared this view. After Vietnam, the general feeling is that any further pullouts of American military force might be upsetting. The Marines are rightly regarded as backup for the force remaining in South Korea, another safeguard against trouble in Japan's closest neighbor.

But, perhaps most important, the Japanese have had more dealings than most with the government of Kim Il Sung in North Korea. Kim's unpredictability is well known to them.

There is no doubt that détente between the Soviet Union and the United States, as it has developed, has been worrisome to Kim's regime. The Chinese rapprochement with the Americans, as that progresses, causes Kim even greater concern. His suspicions of his two Communist senior partners seem to have been reciprocated in recent years. There is comparatively little supportive action for Pyongyang coming from either Russia or China; and one suspects that Kim had to work hard to arrange his last fraternal visit to Peking.

The announcement of an American withdrawal, however, has probably given Kim's personal rule a new lease on life. This is, after all, the moment he had been waiting for and predicting since the end of the Korean War, the first stage in his announced reunification of the Korean peninsula.

Kim, his ambitions and the vise in which he holds North Korea's 16 million people, were and are the best military argument for a continued American military presence in South Korea, on the ground. To Koreans especially, the promise of constant air and sea support is unconvincing. They remember that American air and sea power failed to deter the North in 1950 — and that neither was used in the *Pueblo* incident of 1968.

The real nightmare — to which South Koreans return over and over again in conversation — is a North Korean lightning thrust directed against Seoul. Even granting that the South Korean army is or could soon be superior to the North Koreans in arms as well as in numbers, a capital city just thirty miles from the border is a difficult commodity to insure. There is always the risk that it could be captured — or at least entered in a single surprise rush. With Seoul captured or in ruins, even a South Korean victory in a long drawn-out war would be worse than Pyrrhic. South Korea would have to negotiate, and a cease-fire would probably be imposed. The odds would favor its being backed by the strength of China and the Soviet Union, with predictable results for a then-truncated South Korea.

IV

The second-best reason for keeping an American division on the ground in South Korea is President Park Chung Hee. Since he abrogated the Korean constitution in 1972 — tailoring a new model to allow himself continued autocratic rule — Park has been increasingly hard to deal with, increasingly less receptive to advice in political, as opposed to economic, matters. Able, ruthless, and incorruptible himself, he is a zealot and a driver who sets little store by democratic debate. Although surrounded by cronies and yes-men—many of the bright people around him in Seoul's presidential Blue House have long since excused themselves and gone elsewhere—he is probably too smart and too concerned with long-range goals for the economy to think of adventuring north himself. On this issue at least, he is a far different breed from Syngman Rhee, the old revolutionary patriot whose increasing bent for dictatorial rule in the late 1950s gave Park a recent, if unfortunate, precedent for assuming semi-dictatorial powers.

Park keeps his own counsel and runs his own country. Under the present arrangement, where U.S. troops are deployed north of Seoul, he does not, however, command his own armed forces in the event of conflict. An American four-star general is in charge, as U.N. commander in chief, a holdover from the Korean War days when the war was sanctioned as a United Nations effort. The value of such cautionary control is obvious. It is doubtful, however, whether this command function can be maintained, once we withdraw most of the combat troops. That is a fact that makes Asians extremely nervous. The Japanese, especially, understand and sympathize with Park's problem, facing an unpredictable and avowedly aggressive power on his frontiers. But they would sleep a bit easier if he were not left to handle it by himself.

V

The news about human rights in South Korea is not good. One cannot quarrel with President Carter's campaign statement that "the internal oppression" of the Korean people is repugnant. There should have been more support for political freedoms in Korea by past administrations, either publicly or in the form of pressure applied directly from Washington. The Korean people are watched; they are arrested; they are constantly called in for questioning by the Korean Central Intelligence Agency, which has degenerated under Park's leadership into a combination Praetorian Guard and secret police. KCIA officers and agents have systematically harassed and intimidated Korean opponents of the Park regime, not only in Japan, but also in the United States and in Europe. And in 1973 the KCIA even abducted Kim Dae Jung, the opposition candidate in Korea's last free election, from his hotel in Tokyo, back to constant house arrest in Seoul.

It has not always been so. After leading the group of officers who took over the government in 1961, Park was elected in 1963. For most of his first two terms, he governed and was governed by democratic processes. In his earlier writings, he took pride in restoring a working democracy to Korea after the chaos and factionalism that accompanied Syngman Rhee's fall from power in 1960.

His own instincts, however, were and are authoritarian. When he came to power he set out with the intensity of a Puritan to modernize his country through sweeping economic development, putting his plans into effect the way an engineer works from blueprints. The more power Park acquired, the less he tolerated opposition, especially after Kim Dae Jung, then a relatively obscure young lawyer, almost beat him in the 1967 presidential election. Park suppressed demonstrations, closed down universities, and harassed his opponents, manipulating the constitution to secure his election to a third term in 1971. And in the fall of 1972, he imposed martial law and drastically altered the constitution to make the Assembly a rubber stamp for his personal executive. After his wife, one of the few softening "human" influences around him, was killed in 1974 in an assassination attempt on him, Park became even more inflexible.

Yet, for all the harassment, it must be said that some of the rubrics of democracy persist in the Republic of Korea. The forms have not been emptied of all their content. Most coercion continues to be backhanded, if effective—like the tactic of putting government pressure on business firms not to advertise in *Dong-A Ilbo*, the respected Seoul newspaper, when its editors criticize the government overmuch. The bulk of Korea's citizens go about their business in freedom and are protected by the law. People criticize the government and discussions take place that would not be tolerated in a fully totalitarian country. In comparison to most Socialist countries, including the shining lights of revisionism like Yugoslavia—and to the newly rightist countries like Chile—the degree of repression in Korea is small. The U.S. government could do a great deal by putting private pressure on Park, not to mention the business leaders and the strong Korean bureaucracy, which are developing independent power centers of their own.

While the Kennedy administration did apply such pressures, much less was done during the Kissinger years. That period witnessed almost a public cynicism about human rights, which could only have served to confirm Park in his drift toward absolutism.

President Carter has changed all this. However much the announcement of troop withdrawal is pictured as a purely military decision, it clearly shows Washington's public concern over a bad human rights situation, which, in the president's words during his campaign, "undermines the support for our commitment." He has chosen to work from outside, rather than from within. Park Chung Hee has been put on public warning, so to speak. If he wants the support of the American people—and this is a people's government—he had better behave. This, at least, is "The View from Here."

How clear is that view? Looking at Korea again from an Asian perspective, it would seem to be defective in several ways. The withdrawal announcement has hardly fostered self-confidence among the Korean people, most of whom, rightly or wrongly, see the word "abandonment" written in the fine print behind "withdrawal." Nor can we expect Park to heed the warning and to mitigate the severities of his rule as a reflex action. He may, but the opposite may also happen. Driven into a position of isolation, real or fancied, Park is likely to tighten his grip on authority, not loosen it. He and his government are still amenable to American influence. They must be. But much of this influence was squandered needlessly by publicly announcing that we are pulling out. In a sense, we have given away much of our bargaining power with Park and given it away in advance. In return we have done nothing yet for human rights in Korea but preach about them.

VI

The realities of Korea are complicated—"this free, authoritarian, democratic dictatorship," as wits in Seoul are wont to describe their country. In appraising the Koreans and their modern situation, we must remember that modern nations, despite the world's superficial unities of 747s, common communications networks, satellite TV and shared technology, continue to live in different historical time zones. Developing nations, in particular, are finding this truth a poignant one. The rush into modernity goes slower when you must carry your own past on your back.

Japan, Korea's close geographical and racial neighbor, was fortunate in accomplishing its modernization during the Meiji century, so-called, which began with the Meiji Restoration in 1868. The Meiji modernization was not without pain, but in the end, civil war, industrial revolution, democracy, socialism, colonialism, militarism, big business, mass education, and a disastrous major war were all somehow digested to form the liberal affluent society of today. But the Japanese needed all the time they could get to synthesize the conflicting demands loosed by the Meiji reformers. Their history until the fatal China adventure and Pearl Harbor was one of constant conflict between authority, variously benevolent or ruthless, and an aroused sense of popular rights. At times, in the 1920s, democracy seemed to be winning. In the 1930s democracy lost. It took the shock of a disastrous war and the utterly unexpected beneficence of American military occupation to graft on to the roots of the Meiji reforms the vigorous and workable—if *sui generis*—democracy in Japan today.

In Korea, this century-plus of modernization has been squeezed into roughly thirty years' time, with just about everything happening at once. Park and his fellow officers of the 1961 military revolution are rough parallels to the young Meiji *samurai* of a century ago. Like them, they have found that goals of strength, democracy, popular education, prosperity, and national self-respect often conflict—particularly if you have to achieve them all in a hurry. Worse off than the Meiji reformers, the Korean leadership has had the legacy of Japanese colonialism to deal with, not to mention the destruction of the Korean War. National leadership was stunted and suppressed for generations. Until liberation after World War II, there was no tradition of political democracy to build on. Few Koreans had ever really voted.

The concentration on economic growth and military strength that so impresses the visitor to Korea today is the product of necessity—like the *Fukoku Kyohei* syndrome ("a prosperous country and a strong army"), which the Meiji reformers turned into a slogan. But unlike the Meiji, the Korean reformers include people out of two eras, working in one. The generation of Korean technocrats in their forties, who are responsible for the extraordinary national growth rate, are justly compared to the Japanese 40-year-olds of the 1950s (accidentally thrust into power by the Occupation purge of their elders) who created the economic miracle. But their seniors, notably Park himself, seem spiritually closer to the original Meiji reformers of a century ago.

Park has made his own study of the world's contemporary national revolutions. In one of his widely circulated memoirs, *The Country, The Revolution and I* (copies of which can be found on every prudent businessman's office bookshelf), Park cites the Meiji Restoration, Sun Yat-sen's revolution in China, the Turkey of Atatürk, and Nasser's Egypt as examples, each useful in a different way. Not surprisingly, in a man with a sophisticated grasp of modern industry and economics, he reserves most of his admiration for the "miracle on the Rhine" of postwar Germany.

Yet, business and economics aside, he runs his government in such a way as to justify the jibes of Japanese commentators that he is, politically speaking, a "born-again Confucianist." To justify his maddening paternalism, which is again far closer to the attitudes of the Japanese Meiji leaders than to those of most modern authoritarian leaders, he continually stresses the political weaknesses of Koreans, their almost incurable political factionalism and their consequent need for strong leadership. Many of his countrymen would agree with the thesis, but are nervous about Park's evident desire to stay with the job until he finishes it. "We need strong leadership," a prominent lawyer said to me recently, "at the moment, even a dictator. But when someone thinks he is the one indispensable man, that is dangerous."

VII

As yet Park's internal oppression has been selective and relatively sparing. Although it worries many Koreans, the prevailing mood in the country is the optimism of a business boom. The lot of the average citizen is vastly better than it was ten or even five years ago. The government is associated with the good times. Except for the city of Seoul, Park could probably carry most of the vote if a free election were held tomorrow. The realities of Seoul and the countryside around it, in fact, are different from the picture of tension generally given newspaper readers outside Korea. The military is in evidence, but hardly ubiquitous. The streets of Seoul are packed and traffic-ridden, with Korean-made cars now strikingly in evidence. New housing units are being built with great speed, but not fast enough to overtake demand. Seoul is a city of paradoxes and growing pains. In the city's central square a man walks precariously among the whizzing cars, seven fancy suitcases wrapped in cellophane stacked on an A-frame on his back. Even in a boom economy, A-frames and cars must coexist.

The disordered clatter of Seoul, the new power lines in the countryside, the rough-cut version of a Japanese or American freeway linking the capital with Pusan (a road that manages to serve almost two-thirds of Korea's concentrated, 60 percent urban population), the steel mills at Ulsan, the new technology villages of scientists and engineers pulled back to Korea on the brink of brain drain to Europe or the United States, the *saemul* or new village movement in the subsidized countryside, the assembly lines of low-paid workers turning out calculators cheaper than Japan and shoes and tennis shirts cheaper than Hong Kong—all this, despite the apparent disorder of Korean living patterns, is part of a closely fitted economic plan for growth and national prosperity, which should be a model for every underdeveloped country.

In fact, South Korea can no longer be classed as such. The country, which counted itself lucky enough to export $41 million worth of merchandise in 1961, sent out to the world $7.8 billion worth in 1976—an annual increase of 35 percent per annum. Per capita income, less than $100 in 1961, now stands at more than $800. In the teeth of a worldwide recession, the economy has continued to grow by 9 percent yearly. A country that had to import most of its staples in the early postwar years is now self-sufficient in rice and barley, symptoms of a newly healthy and balanced agricultural sector. As the report of a World Bank investigating mission summarized its conclusions earlier this year:

The sustained high rate of expansion in incomes over 15 years has transformed Korea from one of the poorest developing countries, with heavy dependence on agriculture and a weak balance of payments, financed almost entirely by foreign grants, to a semi-industrialized middle-income nation with an increasingly strong external payments position and the prospect of eliminating the current deficit in the next 5–10 years.

Part of the explanation for this success lies in the impressive abilities of the Koreans themselves. Widely regarded in both East and West as less disciplined reverse images of their Japanese racial cousins, with an objectionable facility for saturating food with garlic, they are in fact just as competent and emotionally more relaxed. The Koreans are driven by the same urge to educate their children at all costs as the Japanese "education mamas" who drive their sons into tutoring schools and universities in Osaka and Tokyo on the other side of the Tsushima Straits. Both high school and university-level education have expanded spectacularly since their release from colonialism. (One-half of Korea's children now attend high school, while the literacy rate has risen to 92 percent.) Koreans are moved by a combination of patriotism and survival. They have lived with the same economy of scarcity as the Japanese.

Starting from scratch as an industrial power, Koreans have nothing but new plants. Their labor force works long and cheaply. The growth of labor unions has been rigidly suppressed under the Park government. And thanks to the bloodbath of 1950–53, which no one ever wants to repeat, the life of a garrison state is tolerated. Besides, benefits are seeping down to the people. Electrification, plumbing, housing are coming. The appetite for rising expectations, if growing, can still be controlled. So the labor productivity rate remains astonishingly high.

And the control of industry, since the first of the four five-year plans began in 1962, has been openly coercive. Park himself is in personal control. He has set out to leave behind a healthy country, agriculturally and industrially sound. He does not brook slacking. The president's personal integrity has rarely been questioned. He has kept the machinery of the economy running remarkably straight and smooth. His economic and financial bureaucrats, many of them American-trained, have cheerfully taken leaves from Japan's book and guided Korea's new bumptious capitalists into efficient channels. At the same time, the Korean Finance Ministry has managed a swinging, high-risk game of international borrowing that might easily have led to disaster, but so far has not.

VIII

Against a background of boom times, internal oppression, and considerable nervousness inside Korea and among its neighbors about a slide in the American commitment, the Carter administration must now consider the consequences of its pullout announcement and learn to live with them. One must assume that the announcement itself is irreversible, in the absence of drastic new developments. By pledging American troops to a front-line position there, we had established a political quiet zone. We have endangered that. To restabilize matters, even partially, we must maintain an active, visible front-line diplomacy.

First, along with Japan, the United States should do everything within its power to assist and to help secure South Korea's extraordinary economic growth. This involves the welfare of the Korean people. It is also a necessary—though not a sufficient—condition for any easing of the regime's authoritarianism. To minimize economic pressures and to help young Korean managers bring on the consumer society of the 1980s can only help.

On the human rights front, it is doubtful if public denunciations of abuses will turn Park around and make him repent. Americans have rarely been successful with this tactic. It is far better to increase cultural and educational influences on Korea, on which this country has hitherto lavished little care, while applying constant, not sporadic pressure—firmly but privately—to expand political freedoms, with a promise, at least, of some return to a parliamentary government. Such unpublicized actions may have some effect. But we cannot win this game from the outside, any more than we can turn the Koreans overnight into responsible partisans and sophisticated independent voters.

The actual troop withdrawal should be slowed, as Washington has already indicated. And now that we have made the basic announcement, we must be careful that any subsequent incident from the North is met with more than normal vigor and severity. Kim Il Sung and his regime do not have a good record in reading American intentions accurately. Nor can we expect Kim to shart his own little détente, in the hope of speeding the U.S. withdrawal. Pyongyang, to put it mildly, lacks the sophistication of Moscow and Beijing. The fact that the North Koreans were almost civil when they returned the bodies of American airmen they had shot down recently over the demilitarized zone hardly seems a sufficient premise for predicting a new era of good feeling.

In Japan, however unconcerned the leadership may appear, the urge to examine the rearmament options will grow stronger. It already has. To the Japanese, Korea is within their defense perimeter. Although the possibility of a substantial Japanese rearmament is still not immediate, the withdrawal from Korea has certainly opened the question, and many thoughtful politicians and bureaucrats in Tokyo will start reviewing their options. Already a consensus may be forming.

Finally, there is the critical issue of stabilizing the Korean situation on a more lasting basis. Given the vast differences that thirty years of Kim Il Sung's brand of Communism have created between the 16 million North Koreans and their 35 million relatives in the South, it is hard to see any true modus vivendi yet in prospect, and still less any reunification of the country. But talks between North and South, aborted since 1971, could open up personal and economic contacts over time. Tensions could also be eased if the Soviet Union and China were to recognize Seoul in return for American recognition of Pyongyang. Ultimately there must be some guarantee of the Korean situation by the four great powers most concerned: Japan, China, the Soviet Union, and the United States. The very similar case of the two Germanies shows fairly precisely what might be done under all three headings.

It is in this diplomatic area that one must especially regret the unilateral character of the American withdrawal announcement, and the failure to make use of it, in private discussions, as leverage toward one or another of these three objectives. Perhaps the later decision not to withdraw most of the combat ground forces until 1981–82 still leaves the way open for some moves of this sort, although they will be less effective than if the situation had been dealt with as a whole from the outset. At any rate the prospect of American withdrawal now makes it more than ever urgent that all six interested parties—but especially the United States as the one with most effective contact among them—seek to break the present deadlock in the next year or two. Geography and ideology have combined to make Korea one of the major danger points in the world. It demands the most imaginative diplomacy that can be brought to bear.

BIBLIOGRAPHY

Amsden, Alice. *Asia's Next Giant*. New York: Oxford University Press, 1989.

An, Tai Sung. *North Korea in Transition: From Dictatorship to Dynasty*. Westport, Conn.: Greenwood Publishing Group, 1983.

Brandt, Vincent S. R. "Korea." *Ideology and National Competitiveness: An Analysis of Nine Countries*, George C. Lodge and Ezra F. Vogel, eds. Cambridge: Harvard Business School Press, 1987.

Cheng Tun-jen, and Haggard, Stephan. *Newly Industrializing Asia in Transition: Policy Reform and American Response*. Policy Paper No. 31. Berkeley: Institute of International Studies, University of California, 1987.

Eckert, Carter. *The Colonial Origins of Korean Capitalism: The Kochang Kims and the Kyongsang Spinning and Weaving Company, 1976–1945*. Seattle: University of Washington Press, 1991.

Eckert, Carter J., Lee Ki-baik, Lew Young Ick, Robinson, Michael, and Wagner, Edward W. *Korea Old and New: A History*. Cambridge: Korea Institute, Harvard University; 1990.

Han Sungjoo. *The Failure of Democracy in South Korea*. Berkeley: University of California Press, 1974.

Jones, Leroy P., and Sakong Il. *Government, Business, and Entrepreneurship in Economic Development: The Korean Case, Studies in the Modernization of the Republic of Korea, 1945–1975*. Cambridge: Council on East Asian Studies, Harvard University, 1980.

205

Kang, T. W. *Is Korea the Next Japan?* New York: Free Press, 1989.

Kihl Young Whan. *Politics and Policies in Divided Korea: Regimes in Contest.* Boulder: Westview, 1984.

Kim Joungwan A. *Divided Korea: The Politics of Development, 1945–1972.* Cambridge: Harvard University Press, 1975.

Kim Ilpyong J. and Kihl Young Whan. *Political Change in South Korea.* New York: Paragon, 1988.

Lee Chong-sik and Robert Scalapino. *Communism in Korea* (2 vols.). Berkeley: University of California Press, 1972.

Lee Chung H. and Blumenthal, Tuvia. "Introduction." *The Economic Development of Japan and Korea,* Chung H. Lee and Ippei Yamazawa, eds. New York: Praeger, 1990.

Mason, Edward S., Kim Mahn Je, Perkins, Dwight H., Kim Kwang Suk, and Cole, David C. *The Economic and Social Modernization of the Republic of Korea.* Cambridge: Council on East Asian Studies, Harvard University, 1980.

McGinn, Noel F., Snodgrass, Donald R., and Kim Young Bong. *Education and Development in Korea, Studies in the Modernization of the Republic of Korea, 1945–1975.* Cambridge: Council on East Asian Studies, Harvard University, 1980.

Myers, Ramon H. and Peattie, Mark R., eds. *The Japanese Colonial Empire, 1895–1945.* Princeton, N.J.: Princeton, 1984.

Song Byung-Nak. *The Rise of the Korean Economy.* New York: Oxford University Press, 1990.

Steers, Richard M., Shin Yoo Keun, and Ungson, Gerardo R. *The Chaebol: Korea's New Industrial Might.* New York: Harper and Row, 1989.

Sutter, Robert and Han Sungjoo, eds. *Korea-U.S. Relations in a Changing World.* Berkeley: University of California Press, 1990.

Vogel, Ezra F. *The Four Little Dragons: The Spread of Industrialization in East Asia.* Cambridge: Harvard University Press, 1991.

INDEX

Agency for National Security Planning, 84
Agriculture, 55, 96, 143
Allen, Rev. Dr. Horace, 43
Amsden, Alice, 1
Anti-Communist Law (1961), 68
Anti-Monopoly and Fair Trade Act (1981), 80
April revolution, 39–42
  forces emerging from, 41–48
Aquino, Cory, 9, 86
Aquino, Ninoy, 135
Army, ROK, 142
  economic growth and, 53–54
  Korean War and, 28, 32–35
  as modernization factor, 44–48
Art, 15–16
Asia Watch, 121

Banking liberalization, 80–81
Bank of Korea, 53, 133
Brandt, Willy, 105, 106
Buddhism, 14–15, 20

Capitalist developmental state, 3
Carter, Jimmy, 92, 142–43, 160, 187–204

Catholics, 18, 43, 70–72, 135
Celadon, 15
Chaebol conglomerates, 4, 54, 56–64, 78, 83, 111, 128, 130, 131, 137, 144
  characteristics of, 63
  democratization and, 93, 96, 97
Cha Ji Chul, 73, 74
Chang Myon, 40, 41, 46–47, 51
Chang To Yong, Lt. Gen., 48
China, 96, 105, 120, 154
  history of Korea and, 13–29, 34–36, 111, 115–20, 141–42
  "northern politics" and, 108–12
  as student of Korea, 149–50, 155–56
Choe Kyu Ha, 74, 76
Cholla provinces, 14, 75, 76, 135
Chonggun (Clean Up the Military movement), 47–48
Cho Soon, 133
Chosun Dynasty, 16–17
Cho Tae Yearn, 58
Christians, 18, 23, 133, 146
  as modernization factor, 42–44
  opposition movement and, 70–72

Chun Doo Hwan, 5–6, 44, 45, 73, 91, 94, 106
  ascent to power, 74–79
  economic reforms of, 79–82, 101
  political repression of, 82–88
  retirement of, 87–88
Chung Ju Yung, 52, 57–58, 97, 109, 127, 135, 137
Chusok, 136
Cold War, 27, 35, 39, 106–12
Communism, 106–7, 118, 122, 137
Confucianism, 17, 19, 20, 36, 44, 70, 72, 92, 95–96, 122, 152, 154
Confucius, 13–14
Construction industry, 57–63, 104, 145
Consumerism, 101–2, 133
Corruption, 5, 52, 134, 135
  Chun and, 82, 83
  Rhee and, 39, 40, 46–47

Daewoo, 97, 130, 148
  corporate empire of, 60–61
Declaration of Democratic Reform, 90–91
Democracy, 6–11, 87–102, 133–36, 152–53
Democratic Front for the Unification of the Fatherland, 32
Democratic Liberal party, 99–100, 134, 135
Democratic party, 135
Deng Xiaoping, 108, 138, 156
Doksu Palace, 21, 22
Dong-A Ilbo, 69
Dong Il Textile Company, 70

Eastern Europe, 107, 108, 120
East Timor, 155
Economic growth, 50–65
  democratization and, 100–102
  economic stability and, 79–82
  high costs of, 67–76
  middle class and, 78–88

problems with, 55–56, 64–65, 69, 78–79
  recession of 1992 and, 134–36
  switch to heavy industries, 56–64, 78
Economic Planning Board, 54, 56, 79, 135
Education, 4–5, 80, 145–46
  effect of, 6, 42, 43, 54, 67
Eighth Army, U.S., 75, 132, 142, 143
Eisenhower, Dwight D., 35
Elections of 1992, 134–36
Electronics industry, 130
Entrepreneurs, 56–64, 96

Financial stabilization, 79–81
Foreign loans, 53, 101
Four Little Tigers (Dragons), 1, 2, 4, 9

General Electric (G.E.), 59, 62
General Motors, 126
Gorbachev, Mikhail, 7, 8, 95, 107, 108–9, 151, 152
Great Han Empire, 21

Han, 21
Hanawehi, 75
Han Dynasty, 14
Hanguk Fertilizer Company, 59
Hangul alphabet, 17
Han Sung Joo, 47
Hayato, Ikeda, 67, 105
Hideyoshi, Toyotomi, 17–18
Hitachi, 62
Hodge, Lt. Gen. John R., 30
Hong Kong, 1, 2, 9, 35, 138, 150
Hong Sung Eun, 62
Housing, 97, 101
Human rights, 98, 135, 145
Hyundai, 1, 70, 92–93, 97, 130, 148
  corporate empire of, 57–58
  Ulsan and, 125–28

Ilhae Foundation, 83
Import liberalization, 80

Income distribution, 82–83
Indonesia, 9, 154–55
Infrastructure, 96, 97
International Atomic Energy Agency (IAEA), 138
Ito, Prince, 21
It's a Big World and There's Lots to be Done (Kim), 60, 61

Japan, 1–2, 36, 104–5
  after World War II, 3
  history of Korea and, 14–30, 42, 43, 111, 131–32, 142, 147–48
Jaruzelski, Wojciech, 107, 157
John, Pope, 71
Joint ventures, 137, 143
Juche ideology, 114, 117, 123, 137
Judicial reform, 98

Kanemaru, Shin, 147
Kanghwa Island, 19
Kang Won Yong, Rev., 121
Kapsin Coup, 20, 43
Kim, Stephen Cardinal, 43
Kim Chi Ha, 71
Kim Dae Jung, 7, 68, 69, 70, 74, 75, 91, 100, 135
Kim Dong Gil, 36, 71
Kil Il Sung, 2, 5, 30–36, 52, 65, 67, 71, 84, 86, 147
  described, 114
  eightieth birthday of, 113–14
  grip on North Korea, 115–23
  names for, 113
  Roh's northern politics and, 106–12, 136–38
Kim Jae Kyu, 74
Kim Jong Il, 114, 118–19, 123, 138, 139
Kim Jong Pil, Lt. Col., 47, 99
Kim Jun Yeop, 85
Kim Ku, 29, 30
Kim Ok Kyun, 20
Kim Su Hwan, Cardinal, 70–71
Kim Woo Choong, 60–61, 137

Kim Yeon Joon, 73
Kim Young Sam, 74, 91, 99, 134–35
Koguryo Kingdom, 14, 15
Kojong, King, 18–22, 29
Konguk University, 86
Koo Cha Kyung, 59–60
Korea:
  history of, 13–37
  modernization of, 18–23, 131, 144
  "opening" of, 19
  powerful neighbors of, 3, 14–37, 106–12, 141–42
  unification of, 2, 3, 46, 86, 96, 107–108, 112, 115, 123, 136–39, 147, 150–52
  wars and occupation of, 26–38, 115–17
Korea, Democratic People's Republic of (North Korea), 2, 14, 27, 30–36
  authoritarian government of, 2, 3
  compared to other countries, 1–2
  described, 115–23, 151
  economic relationship to Japan, 57, 147–49
  establishment of, 31
  important cities of, 125–33
  isolation of, 8, 36, 104, 108, 112, 115, 119–21, 137, 149–50
  major changes in, 140–41
  nuclear weapons and, 120, 123, 138–39
  problems in, 153
  rebuilding of, 40
  statistics on, 1, 8–9
  threat from, 52, 65, 67, 73, 105–6, 108, 137–39
  transformation of, 7–11
  U.S. and, 142–47
  in the world, 140–57
Korean Advanced Institute of Science and Technology (KAIST), 129–30
Korean Central Intelligence Agency (KCIA), 5, 51, 68, 70, 71, 84
"Korean commonwealth," 137–38

"Korean disease," 134–35
Korean War, 2, 4, 26–36, 39–40, 45, 61, 115–17, 132
  article on, 159, 161–72
  effect of on Korea, 28, 36–37
Korea University, 85
Koryo, 15, 16
Kublai Khan, 16, 17
Kungminban (neighborhood associations), 40
Kwangju massacre, 75–76, 86
Kwangyang, 128
Kyongju, 15, 125

Labor-management relations, 83–84, 92–93, 95, 127
Labor unrest, 6, 8, 69, 70, 84, 126, 127
Law for Assembly and Demonstration (1973), 69–70
Lee Bum Suk, 106
Lee Byung Chull, 59
Lee Hu Rak, 70
Lee Kuan Yew, 9
Lee Kun Hee, 59
Lee Teng-hui, 154
Li Hongzhang, 19
Literacy rate, 42
Los Angeles Times, The, 10
Lucky Goldstar, 1, 62, 97, 130
  corporate empire of, 59–60

MacArthur, Gen. Douglas, 28, 33–35
Makoto, Adm. Saito, 29
Malaysia, 9
Manchuria, 18, 26
Mang Hyang-Je, 136
Mao Zedong, 34, 35, 116, 118
Marcos, Ferdinand, 9, 76, 86, 87
M*A*S*H, 2
Mtsushita Konosuke, 57
Meiji Restoration, 18, 19, 21, 22, 54, 56, 131
Middle class, 68, 78–88, 92, 93, 131, 133

Military Academy, 45, 47–48, 75, 94
Min, Queen, 21, 22
Ming Dynasty, 16–17, 18
Ministry of Science and Technology, 130
Miracle on the Han, 51, 74, 78
Mitsubishi, 57, 148
Mongols, 16–17
Moon, Rev. Sung Myung, 122–23
Munmu, King, 26, 126
Myongdong Cathedral, 43, 70, 71, 72

National Assembly, 5, 6, 7, 10, 41, 47, 68, 74, 75, 97, 132, 134, 135
  democratization and, 98–99, 127
National Council for Unification, 69, 76
New York Times, The, 10
Nonaggression agreement, 137
Nonproliferation Treaty, 138
Nuclear Safeguard Accord, 139
Nuclear weapons, 120, 123, 138–39, 143

Olympic Games of 1988, 2, 6, 8, 87, 96, 106–7, 119
  significance of, 104–5

Pacific Rim, 9–10, 35, 111, 150, 152, 153–55
Paekche Kingdom, 14, 75
Paik Sun Yup, 32
Panmunjom, 68, 136
Park Chong Chol, 86–87
Park Chung Hee, 7, 14, 83, 105, 137
  ascent to power of, 47–48
  death of, 74–75
  dictatorial rule of, 4, 5, 8, 37, 44, 67–74, 96
  economic policy of, 50–74, 78, 118, 128
Park Hun Young, 116–17
Park Tae Joon, 128
Peng De Huai, Marshal, 35
Perot, Ross, 135

Philippines, the, 9, 86
Pohang, 128–29, 130
Pohang Iron and Steel Company
  (POSCO), 128–29, 148, 149
Poland, 107, 142, 157
Price controls, 80
Price stabilization, 79
Protestants, 43, 44, 70–72
Pyongyang, 119, 121

Reagan, Ronald, 76
Red Cross, 136
Reform of 1894, 20–21
Research and development (R&D),
  128–31, 149
Research Institute of Industrial Science
  and Technology (RIST), 128–29
Rhee, Syngman, 23–24, 27–41, 45–
  47, 54, 74
  article on, 159–60, 173–86
Ridgeway, Gen. Matthew B., 34–35
Roh Tae Woo, 14, 36, 45, 76, 84, 152–
  53
  described, 94
  merger of political parties and, 99–
    100
  "northern politics" of, 104–12, 123,
    136–38
  political reforms of, 6–10, 87–102,
    134
  unification and, 96, 123
Rostow, Walt W., 51
Russia, 21, 27, 96, 142, 144, 156–57

Saemaul Undong (New Community
  Development Movement), 55, 83
Samsung, 1, 97, 130
  corporate empire of, 58–59
Savings, 79–80, 101
Sejong, King, 17
Seoul, 2, 131–33
Shamanism, 121–22, 123
Shim Shang Chul, 101
Sigur, Gaston, 87
Silla Kingdom, 14–15, 75, 125, 126,
  142

Singapore, 1, 2, 9, 35
Society for Rapid Realization of Inde-
  pendence, 30
Song Byung-Nak, 4, 8
Song Yo-chan, Gen., 41
Soviet Union, 7–8, 27–36, 104, 115–
  17, 120
  "northern politics" and, 108–10
Special economic zones, 139
Special Law for Punishment of Anti-
  State Acts (1977), 70
Special Law for Safeguarding the Na-
  tion (1971), 68
Ssangyong, 62–63
Stalin, Josef, 29, 32, 35, 109
Steel industry, 128–29
Students, 42
  unrest by, 6, 41, 43, 70, 71, 75–76,
    84–88, 90, 98
Suharto, 154, 155
Sung Dynasty, 15
Sunjin choguk changjo (creating an ad-
  vanced fatherland), 82
Sunjong, King, 21–22
Supreme Council for National Recon-
  struction, 48

Taejon, 129
Taewongun, 18, 19, 21, 22, 43
Taiwan, 1, 2, 9, 111–12, 138, 150,
  153–54
Tang Dynasty, 14
Tangun, 13
Technology, 17, 128–31, 148–49
Thailand, 9–10, 154–55
38th parallel, 28, 30–35, 68, 115
"Three lows," 81
"Three sevens," 135–36
Tji Hak Sun, Bishop Daniel, 71
Tokugawa Ieyasu, 18, 19
Tonghak (Eastern Learning), 20, 21
Toyota, 126–27, 148
Trade balance, 101
Treaty of Friendship, 19
Truman, Harry, 32, 34, 35

Ulsan, 125–28, 130
Unification Church, 122–23
Unification Democratic Party, 127
Unification National Party, 135
United Nations, 27, 31, 33–35, 93, 139
  joint Korean entries to, 110–11
United States, 97, 142–47
  aid to Korea, 28, 31, 39–40, 51, 55, 69, 145
  article on withdrawing troops from Korea, 160, 187–204
  Korean immigrants in, 2–3, 146
  Korean War and, 27–35, 115–17
  protectionism of, 1, 8, 64, 143
  repression in Korea and, 72, 75–76, 86
U.S.S. *Pueblo*, 67

Van Fleet, Gen. James, 45
Violent demonstrations, 6, 8, 37, 41–42, 70–76, 83–88, 90, 126

Wilson, Woodrow, 23–24
Women, 43, 70, 95–96
World Peace Conference, 22
World War II, 4, 26–27, 29, 115

Yanan Koreans, 116, 117
Yan Fu, 19
Yangban aristocracy, 19, 20
Yi Dynasty, 15–17, 121
Yi Ki-bung, 40, 41
Yi Song-gye, 16
Yi Sun-shin, 17, 18
Yoido Island, 132–33
Yongbyon, 138–39
Yook Yung-Su, 73
Yoon Pil Yong, Gen., 72–73
Yuan Dynasty, 16
Yu Deuk Hwan, 144
Yun Po-sun, 41
Yushin Constitution, 64–65, 69, 70, 73, 74, 83